CYPRIAN KAMIL NORWID

DRAMATIC WORKS

PUBLICATION SUBSIDIZED BY
THE POLISH BOOK INSTITUTE

THE ©POLAND
TRANSLATION
PROGRAM

BOOK INSTITUTE

©POLAND

GLAGOSLAV PUBLICATIONS

DRAMATIC WORKS

by Cyprian Kamil Norwid

Translated from the Polish and introduced by
Charles S. Kraszewski

**This book has been published with the support
of the ©POLAND Translation Program**

Publishers
Maxim Hodak & Max Mendor

Introduction © 2021, Charles S. Kraszewski

© 2021, Glagoslav Publications

Proofreading by Stephen Dalziel

Book cover and layout by Max Mendor

Cover image:
Photo of Cyprian Norwid by Michał Szweycer, 1856

www.glagoslav.com

ISBN: 978-1-914337-31-4

Published in English by Glagoslav Publications in December 2021

A catalogue record for this book is available from the British Library.

CYPRIAN KAMIL NORWID

DRAMATIC WORKS

TRANSLATED FROM THE POLISH
AND INTRODUCED BY CHARLES S. KRASZEWSKI

Contents

CYPRIAN KAMIL NORWID

(1821-1883)

INFURIATING AND SUBLIME

Notes on Cyprian Kamil Norwid
and his Theatrical Works

Charles S. Kraszewski

Several weeks ago, when I was nearing the end of this translation, I met a friend of mine for coffee. As he too is a poet and translator, and above all, a Pole, he smiled knowingly when I mentioned that I was working on Cyprian Kamil Norwid's dramatic texts in preparation for the bicentennial of the poet's birth.

'What do you think of him?' he asked.

'I find him by turns infuriating and sublime,' I said, although, admittedly, I used some rather less diplomatic language in place of that first term, which I choose not to repeat here.

'Exactly,' he replied, with a laugh.

And this is the general reaction of Poles when confronted with Cyprian Kamil Norwid, the great, quirky, lonely individual talent of the second generation of Polish Romantics. He is a genius — there are moments… check that… actually hours or days of magnificence and brilliance in his work; there are also moments… or, to continue with the metaphor of time, let's say uncomfortable minutes, when his sublime genius outsoars our ability to follow. Norwid has a tendency to twist the Polish language into a form that, while it may — to him — more closely approximate exactly to what he wants to say, can be so strange that — to us — it becomes incomprehensible or (what is worse), cute.

The English reader thus has a firm walking staff with which to steady his tread as he sets out to cross the elevated, yet uneven terrain, of Norwid's poetic highlands — he already knows someone quite like him.

CYPRIAN KAMIL NORWID:
POLAND'S GERARD MANLEY HOPKINS

When Robert Bridges brought out the collected poems of his deceased friend Gerard Manley Hopkins (1844 – 1889) in 1918, he did so, courageously, with a true poet's intuition for great writing. He also did it with trepidation. Bridges was the poet laureate — a position not attained by going against tradition — which is exactly what Hopkins did. Although he was blamed by some of the younger generations of early twentieth century poets for 'suppressing' Hopkins' work for so long, one cannot fault Bridges for his sensitivity to the capabilities of the wider public to digest the exotic fare prepared by the Jesuit poetic genius. One has grown accustomed to smirking at Bridges' apologetic warning to the reader concerning 'The Wreck of the Deutschland', traditionally printed at the very beginning of Hopkins' works, as a 'dragon folded at the gate to forbid all entrance',[1] but that is patently unfair. To switch to a culinary metaphor, Bridges is following soberly in the footsteps of St Paul, who in his letter to the Hebrews warned his auditors that they 'are become such as have need of milk, and not of strong meat.'[2]

Again, our reference to Hopkins is not random. In nineteenth century Poland — or, rather, in the nineteenth century Polish diaspora — Cyprian Kamil Norwid (1821 – 1883) traversed an artistic arc quite similar to that of his British near-contemporary. A serious Catholic, Christianity so forms the basis of Norwid's writings that, as Jan Ryszard Błachnio notes, he 'significantly influenced … both methodologically and conceptually', the formation of John Paul II's personalistic philosophy.[3] As an artist, he was ahead of his time, departing from tradition, coining words as well as using words well-known in startling new contexts, just as Hopkins did in England.

> In order to describe the world more precisely, the poet coined new words, or extracted latent meanings from words that already exist,

---

1   Cited by William Henry Gardner, *Gerard Manley Hopkins, 1844 – 1889: A Study of Poetic Idiosyncrasy in Relation to Poetic Tradition* (London: Secker and Warburg, 1948), Vol. 1, p. 40.

2   Hebrews 5:12.

3   Jan Ryszard Błachnio, *Polskie inspiracje i wartości w nauczaniu Jana Pawła II* [Polish Inspirations and Values in the Teaching of John Paul II] (Bydgość: WSP, 1995), p. 68.

breaking them down into constituent portions or 'coping' words that were previously separate. As some scholars see it, Norwid was to the Polish language what Dante was to the Italian: 'a translator of a theological language' before professional theologians even set themselves to the task.[4]

The statement comparing Norwid to Dante may be true enough as far as their 'theological' content is concerned, but it would be an overstatement to carry the comparison into the literary field. For Dante, known and appreciated in his own time, whether loved or hated by his contemporaries, is also the chief creator of the modern Italian literary idiom itself. Norwid, on the other hand, like Hopkins in England, is indeed of seminal importance to the development of the contemporary poetics of his native speech, but only belatedly. Just as Hopkins had to wait, so to speak, nearly two decades after his decease to join the literary conversation in England and the English-speaking world, so Norwid, though befriending earlier poets of the Romantic generation such as Zygmunt Krasiński and Juliusz Słowacki and corresponding with Józef Ignacy Kraszewski, was generally unknown to the wider public in Poland until the chance discovery in 1897 (and thus, fourteen years after his death), of his work in a Vienna library by Zenon Przesmycki, who first went on to champion it. Ever since his adoption by the poets of the 'Young Poland' movement at the turn of the twentieth century, Norwid's star has been in the ascendant. He is the darling of all aficionados of 'challenging' poetry; those who are fond of T.S. Eliot, Ezra Pound, or the afore-mentioned Gerard Manley Hopkins, will probably be attracted to Norwid's work; fans of the (forgive me) undemanding sort of poet like William Wordsworth or Robert Frost, or the Beats like Allen Ginsberg and Jack Kerouac, will most likely find him a bit too arcane.

The above is not at all intended as a dismissive statement. There is much to be said in favour of clarity and simplicity in poetic expression; Pound himself once stated that 'poetry must be as well written as prose,'[5] and for those who see the Apollonian, or classical, approach to poetry

---

4   Szymon Babuchowski, in a promotional brochure on Norwid prepared by the Book Institute (Kraków, 2021).

5   Ezra Pound, *Selected Letters, 1907 – 1941* (New York: New Directions, 1971), p. 48.

as something of an eternal standard, Norwid's approach could only be taken as a fad, or an aberration. This reputation has dogged Norwid since his earliest years. The neoclassical poet Kajetan Koźmian, who hosted Norwid in 1842 during the latter's trip through Kraków, noted this summation of the younger poet's talents in his *Memoirs* (posthumously published in 1865):

> Carried on the winds of popular opinion [Albert Szeliga Potocki] raved about Norwid, a good and pleasant young man, whom I met personally, in my own home, where I hosted him for several days. But although he drew very prettily, he wrote in too incomprehensible a way. Warsaw was echoing at the time with cries such as 'Norwid, you eagle, your age is approaching!' Potocki sent me his poems, completely incomprehensible, along with effusions of praise. When I charged him with levity in his judgement [*płochość w sądzie*] he began to squirm like a snake, admitting the justice of my charge to my eyes, while behind those eyes saying something else.[6]

The sort of thing that Koźmian finds 'incomprehensible' and many readers today find irritating, at least, is Norwid's penchant for creatively deforming the Polish language by the creation of new words, such as we find in his lyric poetry, like *wszechdoskonałość* ['universalperfection'] *niedośpiewana* ['unsungtotheend'] and *ożałobione* ['mourningshadowed'] all of which occur in one of his most famous poems, 'Fortepian Szopena' [Chopin's Grand Piano], being a lament for both Chopin's death, and the martyrdom of Warsaw at the hands of the Russians. Norwid gives free rein to his imagination in lyric poems — something that might be expected, taking into consideration the intimate nature of the genre, which, given the way communication occurs between poet and reader, may well embolden creative minds to striking linguistic experimentation shunned in other forms of literary composition. Readers of English poetry might be reminded here of E.E. Cummings at his best (or worst, depending on your point of view).[7] In his dramatic works, Norwid

---

6   Cited by Kazimerz Wyka, *Norwid w Krakowie* [Norwid in Kraków] (Kraków: Wydawnictwo Literackie, 1967), p. 71.

7   And not just in his poetry. Consider the following passage from his travel journal to the USSR, *Eimi*: hugest/(andtoadreamstreamlined)

coins words too. For one example, in Zwolon's poetic monologue in the play of the same name — modelled on the Great Improvisation from Mickiewicz's *Dziady* [Forefathers' Eve], Part III (and thus a lyrical monologue) the character employs the metaphor of multi-faceted life as a lyre, or chord, a metaphor which was a favourite of Norwid's. And here, the poet indulges in creative license with the phrase *pierwsza odśpiewa / całostrunna* (which we render as 'the former sings / striking all-strings').

The reader familiar with the Polish originals of these plays might well offer some other examples; the old-Slavic sounding title bestowed upon Prince Rakuz (in *Krakus*), *Włady-Tur*, a calque of ancient Slavonic roots signifying authority and the virile strength of a bull, is one that leaps to mind. However, in general, with a dramatist's intuition, Norwid eschews such verbal gymnastics in his plays. Drama is not only a collaborative genre, obviously, it also relies on the immediacy of verbal communication, and the natural tempo of stage action allows for precious little pausing on the receptors' part to puzzle out strange — if effective and rich — unfamiliar terms. As can be seen from his various introductions and initial *didascalia* to the plays, Norwid was concerned with their proper performance, whether he foresaw them as being staged, or read aloud by amateurs at social gatherings. In the introduction to *Cleopatra and Caesar*, he even goes so far as to warn the performers to pay special attention to the exigencies of metre, as in this poetic drama in blank verse they are deprived of the crutch of rhyme. Consequently, except where such was absolutely necessary — as in the case of the above-mentioned soliloquy from *Zwolon*, so strikingly similar, stylistically, to 'Fortepian Szopena' — I have generally smoothed over Norwid's coinages where they appear, for to retain them would run the risk of creating a preciosity not entirely present in the Polish originals.

As a matter of fact, Norwid himself realised the danger of too violent a racking of everyday speech. In *The Ring of the Grande Dame*, the rather unpalatable character of Judge Durejko is satirised by his grotesque devotion to 'purifying' the Polish language by replacing foreign loan-words, such as 'monologue,' with Slavic coinages like *sobo-słowienie*

---

locomotive-nakedly-floating-most-lazily- / who (throughhanoverstation) slid-whispering-extinction / and framed with / nie wychylać sie [sic] / omwierać [sic] drzwi / podczas biegu pociągu. E.E. Cummings, *Eimi* (New York: William Sloan, 1933), p. 3.

['selfspeaking'] — derived from the works of the 'national philosopher' Bronisław Trentkowski. Just as the fashion for re-Slavicising Polish ended almost as soon as it began (and Norwid knew this, and laughed at it), and Trentkowski is a rather forgotten figure today, so Norwid cannot be said to have had the same sort of linguistic impact on Poland as Dante had on Italy. What characterises much of his poetic idiom — such quirky word-builds as described above — was not accepted into common parlance, except for a brief, though marked, influence on poets of the Young Poland period. And this influence was indeed brief; it did not extend much past the *słopienie* ['wordcrooning'] of Julian Tuwim, and generally grates on the Polish ear today.

Despite all the boldness we usually associate with Cyprian Norwid, as a poet and a man, his great characteristic is modesty. He did not consider himself to be a lawgiver. In the strange unfinished drama *Za kulisami* [In the Wings], the play within this play, *Tyrtaeus*, written by the main character Count Omegitt, is whistled off the stage. Glückschnell, the theatrical promotor who (for reasons unclear) accepted the drama for production, explains its failure as partially arising from the author's long absence from commerce with the living language of his nation:

> In complete confidence, I would not conceal this from an interested party like yourself: by nature of his long and far-distant travels, he's lost the active native pulse that, on the one hand, lends a writer's language its peculiar strength, and on the other, incessantly fortifies his thought with the current needs of our society — and that is, I would say, what pleases… everyone.

If Norwid's poetic language — in these dramas or in his verse and prose — is taken into consideration, I feel that we would be hard put to consider it as a good example of the Polish current in his day. His older friend Zygmunt Krasiński, who most people would agree does not rise to the same level of poetic quality as Norwid, still has a rather limpid style in the prose he employs in his dramas. For example, consider this fragment from Krasiński's *Nieboska komedia* [Undivine Comedy] — an intricate condemnation of the Count's forefathers by the revolutionary Pankracy, as the two debate in the portrait-hung walls of the former's palace:

Oh, sure — praise to thy fathers and grandfathers on earth as in…
Yes, there's quite a lot to look at around here.

That one there, the Subprefect, liked to shoot at women among
the trees, and burned Jews alive. — That one, with the seal in his
hand and the signature, the 'Chancellor,' falsified records, burned
whole archives, bribed judges, hurried on his petty inheritances with
poison. — To him you owe your villages, your income, your power.
That one, the darkish one with the fiery eye, slept with his friends'
wives — that one with the Golden Fleece, in the Italian armour,
fought — not for Fatherland, but for foreign pay. And that pale lady
with the black locks muddied her pedigree with her squire — while
that one reads a lover's letter and smiles because the sun is setting…
That one over there, with the doggie on her farthingale, was whore to
kings. — There's your genealogies for you, endless, stainless! — I like
that chap in the green caftan. He drank and hunted with his brother
aristocrats, and set out the peasants to chase deer with the dogs. The
idiocy and adversity of the whole country — there's your reason,
there's your power. — But the day of judgement is near at hand and
on that day, I promise you, I won't forget a single one of you, a single
one of your fathers, a single scrap of your glory!

Compare this to a direct address of similar length from the *Tyrtaeus*
section of *In the Wings*. Laon, returning home, addresses his stepfather
Cleocarpus:

To see you at rest, O my lord and my father, I don't know how fast
I'd be able to urge my legs, but I was told at the Pnyx (something I
might have surmised myself) that the debates at the Aeropagus on this
pregnant night were to last long (as if they were ever any less weighty,
any different). And so, in order not to be too far distant from your
thoughts and wishes, I gladly accepted the call of my superiors to see
to the men working at the port, to whom a free hand is proper, to the
craftsmen who busy themselves with things which, if I may say so, are
not completely unfamiliar to me. And there, like a fresh nut which,
perfect in its roundness, sloughs off its heavy green coat when it is
golden and ripe, thus did we slide into the waters of the sea a skilfully
constructed, new Corinthian galley — not without the usual libations
and the first gay turn around the harbour.

The first of these, that of Krasiński, reads smoothly, even in English translation, if I may be so bold to suggest; it is easy for us to suspend our disbelief and 'be there' in the chamber listening to the fierce exchange, following the ideas, not burdened at all by strained syntax. But Norwid's fragment? Did even the most pedantic son ever say 'Hi, Dad, sorry I'm late' with such density? In reading through this text we get lost among Laon's intricate tropes. It's a wonder that Cleocarpus knows what his stepson is trying to say, although he goes right on after this with a speech in praise of sailing and maritime commerce — which might well be placed exactly where it is in the play, and make just as much sense, if Laon's speech were completely excised. The reason for the discrepancy between these two works of the poet-friends? Krasiński, warts and all, has a fine ear for dialogue, and is able to create a believable, realistic verbal fencing match between the characters of Pankracy and Count Henryk (which we shall omit here, for considerations of space), no thrust or parry of which can be deleted without harming the whole. In Norwid's play, Laon and Cleocarpus deliver soliloquies, recognising the (unnecessary?) presence of one another merely by waiting for the other to finish his spiel before beginning his own.

Of course, it is not always thus with Norwid's plays. Passages from *Cleopatra and Caesar*, *Wanda*, *Zwolon*, *Krakus*, just about any of the plays here included, sparkle with polished repartee. We must also remember that *Tyrtaeus* is supposed to be a *failure* as a dramatic work, and whereas the conversation in the garden between Tyrtaeus and Eginea is brilliant, theatrically, the citation of Glückschnell's words above might well be a veiled 'note to self' by Norwid.

NORWID AND THE WORD

That said, one of the things that occurs to the reader of Norwid's plays is that there are few Polish poets, certainly none among the Romantics, who pay such close attention to the word and, what we might call for lack of a better term, communication theory. Before we make too great an authority of Glückschnell, we ought to remind ourselves what his character represents. Just as his name suggests, he is after fortune (*Glück*), and quick! (*schnell*). No artist himself, he is a promoter, eager to make money by pleasing the audience, hoping, for example, that the serious, failed tragedy of Omegitt's will not turn the audience away before he can pull them back in with the snappy songs and witty sketches that are slated to follow it. He is not even a competent critic, since, as he admits to another character, he wishes to follow the vacuous popular French author de Fiffraque around a bit to learn from him 'what we are to think and write' about the play that he himself has chosen to produce. Glückschnell sins at the other extreme: trafficking in pleasant banalities. Now, whereas plays, produced as they ought to be, on stage or in dramatic reading, do not afford the receptors much luxury to savour deeply every word presented by the *poeta doctus*, this brief exchange between Zwolon and a peremptory court official might be set forward as an example of the approach to the word that Norwid recommends:

GUARDSMAN
What do we have here? Are you casting spells,
Magician? Drawing runes and warlock wheels
On royal footpaths?

ZWOLON

With great calm.

Those are royal seals.

GUARDSMAN
What?!

ZWOLON
Royal seals. Look closely. Can't you tell?

GUARDSMAN
No!

ZWOLON
The garden implements all bear that mark.

GUARDSMAN

Inspecting the impressions more closely.

Aha — I see…

ZWOLON
             Like God's word. So it goes:
From quire to quire
It flows on ever higher,
And here it sparks, while there it bursts to flame,
And lower still, its fire
Cheers, and feeds the plain
Still lower with lush green.
And there's another might — of stone:
A stupid thing that hastes
About the ruts of waste
Where verdure is unseen
And so it mocks the truth with jibing splutter
And quire on quire slips down the crooked gutter.

Pause. He gazes at the sky.

It looks like we'll have rain again tomorrow.
Goodbye.

He moves off.

The Guardsman sees Zwolon standing near some odd impressions in the dust and jumps to a wild conclusion. Calmly, Zwolon has him look more closely; to pause, and consider the evidence presented before speaking; in short, to take the time to interpret the matter set before him, just as a reader, or critic, ought to bend over a text. The Guardsman — like most of Glückschnell's audience — is too impatient for that; he wants to consume and move on, not savour and delectate. The conclusion of this passage is a masterpiece of dramatic movement. Zwolon pronounces a brief sentence on 'God's word' — an example of dense, challenging poetry — and when he looks at the flummoxed face of the Guardsman, unable to deal with anything more complicated than pleasantries and hasty charges, he breaks off with a — banal — comment on the weather forecast and walks away.

Norwid is a poet who knows the weight of words. It is no coincidence that two of his most sympathetic characters, two queens: Wanda and

Cleopatra, in the plays that bear their names, have periods of silence, of keeping quiet, of not speaking, so long, as a matter of fact, that their subjects and intimates become unnerved. Sometimes, it is better to say nothing than to use speech improperly.[8] In two of his plays, *Zwolon* and *Krakus*, the nineteenth-century Pole displays an uneasy sensitivity to the possible misuse of speech that predates George Orwell by over half a century. In the first of these, Zobor, a ruthless henchman of his absolute monarch, who hesitates not to bring negotiations to a satisfactory end by underhandedly slaughtering the other side, tells the scribe Stylec how he ought to approach recording what has just happened for posterity:

> Describing victory,
> Let your descriptions not be niggardly.
> Use your imagination. Writing is
> An art — these pages are clean canvases.
> And as you write, show some liberality —
> You are the one creating history —
> Be as a trumpet: blaring, thundering,
> And your inventions will become the thing
> Itself. The writer's might is chthonic,
> Creating... truth. Where would Achilles be
> If not for some well-crafted histrionics?

He who controls the past, controls the present and the future as well — for sure. Rakuz, the brutal usurping prince of Norwid's retelling of the foundational myth of Wawel Castle in Kraków, establishes his own Ministry of Truth. First, he suppresses the historical record. When the cringing Szołom approaches him with his record of the final moments of the king's life, which contains no explicit decision regarding the succession to the crown of Kraków, Rakuz commands:

---

8   It is from here, I reckon, that we ought to start in any discussion of the silence of these two women, and not, as Kruszewska and Coleman (following Julian Krzyżanowski) suggest, from a far-fetched interpretation of 'Wanda's desperate plight [as] the plight of the artist in general, whom [Norwid] sees as eternally under bondage to Silence, forever unable to express the whole of what he feels.' Albina I. Kruszewska and Marion M. Coleman, 'The Wanda Theme in Polish Literature and Life,' *The American Slavic and East European Review*, Vol. 6, No. 1/2 (May, 1947): 19-35, p. 32.

You'll no more touch those writings. Give them here.
For all times in his treasury they'll be lain,
Despite the fact his will was none too clear,
And failed to indicate an heir by name.

Or, precisely *because* he failed to indicate an heir by name. If, in his *Undivine Comedy*, Zygmunt Krasiński predicted the class struggles that were to plague most of the twentieth century, in *Krakus* and in *Zwolon* Norwid prophesies the nefarious nature of totalitarianism. Consider how the exchange between Rakuz the usurper and his servile scribe develops following the lines just quoted:

SZOŁOM
When all a man's strength is well-nigh consumed,
He's like a candle as it's burning down —
By this you'll know the man who knows the runes:
For he can clarify, explain, expound —
O, for example, look here: see what I'd
Inscribed with my own hand next to those words:
'By this, clearly, Rakuz is signified,'
Although he was awaiting both young lords...

RAKUZ
Such things, if anyone, the runesman can
Unravel — false appearances from truth —
I do not seek the praise of any man.
The truth is my concern alone.

SZOŁOM
                                        In sooth!

RAKUZ
And truth is...?

SZOŁOM
                        Ah, what is truth?

RAKUZ
                         Truth is a word.
Whatever you redact, don't hesitate
To bring to me...

Now, whereas Communism was little more than a word in the nineteenth century, totalitarianism has always been around, and the Warsaw native Cyprian Kamil Norwid was aware of how words can be used to affect, if not change, reality. Surely, the quip of Alexander Pushkin was known to him,[9] who warned off Western Europeans from intervening in Poland's uprising against Tsarist Russia with his condescending description of the war for national liberation as a mere 'quarrel between brothers.'

But words can also be used as proper weapons, when they are in the service of truth. Krakus returns to Kraków and slays the dragon that Rakuz hardly dared approach, not with the strength of his arm, but by words, as the mystical Spring taught him during his rest in the Sapphire Grotto:

SPRING
Then no more sleep —
This wisdom keep
Ever present in your mind:
Poems can heal
And bite like steel.
Strike the dragon with such rhymes!

And here we have the true import of Norwid's writing: it is in service of something else, something beyond literature. *Chwila myśli* [A Moment of Thought], that early poem in dramatic form with which we open our collection, begins with a young man not understanding the anxiety that grips him. He wants to be a writer, but wonders if he has the talent to succeed as he would like, and if not, will he agree to be 'drawn and quartered' for money, writing the sort of things that the Glückschnells of the world pay good money to produce, and good money to consume? What is he to do? The answer to his anxious queries in that cold garret comes with the cries of some children in the building: 'Mama, mama,

---

9   See T.J. Binyon, *Pushkin: A Biography* (New York: Vintage, 2002), p. 364.

we're hungry! Give us bread!' Norwid is too good a writer to have light-bulbs popping over the character's head here; he is at first obtuse, responding to the cries of the hungry children with a clueless, self-centred thought: 'They suffer in the flesh, and I, in spirit.' Now, whether or not the sufferings of the soul can be as acute as those of the flesh, this is a rather cold and oblivious thing to say to the father of the children, who had just finished describing their plight in the winter. *A Moment of Thought* is exactly what its title suggests: a brief meditation that suggests rather than provides a developed answer to the dramatic conflict — in this case, what is the role, or even sense, of art in a world where hungry children freeze in winter? And although no definitive answer is given, one is certainly suggested: Whatever you do, whatever you busy yourself with, help others, if only you can. Norwid's youth is worried about becoming an author. But what does writing matter? What he should be worried about is being a good man.

In *Krytyka* [Criticism] another of these brief dramatic sketches in verse, a similar question is put to the eponymous character who has just denigrated the use of modern, northern European models for artworks depicting Biblical scenes. The Secretary of the journal for which the Critic writes counters with words that might be considered Norwid's own:

SECRETARY
      One more question, if I may:
Now, is the goal of artworks to disguise
The word, or to reveal it to our eyes?
For truth is born each day; we're ever turning
A new page, and with care: we're ever learning
— Through nineteen centuries — that we're to seek
In each and every person that we meet,
Though they be deeply hidden — Cross and gall,
Nail-head and tomb and glory's ray, and all
The grand account of our salvation — stippled,
Shaded and bright, in both hale and cripple.
How else can virtue speak unto our heart?

Although the clueless Critic, satirised by Norwid, responds with his familiar 'What sense, in that case, has the critic's art?' the message of the

Secretary is as clear and simple as any parable from the New Testament: what is the 'truth' of an authentic setting, or a search for Middle Eastern / Semitic human types for Biblical paintings, in comparison to the truth defended by the Secretary: we are all of us children of God, and we are to see Christ in everyone we meet, not just those who look like Him on the outside. Norwid's critic would find a lot to object to in Gaugin's Tahitian Holy Families, while Norwid and his Secretary, on the other hand, would consider them greater than mere paintings: icons, which visually and immediately present a profound theological lesson concerning God's love for us, all of us, and the love and respect He expects us to have for one another.

NORWID, CRITICISM, AND TRUTH

Speaking of critics, in general, Norwid has few kind words to offer them. The master-builder Psymmachus sums them up thus in *Cleopatra and Caesar*:

> O, there's no lack of critics, but the learned?
> The competent ones? It's like aboard ship:
> Those without sea-legs tumble to the rail
> To bark into the waves… their morning meal.
> So much for critics. They know how to clap
> Or piss at one's foundations. Spasmatics
> With bladders full…

And in the play *In the Wings*, Norwid repeats the familiar canard of the critic as a failed writer — unable to be creative himself, he criticises the creativity of others. This argument, while it overlooks Samuel Johnson's *bon mot*, that one needn't be a joiner in order to tell when a table is crooked, is not the main philosophical reason behind Norwid's disdain for critics. It is, rather, their lack of charity. As he puts it in the brief introduction to *Krakus*:

> Today's critics, dispossessed of that informality, simple, not to say Christian, which permits a person to respond directly to direct questions, are very defective in that first great virtue of brokering and mediating between works of literature and the readership.

One might think that they preserve unto themselves a mandate of *casual and persistent review and censorship,* at the cost, indeed, of readers to whom the chief principles and truth of the literary art are unfamiliar — and who thus are presented merely with the particular works or reputations of such persons as they have permitted to exist!

As Norwid sees it, the critic has a 'sacred' obligation to help those who need him, the readers as defined above, and not to use the texts they criticise in order to further their own agenda; pulling others down, so as to appear to be above them. It is the careful critic who is needed, one who patiently bends over the given text, and after sensitive study, is able to extract the one important thing from it, the truth, for those who can't access it otherwise.

Here we find another point of contact with Hopkins. The critics castigated by Norwid are like the interpreters of Sibylline oracles: the truth is there, but they are unable to suss it out. In *Wanda*, after Rytyger tosses the chalice he'd been drinking from into the woods, and an aerie of eagles take wing, the German runesmen opine:

The queen shall fall in love, and with such might
Not seen since ages hoary.
Four eagles, at your throw, took flight.
Great shall be her glory.
She'll fall in love, and bathe her body white.

Ironically, their interpretation is correct, but in the most essential sense, they get it all horribly wrong. Wanda shall fall in love indeed — but with her nation, not with Rytyger. She will bathe her body white, but not in preparation for her nuptials, rather, she will cast herself into the Vistula, self-immolating in Christ-like fashion, to save her people the Wiślanie, and, by extension, Poland, from becoming subsumed into the German element through an unconsidered marriage to the German prince.

The truth is a slippery thing, but it is perceptible to those who follow it with humility. This is effectively borne out in that scene from *Wanda*'s twin Cracovian tragedy, *Krakus*. When Krakus, spurned and wounded by his own power-hungry brother and left in the forest, returns incognito to deal with the dragon plaguing the royal castle of Wawel, he finds his brother Rakuz, exhausted with watching, asleep in a chair. Gazing at him tenderly, from the new heights of his sublime, mystical enlightenment, Krakus whispers: 'Mere presence at the crucial hour — what dare / Man hazard without peace, conscience, and prayer?' Thinking to approach his brother, he decides better of it — let him rest, worn out, as Krakus mistakenly infers, with weeping for their dead father — and goes off to slay the dragon. The ironic thing is that these very same words were on the lips of Rakuz just before he dozed. However, he continues them, confessing that they are 'Three things, of which [he's] never had the pleasure / Of personal acquaintance...'

The truth, like our conscience, is inborn in all of us. That is what is suggested by this curious repetition. What we *do* with the truth makes all the difference, in our own lives, and in the life of the world, to say nothing of our eternal destiny. Norwid here is dramatically presenting the lesson given us on faith by St James. Faith? Without works? 'Thou believest that there is one God. Thou dost well: the devils also believe and tremble.'[10]

NORWID AND THE DANTEAN APPROACH TO LITERATURE

At the base of Norwid's writing is the Christian conviction that this life is not all there is, that happiness in this life is not man's supreme aim, and that the eternal destiny of man, which is a gift from God, also carries with it responsibilities. This is what, in shorthand, we might call the Dantean tradition, after its greatest literary practitioner, although it can be found, of course, before the *Divine Comedy* and after, as it stretches into our own day — in the works of T.S. Eliot and Jan Zahradníček, to give but two examples. And so, in *Zwolon*, while Norwid does not push aside ideas of justice here and now (his 'improvisation' on the two colours — red and white — is a yearning for a just and free Poland) it is not something that should be fought for at all costs. There are more important considerations. The character of Szołom, whom we meet up with in *Krakus* as well as here,[11] is a stirrer-up of strife, a person playing

---

10   James 2:19.

11   More precisely, we meet up with the name, and a character so similar as to be the same person. For *Krakus* is set in the early mediaeval period, and *Zwolon* seems to have a contemporary, nineteenth-century setting. This makes the

two sides of the same game for his own benefit, or, worse, the benefit of the destructive powers of the air. It is for this reason that, after the defeat of the rebels, when Szołom is skipping round Zwolon, seeking to engage him in conversation, alternatively fawning over and tempting him (if subtly), Zwolon first ignores him, and at last asks him 'what is your name?' — approaching the character as an exorcist might. Szołom, 'bound,' reveals his name (he is a servant of Spirit — but which 'Spirit?') and disappears.

Again, it's not enough to recognise the truth; one must also use it, correctly. Gaius Valerius, in the dramatic poem *Słodycz* [Sweetness] is not necessarily an evil man. He keeps Julia Murtia imprisoned not because he is a sadist deriving pleasure from tormenting her. Rather, he is busied with an experiment: he has heard of these Christians, and wants to find out what makes them tick:

> Should I declare her Christian, she's undone.
> She's executed and… what would I have won?
> Will that in some way heighten my control
> Over her? Or will it transform her soul
> Into a flower (if Plato is proved
> Correct) — and if so, can a flower be moved?
> [...]
> … Where do these Christians get that inner strength?
> I've seen troops hopelessly beset, veterans
> Of ancient legions; I've known gladiators…
> It's something more than bravery —

He's not after her death, he's after understanding. However, when that opportunity is presented to him, in a dream, when St Paul appears to him, he reveals his true colours:

> Old man — you, in that cloak of red you wear,
> Barefoot, with flashing sword there at your side

---

repeated use all the more intriguing, as it suggests a type of person — a family; in *Krakus* Szołom himself refers to the generations of his kind — and thus, the persistent endurance of evil and servility eating at society throughout all time, like a cancer.

CYPRIAN KAMIL NORWID

Where we've but dark and empty pleats, who cried
That I might be entangled too — speak on!
I'm listening…

ST PAUL

In Gaius Veletrius' dream.

                    The grace over which none
Of your fierce tormentings can prevail
I can give you — and with it, you might heal.
But why do you seek it?

GAIUS VELETRIUS

Quickly, unconsciously.

                    So I might overcome
Her!

ST PAUL

Touching Gaius Veletrius' shoulder with the point of his sword.

        Julia Murtia has died.

He sought it not for his own salvation, or to become one with her. He sought it as some unvanquishable talisman, with which he might overcome her — and in the end she overcomes him, by escaping in death to a greater freedom than he can imagine; a freedom he himself will never taste at his own passing, since he refused the one opportunity afforded him to grasp it. His death will lead to a deeper prison than hers in the Vestals' gaol. For we live in an eternal moment of decision — as Eliot will say, each of our acts, however trivial, is a moral decision, for good or evil, with eternal consequences. The thrust of Norwid's dramatic works, like the *Divine Comedy* of Dante, is to prompt us to choose wisely, so that we should not end up like his Roman high priest.

Though I hope not to become another Glückschnell, who would tell the reader 'how we are to judge and how we are to write about' the plays included in these *Dramatic Works* of Cyprian Kamil Norwid, I still would like to present a few short paragraphs on each of them, so as to set them in a more particular context than the general thoughts we have presented so far.

THE SHORTER WORKS

For most Poles, Norwid is above all a lyric poet. He seems to have approached the theatre with timid steps, as, in our chronological arrangement, we note that the first four plays are short sketches — scenes or tiny dramas (a genre initiated among the Slavs by Pushkin with his *Little Tragedies*), which can just as well be considered lyric poems in dramatic form,[12] as small dramas in verse: *A Moment of Thought*, *Sweetness*, *Auto-da-fé* and *Criticism*.

The Christian themes present in Norwid's poetry, which we have noted above, can already be found in these first tentative dramatic sketches. Not only is *Sweetness* a story of Christian patience *usque ad sanguinem*, but *A Moment of Thought* is as well, even though it does not end with a definitive picture of the Youth's next step, concludes with an expression of the sense of the universe, which indicates the path that will lead him to his answer:

> We've still learned nothing. Nothing but the cross
> That stretches wide its arms old folks to greet,
> The youth to bless, and, bending through the rent
> Clouds, peers to spell out from the children's eyes
> Whether these ribbons, which so thickly flow
> Will be worth anything? Or disappear?
> No! They won't disappear. For deep inside
> As long as — in thought, not in screams — grows

---

12   Or 'Romantic lyrical scenes' [lyrischen Szene der Romantik], as J. Łuczak-Wild terms them, following Gomulicki. See J. Łuczak-Wild, 'Polnische Norwidiana 1945 – 1969: Teil II,' *Zeitschrift für Slavische Philologie*, Vol. 36, No. 1 (1971): 153-226, p. 159.

Pain, it shall burst into bloom, a thorny bow
To ply the heartstrings of all who live below!

As individual as Norwid is, he does emerge from a tradition that cannot but leave its mark on him. The tradition to which I refer here is not just Christian culture, but the works of the first generation of Polish Romantics. In Adam Mickiewicz's *Forefathers' Eve,* Part III, the Promethean hero Konrad learns that, even if we cannot fly before the throne of God to solve the problems of the world, we can make the world a slightly better place by small acts of charity. His selling of his signet ring as he heads off into exile in Russia, with half of the proceeds to go to the poor, and half for Masses on behalf of the souls suffering in Purgatory, is a concrete act of charity which outweighs by a thousandfold all the bombastic cosmic plans of saving his nation, which are doomed to failure from the start. Norwid learns from this, as here, his hero slowly comes to understand that our mere sensitivity to suffering prods us to ask questions and try to help others, and this, like Konrad's humble gift of his ring, is sometimes quite enough.

A Moment of Thought is a work in which the main character asks himself what can fame, and writing itself, be worth in a world so full of human suffering. This questioning of the sense of writing (when there are so many more important things to do) is part of a current of self-criticism that runs through Norwid's plays. It is taken up in *Auto-da-fé,* in which the main character, a writer named Protazy, uses books as kindling. At one point, considering the glut of printed works in the world (one can only wonder what he would think of our days of print-on-demand and electronic self-publishing!), he muses:

> I don't understand
> This strange world any more. Each writer sets
> A pen in his wife's mouth; talking with friends
> He thinks: 'There's a new page!' And off he jets
> To write it down. Men are no longer ends
> In themselves, but merely means to spill some ink!
> And for what? For a plasma ball that sparks,
> Spitting some dim electrodes in the dark.

Writers, he suggests, are so in love with writing, that it elbows out *living*. People are not to be loved, experiences are not to be savoured, they are all but the raw material of literature. It's hard not to agree that books written in this fashion are better tossed into the stove than set on the shelf.

This thought, too, is derived from an earlier work, the *Undivine Comedy* of Norwid's older friend Zygmunt Krasiński. There, Count Henryk, a poet, is so enamoured of the make-believe world of the poetic ideal, that he drives his real family — a real wife and a real son — into tragedy on account of his mania. Norwid's Protazy, unlike Count Henryk, is clear-eyed. Though he may have his own problems to deal with in respect to how he treats people (and how he thinks of himself) his burning of the books seems an almost subconscious desire on Norwid's part to put art in its place.

Yet it is not only poets and writers who are to blame here. In *Criticism*, Norwid sounds a theme that he will repeat in *Auto-da-fé*: critics and readers rarely approach a book on its own merits. Rather, they seek out works, authors, and themes which validate their own way of thinking. In the former, the critic responds to criticism of his assessment of a book, which he judged not on its artistic merits, but on the 'lesson' it presents:

CRITIC
What? Virtue
Is not sufficient for a worthy book?

SOMEONE
Perhaps, but, for a work of fiction? Look —
Would you call that a novel, or a chart
Of your own views?

CRITIC
What else is the critic's art?

And in the latter, Protazy, again:

As the lightning splits the air,
Leaping great distances to spread its light,
So, people say, is print. They may be right,
But when a person takes a book back home

And sits down on his chair or in his bed
To slice through page-ends with his knife, instead
Of reading, he but searches for his own
Thoughts in the author's words, which, should he find,
He's satisfied. This reader is a kind
Of writer, but a lazy one; from this,
It's plain to see that readers... don't exist!

In this, the little dramas are most similar to dramatised lyrics: there is not space enough for too many themes; most often, it is one thought, one idea, that the poet seeks to delve into with a pithy directness.

THE 1002ND NIGHT

This early play, a comedy, is one of Norwid's few completely finished works for the stage. With it, he introduces a motif that will accompany his dramatic writing to the very end: that of a hidden truth, masquerading, concealment. On the one hand, this reveals Norwid to be a very nineteenth-century artist, naively operatic, in the manner of Mozart/ Da Ponte's *Marriage of Figaro* or Shakespeare's *Two Gentlemen of Verona*.

The Count (why are these people always counts?) believes that the mysterious woman who has arrived at the inn where he is staying in Verona is the same one who, as he understands it, rejected his proposal of love in a very insulting way — by sending him a letter that ends with 'and here's my reply —' which reply is his own letter, returned to him. (We pass by the fact that a proposal of love sent to a woman *by letter* is itself a rather clumsy thing, if not adolescent). The woman wishes to look out on a storm from the window of the room occupied by the Count, in which she once stayed herself, and the Count plans on taking his revenge by hiding in the closet and then leaping out to confront her and her supposed husband when they arrive:

I — shall emerge, calmly, coldly — no exaggerations — and ask her to introduce me to her husband. I'll fill in whatever she leaves out... with a smile... And then I'll wish her *bon voyage*...

We'll change the play into a still, deep, drama, or a casual comedy... at any rate... *alea iacta est...*

Some Caesar! At this point, we are beginning to wonder if the Count is fourteen...

He will confront her with... the second half of her letter, which she, distractedly, left in that very room, and which he — by improbable coincidence — found there... And yet Norwid shows a surprisingly mature theatrical sensibility by veering the story left at the very last moment. For when the Count leaps out crying triumphantly 'A masterpiece of recklessness...!' his voice dies off in embarrassment, for — the woman is a complete stranger. The masterpiece of recklessness turns out to be not the letter 'she' wrote him, but the *opera buffa* trap he laid. And thus, a play which seemed to be rolling in the well-oiled grooves of convention, with improbabilities that do not necessarily arise in a logical fashion, and melodramatic elements such as the closet-trap, are completely destroyed. Melodrama becomes absurdity, and in a way that underscores the primacy of unpredictable, real life over the contrived imagination that wishes to control it.

ZWOLON

If we were providing more than just the titles of the plays for dividers in these notes, here we would probably have something like '*Zwolon*, or a Guided Tour of the Polish Romantic Stage.' For it is in this unfinished drama — still perhaps the most intriguing of Norwid's works for the stage — where the great, idiosyncratic poet uncovers to our eyes the sources of his inspiration. *Zwolon* contains so many palpable allusions to the theatrical works of Mickiewicz, Słowacki, and Krasiński, topped off with Byron, as to seem something of a show-piece of a virtuoso musician, setting forth the range and variety of his skills.

It is a veritable anthology of influences.[13] We have a meeting of conspirators under the leadership of a timid cénacle chief such as we find in Słowacki's *Kordian*, a blind boy-poet of the Orcio type (an allusion to Krasiński's *Undivine Comedy* — although, it seems, this blind boy is not doomed to fade away; he triumphs in the end), a nod to the very roots of the great-souled Byronic traditions with the addition of a sardonic character named Harold, and — most tellingly — a long

---

13   Kazimierz Braun speaks of 'mannerism.' See Kazimierz Braun, 'Poetycki teatr Norwida' [Norwid's Poetical Theatre], in Inglot, 359-376.

soliloquy spoken by the main character, Zwolon, which is a clear homage to the greatest improvisations of the Polish Monumental stage: Kordian's soliloquy on Mont Blanc and — of course, the greatest of them all — Konrad's fierce, despairing (and wrongheaded) diatribe against God in Part III of *Forefathers' Eve*.

However, Norwid's Zwolon differs from the romantic heroes such as Konrad and Kordian in this, that *he is not a rebel*. This should not be misunderstood as to suggest that Norwid was any sort of loyalist. Nothing can be farther from the truth. Norwid was no less an advocate of national self-determination, yearning after the independence of partitioned Poland, than the great Romantics, whose exile from the fatherland he shared. But whether it be because Norwid came of a later generation that witnessed (as a child and as an adult) two armed uprisings end in tragedy, or because of his authentic Christian faith, which, while not necessarily quiescent or pacifistic, preferred the arms of the Spirit to those produced by armament factories, he longs for the reconquest of Polish independence through victory in the moral struggle. And so, to give but one lyrical passage from Zwolon's 'great improvisation,' striking in its similarity to the more exalted bits of 'Chopin's Grand Piano' with its longing for a Poland of 'transfigured wheelwrights,' where Christ rules 'incarnate upon Tabor,' Norwid's hero exults in a mystical vision of his country:

> From her I lived, and lived with her. Her I now wish to see
> So perfect, and full of being, to be
> Like the nation's eagle, in a flash, like a young thing
> Of another world… leading the rushing throng,
> And psalter-in-hand, leading the nation in song!
> Like streaming choruses, with rhythm angelic,
> Aquiline, lyric,
> From Lech to Lech the national glory
> And she, with outstretched hand, toward the wings falling there,
> Gathering from the air
> The echoes of history,
> That might tangle-twine in wreaths, of this land!…

Again, this is not quiescence by any measure. Norwid castigates evil directly where he finds it, and the very fact that the revolutionary party succeeds in violently overthrowing the unnamed, quasi-tyrannical king at the conclusion of the play is evidence enough of his understanding that, yes, at times, violence can be justified (as in a just war) to achieve moral aims. But just as the definition of a just war requires a careful ascertainment of war aims before the battle is joined, so in *Zwolon* Norwid cautions the hotheads against mistaking simple adrenaline and bloodlust for righteous ire. After the chilling character Bolej is introduced, who cannot sleep because of his desire to slash and kill and burn, Zwolon appeals to the crowd:

ZWOLON

Gesturing at Bolej.

This young man, nourished, as he says, on gore,
Is no son of freedom — he's nothing more
Than judgement's slave. And you, and those
Beneath that flag unfurled — which of you knows
Exactly what it means?

SZOŁOM
                    Traitor! Be gone!
His words would douse the ardour of the throng!

ZWOLON
Citizens! Citizens — but of what state?
The fatherland, or despair?

SOME
                    Ah — hear him prate!

ZWOLON
For I'm not sure — you're rushing off to die;
Is there any among you fit to seek
Life? Everyone would die for freedom's sake,
As if only the tomb were liberty,
And any sort of perishing, the gate
To immortality. Ah, but revenge

And liberty — these are quite different ends!
And often, when the two are so entwined,
And vengeance is achieved, avengers find
They've lost their freedom…

The argument is both practical and Christian. Practical, in that one can never tell whether violence may not lead to even greater oppression (of which the recent history of Norwid's Poland offered ample evidence) and Christian, in that it reminds the mob of the fact that their enemies are people too. The laws of God must always be respected, especially in cases where one finds oneself in a desperate situation that calls for violent action. In other words, there are things even more important than national independence. This sentiment veers quite near heresy in the ears of the earlier generation of Polish Romantics, and it is no surprise that Zwolon's words not only fall on deaf ears, they arouse the people against him — and this will eventually lead to his death.

Norwid's Zwolon, again, is no Byronic rebel. He is, rather, a prophetic spokesman of Christian truth — a representative of the King of Kings, the Order of all orders, against which Mickiewicz, boldly and beautifully, had his Konrad arise on behalf of justice for the nation he loves.

Zwolon's diametrical opposite in the play is the character named Szołom. Just as Zwolon's name suggests his character as one 'called, elected,' so does that of Szołom, from the verb oszołomić ['stun, bewilder,' by extension: 'lead astray by obfuscation'], aptly summing up the character of this figure, who appears in Norwid's works like the wandering Jew. In both this play and the later Krakus, Szołom is a servile tool of power, more than willing to set aside morality in order to serve a strongman. In Zwolon, his character is that of an agent provocateur: he stirs up the rabble to their rebellion in order to give the King an excuse to set his realm in iron order by moving strongly against an uprising. It is significant that, towards the end of the play, when everything seems to have gone wrong for him, the rat leaps from the sinking ship. Coming across Zwolon, he starts to skip round him with blandishments:

SZOŁOM

In travelling attire.

What have they won for us? Ruins on all sides,
Great man — blood, shame, and poverty, and waste!
In vain I begged, yes, in vain I cried
'Brothers! I like not the look on their faces,
Those fighting boys!' Destruction and disgrace!

*Pause. He continues following the silent Zwolon, peering continually
into his eyes.*

There was more courage by far in negation
Than in stoking just ire into the elation
Of bloody vengeance! Knowledge directs lives
Better than swords — a mere temptation
For children! What are swords? Are kitchen knives
Not made of the same steel? And so, why not
Make flags of tablecloths, with which to march
To cheering crowds through a triumphal arch
For having nobly with a pork-chop fought?

*Pause. Szołom continues to skip at Zwolon's side, glancing up at his face
beneath the brim of his hat.*

Am I not right, sir? Wise men know it's all
Spirit, yes, the Spirit's what it's all about!
But those men! They're unlearned — like some pagan rout!
And in the end, upon the learned falls
The blame, and we, what can we do but bear it?

With a sad gesture, he halts Zwolon.

So let us suffer. Meanwhile, in that spirit,
I bid farewell to you.

ZWOLON

> Tell me your name.

SZOŁOM

Dodging aside.

Szołom, a servant of the Spirit.

What is worth pointing out here is not so much the cringing nature of Szołom as Zwolon's calm, though stern, engagement with the lackey. As mentioned above, 'Tell me your name' is an allusion to the rite of exorcism. Commanded to reveal his identity, the demonic spirit (what 'Spirit,' indeed, does a wretch like Szołom serve?) falls under the control of the exorcist, who moves on to expel him. Szołom's sudden disappearance after telling his name — even though he previously announced his desire to leave, after his attempt at self-justification — sets this scene in the context of the exorcism of Mickiewicz's Konrad by Fr Piotr. And once more, the distinction between Norwid's Christian hero and the rebels of the earlier Romantics is set in high relief.

THE KRAKÓW PLAYS

In 1842, on his way to further artistic studies in western Europe, Norwid passed through Kraków. As Kazimierz Wyka tells us:

> Such a journey of several months constituted the realisation of the programme of the Romantic grand tour [...] Due to different political conditions, this programme could be realised by the first generation of Polish Romantics [such as Mickiewicz, Słowacki and Krasiński...] in a manner different to that in which it was by the second romantic generation, to which Norwid belonged. [...] The former were still capable of truly grand romantic voyages — one example of which is presented by the second act of *Kordian*: Italy, Rome, London, Mont Blanc. [...] The Romantics at home in Poland could not indulge in such journeys because of political concerns — ever-present police observation, the necessity of obtaining a foreign passport, and also monetary worries. [...] All that remained in place of this was to

wander about the country. [...] A trip through Poland, however, had its own justifications and nomenclature. Because Romanticism awakened lively interest in the historical past of the country as well as the material relics and other testimonies to that history — called *the fatherland's antiquities* — these journeys were known as 'travels into antiquity.'[14]

No other region of Poland presented the 'traveller into antiquity' with so many witnesses and relics to the historical past of Poland than Kraków. The mediaeval core of the city, crowned by Wawel, that royal necropolis and treasury, as well as traditions such as the Lajkonik, impressed Norwid to such an extent that, in Wyka's estimation, he becomes the first of a long line of Cracovian poets, including Wyspiański, Czyżewski and Gałczyński, who poeticised the city and its celebrations.[15]

Among the relics in the region of Kraków are the ancient mounds of Krak and Wanda. These neolithic tumuli have been associated from ancient times with the pre-Christian rulers of the Wiślanie: Wanda, who rejected the hand of a German prince in order to guarantee the national autonomy of her people, and Krak, who founded the city that bears his name after overcoming a dragon laying waste to the surrounding countryside. These mounds inspired Norwid so, that he not only created two of his most successful, and complete, dramas, *Wanda* and *Krakus, the Unknown Prince*, but dedicated the first, in gratitude — not to any person, but to the mound of Wanda itself! This very fact opens our eyes to his spiritual kinship with Wyspiański, who also testified to his love of the 'stones' of Kraków. As Wyka points out, 'After all, both of these compositions close with an apotheosis of place, apotheoses played out in a manner that cannot but have attracted Wyspiański, as they are in such great agreement with his own theatrical imagination.'[16]

---

14   Wyka, pp. 35-36.

15   Wyka, p. 24. Wyka also reminds us that had Wyspiański succeeded in obtaining directorship of the Municipal Theatre in Kraków, he planned to inaugurate his initial season with none other than Norwid's *Wanda* (p. 86). Of course, the great poet of Young Poland also created his own plays based on the Wanda myth: *Legenda* and *Legenda II*.

16   Wyka, p. 82.

CYPRIAN KAMIL NORWID

Who can say if Wyspiański's great theatrical triumph *Acropolis* — in which there are no human characters, but only vivified statues and tapestries from the Wawel palace and cathedral complex, to say nothing of the enlivened tomb of St Stanisław, which (or 'who?') falls upon King Bolesław Śmiały in Wyspiański's retelling of that conflict — would have come about, if it were not for the anthropomorphosised characters of the Threshold and the Spring, who play such a key role in the mystical scenes of *Krakus*?

This play, which, as Norwid himself notes, forms a dramatic diptych with *Wanda*, provides us with a glimpse into the poet's theoretical musings. In his introduction to *Krakus*, Norwid defines tragedy thus:

> As far as I am personally concerned, I believe tragedy to be *the making apparent of the fatal nature of history, society, the nation, or the age proper thereunto.* Consequent to this definition, it plays an auxiliary role in the progress of morality and truth. For this reason, it is no wonder at all that tragedy could, and indeed had to, be possessed of an almost ritual gravity.

These words should be borne in mind when considering Krakus' triumph over the dragon — defined by the elderly Hermit (a nod, again, towards Słowacki's *Balladyna*) as a progeny of 'the first snake, by Virgin's foot / [...] crushed; / your dragon's merely an offshoot / Of that first evil', where, it is not with steel, but with grace and virtue — and song — and truth — that the victory is won:

KRAKUS

Song.

Come forth! Now! By the faith of faiths
I conjure you, who gnaw the soul —
Your spell is gone with your last breaths;
My spell, it is no spell at all!

God knows how much sin, foul and black
Impels me here to sling this word

Into your face — my only sword
This lyre; this song — my only act —

My song is now no song at all!

Although this play is set in the ancient pagan past, and we do not witness Krakus' baptism, it is the 'faith of faiths' — Christianity — that triumphs over the enemy of all mankind, the devil; Rakuz, who remains in paganism (even after the victory over the dragon) is not only impotent in face of the evil, but *becomes* the evil after the death of the dragon by his jealous murder of his own brother. Krakus, who slays the snake, triumphs as a Christian hero.

Likewise, Wanda, a princess of an even earlier age than Krak, does not merely commit suicide in order to avoid an unwelcome marriage; in Norwid's retelling of the story, at the key moment of the drama, she is granted a vision of Christ's sacrifice on Calvary, and this indicates to her what she is to do. Her death is not a suicide, it is a sacrifice on behalf of the good of her people, and thus raises her to the dignity of a Christian martyr:

WANDA
My good people — I've seen above our land
God's immense shadow, like a straight road, run;
It was but the shadow of His hand,
And that hand — pierced — for through the palm the sun
Shone unimpeded... Staring like a bird
Flying in darkness toward that chink of light,
Suddenly, something in my spirit stirred
To a sure knowledge of what I must do...

She takes a candle from the hand of Piast, and ascends the pile.
Then, more quietly:

The knowledge that I must now... die for you...

I don't think we'd be going too far if we were to suggest that her dramatic, fatal plunge into the Vistula, as presented in Norwid's play, could be read as a sort of baptism.

At any rate, considering Norwid's definition of tragedy as the 'making apparent of the fatal nature of history, society, the nation, or the age proper thereunto,' we would be hard pressed to find better examples of the philosophy behind Norwid's poetics: his conviction that the nature of his nation, Poland, is Christian — and that that Christian nature of the country should determine the behaviour of Poles, in all situations with which they are faced, at all crossroads, where they are to take a decision.

IN THE WINGS; TYRTAEUS

Formally speaking, Norwid's *In the Wings* is arguably his most ambitious stagework. In an oeuvre dominated by disguise and hidden identities — let us add to the catalogue the King and Szołom's various disguises in *Zwolon*, employed to facilitate free movement among circles inimical to them, and Krakus' disguise as the 'hooded saviour' upon his incognito return to Kraków — *In the Wings* takes questions of hidden identity to an extreme. The play is set one evening during a masquerade, where everyone is disguised and not necessarily recognisable to one another; it is set in a Poland dominated by various secret societies and competing police agencies, all of which have their spies circling among the crowd, dressed as waiters; finally, there is the matter of *Tyrtaeus* itself, presented as a play by an anonymous author (which turns out to be Count [again, a Count!] Omegitt), within the context of the masquerade. So, in the audience, we are watching a play unfold on stage (the masquerade), during which the characters move off to another hall to watch the play *Tyrtaeus* (and so, where is reality in this *mise-en-abîme* of stages and plays?). As if this were not confusing enough, when we ourselves finally see a fragment of *Tyrtaeus* played out before us, the characters of Omegitt's Greek play enter the stage when Omegitt, exhausted, lays down to rest in the early morning. And so, one more Chinese box: are we watching a play, or witnessing a character's dream? To muddy the waters further, Omegitt's servant seems to have taken note of the presence of these ancient characters, too…

In the Wings is a problematic work, not only because it is unfinished. It seems as if here Norwid's reach exceeded his grasp, and, failing to create the gigantic, epic masterpiece he envisioned, what remains is less successful than had he parcelled out his ideas into a few, smaller works of less ambitious scope.

That said, even the less successful products of genius are well worth our regard, and in this implied questioning of reality and pretence we find something truly remarkable. That Norwid intended to confront his receptors with the matter of what is true and what is fool's gold in us and in our world can be intimated from the opening introductory scenes, where Quidam (a sage guide not entirely unlike Zwolon) uncovers to the 'Traveller's' eyes (Omegitt) the shabby truth that lies beneath the gaudy exterior of things:

TRAVELLER
What do you mean, modern? Modern, how…? This multi-coloured African marble, the slim Lombard columns? They don't make any more marble like this…

QUIDAM
Indeed they do. That's nothing but brick plastered over and painted.

TRAVELLER
That rectangular capital, carved with pious chisel by some master stonemason of the twelfth century?

QUIDAM
Was poured of zinc, one of a mass of factory-produced copies from the same mould, and subsequently gilded by a galvanising process. A structure such as what you look upon is built, these days, in the space of eight months.

'Is there no longer man or woman here, but mere phenomena of coincidental custom and the technical balance of the senses…?' Omegitt cries, at a key moment in his play. Thus, *In the Wings* can be considered a play of uncoverings. I would rather use the word 'discoveries' here, but one of the things we come away with upon finishing our lecture of this unfinished play is — the layers have not been peeled away sufficiently anywhere, to uncover an unvarnished truth to our eyes. Omegitt's question remains unanswered. Are all the people he deals with throughout the evening we witness, mere behavioural automatons, programmed by cultural mores? Or are there at least some real 'men and women' among them?

One of the 'peelings away' happens very much in the vicinity of Omegitt. At the beginning of the play, he is to be engaged to Lia. At the end of the play, she returns his ring to him and marries someone else — what's more, a Russian. Has she made a mistake, or was the 'reality' of Omegitt revealed to her eyes so, that she can now wipe the sweat from her brow at the bullet of fate missing her by centimetres? We cannot know — and never will, since the work is unfinished. One would not wish to consider Norwid a proponent of modern ideas such as the relativity of truth, or the impossibility of man to arrive at any objective knowledge. However, in its present form, *In the Wings* seems to suggest just that: we cannot know anything for sure. On this earth, at least, we are always 'in the wings,' never at centre stage, under the harsh glow of truth.

THE DRAWING ROOM PLAYS

Thus, generically at least, would we group the finished *Miłość czysta u kąpieli morskich* [Pure Love at the Sea-Baths] and *Pierścień wielkiej damy* [The Ring of the Grande Dame], two works revolving around the proper crystallisation of male and female attraction, the course of which, as the saying goes, never runs smooth. However, in both plays, everyone ends up where they ought to be, at least ostensibly, and here we run into a little problem. For, while *Pure Love at the Sea-Baths* is subtitled by Norwid 'A Comedy' — as indeed it is, in both an Aristotelian sense, and in the modern sense of a work producing smiles, if not belly-laughs, with *The Ring of the Grande Dame*, Norwid wished to create some new genre for the stage, which he calls a *biała tragedia* — a 'white tragedy.'

How this work might be considered a 'tragedy' at all is a quandary. The lovelorn Mac-X achieves his goal, at last, of betrothing the Countess Harrys (Yes. Another peer); he does *not* shoot himself, as he had planned, and Count (how tiresome) Szeliga, who was also obsessed with Countess Harrys, finds happiness in the end with her companion Małgorzata, who, it turns out, was a kindred soul to him all along. Even Judge Durejko, who seemed rather a money-grubbing villain in the earlier parts of the play, and the persecutor of poor Mac-X, turns out to be a rubber-toothed cur, and even a likeable one, who takes credit at the end (the subtitle is, after all, 'Durejko ex machina') for conducting it all to a happy end. Well, in his very long introduction to the play, Norwid describes the genre in this fashion:

I believe that this genre, for which we do not have an adequate term in Polish (as the *thing itself* has not yet appeared amongst us) is — *la haute comédie.* It is that which lays open, mainly, the field to edifying drama in our Christian society. At least it seems that it should be so, since this is to be a period of *societal-self-reflection* as a whole, of self-examination, I say, from the highest summits.

The whole of society!... I say, for it is here, and not in the comedies *buffo* (such as are masterfully sketched by the pen of Count Fredro), where one social caste examines another, discovers its ridiculousness, but as such acts as a civilisational-societal whole, as if a reflection of the universal conscience, examining itself.

This is an archly-difficult task for this reason, that the great, naked *Serious* here takes the place of those sensitive moments which tragedy is capable of drowning in blood, palpable and red. In accord with such a mood, all shadings must be indescribably subtle.

And so, the 'tragedy' does not lie in the dramatic movement of the main character from good fortune to bad, as on the Greek stage, but rather in the 'seriousness' of the subject, which does not preclude a happy end. Hence the one term he finds most suitable: *la haute comédie,* in which 'comedy' is used in the French sense of a serious stagework, or, as Norwid goes on to say, in the Dantean sense of the *Divine Comedy*, which has nothing funny about it at all, and — in its deepest sense — is to convey a very serious message to the reader. (It is in this sense — the *Divine Comedy*, as a writing that we know to be fictional, yet the aim of which is not to entertain, but rather to awaken us to the most important ontological truths of human life: sin and repentance, Heaven and Hell — that Dante's great work defies generic classification, and can only be compared, as far as purpose is concerned, with Holy Scripture. It is in this sense too that Norwid's writing, as we alluded above, is like unto Dante's. Norwid sees literature as a vehicle for Christian truth, not as an end in itself, and in this didactic approach to art he is, again, far from the Romantic norm). The only question that remains is this: what is the serious message that Norwid is trying to convey in *The Ring of the Grande Dame?*

There may be more than one answer to this question. I would offer the following, from the very end of the play. Mac-X, hopelessly in love with the Countess since the death of her husband, hears, at last, the words he has been longing to hear: Countess Harrys proposes marriage.

And yet, why is she doing this? Does she really love him? Or is this just her solution to a problem that has suddenly cast a shadow on both Mac-X, and the reputation of her own house? So the response of Mac-X is surprising:

> No, Madame, I'd be leading you astray.
> Perhaps I'd even become a liar, like
> The fellow who claimed to be a great marksman,
> Finding a hawk stretched dead upon the ground,
> Felled by a lightning bolt, by chance, after he
> Shot, and missed the mark! Ah no, my noble cousin!
> You err sublimely, but even so, you err.
> What we call the sublime is so for this reason:
> Sublime, in that it is above all hap.
> It spills forth from a heavenly fountainhead,
> Everywhere self-inspired, and always free.
> Can one be coerced to magnanimity
> Without once playing false to one's own will —
> Which, in revenge, will deceive one too, in time?
> The sort of man who would accept so great,
> So tempting an excess of such a heart
> Would be a cunning fellow merely. I,
> In this age, in this nineteenth century,
> Would rather not be skilled in cleverness.

What, in short, is the truth of her feelings? What do we find when we 'peel back' the drastic offer (for marriage is a drastic thing) of herself to Mac-X? This is what Mac-X needs to know, and this is the heavy message that Norwid wishes to convey via his 'white tragedy' to the society he forces to look upon itself in this dramatic mirror. It may also be found in a brief exchange between the Countess and Mac-X right before this long reply. Wishing to repair the damage done to Mac-X's public reputation by his false arrest, the Countess proposes: 'I'll submit your name / To the committees, and you'll be inscribed / A member of the board — a permanent one — / In our Society of Mercy!' to which Mac-X replies, without the slightest tinge of sarcasm: 'I'm one already. / I'm a Christian.' If tragedy, 'white' or otherwise, is to set a question before the society it wishes to challenge, in Norwid's work, once more, society is challenged to consider the worth of the social veneer it so prizes — the avoidance of the 'blot on the escutcheon,' to which one of the police officers makes reference during the arrest scenes — in reference to something human and real, such as love. Nature must be followed, not convention.

And what is convention anyway, if not self-absorption? What is any sense of disgrace and propriety, but a sick concern with oneself, and how one is seen? In this very brief treatment of the play, we seem to be making a hero out of Mac-X. But it's worth remembering a conversation he had early on in the play with the kind, simple housekeeper Salome, who asked Mac-X to put in a good word with the Countess for her son, who is far away in Japan with the navy. Although Mac-X promises to do this, his own love-problems are so all-encompassing that he forgets, as soon as the scene ends. Three solutions to his problem present themselves at various parts of the play, all three of which he seriously considers adopting: suicide, emigration to America, and marriage with Countess Harrys. Had he gone through with either of the first two, his promise to Salome would of course have gone unfulfilled. In the end, it turns out that the last, happy, possibility will be embraced after all. And now it is his own fulfilment that stands in the way of his helping the kindly old woman. And so — is this the subtlety that Norwid was referring to? So subtle as to be unnoticed by the reader, forgotten by the playgoer, the real message that makes all of the other, 'bigger' issues just red herrings? — what about that 'Society of Mercy?' How much of a Christian is Mac-X, really?

CLEOPATRA AND CAESAR

I would like to spend a little more time on Norwid's unfinished Shakespearean drama, because it was the motor behind this entire project.

To set her in the context of Shakespeare's Cleopatra, since that is unavoidable, we see that Norwid's heroine is a tragic figure because she is, above all, not solely a queen, not even a woman, but a girl — a young, attractive, normal girl in search of the most basic fulfilment of all: love. She is not Shakespeare's Cleopatra — one of the Bard's 'strumpets royal' as Charles Beauclerk[17] puts it perhaps a bit too harshly; she is a chaste,

---

17   Charles Beauclerk, *Shakespeare's Lost Kingdom. The True History of*

if willing, teenager, whose precocious, and intelligent, investigation of human love and human loneliness separates her from the Gertrudes, Titanias, and Cressidas to set her among the Lears and — above all — the Hamlets. Just as the Danish prince has his skull, the Egyptian princess has her mummy, whom she addresses in this same scene:

> So, to the judges of the underworld
> I spill libation, as a recompense,
> For you, the dead, and peer into your skull,
> Dead man — or woman — I, who've never lived,
> Might greet you with a hug, who live no more,
> Like old friends meeting — both of whom belong
> To that same heartless caste... though of you, perhaps,
> The wordsmiths might concoct the oddest tales
> As they do of me. And that old gossip
> That they call History, half decrepit, who
> Forgets her yarns before she's finished the telling...
> But praiseworthy she is, and for the age
> Peculiar in her affections.

Of course, this play is Cleopatra — *and* — *Caesar*. The motif of 'the greatest love story of all time' as Joseph Mankiewicz's 1963 film with Taylor and Burton is pitched can't, of course, be overlooked. But how splendidly it is handled by Norwid, and how unexpectedly. Mieczysław Inglot is not wrong when he states that 'the union of Cleopatra and Caesar was intended to give new birth to ancient civilisations. For Caesar represents the idea of the union of politics with morality. He symbolises progress in history [...] Cleopatra's love for Caesar is the union of two great personalities. It is the unification of beauty and profound idea.'[18] Yet it is something different, and more visceral, for both of them. Inglot illustrates his comment with the following exchange from the end of Act I:

Shakespeare and Elizabeth (New York: Grove Press, 2010), p. 12.

18   Mieczysław Inglot, 'Ogólna charakterystyka twórczości dramatycznej Cypriana Norwida' [The General Characteristics of the Dramatic Oeuvre of Cyprian Norwid], in Inglot: 134-169, p. 156.

CLEOPATRA
I rest upon your arm. For the first time
I feel as if I had the world's support.

CAESAR
'Tis not the arm of Caesar that you feel,
Madame, but that of a Roman consul.

Yet this has little, if anything, to do with geopolitics, at least from Cleopatra's perspective. This is the same girl — the same human being — whose erotic experience has been restricted to the strange ritual marriage to her brother, as dictated by Egyptian dynastic tradition. What does she know about love, 'betrothed unto a child, who shared my bed / But as a pet gazelle?' What does she know of love, indeed. But she is curious, and very curious is her confession of having been strangely stirred by the phenomenon, when she observed it among others:

In those eyes, that mouth, in those sun-bronzed cheeks,
Wind-tousled hair and swelling chest, I saw
Some unknown movements... of the soul...

Her fascination with Caesar is real. For her, he is 'a real man, / The first essential man [these] eyes have seen!' He is the key to unlock this mystery to her.

As for Caesar, certainly, in Norwid's telling he never ceases to be that historic man of destiny; he is sure of his mission and his significance, and that of Rome, in his speech and in his writings. *That* Caesar is familiar to us all. The side of him of which we know much less, and which Norwid reveals to us in his play, is a striking one indeed. As Cleopatra reluctantly departs from him, on the eve of her wedding to her second (!) brother, he senses both the cruelty of those geopolitics that tolerate, and make use of, such dodgy ceremonial, as well as the subtle reproach she tosses in his lap as she leaves. As she goes off, uncharacteristically, Caesar erupts:

CAESAR

Calling after her.

It is not my will that you marry him!…

CLEOPATRA
It's Rome's.

CAESAR
              No, it's not on account of Rome!
Along with you, he would be sent to hell
Were it not for Dynastic reasons. Ha!
You'd be a Roman slave, and not your people's
Mediatrix… The dead king's impotence,
The plotting of your own sister, your brother-
Spouse's vacuity… It's on account
Of these — and furthermore, it's on account
Of your Egyptian people! Bred between
Sphinx and Mummy!

CLEOPATRA
              Consul! Egypt's queen
Has not time for such speech to be prolonged.

His outburst — that of a frustrated lover, not a Roman consul — is just
as surprising and revealing as her cutting him off when he ventures too
far in his complaint, past dissatisfaction with the (somewhat perverse)
ceremonial, to attack the nation itself. Caesar gives vent to his emotions
as a man at the same time as he bows to the necessity of personal sacrifice
on behalf of political advantage. Cleopatra expresses her frustration with
her role, as a woman, but then, as soon as he goes too far, she puts him
in his place as a queen.

  This is the crux of Norwid's love-tragedy. A royal person is the most
unfortunate prisoner of office. Mateusz Grabowski describes it well,
when he says:

Caesar's action is dependent on the will of the Senate. Cleopatra's will
is overcome by tradition and her father's testament. The heroes are
representatives of their respective states, and simultaneously their
slaves, enmeshed in a string of political accords. Both are subjected

to a tragic destiny, the essence of which is the conflict of two separate cultural orders.[19]

As Beauclerk points out, queens have both a private body and a public one, the latter being their incarnation as the state. While this (he suggests) was effectively manipulated by Elizabeth I so that the (public) Virgin Queen shielded — and liberated — the private Elizabeth Tudor to enjoy the favours of Dudley, seeing no contradiction in what for any ordinary person would at least deserve the name of hypocrisy,[20] this is a source of pain to Norwid's Cleopatra — a normal girl if there ever was one, who chafes against hated, artificial, ceremonial:

CLEOPATRA
Caesar — a napkin, please — the woman asks.

She rises and moves to exit.

The Queen of Egypt now presents herself
To her expectant people, who await
The news of her marriage to… her brother-spouse,
The king… and that the plenipotentiary
Of the Roman Republic should announce
The testament of the monarch deceased.

The stalemate situation that exists between them can only result in catastrophe for two people who want to be together but cannot because they will not choose to cease being institutions. Well, they *could*, but history has no lack of royal figureheads abjuring their responsibilities on behalf of the persons they love (England has had two Edwards try this: the Second and the Eighth of that name) and this hardly ever turns out well… Alina Witkowska is probably not far wrong when she sums up

---

19   Mateusz Grabowski, 'Historiozofia zagłady. Uwagi do *Kleopatry i Cezara* Norwida' [Historiosophical Destruction. Some Comments on Norwid's *Cleopatra and Caesar*], *Acta Universitatis Lodziensis, Folia Litteraria Polonica*, Vol. 1, No. 27 (2015): 79-91, p. 86.

20   Beauclerk, pp. 42-43.

the personal tragedy of Cleopatra and Caesar as a case of 'wrong place, wrong time:'

> [Norwid's] general principle of the tragic nature of history also encompasses the love of Caesar and Cleopatra. Their feelings also bear the stigma of the times. It is a happy love, and one simultaneously sentenced to remain unfulfilled. Not only because Caesar is shortly to perish, but because — as one is free to assume — of the irony of two people meeting 'not at the right time,' 'not in time;' these two people otherwise being true discoveries to one another: in Cleopatra Caesar discovers Woman, and in Caesar, the queen of Egypt discovers Man.[21]

The fatal dichotomy between private and public is expressed by Cleopatra, as here, in her various speeches, when she makes a distinction between *Caesar* and *Julius*. For another example:

> While Julius and Cleopatra yet remained
> Together, they were like two living beings.
> But with a woman, Caesar is a stone
> That casts its shadow broadly on the sand,
> The greatness that was Rome obliterating
> All commonality…

Their quest for love is a quest for reality. Cleopatra no more wants 'Caesar' than she wants her ritual brother-spouse. She wants the experience that intrigues her in Faleg-Mun and Abdala Ganymedion, so in love with real persons, that they are unable to notice the queen's presence in their midst. She wants to have the same experience as they, for which she needs a man just like them, in short: 'Julius.'

> I gave no thought to Rome — For what Rome is,
> The great man, with a word, or in the still
> Majesty of his being kept from me,
> Blocking my sight by gesture, or a nod —
> Just like when someone sits down at a sill

---

21   Alina Witkowska, *Literatura romantyzmu* [The Literature of Romanticism] (Warsaw: PWN, 1987), p. 233.

Beyond which lies a city, and with elbow
Or fabric softly falling from a shoulder
Cuts off the view of millions of townsmen,
One finger blotting out a battlement,
Eclipsing a huge temple with an arm…

Her Julius fills up the window of her sight — blotting out Rome itself. Caesar too, that 'great man,' 'kept this from her' — for, as he says in that moment cited above, when he was caught off guard and angrily protests against the ceremonial laws which constrain the woman he loves to a hateful ritual marriage, he is after the same thing: at least a respite from history and custom, in the common glory of simple manhood.

Norwid's *Cleopatra and Caesar* is, above all, a realistic play. Shakespearean in conception and expression, it is yet far from the English playwright's general practice in that Shakespeare's dramas have a discernible arc to their stories. Whether we are talking about strict tragedies such as *Othello* and *Macbeth*, where tragic complications are tidied up at the end (*Hamlet* and *King Lear* are possible exceptions here; are the central questions of those plays ever truly resolved?), or the histories, which tend to lead to the reimposition of order after chaos, Norwid's work seems to *have no plot*. This, in short, is how Tadeusz Pini's reading of the play might be summed up. However exaggerated it may sound, there is some truth to it:

In this great 'historical tragedy,' Norwid's most compendious, and last, dramatic work […] nothing, generally speaking, happens. There is no intrigue, no action. And so despite the fact that the style is worked out with extraordinary care, clear, fluent and colourful; despite some beautiful situations and even effectively and profoundly thought-out scenes in their entirety, it is really torturous for the reader to attempt this tragedy, as he struggles in torment to discover a thread or tragic conflict that doesn't exist.[22]

When considered more closely, I believe that there is more method to Norwid's madness than his otherwise exuberant critic gives him credit

---

22   Tadeusz Pini, ed. *Dzieła Cyprjana Norwida* [The Works of Cyprian Norwid] (Warsaw: 'Parnas Polski,' 1934), p. xliv.

for. Granted, the work is unfinished. Yet it can be performed or read as a completed work for the very reason that it lacks a plot. Coming to the end of Act III, on which the curtain rings down dramatically with the suicide-by-servant of Antony, the spectator is not left wondering 'what next?' It's not as if Shakespeare broke off Othello in Act IV, right after the scene in the garden, and we're uncertain as to whether Iago's ruse will work, or come crumbling down around his own ears. There is enough of the play for us to hypothesise that Norwid was *consciously* working out a play in which 'nothing happens,' and would have continued in this manner even had he finished and polished it. Why? There are at least two reasons. On the one hand, it may be, as Grabowski points out in another article, that we are witnessing the death throes of two moribund civilisations,[23] and this lack of activity, lack of plot, is intended to underscore the progressive necrosis of a world ending, not with a bang, but a whimper. On the other hand, this lack of action emphasises the quotidian with which we are all familiar: that of long days during which 'nothing happens.' What this would lead to is an emphasis on reality and — like it or not — a meditation on human life in general.

NORWID TRIUMPHANT

In September 2021, two hundred years will have passed from the birth of Cyprian Kamil Norwid. And so it seems that Warsaw and Potocki, not Koźmian, were right after all. The twentieth century was the 'age' of that 'eagle' Norwid, and his ascent shows no signs of flattening, to say nothing of a descent. Despite all the things that set him apart from the other Romantics, Norwid is the quintessential Romantic in that, influenced he may be, but he scorns imitation (the hallmark of Neoclassicists such as Koźmian). His poetic personality is too strong, like young wine, such as will burst any old wineskins that it should be poured into.

There is an interesting passage in *Cleopatra and Caesar* that touches upon individuality and mimesis in art. Psymmachus, the master builder,

---

23   See Mateusz Grabowski, 'Dialektyka przemocy w ofiarniczych tragediach Cypriana Norwida' [The Dialectics of Violence in the Sacrificial Tragedies of Cyprian Norwid], *Czytanie Literatury. Łódzkie Studia Literaturoznawcze*, No. 5 (2016): 139-160.

recalls a slave from his days in Athens, who was so adept at copying others, that it ended poorly for him:

> I know no better mynahs then the tribe
> Of Wendo-Scythians. In Athens, once,
> While I was studying geometry,
> I had a slave of that far distant nation,
> A northern tribe… His name was Imitalski —
> And so protean was his mimesis
> That — sell him to a cobbler, and behold:
> The finest cothurn was stitched on his anvil.
> Pass him on to a tailor: in a trice
> Garments flow through his hands with weft out-spinning
> Rhapso or Ariadne. A looking-glass
> The fellow was — empty when left alone,
> But should a man come near, becoming him.
> He could do anything except invent.
> And for that reason he remained a slave.
> He needed a master just to exist.
> Once, two masters vied for his industry,
> And left the matter of whom he should serve
> To his own arbitration, the poor chap —
> That did him in. He simply couldn't choose
> Between this and that, both worthy men.

> OLYMPOS
> So, like the fabled ass, he died of hunger,
> Between two bushels of cracked oats?

> PSYMMACHUS
>   Not quite;
> The poor man tore himself in two halves
> In straining so, now east, now west.

In this wry reference to the slave as a 'Wendo-Scythian' named Imitalski (and thus, a Pole), who dies by a violent partitioning, Norwid is levelling a daring charge at both his nation's recent history and its artistic traditions. It is also something of an ironic statement, coming from a nineteenth century poet writing a pseudo-Shakespearean drama. Yet the message is an intriguing one concerning Norwid's own idea of artistic individuality, not to say idiosyncrasy: like Hopkins, he is by nature a poet of inscape and instress, a confessor to Duns Scotus' idea of *haecceitas*. As Norwid sees it, the artist, like Hopkin's kingfisher, 'Selves — goes [him]self; *myself* [he] speaks and spells, / Crying *Whát I dó is me: for that I came*.'[24] And this is why we are celebrating Norwid this year, and will continue to do so as the years pass; for he, like Hopkins, is timeless.

THIS COLLECTION

This collection of Cyprian Kamil Norwid's dramatic works presents the English reader with the majority of Norwid's theatrical corpus. Nearly every work he wrote for the stage, or for dramatic reading, is translated and included here. The reader will not find *Aktor* [The Actor] here, nor every one of the small, dramatised lyrics that Norwid produced in his relatively long life, although a few of the latter, such as *A Moment of Thought,* for example, and *Auto-da-fé*, should give the reader some inkling of that current in Norwid's creativity.

There are several ways in which the works contained in this anthology might be arranged. *Cleopatra and Caesar* is a work modelled after Shakespeare's histories; *Pure Love at the Sea Baths* is a comedy; *Krakus, the Unknown Prince* has elements of romance in its fantastic elements, in which inanimate objects such as a Threshold take on speaking roles. Yet generic distinctions in the world of Cyprian Norwid are fluid. *Krakus* has elements of a tragedy, as does its twin *Wanda*, yet both of them are Christian tragedies, if one might put it so, and the deaths of the titular heroes are sacrificial — not something necessarily 'tragic' to be mourned. Indeed, the genre of tragedy is difficult to pin down in Norwid's writing: *The Ring of the Grande Dame* is intended to be something Norwid terms a 'white tragedy,' and yet — especially considering its conclusion — the dramatic movement is from complication to happy resolution, which is the classical definition of comedy, and the character of Judge Durejko is one broadly cut from the cloth of farce.

If generic ordering is a debatable strategy, chronology might be a better way to go. But even here we run into problems. Generally

---

24   Gerard Manley Hopkins, 'As Kingfishers Catch Fire,' Vol. 7-8.

speaking, Norwid's dramatic career spans some thirty years: the first datable dramatic work from his pen is the short *Moment of Thought*, dated 1841, and his last, and most complete play, *The Ring of the Grande Dame*, is dated 1872. That is, unless the magnificent torso of *Cleopatra and Caesar* is taken into account, which was begun around 1870, and taken up again toward the end of the poet's life in 1878/1879. With most dramatists, we are able to create a hard and fast chronology based on productions or publications. This is not true of Norwid's work, most of which remained in manuscript until collected by others and printed in the early twentieth century. It is difficult in such a case to definitively date many of these works, which seem not to have been intended by the poet to be romantic mystifications, 'finished' in their unfinished form, the literary equivalent to 'ruins' constructed in a suitably romantic, dilapidated state in nineteenth-century parks, but writing that he set aside, and returned to at different times in his life. Thus, though the progression of texts in our volume is basically chronological, we cannot vouch for its precision. The order we follow is that presented by one of the greatest editors of Norwid's works, Tadeusz Pini, in his one-volume edition of Norwid's writings published in Warsaw in 1934. Many of the notes indicating lacunae in the texts are also reproduced from Pini's edition.

ACKNOWLEDGEMENTS

I would like to thank everyone at the Polish Cultural Institute, London, who first proposed the translation of *Cleopatra and Caesar* as part of the celebrations of the bicentennial of Cyprian Kamil Norwid's birth in 2021. To Natalia Purchalska, and Marta de Zuniga in particular, who also facilitated the production of my translation of Jan Kochanowski's *Dismissal of the Grecian Envoys* at the Globe Theatre as part of the 2019 'Shakespeare is Poland' festival, I owe a deep debt of gratitude, as I do to the people at the Globe, for their interest in promoting Renaissance and Shakespearean plays off the beaten path. As always, I am deeply indebted to Ksenia Papazova and everyone at Glagoslav for their interest in bringing Polish literature to the English-speaking world, and to the Polish Book Institute for their generous financial support.

Prague, 22 July 2021

A MOMENT OF THOUGHT

A FANTASY

A little garret room. Windows, thickly covered with frost, admit some pale light. A few embers are faintly glowing in the stove, next to which stands a table with books and torn papers in a jumble. To the rear is a glass door that gives on to a hallway. Evening. All is quiet.

YOUTH

Pacing the floor.

What is it scalds me, what so swells my breast
That I must hold my tongue, yet I must weep?
Cold is the speech, but powerful, to keep
This errant soul in fleshly chains impressed.
Would that it were to the young heart befitting
To tread with light foot the flowery swale
And not despair — for such a thing's upsetting:
People get bored, and cheeks are known to pale!

Paces, pauses, looks at the papers.

And quills? Well, if they scorn the vales below
And as the eagle, soar on mighty wing,
Yes! But to furrow the brow like a hoe,
And turn the dust to uncover — nothing?
Blessed are those who utter words aloud
And sing! Just like that! Who only need a hand
To write… For my words — dull syllabic crowd! —
Come not to christen, but to toss some sand
Upon thought's coffin. What good is a scythe
When the whole harvest won't make up a tithe?

Paces, halts, looks at the window.

And who said you should scribble anyway?
There's lots of other work: look! the doormen hew
Firewood — and you can chop as well as they —
There's firewood enough, and doors, too…

Suddenly.

So it's addiction, warmed beside the coals
That coaxes you to vanity, great soul?

DOORMAN

Enters to light the candle.

Evening sir. How's this for bitter weather?
I… Sir? Are you not well? The veins, like tethers
Tremble on your brow…

YOUTH

Striving to hide his embarrassment.

                Ah, nothing to fear!
The smoke backed up into the room. I lit
The stove without checking if the flue was clear —
It's in old stoves like that the devil sits!

DOORMAN

Inspecting the stove.

Sometimes the sparks leap out onto the floor
And start a conflagration… But this is
Unlit!… Now, frost don't respect persons, be't lord
Or beggar — Ah, me, three kids and the missus —
To hear so many teeth a-chatter! Breath

Freezes before your nose; the walls are white
With frost — the kids cling together, as if death
Had bound 'em for quick lading — what a sight!

YOUTH
They suffer in the flesh, and I, in spirit.

DOORMAN

Lights the candle, continues.

I tell you sir — if you should care to hear it —
It's that what sparked my quarrel with my wife.
So cold was I, needing to warm the bones,
I took a little nip… Upon my life,
A little dram hurts no one! Yet here she comes
And don't she lay into me…?

Noticing how distracted the youth is.

Well, good night.

Shielding the flame against the draught with one hand, he goes out.

YOUTH

After a pause.

Such the mirages that dupe our human sight —
What rules the world but money? Oh, that gold
Should rust and lose all value! Yet instead
Of life, we're drawn and quartered, cheaply sold…

CHILDREN

Past the wall, weeping.

Mama, mama, we're hungry! Give us bread!

YOUTH

Listening, he looks around and searches through his pockets.

And I have nothing, bread or coin, to give!
So I must be quartered, and sold, and then
I'll be of some use to my fellow men —
For what's the reason, tell me, that I live?
My flesh is frozen, while my empty thought
Bobs through the heavens; my hands smoke like tar
While I rinse them of earthly things; I'm caught
In the embrace of a drowned man and far,
Far away into the depths we sink,
While like a hanged man withered is my heart
Who senses yet, while dangling dead below
The branch, a bird above him — dove, or crow?

Paces, halts, grabs his pen.

As if I didn't know what I'm to do!
Write for the mob, for cash! That's nothing new!
Pander the word, until each page will chime
With silver bullion, like a silver mine,
And you must prop your head, which burdened, sinks
Not overcome with thought, but gold chain-links!

Paces, then halts.

O, wretched man! Again we've fallen thus?
My fervour sick, my strength a child's, yet I
Enthuse… Well, magnets even attract rust…
With hope alone, so cheaply, you might buy
Body and soul — and look here: you're still young
And fresh, but know: just like the blight that duns
The rose, a thorny tendril loops your brain,
To form — no wreath of bay, but — a choker-chain!

Pause.

So, write and write, and hock your words retail,
Herding your thoughts to market like fat beeves.
And when the coin falls in downpours like hail,
Instead of strong flour milled from hearty sheaves,
Toss candy to the hungry, to those that thirst,
Sweet drinks that cloy, not slake — May it be cursed,
The moment I should so befoul my thought,
Blinding its pure eyes with soiled rags, to plot
Schemes to filch bags of coin!

CHILDREN

Sobbing, past the wall.

Mama — bread, bread!

YOUTH

In a paroxysm of despair.

Sterile pity will be the end of me!
It's not enough to crush one's enemy —
As long as the heart beats, it must get dirty,
Sold to the world for silver pieces thirty,
And then… Lean back and laugh!

He goes over to the glass door, stands there gazing a moment, then calls.

Hey son! Come here!

CHILD
You calling me?

YOUTH
I am, but mind your tongue!
Be more polite addressing elders, dear.

Trying to divert the boy.

When I was just a boy, about as young
As you are, I would skip and laugh and play…

Hiding his tears.

What's all this moaning? Have you ever known
Any of us to cry? You should be gay!
Tears get you nowhere — Play! Leave off your moans
And play!

CHILD
    When it's below freezing outside!

YOUTH
That doesn't matter. You have got to try
To be happy, or Jesus will get mad.

CHILD
My mama says that Jesus too got sad.

DOORMAN

From the hallway.

Hey, boy!

CHILD
    I'm coming!

Runs off.

YOUTH
               Judging from the rags
And misery, who would expect such alms?

Deep in thought.

His Mama says that 'Jesus too got sad.'

Pause.

All our life long, we know — nothing at all.
We want to know, yet we know — not a thing.
We grow, indeed, but so does our swaddling,
And we will never beat it in this race,
The world our swaddling clouts, and we — eternal babes
Who play in the shadows and fear the dark;
Then terror evaporates with lightning speed
And all is well once more, although, indeed,
We've still learned nothing. Nothing but the cross
That stretches wide its arms old folks to greet,
The youth to bless, and, bruised forehead bent
Earthward, would spell out from the children's eyes
Whether the bloody ribbons, which so thickly flow
Will be worth anything? Or disappear?
No! They won't disappear. For deep inside
As long as — in thought, not in screams — grows
Pain, it shall burst into bloom, a thorny bow
To ply the heartstrings of all who live below!

(1841)

SWEETNESS

A TRAGEDY IN ONE SCENE

TO THE READER

After some brief reflection, the gentle reader should become convinced of the fact that the only reason he would deny these few pages the name of 'tragedy' is because… they are but a few pages. The author is not concerned with this.

Persons: Gaius Veletrius, high priest of Jove and senator. Pamphilius, a grammarian and client of Veletrius. The Turnkey of the prison of Vesta. St Paul, apostle.

The setting of the play is Veletrius' villa near Rome, during the reign of Emperor Nero.

The baths in Veletrius' garden. To the rear, a pathway, beyond which we see the green of trees. To the left, a bath of porphyry, into which water falls from beneath the feet of a statue set above it. To the right: a sofa, upon which Veletrius is seated. At his feet, a low stool.

GAIUS VELETRIUS
And what did Julia Murtia say, when brought
That bread?

TURNKEY
        She raised her eyes, then, deep in thought,
She said 'thank you,' — and gave it to the rat
Which has its hole there in the dungeon wall.

GAIUS VELETRIUS
A week of strict starvation, and that is all?

I reckoned you'd have more for me than that…
Dismissed!…

TURNKEY
        I go.

GAIUS VELETRIUS
                There in the holy Vestals' gaol
There ought to be nor rat, nor even rat's tail,
Nor any hole or crack in the smooth stone!
Go! Have Pamphilius, or some other come
To read me Aristophanes. Have him dressed
In kirtle, to match his gestures to the text.

Exit Turnkey.

Who is this God who keeps her in His care?

Pause.

Should I declare her Christian, she's undone.
She's executed and… what would I have won?
Will that in some way heighten my control
Over her? Or will it transform her soul
Into a flower (if Plato is proved
Correct) — and if so, can a flower be moved?

PAMPHILIUS

Enters carrying a vase.

I've brought *Frogs, Wasps, Birds*…

GAIUS VELETRIUS
                And *Assemblywomen* —
Let's have that. Sit!

PAMPHILIUS

Sitting at Gaius Veletrius' feet.

>It's proper to set them in
The same caste as female bugs and reptiles…
The thought is bold, bitter, but makes one smile.

Pause. He follows Veletrius' eyes.

It's too bad that — the priestly dignity
Deprives one of a certain amenity,
That is, a certain joy…

GAIUS VELETRIUS
>What?

PAMPHILIUS
>If you please…
You might have been an Aristophanes!

Pause, then, changing gesture and accent.

How many fit inside the new arena?

GAIUS VELETRIUS
It's better than the Flavian. I mean — a
Smaller venue, but a more select crowd.

PAMPHILIUS

Aside, but loudly.

Such precise terms! Laconia would be proud…!

GAIUS VELETRIUS
Listen, Pamphilius — tell me: no nonsense…

PAMPHILIUS

Interrupting.

O, by Minerva!

GAIUS VELETRIUS
…Where do these Christians get that inner strength?
I've seen troops hopelessly beset, veterans
Of ancient legions; I've known gladiators…
It's something more than bravery —

PAMPHILIUS

Assuming a serious mien and accent.

                    The source
Of virtue, among us, is inspiration:
A spark divine, whereas in that dark nation
Known as the Christians, well, to be precise,
It's aether. A liquid, clear as panes of ice.
Instead of fire, they're water. Hence the reason
They are so cold and harden unto treason,
And yet, a certain… sweetness… but the name
I don't quite know… more than the bruit of fame…

GAIUS VELETRIUS
Indeed — a precise terminology
Would be a good first step; for now, let's say —

PAMPHILIUS

Catching up.

The aquatic-combustive, if I may
Suggest, by way of etymology,
For this system of mine…

GAIUS VELETRIUS

                    Good! Considering
The self-destructive tendencies they bring
To their ontology…

PAMPHILIUS

Aside, but loudly.

                    You Socrates!

GAIUS VELETRIUS
In short, use what nomenclature you please,
The thing remains itself. I wouldn't say
A thing civil, but natural… or do I stray…?

PAMPHILIUS

Bowing his head.

What shall I say to Plato?

Pause.

                              Once when I'd
Strayed over the Tiber on a walk, I passed a
Shoplet of cast-off goods, and there I spied
Two jars — of basalt and alabaster —
The first held balsam, and some shards of clay,
The second — the lid of which bore a sphinx —
Held manuscripts: of Christian sufferings,
And of their Christ Himself — his *Odyssey*,
If I might speak of that vain screed this way,
Though it contains — I grant you — something… sweet,
Something that they call grace…

GAIUS VELETRIUS

                    Something…

Tossing the hem of his toga over his eyes he drowses. Pamphilius tiptoes off.

GAIUS VELETRIUS

In half sleep.

                                    Something…
Something that gives them strength… I've seen them pat
The famished lions sent against them, and
The beast becomes as gentle as a cat,
Rubbing against their legs, licking their hand…
The strength that fills their hymns until fierce death
Closes their smiling lips — Or Murtia… strength…
Old man — you, in that cloak of red you wear,
Barefoot, with flashing sword there at your side
Where we've but dark and empty pleats, who cried
That I might be entangled too — speak on!
I'm listening…

ST PAUL

In Gaius Veletrius' dream.

                The grace over which none
Of your fierce tormentings can prevail
I can give you — and with it, you might heal.
But why do you seek it?

GAIUS VELETRIUS

Quickly, unconsciously.

                So I might overcome
Her!

ST PAUL

Touching Gaius Veletrius' shoulder with the point of his sword.

Julia Murtia has died.

St Paul vanishes. Enter Turnkey.

GAIUS VELETRIUS

Leaping to his feet, to Turnkey.

She's dead?

TURNKEY

Just now.

AUTO-DA-FE

A COMEDY IN ONE ACT AND ONE SCENE

This bronze is a deceiver, for it pretended to be God before the eyes of men, and only God can put an end to suffering, and calm the heart forever, etc.

Juliusz Słowacki, 'Anhelli,' p. 43, fragment 4.

PERSONS

PROTAZY, a poet
GERWAZY, Protazy's confidant
FUNERAL CHORUSES of a deceased person
READERS
TWO STOVES — etc.

Act 1 Scene 1

The theatre is set up to represent the author's home — Protazy is stoking the stove — Gerwazy is binding up packages of new books.

PROTAZY

Leaning away from the fire.

See what the world is coming to with books!
Each month my editor sends me new kindling,
As if my library shelves needed stuffing.
Bound up and gilt — Presto! *Collected Works.*
But noblesse oblige… Wait… Here's my newest thing…

He gets up, picks up a book and writes on the flyleaf.

'From — the — author.' Good, then. Now, send some man,
Or hop along and send it through the post.
Reciprocal politeness — that's the most
One can do, sometimes…

Gerwazy exits.

PROTAZY

Aside.

                  I don't understand
This strange world any more. Each writer sets
A pen in his wife's mouth; talking with friends
He thinks: 'There's a new page!' And off he jets
To write it down. Men are no longer ends
In themselves, but merely means to spill some ink!
And for what? For a plasma ball that sparks,
Spitting some dim electrodes in the dark.

GERWAZY

Entering.

I sent it.

PROTAZY
    And I'm burning the last one.

GERWAZY
'With love, from your brother,' you might have sent —

PROTAZY
I see no reason for dishonesty!

GERWAZY
Deeds are dumb thoughts, while thoughts — deeds eloquent.

PROTAZY
I sent it — what else do you want from me?

A knocking at the door. Gerwazy opens and receives a letter, which he hands to Protazy.

PROTAZY

Reading the letter.

It's from him! Look how dangerous it can be
To hurry! Something's come into his head —
He says 'Send nothing to me here; instead,
Hold on — I'm moving, closer by, you see,
And my apartment's small.' Sit down, quick! Write:

Dictating.

'I put my new book in the mail before
I opened yours. Return it, at my cost.'
End, full stop, there's nothing more to say, by...
But have the courier bring back a reply.

GERWAZY

Exiting with the letter.

Thus do we unto others, as we would...

PROTAZY

Solus.

I'd be most happy if that letter should
Arrive no later than the book. But where's
Gerwazy?

He paces, halts from time to time.

            As the lightning splits the air,
Leaping great distances to spread its light,
So, people say, is print. They may be right,
But when a person takes a book back home
And sits down on his chair or in his bed
To slice through page-ends with his knife, instead
Of reading, he but searches for his own
Thoughts in the author's words, which, should he find,
He's satisfied. This reader is a kind
Of writer, but a lazy one; from this,
It's plain to see that readers… don't exist!

Paces, halts in front of the stove.

There is another type, who doesn't know
His own mind — this one bends over the book
With open mouth, as if it were a brook
And he, thirsty, gulps down whatever flows
Upon the current — be it jokes or tears,
Laughter or melancholy, comfort, fears…
The author pours on, till he's surfeited,
Loses his sense of taste…

Pause.

            And both are… dead!
Help!

               · · ·

Where is Gerwazy?

A knocking at the door. Gerwazy enters, exhausted, seeks out a chair and sits down.

GERWAZY
I wanted to forestall today's post-chaise,
I wanted to head off your hurried thanks,
But then — a funeral put paid to my haste —
And how long the procession! Ranks and ranks
Of priests and monks of every sort of cowl,
And mourners? Crowds! How slowly did they crawl —
Forests of glowing tapers around the bier
That bore the dead! I watched the legions flow
Past, squeezed into an old niche where I'd pushed
Myself out of the trample — Apollo
Once had his idol there — thanks be to him —
And when they passed me by, again I rushed
Upon my way, but, when I reached his house…

He pauses to catch his breath.

PROTAZY

Finishing his sentence.

He wasn't home — he'd already cleared out!

GERWAZY
No, not at all. That move was just a whim —
He's staying put. He greeted me and bade
Me greet you in his name; he says he's well
— I've never seen the man so gaily clad
Or ever in a better state of health —
Only, it seems, the hour at which I came
Was awkward… for I found him feeding flames
With — just as you do! So I thought it better
Not, after all, to deliver your letter…

PROTAZY

Sighing, gazing at his stove.

Well then, if we're not peers in wisdom, say:
At least we show our thanks in the same way!

End of Act the First, Scene the First and Last.

CRITICISM

A DRAMATIC POEM IN THREE IMAGES

I.

EDITOR
We've got our newspaper, now, who will be
Our critic?

SECRETARY
   Of what?

EDITOR
      Books, life, art — all three.
Here facts, there theory, and here — the ideal,
All explicated in a lettered row.

SECRETARY
Let's start with literature.

CRITIC
      Here we go:

Reads.

'A novel with a folk-national theme
Describing local customs. So, it seems
The author, through his Wacław, means to sing
Of too much loving as a tragic thing.
Wacław, the castellan's son, is in love
With Doloroza. But — like hand in glove:
Her father with his father is at odds.
He grants his daughter's wish but — it's a dodge:

For this love's none to his liking. Instead
Of married to Wacław, he'll see her dead.
(Both families are proud, as well as sore).
In the meanwhile, the nation is at war.
Wacław and the sire of his bride to be
Conspicuously rout the enemy.
Wacław, while dealing blows both left and right
Does so, day-dreaming of his wedding night
(Which is no good example for a knight! —
Love when you've time to cuddle, in battle: fight!
But I'll forgive him this). When they return,
What does the young lover, to his sorrow, learn,
But that no bride awaits him — but a corpse!
Her father weeps; Wacław springs to his horse
And vanishes. Meanwhile, the old man dies,
Kneeling at daughter's graveside, drowning his eyes
In bitter tears. At this, the reader asks:
Was Wacław simply not up to the task
Set him by fate? For in the end it proved
That, more than virtue, 'twas himself he loved?
So: a weak hero, a maiden too romantic
Who, had he let her be, and ceased from antics
Of passion immature, she would live still,
Unthrottled by the servants sent to kill
Her by her father, who would not have died
For having thus the fatal match denied,
Later to fall into morbid remorse.
Thus, had our author chosen such a course,
His book had been greater, as well as meeter;
As it is, it's not fit for every reader.'

SOMEONE
I beg your pardon, but if such be true,
Would it still be a novel?

CRITIC
                    What? Virtue
Is not sufficient for a worthy book?

SOMEONE
Perhaps, but, for a work of fiction? Look —
Would you call that a novel, or a chart
Of your own views?

CRITIC
                    What else is the critic's art?

II.

SECRETARY
Let's have a look at social commentary.

CRITIC

Reads.

'No bagatelle can escape the wary
Eye of the censor, and thus we make bold
To comment on the carnival (all told
A fine affair, as entertainments go,
With dancing — dances fast and dances slow,
Proper to age and number, one might say,
For there's a way to dance, and dancing's way
Of being…)' Here the author halts and slips
Into the text a meaningful ellipse,
Then: 'Who might be the gentleman who wore
The Domino mask, gold, with crimson lined,
Who stood at the buffet for such a time,
Statuesquely, and crying out "More! More!"
Tinkling his glass — "Come! fill it to the brim!"
Unless we are mistaken: a pilgrim
Just recently returned from sacred sites?
It *can't* have been him, no, for it's not right
That pilgrims dabble with such earthly rot
As wine and the fair sex…' Then, dot-dot-dot:
Ellipses to provoke the reader's thought…

SOMEONE

Once more I have a question for you: Now,
Is it thought you're provoking, or a row
With commentary leading to surmises,
Offence, polemics, and nasty surprises?
Sure, faults exist — but should we crucify
The errant, or inspire, and edify?
Is scandalmongering a noble part
Of journalism?

CRITIC

What else is the critic's art?

III.

SECRETARY

Read us your thoughts about the arts now.

CRITIC

Sure!
'First Fruits of the New School of Miniatures
Is our first topic, sensing what the times
Demand, the temperaments of varied climes
And nations bearing witness in the arts
To their devotion thereto; for our part,
Let us permit our careful eyes to settle
On each bloom, and then, let's, petal by petal,
Dissect its composition. So, the craft
(Bypassing other genres) of *Landschaft*.
What is a landscape? Let the artist's view
Of Nature ravish us, pierce us through and through
As does the bolt from on high; otherwise,
Let it swell in us deeply, to the skies
Impelling elevated thought. The aims,
You see, of painting too are varied; varied claims
The vulgar and the sacred styles require
Of the artist; the first of these inspired

78

By life, the second by a higher sphere.
I offer one example to you here:
How can a subject apostolical,
That's set in Syria or ancient Rome
Be worked up properly from such local
Patterns as may be found right here, at home,
Such as the soapbox-orator, or the poor
Maid drowsing at some German tavern's door?
How can the master take in hand some trull
And with her, deutschify a parable?
The patterns that he needs are to be found
Not here, but in the deserts that surround
Tyre and Sidon, or even south from there,
Where palm trees droop their fronds in the blue air
Like humble tresses, or farther still,
Where three crosses were searched out on that Hill
Of our salvation…' That's what I have to say
Of painting.

SECRETARY
                    One more question, if I may:
Now, is the goal of artworks to disguise
The word, or to reveal it to our eyes?
For truth is born each day; we're ever turning
A new page, and with care: we're ever learning
— Through nineteen centuries — that we're to seek
In each and every person that we meet,
Though they be deeply hidden — Cross and gall,
Nail-head and tomb and glory's ray, and all
The grand account of our salvation — stippled,
Shaded and bright, in both hale and cripple.
How else can virtue speak unto our heart?

CRITIC
What sense, in that case, has the critic's art?

THE 1002ND NIGHT

A COMEDY IN ONE ACT

This play is dedicated
To M. T.
The closest person to me not born of the same blood

... e maestra mi fu l'anima mia

PERSONS

Roger*	of Czarnolesie
Lady	on her travels
Doctor	accompanying the Lady
Lucio	innkeeper

* The name Roger may be changed to another, more euphonious one.

The action takes place in Castel-Fermo, near Verona.

THE INN, CASTEL-FERMO

An upper room.

LUCIO
By good St Anthony of Padua, my lord, this is the tenth vetturino
that's pulled into our courtyard today — There are more spacious
rooms on the left, but...

Drawing near the window.

... none of them has such a treasure... What a view! Perhaps you
paint?... Perhaps my lord's an artist?... A certain Signor Calame, who
paints landscapes, once stayed with us... here... a full two weeks and
in this very room... all of our returning guests who know of it, they
always ask about this room...

Thunder. The window is closed — the lower panes papered over.

If only the storm would pass, by Bacchus! By the Most Holy Virgin!
By St Anthony of Padua! I ought to set my wife upon the roof with
the Loretto bell...

WOMAN'S VOICE

Offstage.

Lucio! Lucio!...

LUCIO

Setting chairs here and there, putting things in order lazily.

What, again?... I'm coming, I'm coming!

VOICE
Lucio!

LUCIO
I'm on my way!

He exits.

ROGER
Most curious of nations... No matter how firmly I might have sworn
to have no more to do with the ideal, and enter onto a more practical
life... All it takes is one fleeting consideration of the moral character of
this archly-classical people... the mosaic floor... the lamp, unchanged
in shape from the times of the Etruscans... the cobwebs trembling
in the corners, which still remember the Lombard invasions... the
coverlet there, tossed upon the bed, of purple velvet — perhaps the
property, once, of some Verona nobleman, some Scaliger, bought by
the innkeeper as a pawn at public auction... and the disorder... and
the laziness!

   Speaking of which — and of practicality — here you sit, Roger,
listening to the storm that rumbles above the towers of Verona...
composing verses. Oh! You silly man...

   You wretched man — you wretch! Yes, shame on you, unable to
keep a trifling promise — to yourself! Right now you ought to leave
behind this land of illusions, this still, soft land of laurel groves... this
cemetery of both men and giants... Here on the threshold of Italy...
Just fling your thought over the Alps there... it's there you ought to
be... ought to return... having made that promise to yourself...

Slowly and solemnly.

... that you would be, from now on, practical... Come now, I say, you
ought to beat your breast and look one last time, one very last time,
upon the realm of the ideal...

Pause.

How beautiful — how beautiful this realm of dreams, mistakes...
mistaken dreams, that spreads before me now like vales and hillocks,
lakes reflecting the dawn...

CYPRIAN KAMIL NORWID

Thus I address you — You! Ideal future! You, delightful region… hear me now! It's over between us.

With a smile.

Thus Hannibal, upon the Alpine summits, raised his visor and cast his eyes upon Italy, and said 'I bring you your grave.' Thus Hannibal…
No! Not at all! Hannibal was no baby…
Thou shalt not take the names of great men in vain.

He paces the room. Lucio Enters.

LUCIO
With your permission, with your permission, by Bacchus…! A certain lady, an Englishwoman, asks if it might not be possible for her to watch the dying storm from this window…

With a smile.

… A nation of madmen, the British!… With the rain pouring down more fiercely than before!… I beg your pardon, but we don't like to refuse our foreign guests…

ROGER
Go tell that lady that I'm snoring. Sleeping the sleep of the dead. But that I keep two loaded pistols by my bed, and can't answer for what might happen should I be awakened suddenly. And tell her that from tomorrow on she may glut her eyes on atmospheric phenomena from this window, after I've left for Verona… A strange nation indeed… lunatics and dreamers…
What does she look like, this lady of yours?

LUCIO
She's the most beautiful woman I've ever seen… majestic… She passed this way before, two springs ago, accompanied by the same cavalier… or husband… she's the most perfect woman — hah! She stayed here in this very room — but that was when we were

remodelling everything. The inn was crowded, all the rooms were full, just like today…

ROGER
Please tell the lady that I'm fast asleep.

LUCIO
That's just what I'd reckoned, so I gave her a doubtful reply. You see, I'd never dare disturb a guest at this late hour… However that may be — we don't like to refuse our foreign travellers anything… especially a lady who is lodging with us… the most beautiful lady…

ROGER
Tomorrow morning, please wake me at five.

LUCIO
Good night… the best of nights…

ROGER
Good night.

Pacing.

Good, good, at last, something practical, for once in my life. I'm sleeping — I'm sleeping — night is for sleeping, and that's that.

Sits at the table and leafs through an album.

How many sleepless nights have there been, after all? And all in vain. When she… 'She.' How come I cannot say her name? Is it that I'd not have the dust motes in the air of this untidy chamber alight upon the breath that bears her name? Her name, like some sort of flower freshly burst… fresh, white, and pure — created by the mind of God as He passed along the garden for the first time?

So while… She… was surrounded by gallant haberdashery, exquisite formalists, soft, and repetitive! — When she was casting the pearls of her graces all around her — to whom? To whom? The wearied and the bored!… Then was I peopling these white nights

CYPRIAN KAMIL NORWID

of mine with fitting phantoms — the sort that slay one's powers in embryo, forestalling the flash of eyes in streams of tears! That take hearts in hand like new books, with pages yet uncut — and read into them, ever more deeply... tear them apart... the leaves... the hearts... and...

Covering his eyes.

Oh, wretched me...

Paging through the album.

A flower plucked along the road to Amalfi... I can still see that light hand of hers, dangling alongside her horse as we rode on beside the cliffs... the flowers clutching both sides of the abyss, on both sides of the path... she sent that flower back to me by the hand of the guide, who walked beside her horse... It was a pink blossom back then... in the immaculate purity of its sheen...

Today it's wilted yellow... the petals drop away, which once had formed its crown... And now it more resembles a spider, who's spun all of the silk from out her breast and hangs there, empty, dries and perishes, never more to return...

Pause.

And here — and here that letter written in response to my last question, which I could no longer carry in my bosom in secret...

For sure — no one has ever received such a reply — Not even one remotely similar among all those ever given to man... an elegant letter... beautiful... A gorgeous letter...

I would have wanted to burn it... but it would just have melted like a piece of ice to become... a handful of filth.

I wanted to tear it, but it wounded my hands.

And so it remains to this very day. Such things are of just that sort of quality. They hold up well. It's hard to lose them, difficult to cast them away.

Looks through the letter.

'Castel-Fermo.'

Right — I remember — that the letter was sent from here…

'Castel-Fermo… etc.

'I've just received Your beautiful letter, my dear…!'

My beautiful letter!

That's just like someone who comes across a wretch, speechless with pain, and says: 'What a beautiful effect, the pallor of that face, those dull eyes… What a beautiful subject for an artist…' And then, coming up to that same 'subject' claps him on the shoulder and goes on his way, whistling a tune…

Reads on.

'I've just received Your beautiful latter, my dear Roger… Please, I beg you, will you kindly drop in on Princess Olympia when you'll be in Naples…? She has some books of mine… I'm not concerned with most of them, but she does still have my third volume of Richter… A work like that loses so much when a volume is missing from the middle…'

Pausing in his reading.

Ha! And if a heart is missing?

Reads on.

'…missing from the middle — and now, for my mare. Should she be sent on by rail, or by sea? Please, if you would be so kind, give this all a moment's thought, all right? Oh — and those few sketches that were brought to me on the day of my departure, and the Papal blessing with the rosaries — they're on the hearth-mantle in the lesser salon — I forgot those, too. Everyone here remembers you most fondly, especially at tea-time… *à propos*… I seem to have lost a portion of your letter somehow, half of it, actually, as I've only the second half before my eyes right now… But I remember you mentioning something about your heart, and love… Oh, there's so little space in this room — such before-departure clutter — there's the culprit! But the view, Ah, the view is splendid! I'm going to

make haste and set the seal now, because we're just about to leave…
Mille tendresses… mille amitiés… etc. P.S. Please remember to take
care of yourself! Watch your health! Be well…'

And once more, at the bottom of the page:

'As for the love you have for me, and have had for so many years,
I can only say in reply…'

… and here she inserts the second half of my letter.

Pause.

If it's an ironic coincidence, well, she's taking a matter of the
heart in hand with such recklessness… Considering the possible
consequences, and serious ones, of such an attachment…

Or if she reckoned that this would be the *easiest* way to reply…
I mean really! She might have chosen one *more difficult* but more
conscientious… I deserve at least so much, as a human being… as
any other man…

*He gets up and paces about the room, very slowly. Then he sets his chair
near the window, and opens it.*

IMPROVISATION, IN A HALF-WHISPER

Above both Capulet and Montague,
Where thunderclaps raged, and sheets of rain beat down,
The becalmed eye of blue
That sweeps the ruins of the feuding town,
Its shattered garden gates, its seedy park,
Lets fall, from its calm heights, an errant spark…

'For Juliet,' the cypresses all say;
'For Romeo' this cosmic tear is shed,
'To plummet its sad way
Into their tomb.' But those of cooler head
State that it's nothing but a senseless rock,
On which no one is waiting in the dark…

He closes the window. The town clock strikes one.

Bravo! That's the way to keep your word, Roger! What's happened with your rebirth to practicality? Enough... enough!

One o'clock. High time to get your things ready for tomorrow...

Noticing that the window's not quite closed.

... shut the window, lock the door... and get some proper sleep.

Struggling with the window.

O, these classical windows, classical doors! The jambs and sashes always out of skew...

He brings the lamp nearer to inspect the stubborn window.

Ha! *Deus ex machina!* Oh, Shakespeare, you titan! Now I understand your greatness — as this lamp uncovers to my eyes the drama of my heart entire! The windows — papered over...

Draws yet nearer, with the lamp.

... as tightly as the leaves of my own heart, smashed, perhaps, by a stone cast by some naughty hand... Here is the first half of my letter! Lucio used it to mend the pane... And here, the second half of Hers — it was in this room she was staying — this is the lovely view she gushed about... As frivolous as always! here she forgot the letters, just like that Papal blessing on the hearth-mantle of the lesser salon, and the rosaries, like those rosaries of the tears I strung together... like her mare in Naples, and volume three of Jean-Paul...

'Woman! You fluff of vanity...'

He returns to the table on which the album rests, takes out the letter, and returns with it to the window, with the lamp.

So let's touch gold to gold...

'Castel-Fermo... etc.

'I've just received Your beautiful letter, my dear Roger… Please, I beg you, will you kindly drop in on Princess Olympia when you'll be in Naples…? She has some books of mine… I'm not concerned with most of them, but she does still have my third volume of Richter… A work like that loses so much when a volume is missing from the middle… and now, for my mare. Should she be sent on by rail, or by sea? Please, if you would be so kind, give this all a moment's thought, all right? Oh — and those few sketches that were brought me on the day of my departure, and the Papal blessing with the rosaries — they're on the hearth-mantle in the lesser salon — I forgot those, too. Everyone here remembers you most fondly, especially at tea-time… *à propos*… I seem to have lost a portion of your letter somehow…'

Ha!

'… half of it, actually, as I've only the second half before my eyes right now…'

So here, after so many years, I have the whole thing in front of me… Onward!

'… But I remember you mentioning something about your heart, and love…' Onward! Here, on the broken pane, what I write of my heart and my love… Onward…

'… something about your heart, and love…Oh, there's so little space in this room —' True enough! On…

'… such before-departure clutter — there's the culprit! But the view, Ah, the view is splendid! I'm going to make haste and set the seal now, because we're just about to leave… *Mille tendresses… mille amitiés…* etc. P.S. Please remember to take care of yourself! Watch your health! Be well… As for the love you have for me, and have had for so many years, I can only say in reply…'

He tosses aside the letter and continues to read that pasted to the window.

'… I can only say in reply what an old acquaintance of mine once wrote in my album: that you, the young men of the nineteenth century, begin from a largesse of the heart. You love passionately, truly and purely at the dawn of your days, and later, by degrees, slowly, that gem is worn away, the spring runs dry, and you settle into an opulence of form, which replaces the inborn tenderness of your hearts.

'Now we, the women of the nineteenth century, on the contrary — snub your ardour at the start, while we are in the full blossom of our youth, and only later, slowly, by degrees, after so many disappointments, so many graves, which close at our feet along our path through life, arrive at a respect for that holy spark of yours... Your starting point is our finish-line...

'How then are we to meet up with one another on this earth?

'It is for this reason that we are in constant pursuit of one another, that we merely chase each other, deceive each other... Farewell, farewell, Claudia...'

That's the truth!

Or at least the truth of one Epoch...

And yet the truth has a balsamic strength... That's right — the truth...

Pause.

What night is this?... It is... of the thousand and one nights, this is the thousandth and second — the one tale that Scheherazade forgot to add to her entertainments, just as Claudia forgot the second half of her letter... Most curious woman! *Recklessness*, that drags *profound reflection* at its heels like a prisoner his ball and chain... Sad, sad, sad — He only, who holds the measure of time in His right hand, might help, perhaps. This drama of hearts has become a drama of time...

He repeats aloud the words of the letter.

'... in constant pursuit of one another... we merely chase each other... Farewell.'

The city clock strikes two.

LUCIO

Knocking at the door.

With your permission...

ROGER
Come in.

LUCIO
It seems my lord is having trouble with the window. I heard the panes
rattle, and some footsteps in the room — I saw your light — and so I
made bold to knock… You see, I forgot to ask you for your passport;
I'd need it now, if all is to be in order before five.

ROGER

*Paces the room slowly. Arriving at Lucio, he claps him on the shoulder
and says, emphasising his words.*

The lady of whom you spoke is no Englishwoman. Nor did she wish
to come here for the view. All of that — is lies.
    Who is that woman? What did she tell you? Speak!

LUCIO
We, *Italiani, per Bacco!* we say: 'British' for every foreigner, you know:
'she's British,' meaning 'she's from beyond the Alps, from some cold
country…'
    As soon as she arrived, she greeted me with '*Caro Lucio,*' and
then she spoke with the cavalier who's accompanying her — her
husband, maybe — for a long, long time, and then again to me: '*Caro
mio,* I wish to look upon Verona from that window when the storm
is over,' and I at that: '*Benissimo!*' and off she goes to her own room
and tea is sent up — and you can still hear them talking in there…

ROGER
This is the thousandth and second night, you understand?

LUCIO
You don't say? Tomorrow is the feast of the Assumption of the Most
Blessed Virgin Mary.

ROGER

Aside.

It's her! — good —

LUCIO

Taking a paper from the table.

My lord's passport…

ROGER
The lady is beautiful…

LUCIO
Si.

ROGER
Her face is something like those of your madonnas…

LUCIO
… Exciting piety… *Si, signore…*

ROGER
She's got light hair, golden… and eyes — dark…

LUCIO
Si, signore conte… Si…

ROGER
And she once stayed in this very room —

LUCIO
… *Bravissimo!… Si!…*

ROGER
She's got an ugly husband... who is much older than she... When she first arrived here, she came with no husband... She was a widow, then...

LUCIO
... Si... si... si, bravissimo...

ROGER
Lucio!

LUCIO
Signore...

ROGER
You see those pistols there? Check if they're loaded.

LUCIO
They are...

ROGER
No, take them in hand and check.

LUCIO
We *Italiani* can tell such things at a glance. We know our way around, *per Bacco!* They're loaded all right, bloody well loaded... Anybody else would have to pick them up and handle them — test them, and later — We have a sacred custom here: 'A place for everything, and everything in its place...'

ROGER
Va bene, Lucio.

LUCIO
Signore...

ROGER
You see that pile of piastres on the table?

LUCIO
… Benissimo…

ROGER
They are for you. Go on now, pocket them —

LUCIO

Scoops them up.

Your wish is my command, my lord.

ROGER
And now?

LUCIO
Si… signore… Va bene…

ROGER
Tomorrow — morning — my things will be taken downstairs — my
passport made ready — and this window closed, closed properly —

LUCIO
Closed properly — *si…*

ROGER
Then you will go to that lady and tell her that the traveller who'd been
staying in this room has departed. Look, there where the pistols are…
that wardrobe? I shall be there, inside. But of that, not a word!

LUCIO
I shall be as silent as the grave, *si…*

ROGER
Remember, now — You are to say to her:

Lucio notes down the words.

'The traveller — who'd been staying in that room upstairs — has gone, bidding Madame farewell — He's left the room unoccupied. However, if you wish to look out upon the landscape from that window, know that it is shut, and cannot be opened by any other hand except yours.'

LUCIO
Word for word, as in the *Ave Maria*…

ROGER
Buona notte… Lucio…

LUCIO
… Felicissima notte, signor conte…

ROGER
And now let the events take their proper course — Let her play out the final scene by herself — Let her see with her own eyes the work of her reckless hands — Let us complete her letter now…

He takes the first half of her letter and affixes it with some wax beside the first half pasted over the window-pane.

She'll see it — recognise it — and remember. She'll have a lot of explaining to do to her husband… A little… unpleasantness that lasts but a moment, but which will fix her for ages…

    I — shall not emerge from my hiding place. I shan't look on her ever again…

Pause.

I — shall emerge, calmly, coldly — no exaggerations — and ask her to introduce me to her husband. I'll fill in whatever she leaves out… with a smile… And then I'll wish her *bon voyage*…

    We'll change the play into a still, deep, drama, or a casual comedy… at any rate… *alea iacta est*…

He parts the curtains round the bed and enters in.

THE INN, CASTEL-FERMO

A salon; the darkness of early morning, candles lit.

DOCTOR
Ever since I've had the pleasure of accompanying you on your travels, my memoirs, and my medical research, have been greatly enriched.

LADY
Perhaps, Doctor, from time to time, you also note down some little tidbits of gossip *sul mio conto*?

DOCTOR
Madame… I had begun a serious monologue.

LADY
Please continue…

DOCTOR
By degrees, my medical studies have taken a turn towards psychology: psychological observations… and tonight, they've given rise to some meteorological insights, too… Ladies (by this I mean you women of the nineteenth century) are the most curious phenomena of your genus. A thunderstorm, for example, evoked by the electricity in the atmosphere, starts you humming like telegraph wires, vibrating with harmonies of the imagination…

LADY
That's so childish! What silliness you babble, Doctor! Call things by their names — describe them as they are — your scientific talk is like a foreign language to me. Let's speak plainly…
    You know how much respect I have for the sciences, their profundity… Yet every time I catch too strong a whiff, I call to mind some verses I once heard a poet intone — I can never recall which poet wrote them, or where I first came across them, but they speak of falling stars…

DOCTOR
Of aerolites.

LADY
Yes, yes, something like that.

Sings.

'For Juliet,' the cypresses all say;
'For Romeo' this cosmic tear is shed,
'To plummet its sad way
Into their tomb.' But those of cooler head
State that it's nothing but a senseless rock,
On which no one is waiting in the dark…

DOCTOR
Here I can be of no aid to you, Madame. Such questions are beyond
my practice.

LADY
Excellent, Doctor! You repeat almost word for word what the Doctor
says in *Macbeth!*
    Splendid!

DOCTOR
My wonder at that surpasses his, who was astonished to learn that,
all his life long, he'd been speaking prose…

LADY
Let us speak prose, then… Tell me about these medical insights of
yours…?

DOCTOR
I've learned that I must approach my art soberly, conscientiously, and
with disinterested friendship, in order to accompany you on your
travels, and serve you with advice.

LADY
I'm deeply aware of these difficulties, and for that reason I heartily repay your friendship, Doctor, in kind.

She extends her hand to him. Pause.

Yes — really — you are something of my father confessor, insofar as health depends on moral disposition… You know what I've been through… I've been through — all that the others have, who are possessed of a little more heart than usual… and are a little more disposed to the development of the intellectual powers… My separation from my husband, which has, at last, received apostolic sanction, returns me… To what, really? To whom? I sense myself to be an unformed creature, unfulfilled… Now, I trust men even less than I ever have. What man has ever experienced so many hidden, unseen, profound dramas of the heart? One would needs have loved an individual — beautiful, full of alluring charms of a more elevated sort, noble, proud, perhaps — certainly vain and inclined to profound reflections — but belated ones — and infinitely flighty of sentiment, when it matters. A bitter knowledge, this, and dearly paid for… After long residence in the realm of the ideal, what man ever feels that conscientious and at the same time heart-felt need of communing with the simple truth of life?… Who has ever been quit, as I have been quit — speaking of my race horses, my hunting dogs, and my heart?

And who, despite it all, has perceived at least a spark of life yet — the need to live…?

Ah, really. I don't mean to carry on any longer. I fear I might fall into self-adulation. But I only say such things to you, Doctor… You comprehend — you feel — and even if you felt not, you understand… The physician and the confessor are the two poles of our individuality…

DOCTOR
Madame, the only way I might respond is… If ever I found such a man for you, I would at once return to my own family, for whom I've been yearning now, for so long.

LADY
Doctor, you've promised me your company to the very borders of my homeland...

DOCTOR
I'd happily accompany you to the very turnpike of happiness... That's not a very poetic expression, yet the sense is — profoundly poetic.

LADY
We made a pact that we would speak in prose...

LUCIO

Offstage.

With your permission...

DOCTOR
Come in.

LUCIO
In an hour's time — one hour from now — you will have the most beautiful view from the room that we call *Il Museo*... The room will be all yours...

LADY
But, *caro* Lucio — I wished to gaze upon the moon...

LUCIO
Hardly at this hour, Madame. The sun is rising. My lady the countess simply can't imagine the battle I had to wage just now... A magnanimous soul might reckon I deserved a reward for my valour... a few scudi...

LADY
What? What do you mean?

LUCIO

Well, Madame, as soon as I learned of your wish, I rushed, I leaped, I lunged into the *Museo* (that is, the room that we call *Il Museo*); the British gentleman who occupied it — a noble young man, a count himself — was sleeping… 'Who's there?' he bellows, 'Who seeks entrance here?' he cries, leaping to his feet, with two loaded pistols, as long as andirons the barrels were! But I, ah, no! A Lombard born and bred — I didn't retreat an inch! 'My name — is Lucio!' I thus declared, 'and I come from the countess, demanding that you cede your place to her!'

LADY

But Lucio! You never…!

LUCIO

Yes, I did! Lucio never takes on a mission in vain…!

LADY

But…

LUCIO

The Englishman says, 'Please explain yourself!' And I — I ignore the question, just: 'Sir, if you please, you'll cede the room to Madame the Countess for a spell.' He stands there with his pistols aimed at me — here, at my heart! But I don't budge an inch — and thus we face each other, until two!

At last, at last — he asks me who the lady is, who wishes to look out upon the landscape? And I reply: 'The most beautiful countess the walls of this inn have ever seen… and he… lets drop the pistols, and falls fast asleep.

O! Didn't I laugh then!

Now, in an hour, he's off to Verona. He's a young man, a little, as we say, *pazzo*, who paces the floorboards till late at night, and writes…

Now — my lady — this is what he bade me tell you, verbatim:

'Lucio, you woke me in the middle of the night! You stirred me up! And so — I close the window! Now, if this lady of yours wishes to look at this beautiful vista, tell her that the traveller who'd been staying in this room has gone, bidding Madame farewell. The room is at her disposal, but under one condition: the window must not be opened by any other hand except hers.'

LADY
Most curious metaphysics…

DOCTOR
Rather queer…

LADY
Please take upon yourself your guest's unease — Do you know what his name is?

LUCIO
Here is his passport, which I've just retrieved from the constabulary.

DOCTOR

Taking the paper from his hand and unfolding it.

This is not a British passport…

Reads.

Roger of Czarnolesie.

LADY
I've never heard the name.

DOCTOR

Hands the passport back to Lucio. Exit Lucio.

Ha! I'll tell you who he is… Do you recall Madame Claudia's salon, in Naples?

LADY
That young man... What...?

DOCTOR
One of those lunatics, or, rather, mopers, whom good people seek
to cure by mockery, if they won't be ignored... The reasonable call
them 'children of the times'... such as those who've really suffered in
the world, love — I say this, for in such terms I wrote him down in
my journal...

LADY
I've never met him — but he's no stranger to me from the telling.

DOCTOR
It's getting light... the mist is lifting; now we can snuff the candles.

He does so, with puffs of breath.

LADY
Your words, Doctor, sounded so grave, as if you were deciding
someone's fate.

DOCTOR
You don't say? It's a habit acquired through consultations... How
often are we physicians led to consider people's fate as a purely
material phenomenon... something almost mechanical.

LADY
The first moments of the dawn have something... peculiarly...

DOCTOR
... Peculiarly...?

LADY
Help me to express myself, Doctor...

DOCTOR
Peculiarly... initial. Refreshing.

LADY

Rises and paces slowly about the room. Coming to the table, she leafs through some books there. Then she reads:

And when the gloomy shadows of the night
Melt in the golden morn,
Remember the creation of the light
And be no more forlorn…

LUCIO

Enters.

Il Museo is open — the window is closed.

THE UPPER ROOM

Just as it was at the beginning of the comedy.

LUCIO

Makes a sign to Roger.

They're coming… They're coming!

Exit Lucio, Roger conceals himself.

DOCTOR
And so, this is that famous room…

LADY
Enchanted, rather!

She draws near the window, takes the letter in hand, and reads. Then she hands it to the Doctor. A moment of silence, as they read it through. They look at one another for a moment without speaking.

DOCTOR
It's signed: Claudia!!

ROGER

Opens the door suddenly and leaps out into the room.

A masterpiece of recklessness…!

DOCTOR
My dear sir!

LADY
What does this mean?

ROGER
Just as I said — a masterpiece of recklessness… This time, my own…

Pause.

What you've read, please be kind enough to forget —

LADY
You were mistaken…

ROGER
I reckoned that… that every woman I meet, wherever, is… the author
of that letter… the other half of which, pasted on the window-pane, I
never received in answer to a proposal of mine, whereas the first half,
which you've dropped on the floor… I certainly did.

If you're unable, madame, and sir, to understand this… intrigue
of mine, this desire of taking revenge — that's it, I wanted to wreak
a… cordial revenge; then, I can't explain it to you… Someday —
someone — for somewhere there does exist someone for whom
nothing is too great, nothing too petty — that someone will explain
and clarify this, which now surpasses my capabilities…

DOCTOR
Your name is not unknown to me, sir.

Turning to his patient.

Madame, I'd like to introduce Roger of Czarnolesie.

LADY
I've heard your monologue before sir... on the lips of a woman.

DOCTOR
Tonight...

ROGER

Extending his hand to the Lady to whom he's just been introduced.

Men — if they're silent, it's because, they're silent...

He opens the window.

... Behold the view! — And look, that rainbow, one end of which rests on the ruins of the house of Capulet, while the other spills down upon that of the Montagues. A bridge in the abyss of the ages...

LADY
There are chords in life, which only at certain times can meld in harmony...

DOCTOR
Thus one must never drag one's feet...

ROGER
How do you know, madame?

LADY
The rainbow told me.

ROGER

And there are pains, unspoken merely because… happiness was never to utter them… Pains of joy…

LADY

… And sometimes — of necessity…

ROGER

So there must also be others, quite contrary, that is — when there is reciprocal permeation…

DOCTOR

Nothing's more logical…

Aside, rubbing his hands.

I'm going home… back to my family…!

LADY

I've got something quite original to tell you, sir — that such pains, those contrary to the others, the incomprehensible ones…

ROGER

… Those which are reciprocally understandable, you say…

LADY

… Are not pains at all…

ROGER

… Are not pains at all…

Pause.

DOCTOR

Where there's no pain, there is no need of doctors…

All join hands.

CYPRIAN KAMIL NORWID

CURTAIN — THE END

Written in 1850.

ZWOLON[25]

A MONOLOGUE

WHICH I
DEDICATE TO MY BROTHER
KSAWERY

TO THE READER

Neither the idea of this fantasy, nor its individual characters and their actions, are in any way intended to touch upon any real persons.

However, we feel it incumbent upon ourselves to state this, so that the author's composition might be all the more properly understood according to his thought. There is no part of this work that might have the honour of settling scores with any Party.

Two verses: 'Vengeance, vengeance on our enemies,'[26] etc., are employed here in a way that differs from that in which the great writer presented them in his work, and ought not to serve as evidence that we are abusing quotations. For it would be difficult, if not improbable, to find a stronger expression of pain and the influence of suffering than these — for which reason we appropriate them. The rest we leave to the reader's good will and indulgence.

C.K.N.

---

25   The name is derived from the adjective *zwolony*, i.e. 'called, chosen, elect.'

26   From Adam Mickiewicz's *Dziady* [Forefathers' Eve, Part III, 1832]. The reference is to the refrain of a song sung by Polish political prisoners fantasising about the killing the Tsar: 'Vengeance, vengeance, vengeance on our enemies / With or without God's sanction, as the Lord may please.'

... e poi chiamarle
O Tragedie o Comedie...
E se le s'useranno ducent'anni
Le non saranno cose nuove a quelli
Che questo tempo chiameranno antico —?!

Cecchi[27]

29 September 1662
Then to the King's Theatre, where we saw
'A Midsummer Night's Dream,' which I had
never seen before, nor shall ever again, *for
it is the most insipid and ridiculous play that
ever I saw in my life.*

Pepys[28]

INTRODUCTION

Since up till now the world has never seen
A monologue for varied parts composed,
I stand here now, before the opening scene,
To let you in on how the matter goes.
I will hold nothing back of what you'll be
Presented with in dialogic fashion:
Men and courtiers, knaves and His Majesty
Shall bellow past like thunderstorms in passion,
In expedited speech, energetically,
For this was written amidst lightning flashes,

---

27   Giommaria Cecchi (1580 – 1587), Italian dramatist. 'And then to call them /
Either Tragedies or Comedies / And even should these terms be used a full two
hundred years from now / They will be no different things from those / Which
were at the time called Ancient—?!'

28   Samuel Pepys (1633 – 1703), English diarist, Secretary of the Admiralty under
Charles II and James II. Norwid cites this entry in French translation, giving the
date mistakenly as 1659 – 1660. The italics are Norwid's own.

Some in Ercolano, Italy,
Some on a ship, trailing the bitter splashes
Of tears adding their salt unto the ocean,
The rest at home — somewhat like Charon's barge.
In short, the drama is an exile's notion,
Unmeet, perhaps, for Tragedy writ large,
For it would soil the stage where cothurns tread
Amongst white marbles set up in a ring
On graded risers, such as may have fed
Your eyes in Tusculum, where softly sing
The breezes through the withered leaves of bay,
Teasing the lizard who leans through the lips
Of ancient comic mask… A folkish lay!
But it shall be a song that stately slips,
As morally as possible, although
That sense is none too bright; romantic, yes —
But friable, like bleak December clods.
But there'll be roaring cannon none the less;
(To spoil the children we shall spare no rods).

There'll be some space for those who like to cry,
Appropriate and sweet — a little while;
For those who rather the yellow butterfly-
Type of easily spooked flitting, fluttering smile,
We have nothing against such things, for why?
There's nothing there to jibe at. And, of course,
Every feeling shall shoot forth in ray
Of elemental pure emotive force,
Each one its motive role unchecked to play.
And even those of that cold-blooded nation
Whom research and experiment set afire
Will find something to thrill them — punctuation.

So this is not of play of hearts, with choirs
Massed chorally, and twined like tangling vines
Through which the heavens' azure winks and shines,
Nor is it a monologuish gloomy grotto
Fit only for Cain or Iscariot, O

No — rather (may its tang be none to sour):
A mob of husks, a distant, empty stour.

A GARDEN ON THE RAMPARTS

The King and Zabór are walking along a trench.

KING
All those who march on my omnipotent throne
Will by my rod be shattered like clay shards.
Destroy the upper town. No single bone
Unshattered, burn it; merciless and hard
You must be to all — even to babes in arms.
I'll name it Ugolino, for we'll shave
Its walls unto the level of the grave.[29]
Wash out all the street names in waves of blood.
Henceforth, there'll only be a field of stones
Split and unmortared that no hearthfire warms —
Ruins and pools of blood and nothing else,
Except...

Pauses. Then points at something at a distance.

                    ... those poplars standing by themselves,
Three witnesses to what once had been here —
A diorama!

As the King moves on, trumpets sound from the tower.

ZABÓR

Glances up at the tower, then approaches the king.

---

29   The Dantean reference will be explained in the work itself, later on. However,
the Polish ear also hears echoes of devastation in the work — *goły* — indicating
a denuding. *Ogolić* — to shave, to raze.

Someone's rushing near.

KING

Entering a building.

If it be news of new conspiracies,
Remember what I said…

COURIER

                    Hetman divine,
O great man…

ZABÓR

          Well, what is it? Say your piece!

COURIER
The royal troops were spooked and broke the line
At the people's approach — by thirty men
They're led, from the most distant villages
And suburbs, cities — from the battlements
As far as you can see the mad swarm rages —
Plebeians, as if sheaves to standards turned,
And threshing-flails to spears, and every grain
Into a soldier was transformed, who burns
With flaming vengeance!

ZABÓR

                    Should royal ears
Be fouled with such rot? You are spreading treason!

The clock strikes six. The swordsman pauses, then:

ZABÓR
It's the sixth hour. And that's the only reason
I grant you your life. Thank the number six.
I've got a respect for that cipher, so
A stouter head than yours would need be fixed

On that neck to move me to lop it off
At such an early hour. Live then, now go!

*On one side, Zabór recedes into the depths of the terrace, while on the
other a Guardsman rushes up. The Courier remains.*

COURIER

To Guardsman.

Whence? What? And why?

GUARDSMAN
                        One of the palace watch —
On officer, a sober man, with men
At his command… O, a frightful omen…!

COURIER
Some folk wisdom? The kind that ancient women —

GUARDSMAN
The tree, the one called Titan, the royal ash —
The one that threw its shade upon the stream —
Stands there no more! It groaned, tottered, and crashed…

COURIER
Out of my sight! And if you come again
With more old wives' tales, more prophetic dreams
Unsummoned, spreading such treasonous trash
That has no merit, be it oak or ash,
I'll take some birch and have you soundly thrashed!

*The Courier moves away, the Guardsman remains — flummoxed.
Meanwhile a Boy who tends the gardens runs up with two jugs.*

BOY
O, great Sunflower of the garden rows…!

GUARDSMAN
What's wrong?

BOY
        Only the purest water flows
Through the suburban pipes that feed the fountains...

GUARDSMAN

Impatiently.

So?

BOY
They must be crushing sloe upon the mountains,
'Cos when I went to fill my jugs to bring
Fresh water to the palace tulip bed,
The water... Through the garden sluices running...
Was not clear! O no — it was bloody red!

GUARDSMAN
Shh! Say no more, you bastard, or I'll nail
Your tongue to a barn like pelt that's being dried
So you won't alarm the wounded with your wail!
Be off! Before I flay you of your hide!

The Guardsman moves off. The Boy remains, frightened. A brief pause.

BOY

Turning to his jugs.

Damned jugs! Just wait! I'll give you what for!

He sets the jugs down on the dusty path, moves away, then addresses one of them.

You first, you wretched clown! You mud-baked shell!

To the other, kicking it with his foot.

And then you, fatso! Yes! Why do you swell
Your belly at me like that! Wait till I
Grab you by the ear and let you fly!
You'll see it gets you nowhere to tell lies!
I'll bonk you on the pavement till you burst!

He snatches up one jug by the ear and runs off, kicking the other before him.

What business is it of yours, what goes on
Up in the mountains? Water white or red?
It's all the same to those we pour it on —
You big-mouths! I'm a wretched servant too, but
I know enough to keep my big mouth shut!
Just look what comes out of such empty heads!

He goes off. Enter Zwolon, slowly, wearing a cloak tossed over his shoulder pilgrim-style; meanwhile, from the rear, the Guardsman re-enters, examines the circles impressed on the dust by the Boy's jars and then rushes up to Zwolon.

GUARDSMAN
What do we have here? Are you casting spells,
Magician? Drawing runes and warlock wheels
On royal footpaths?

ZWOLON

With great calm.

                    Those are royal seals.

GUARDSMAN
What?!

ZWOLON
　　Royal seals. Look closely. Can't you tell?

GUARDSMAN
No!

ZWOLON
The garden implements all bear that mark.

GUARDSMAN

Inspecting the impressions more closely.

Aha — I see…

ZWOLON
　　　　Like God's word. So it goes:
From quire to quire
It flows on ever higher,
And here it sparks, while there it bursts to flame,
And lower still, its fire
Cheers, and feeds the plain
Still lower with lush green.
And there's another might — of stone:
A stupid thing that hastes
About the ruts of waste
Where verdure is unseen
And so it mocks the truth with jibing splutter
And quire on quire slips down the crooked gutter.

Pause. He gazes at the sky.

It looks like we'll have rain again tomorrow.
Goodbye.

He moves off.

GUARDSMAN
That fellow's strange. He's got a creepy aura.

A suburban market square. To the rear, a Gothic church — abandoned. Crowds of people on the square, brandishing weapons of all sorts, drawn up in ranks divided up into units under banners of different colours. There is a leader at each of the banners, and a speaker. Hum, clatter, confusion. The picture is completed by women and children. Szołom, dressed up as an insurrectionist, is running here and there, preaching loudly.

SZOŁOM

To the women.

Which of you has beheld the welts that blows
Of knouts upon the flesh of sons have raised?

WIDOW
I have, for one, and now, through all my days
Cascades of blood and gore incessant flow
Athwart my path; my bruised heart is rocked
By every branch against my thatch that knocks!

SZOŁOM

Racing up to the youths.

And who amongst you saw his mother freeze
With fright at midnight, when they came to seize
You, dragging you from out your warm bedclothes?

CHORUS OF YOUTHS
O, I — and I too — I as well — a flock
Of eaglets harried from our native wood;
Here we have flown on rushing wing to make good
Our vow of angry vengeance upon those
Who would have extirpated our whole stock!

SZOŁOM

In their midst.

And which of you, fired by prophetic dream,
Or in the misty hours, when the town sleeps,
Has heard the avenging angels' angry scream,
Or felt them set upon his brow a wreath,
Or heard an old man passing whisper — 'Son,
Be watchful, for the hour is at hand,
And she comes in the name of oppressed man!'

BOLEJ[30]
You speak of me, nourished on vengeance raw,
To whom the daemon sends peculiar dreams,
That I am nauseous without blood-splashed maw,
And doves and olive branches to me seem
A mockery of insult, every smile
A jeer. So that I greet each thunderhead
That masses in the sky with joyous bile,
And every plague that creeps near, not with dread,
But as a friend. No wildfire tincts the skies
But I hail it from afar and call it near;
I am the gossip of each pain, each fear;
Even when I speak with men my soft voice burrs
Violent, so that the village curs
Foam rabid at the timbre, and high vaults
Crumble, as if beneath a giant's blows.
And even now…

SZOŁOM

Placing his hands on Bolej's shoulders.

O man of destiny!

---

30   A name coined by Norwid, on the basis of the noun *ból* [pain] or *boleć, boleje* [to ache], *ubolewać* [to complain].

ZWOLON

In the crowd.

O child of woe!

SZOŁOM

To the people milling about.

       Who might lead an assault
Of retribution more surely than he,
More firmly than a man who's truly free?
Indeed, the future nourishes his arm —
It's not enough to say of him 'he can,'
Since his strength surpasses the impossible;
He sees what's hidden from all other men…

ZWOLON
O, brother, this election of the seer is
Unripe for these times!

SOME
               Down with the theorist!

OTHERS
Down with the pedant, who can only gall
Our passions with dry thought!

SZOŁOM
              When the storm rages,
It makes a pact with no man.

ZWOLON
          If one can,
Still hope, brothers, that the unfettered word,
Raised for the good of all, would still be heard,
Permit me —

ALL

        Enough, enough! The same old song!

SERGEANT
Speak! Let him speak! Go on, but don't be long!

ZWOLON

Gesturing at Bolej.

This young man, nourished, as he says, on gore,
Is no son of freedom — he's nothing more
Than judgement's slave. And you, and those
Beneath that flag unfurled — which of you knows
Exactly what it means?

SZOŁOM

        Traitor! Be gone!
His words would douse the ardour of the throng!

ZWOLON
Citizens! Citizens — but of what state?
The fatherland, or despair?

SOME

        Ah — hear him prate!

ZWOLON
For I'm not sure — you're rushing off to die;
Is there any among you fit to seek
Life? Everyone would die for freedom's sake,
As if only the tomb were liberty,
And any sort of perishing, the gate
To immortality. Ah, but revenge
And liberty — these are quite different ends!
And often, when the two are so entwined,
And vengeance is achieved, avengers find
They've lost their freedom…

         CYPRIAN KAMIL NORWID

SZOŁOM

Have you seen the signs

In the heavens?

SOME

Away with him!

OTHERS

Be gone!

Weapons clattering, they prepare to march off.

BOLEJ
The introduction, sir, was overlong;
The tale itself — a plodding, tiresome rede;
And the summation, like the prologue, I fear.
And so, farewell.

SOME

Ha, ha, ha, ha!

ZWOLON

Sadly.

God speed

SERGEANT
You're coming with us, or you're staying here,
Sir poet? You're not eager for the fight?

Pipes and timbrels, cries, and horses neighing. The people group together, form up in ranks, and march off.

CHORUS
Vengeance, vengeance on our enemies!
With or without God's sanction, as the Lord shall please!

ECHO
Vengeance, vengeance!

SERGEANT

To Zwolon.

Hey friend! You're a good fellow!
Come back! You've felt the weight of chains;
You've shed some blood, you've felt the blows
Of scourges lashing — so, come back!
If we don't win, there'll be no lack
Of chains, scourges, and blood again!

CHORUS I
Siege ladders! Overtop the walls!
And when you've surmounted them, fall
To hewing, hacking, slaying all!

CHORUS II
Slash them, tear them with your teeth!
Trample your enemies beneath your feet!
Transform the docile herd into wild beasts!

Afar.

Hurrah, hurrah! Come, at our enemies!
With or without God's sanction, as the Lord shall please!

Single shots, cries, the choruses die off in the distance.

ANOTHER PART OF THE SQUARE,
IN FRONT OF THE CHURCH

To one side, the market square can be seen, along with the streets that radiate from it; to the other side: a cemetery, and trenches.

ZWOLON

Solus.

Pursued by two flames, hounded I go;
One white, one — in livid, red shadow.
That of the bloody shade… evaporates;
The while the white, from inside out escapes,
And like the narcissus' quiet star,
Like an envelope
When the seal is broke,
Like a white figure that spreads wide her arms
And sighs, then wrings her hands,
Or a lightning bolt flashing, thus expands
That flower's cup:
The glow flares up;
That envelope,
That white form, aching hope,
Torn from the world
With arms unfurled
About her blushing, fevered countenance,
That thought, that figure — I don't know, perchance
That unity of being,
Ever present, ever fleeing
From earth to sky, and from the heaven's blue
To the green plains — a cradle, and a tomb!
No, as long as they are silent in the soughing trees…
But when the latter weeps, and the former sings,
Striking all-strings!…

*   *   *

From her I lived, and lived with her. Her I now wish to see
So perfect, and full of being, to be
Like the nation's eagle, in a flash, like a young thing
Of another world… leading the rushing throng,
And psalter-in-hand, leading the nation in song!
Like streaming choruses, with rhythm angelic,

Aquiline, lyric,
From Lech to Lech the national glory
And she, with outstretched hand, toward the wings falling there,
Gathering from the air
The echoes of history,
That might tangle-twine in wreaths, of this land!…

*   *   *

From her I lived, and lived with her. Her now I wish to see,
For I've a will,
So many tears and pains and slaveries
Evoked, I ask no more who might give her me…

*   *   *

I only ask who's stained
And stains each hazard of each game,
By every speech, wordless each,
By every falsehood, each livid spark of Hell…

CHORUS

Afar, amidst the clashing of weapons.

         … the people's thought, the people well
In song: Vengeance — vengeance — vengeance!…

ZWOLON
And as for the nation's anthem?
Angels! What song gives this nation life?
Is it carved on the bark of tree by knife?
Or on our breast by the fang of famine?
Angels! What song soothes
Its thirst? Where is that song? Whose?

CHORUS OF MANY VOICES

FIRST VOICE
Boga Rodzica, Dziewica —[31]

SECOND VOICE
Bogiem sławiena Maryja —

THIRD VOICE
Twego Syna, hospodyna,
Matko Zwolena, Maryja —

ALL
Ziści nam, spuści nam
    Kyrie Elejson.
Twego Syna Chrzciciela zbożny czas...

FIRST VOICE
Usłysz głosy, napełń myśli człowiecze,
Słysz modlitwę jąż nosimy
A dać raczy jegoż prosimy

ALL
Twego Syna, hospodyna,
Ziści nam, spuści nam

---

31   The chorus of voices sings the ancient Polish Marian hymn 'Bogurodzica' [Mother of God]. This is one of the oldest lyrics in Polish; it was sung before the victorious battle against the German Knights of the Cross at Grunwald in 1410. Because it is so well known to all Poles, and its melody, especially when sung in massed chorus, is so moving in and of itself, I have chosen to reproduce it untranslated from the Polish. Here is an English translation, which may replace it, if the performers see fit: 'Mother of God, Maiden, / God-glorified Lady, Maria / Thy Son, our Lord, / Chosen Mother, Maria, / Win for us, Send to us / Kyrie Eleison!/ Through Thy Son's Baptiser, in meet time... / Hear our voices, inspire the minds of men / Hear the prayer we bring before Thee... / Thy Son, our Lord, / Chosen Mother, Maria, / Win for us, Send to us / Kyrie Eleison!/ Through Thy son's Baptiser, in meet time... / Kyrie Eleison!'

Twego Syna Chrzciciela zbożny czas…
    Kyrie Elejson.

ZWOLON

Lifting his arms, in a loud voice.

It creates, it creates
Until wide then gapes
The seal, the tomb here —
No vengeance
But on all hands —
The shadow of Her resurrected — and fear!

To those who foam
Rabid and roam
Like storms blaspheming — chance.
To those who start
From thought and heart
Heaven's law power grants.

To those who mock
With forge and lock
When Glory opens graves —
Benediction
Oblivion
And the Resurrected's shade.

Create, create,
Open, dilate!
I'm faithful, for faithful is He!
Nor dawns nor seas
He's locked with keys —
Life, death, eternity…

THE LOWER CHAMBERS OF THE CASTLE

Zabór and Stylec.

ZABÓR
The townsmen's deputation that arrived
Has now been dealt with…

STYLEC
                    What should I write?
'Those who remained,' or 'those who survived?'

ZABÓR
'Those who remained.'

Pause.

                    Or just a moment, wait:
'Those who survived' is better, for there should be
No doubt when it's read to His Majesty
That we took care of the rebellious factions,
Slicing the rot off in exemplary fashion;
And so, 'those who survived.'

STYLEC
                              'Those who survived…
Town envoys… handled, as soon as arrived…'

ZABÓR
To which, by duty bound, the undersigned
Reports the method, and the place and time
Where this was carried out. My Lord's most true —
'Lord' with a capital 'L.'…

STYLEC
                    … capital 'L.'…

ZABÓR
My Lord's most true… most true… Give us some help…

STYLEC
'My Lord's most true retainer.' Or would you
Prefer I wrote 'knight'?

ZABÓR
                    Set down 'patriot,'
With a small 'p.'

STYLEC
            A small 'p.'

ZABÓR
                                While those who fought
Beneath a captain base achieved great things…

A bell strikes. Zabór pauses.

STYLEC
They're coming in…

ZABÓR
                            Two — four — eight — from the rings
I guess some noble party; ministers
Or of that ilk. And so, the rest, good sir,
I leave to your invention, to your pen.
Read it through, copy it, and once again
In a clean hand…

He moves toward the door. Then turns back.

                        Describing victory,
Let your descriptions not be niggardly.
Use your imagination. Writing is
An art — these pages are clean canvases.
And as you write, show some liberality —

CYPRIAN KAMIL NORWID

You are the one creating history —
Be as a trumpet: blaring, thundering,
And your inventions will become the thing
Itself. The writer's might is chthonic,
Creating... truth. Where would Achilles be
If not for some well-crafted histrionics?
Xerxes and Sulla knew the weight of words
And fostered artists; Homer, all the bards
Through Corneille and Racine — each one of them
Indebted to the work of earlier men,
Each of them great — for standing on the shoulders
Of those who came before. Thus history
Turns rhetoric, and ends up — poetry.
Now it's your turn to... build a little bolder,
You understand?

STYLEC

Aside, his notebook in hand. Pause.

                    Well, I am to be bold...
Stenography from thought out-squeezes gold;
Rarely the scribe stumbles upon a treasure...

ZABÓR

Rests his hand on Stylec's shoulder.

I'll never blame a man for industry —
I like your eagerness. Perhaps it's not
The greatest token of my admiration,
But I'm on duty now... Go. Serve your nation
By making something out of... poetry.

A suburban market square.

To the rear, a Gothic church, its doors wide open. Wounded are being carried in, corpses carried out, of which there are many lying about around the church.
To the right, heaps of blowing ash, to the left, the road that leads to the castle. Various people walk about alone.

SZOŁOM

In travelling attire.

What have they won for us? Ruins on all sides,
Great man — blood, shame, and poverty, and waste!
In vain I begged, yes, in vain I cried
'Brothers! I like not the look on their faces,
Those fighting boys!' Destruction and disgrace!

Pause. He continues following the silent Zwolon, peering continually into his eyes.

There was more courage by far in negation
Than in stoking just ire into the elation
Of bloody vengeance! Knowledge directs lives
Better than swords — a mere temptation
For children! What are swords? Are kitchen knives
Not made of the same steel? And so, why not
Make flags of tablecloths, with which to march
To cheering crowds through a triumphal arch
For having nobly with a pork-chop fought?

Pause. Szołom continues to skip at Zwolon's side, glancing up at his face beneath the brim of his hat.

Am I not right, sir? Wise men know it's all
Spirit, yes, the Spirit's what it's all about!
But those men! They're unlearned — like some pagan rout!
And in the end, upon the learned falls
The blame, and we, what can we do but bear it?

With a sad gesture, he halts Zwolon.

So let us suffer. Meanwhile, in that spirit,
I bid farewell to you.

ZWOLON

                    Tell me your name.

SZOŁOM

Dodging aside.

Szołom, a servant of the Spirit.

As Szołom plunges down a side-street, the Sergeant approaches on crutches.

SERGEANT
                        Hey!
You villain! It was you who sapped our might
When we were drawn up, marching to the fight!
With but a few words, sharpened cunningly,
You bled the ranks of electricity
And they collapsed! I hope you're satisfied
Like they are! Can your laurel chaplets hide
These pools of blood? Is your wisdom as large
As the heaps of them, fallen in the charge?

People begin to mill around them.

I'm not, like you, a man of empty words —
They used me as a whetstone for their swords!

Zwolon raises his hand to take off his hat, at which the Sergeant makes a quick motion towards him.

What?!
You'll raise your hand against a crippled wreck?!

ZWOLON
I do but doff my hat out of respect…

ALL
Ha, ha!
We know you well! Safe in bed he lolls
While with siege-ladders we're storming the walls!

SZOŁOM

From the crowd.

That fellow needs a lesson now — and quick!

SERGEANT
There is no lamppost here —

WOMAN
                              But there's some brick!
Let's pelt him with a hailstorm — nice and thick!

Zwolon moves off, with the crowd following.

CROWD

In pursuit.

Now there's a practical philosopher!
He moves so quickly, his legs are a blur!

They disappear down a side street. Enter a woman in mourning, accompanied by a boy.

BOY
Mama! Tell those people not to throw
Stones at that man! Scold them, just as you do
When in the morning at the pond

I swing a reed and chase away the swans —
Tell them to stop! It isn't fair!

MOTHER
Adults can do what little boys don't dare…

BOY

Raising his hand.

When I get big, just wait and see!
I'll climb up on that hill — instead
Of bricks I'll toss boulders on your heads!

MOTHER
Go pick some flowers for sister, meanwhile!

BOY
Mama, no!

Rushing off after the crowd.

MOTHER
He's a devil, that naughty child!

A CASTLE COURTYARD

The king and queen, their court, and various ministers are seated on a wide balcony beneath a baldachin. Beneath them, on the courtyard, crowds of people mill among fountains, gaily dressed with wreaths on their heads. Music, noise, and cheers, punctuated from time to time by a deep, deaf silence.

KING

Loftily.

Now lawlessness is punished, justice praised;
The just rewarded, and my royal grace
Spills forth in floods, in broadly stretching spans
Which clear the sharp stones from the fertile land.
Let us rejoice! This ought to cheer you well,
And make your hearts with happiness to swell!
Our ancient throne, though stable and exempt
From vulgar rumblings, holds not in contempt
Our humble subjects! We gaze with delight
At all that chains of compassion bind tight.

CROWD
Long live the King!

SOMEONE FROM THE CROWD
           The master orator!

PROFESSOR
The master orator! For when he speaks
In lapidary style, I would say, each
Word is as if carved on granite gravestone, or
Marble — happy the nation that he heads!

ARTIST[32]
How sweet it is, to lie in one's last bed
Beneath so mottoed a sarcophagus.

HARALD
In Rome, on Scipio's grave, asparagus
Is growing, I recall…

---

32   Norwid has *Sztukmistrz* here, which often connotes a prestidigitator or mountebank. However, considering the character's words on sculpture, the word is not intended to be sarcastic, though there seems to be irony in what he says. In a private letter, Norwid uses the term *sztukmistrz* in the sense of 'master artist' in reference to Bronisław Zaleski, an artist he respected. See Kazimierz Wyka, *Norwid w Krakowie*, p. 94.

CITIZEN
                    I doubt it not —
The soil is thick, the climate moist and hot.

Trumpets. All grow silent. The queen rises from her seat.

HERALD
Her Majesty the Queen rises to speak!

QUEEN
Justice belongs to kings; to queens: clemency.
Throughout the realm now let it be announced
That I have swayed the king to amnesty
For all penitent rebels, who renounce
Further insurgency and such misprision.

CROWD
— Hurrah, long live her majesty!
— Sh! Listen!

QUEEN
You may have heard the town's name was to be
Changed to 'Ugolino' as a testament
To what Providence sends as punishment
For breaking faith. But it shall be for me
Renamed Elverino, so that, in after-days
It shall recall not punishment, but grace.

CROWD
Long live the Queen!

SZOŁOM
                    What? Did I hear aright?
An amnesty? Mercy, instead of spite?

HAROLD
I was in Thebes once; strolling by the Nile,
I chanced upon a weeping crocodile.

But — Węžyk[33] cautions — take note of her smile…

HERALD
His Grace the Lord Prime Minister will speak.

PRIME MINISTER
Cognisant of the fact (so often proved
Throughout the ages) that great felicity
Lies in the welfare of the community,
The State council (which I direct) has moved
With no ulterior motives, to advise —

CROWD
Hurrah!

PRIME MINISTER
Cognisant of that fact, I say, and wise —

CROWD
Long live the Council of State!

PRIME MINISTER
                              … wise to the fact
That this suburb, now Elverino hight,
Has, in the past, been famed for vibrant trade —

CROWD
Hurrah!

PRIME MINISTER
…With no ulterior motives, as I've said,
In the disinterested, pure desire

---

33 *Author's note:* Władysław Węžyk, of blessed memory, well-known among the Polish youth for the original talent of his pen (and even more for his personal attributes) — placed in the Warsaw Library a fragment from his memoirs of travelling in the east (after the fashion of Pliny the Younger), in which his romance 'The Crocodile' is to be found, describing the animal's lamentations.

That the townspeople — loyal to you, Sire —
Shall be permitted, *primo*, to dry planks
On all the squares, and firm with sands the mire
That fouls the muddy places; lantern ranks
Along the streets will soon brighten the nights
With all the blessings of new-rigged gaslights;
Et caetera: and further, since the river
That now suburb from capital divides,
Impeding smooth transit to those who deliver
Goods and services from this side to that,
We shall allow bridge-pylons to be fixed[34]
There, near the royal harbour, on our side,
So that a bridge might stretch across, to this.
After deliberations long, an act is
Now to be endorsed repealing taxes
On custom-goods; and passports, furthermore,
Once needed to cross from shore to shore,
Shall be replaced by the citizen's I.D....

CROWD
Hurrah!

ONE PRESENT
    What did he say? And who is he?

---

34   *Author's note*: One of the boons conferred so gracefully upon the inhabitants of Kraków by the Congress of Vienna, in the name of the Holy Trinity, so announced: *Par une suite de cette concession S.M.I. et R. apostolique a résolu de permettre également à la ville libre de Cracovie d'appuyer ses ponts à la rive droit de la Vistule — et d'y attacher ses bateaux* [According to the sense of this concession, His Imperial and Royal Majesty has also determined to allow the Free City of Kraków to rest one extremity of its bridges to the right bank of the Vistula, and to moor its boats there]. The art of building bridges (which cannot stand by resting on one bank alone) had a noble influence on the keeping of this promise. The act mentioned here was affirmed by the signatures of Princes Metternich and Hardenberg, and Count Razumoffski *on his part*. We introduce this note here so that no one would accuse us of invention for mere comic effect.

HAROLD

Once, while in Sparta, I had the mischance
Of falling into some highwaymen's hands.
One took my clothing, another stole my purse,
Which, rifling, he chanced on a button hook.
This he returned me, after one brief look
And shrug, as something valueless. And yet,
Before they left, they were themselves beset
By troops who had been in their hot pursuit
For many weeks. They dropped all of their loot
And took to fighting with the horsemen. I
Sat naked, watching the brawl; by and by
I filched my clothes back, and with button hook,
Snared my purse-strings, recovered what they took,
Got dressed — button by button — and escaped.
A moral can be learnt from this my scrape…

CITIZEN

Of what sort?

HAROLD

        Well, that one should not abuse
The button-hook, for it can be of use.

CITIZEN

And?

HAROLD

Take care while travelling. But that's hardly news…

NIGHT, A SUBTERRANEAN SPACE

Conspirators gather in silence, taking their places by turns. Flickering, dim light. In the centre, a large urn. Next to it sits the President of the association.

PRESIDENT
Enough revenge, enough lament,
Let love now sway us sweetly.
Everything will be different;
All things transformed completely.

Murmurs of satisfaction.

The late rebellion, and its crew
Had little solid content.
Now, we're creating something new —
New strength and better intent.

CHORUS.
So how will it be?

PRESIDENT
First, we must love one another…

ALL
Hurrah!

EDGAR
Of that, it seems, we've a great quantity!

PRESIDENT
All selfishness we must remove
And vow, in complete trust,
To love each other as we're loved.
Those other chaps — they are not us!

CHORUS
Hurrah! Let's love each other! Yes!
And let's abjure all selfishness!

They throw themselves into one another's embrace, then, silence falls again.

KALASANTY
My brothers! I propose we wear
As a sign of our agreement,
A ring set with a heart.

SOMEONE
                              No, no
It would be better not to bear
Any such sign or ornament.

KALASANTY
As envoy of my region, though
My motion be outvoted, so
I make the motion once again.
The heart! The heart, dear gentlemen!

EDGAR
I vote yes, if engraved thereon
There be the letters Y, E, S,
And next to each a skeleton.

SOMEONE
What's the point of such morbidness?

SERGEANT
I'm not surprised, much, at the sort
Of squeamishness you display;
For in our war — however short —
The squeamish… where were they?

SOME
He cut him down to size, indeed!

SOMEONE
If I've friends here, hey! To my aid!

SERGEANT
To me, all those who've swung a blade!

CYPRIAN KAMIL NORWID

Chaos erupts, and a general brawl ensues. Individual voices are lost in the hubbub.

VARIOUS
Hurrah!

PRESIDENT
    For God's sake, gentlemen!
The guard will hear us up above!

SERGEANT
And if he does, what's there to fear?
We're not discussing trifles here,
But honour, and the wounds we bear.
The fatherland our only care!

The noise ebbs and grows, ebbs and grows. Complete chaos.

SZOŁOM

To a Mask, leaning near his shoulder.

The guards will pounce, Sire, in no time!
I've only to give them the sign…

MASK
Hush! I doubt it not, but I'd rather
Hear them out, and come to know
What they are planning — the whole matter.
From which quarter the foul winds blow.

SZOŁOM
All monarchs, and the greatest lords,
And celebrated emperors
Marched fearless at cannons and swords
With just such bravery as yours,
With no retainers at their side,
But the most faithful squire or scribe —

For sacred to them is their king
And yet, I think it no bad thing
To have some stout arms in reserve —
The prudent soul the Lord preserves!
And so I've cached some trusty men
Nearby, and for that very reason:
Your Majesty is brave, but then,
No stronger than the weakest treason…

MASK
Quiet! You've got my gratitude…

The chaos subsides somewhat, and some of the conspirators return to their places.

PRESIDENT
                        All told,
Five balls are for the hearts, and ten against.

OŻÓG
He tore the vote up by the roots, the bold
Objector!

KALASANTY
      Gathering his party quick —
I'll think up something else to make it stick…

Whispering, the group breaks up into parties.

SZOŁOM
… Might be better at the start,
Since they've cast away the heart…

KALASANTY
Alas, no, you don't know, my friends,
Wherein the matter really lies.
'The head, the head!' That only tends
To reckon coldly, philosophise,

Until out of the breast it wring
The heart, which is the only spring
Of all true fervour, from of old!
And so the answer, when all's told
Is to knock off the head. Commit
It to the flames, yes, build a pyre
As Arabs use — they kindle fire
With mummy — and be done with it!

ALL
Hurrah!

SOMEONE
For God's sake, sirs, let's not begin
To set heads rolling! Upon my word,
You've really set my head a-spin!
Knock off the head? The thought's absurd!
For reason's housed — where? In the head!
You see? Without eyes? You'll be led
Straight to the chopping block, the blind
Leading the sightless…

SOME
                Aye! Well said!
All's from the head, and not the breast!

OTHERS
The head's nothing! The heart is best!

OŻÓG
So many thoughts about are bandied —
Let's all calm down and be more candid.
Folk-wisdom may be simple but,
It's true: we ought to heed the gut!

ALL
Ooh, ha!

OŻÓG

    It won't take much for me
To prove the point, if you'll but listen —

KALASANTY

You merely tout materialism!

OŻÓG

What? I speak for nobility!

EDGAR

A credo from some looting lummox!

SERGEANT

… Yes… But armies march on stomachs…

PRESIDENT

The key question deals with finance.
That's something everybody grants?

OŻÓG

Finance and vacance and advance…
And once again, the same old dance!
But where is progress?

PRESIDENT

              Gentlemen!
Of old, all those who have won fame
Above all else, one and the same
Thing they've prized; that, sirs: regimen.
And so, conspirators, I call
You all to order — one and all —
At the conspiratory pipe…

*He gives a low toot on a whistle and they all form up, each with his own
badge. Szołom and the Mask retire.*

There, good.

We end in order, as we should.

He puts on his hat.

UPPER ROOMS IN THE PALACE

Midnight. Enter the King, followed by Szołom, both wrapped in cloaks.

KING
My queen!

QUEEN
   My lord!

KING

Tossing his cloak onto Szołom's shoulder.

      No flowers from my stroll
Have I to offer you, or any droll
Gossip or rustic anecdotes. I've been
In caverns of profane conspiracy…

QUEEN
Good Lord!

KING
      No fear, as I was there unseen,
And I return hale, unharmed, and… oddly gay —
Odd, but I nearly sang along the way.

QUEEN
What do you mean?

KING

With classical exaggeration.

              I've seen repulsive things,
No, worse: I've peered into a vacuum, flat —
The depthless veins from which all folly springs,
So that I'm glad I crushed the mob; so that
The clouds are gone, and now I clearly see
The ruthless vigour of my mailed hand
Was more than kingship — it was prophecy.
My purple cloak and crown! Fill full my cup.
We move ahead with them as we had planned.

SZOŁOM

*Taking the cloak and royal insignias from a table and presenting them
to the King.*

Your Majesty — such are the things of song,
Which rush to rhyme's embrace as to their home —
From these, great epics grow before too long,
Like rivers flooding through great groves of bay.
Those who in later years will sip their tones
Will gasp, 'What happy folk lived in those days
Beneath so great a lord — those passed away!'

KING

Clothing himself in purple, theatrically.

Stop with the swelling tears. Sit down and write
What flashes through my eyes with flaming light.

Szołom sits down at a desk to write.

My subjects! The evil by which you were seduced
And led off into trackless wastes of vice

CYPRIAN KAMIL NORWID

Has pled contrary with us, and induced
Us to take love as our realm's new device.
A tight halter of... magnanimity
We shall impose upon the rebels' necks.
Our coat of arms from henceforth shall reflect
This new determination. There shall be
Two hearts carnelian set upon a ring
Of gold, one bearing the emblem of state
Historical, with griffin, from this date
Now superseded by the new, which king
And nation now shall signify. *Scripsi.*
Tomorrow trumpets blaring, by tympani
Accompanied, this news shall publicly
Declare... supported by the cavalry.
That'll shake up the city...

SZOŁOM

Bowing.

                              And move them, too.

KING
Enough. Szołom, return.

Szołom departs. The King, in purple and gold, remains a while motionless. The Queen stands to the rear of the stage, her eyes fixed upon him.

KING

Rising, to the Queen.

On the high tower, beneath the moon and stars,
I would curse fate, Elvira, in your arms.

QUEEN
The boy's already there, and with his lyre
Awaits you, prince, where the roses respire
Their sweetness to the night…

The King and Queen move toward the rear door.

KING

                              That boy — still pale?

QUEEN
Fading before one's eyes. Even when he sings.

KING

Showing some emotion.

When he… fades, it will be a bitter thing!

QUEEN
The doctors all… Well, it's the same old tale.
We've gathered all the experts we could bring
To consultation… But their powers fail.
They work to palliate his suffering.

KING
And so? That means I'll lose my nightingale?

QUEEN
Yes, lord…

KING

Gloomily.

And once again you yawn, voracious tomb!

*   *   *

I have permitted his mother to come.

*   *   *

The widow of a general. One of my best.

QUEEN
And yet — with your permission — nonetheless
A sickly man himself.

KING
                    Yes, but he won
So many great pitched battles for this throne.

QUEEN
He had a talent for war all his own —
Wielding his staff as lightly as his son
The lyre…

They vanish through the doors to the rear.

ON THE CASTLE TOWER

To the right, a balustrade and stairs leading down into the castle; to the left, a table and chairs covered in cloth; the table is lavishly set. The entire terrace is full of flowers — to the rear, a view towards the city, lit by the full moon.

BOY

Half reclining on the floor, half on the stereobate of a column (as if sleeping) every now and then he strums the lyre lying next to him.

SONG

He dries and vanishes, so pale!
Soon he shall rest beneath the sod.

There shall be no more nightingale
Unless the angry arm of God
Retains the music-clerk!

The learned doctors, one by one
Held whispered conference with the queen.
Already they've purchased the stone
Beneath which he'll be drolly lain
When fall days grow dark!
And yet the angel makes a sign
And says 'You're better ill,
A songbird caged to please the lion,
Fleshed here in mist until
The world shall be renewed.

'Play at the child, play at the child,
But then moult into power
To sob out thunderheads wild —
A life crammed into one hour —
And unchain the bolt you've brewed!'

BOY

Rising, extending his hands.

 Angel unseen, what is your name?

Turning to face the column.

Judith! — Judith!

The King and Queen, half seen, stand by the staircase to the right, leaning on the balustrade.

QUEEN
He's got an ideal voice — perfect for rhyme.

KING
He's singing ballads, or panegyrics?

QUEEN
At the very lip of the tomb, his lyrics
Arise from within.

KING

To the Queen, as he emerges onto the tower.

A peculiar bard.

Nearing the child.

To look upon him in this state is… hard.

QUEEN
Lord, be, as you well know how to be — mild
And sweet when faced with suffering…

KING

Taking a cup from the table.

Poor child.

THE INTERIOR OF A TOWNHOUSE

A moment before sunrise. A lamp on the table is dying down; beneath it, a cradle, half covered, and next to it, Portia. Enter Wacław.

WACŁAW

Throwing himself onto a chair.

Portia! I've loved everything, in everything believed,
Asleep, awake, in the masses' strength, in my own might,
And today, I swear to you, tell me — I was deceived!
I'm back from the cenacle — everything there: so tight,
Sickroom-like inadequate, and so boringly roiled,
And consumptively furious (maybe even soiled),
So much so that from my body I would like to flee
Into some dark abyss, if only you fled with me.

PORTIA
Every day these same explosive outbursts. Why?
You curse, create, endure…

WACŁAW

Covers his face with his hands.

                              In a sublime lie!

PORTIA
O, how you frighten me, Wacław, sometimes…!

WACŁAW
And so let's talk of something else — whatever comes to mind!
Of anything… of nothing… as long as I might gaze
Upon your countenance, and see there a happy face…

Long pause.

WACŁAW

Rises, paces, then returns to the same place and sits back down.

The night that ebbs away, the light of dawn, the tallow
Faint with watching, amuse me. I'd sway like a mallow
Musing among the flowers, beneath a golden rain
That slakes the thirsty blooms as it blows across the plain;
I'd love small things with a great love, I'd love a small life

Hidden, unapproachable, but known in you, my wife.
And I would like… despite the bitter fruit the times blight
That day should become just day, and that night be merely night,
And music not a screeching, sobbing, or lunacy,
That sculpture not be painting, sweetness unwounded be;
That tragedy be no mosaic set by a hand uncouth;
That fables deigned be merely fables, and the truth — the truth.

*   *   *

But all this…

Stretching out his hand toward his wife.

Portia, are we alone here?

Looking around wildly.

Ha! — One thing's as I'd wish it!

PORTIA

What?

WACŁAW

A tear's a — tear.

The light grows strong in the main window, the lamp dies, the doors open with a crash and a child runs in.

BOY
Wacław!

WACŁAW
What's happened?

PORTIA

Where is your mother?

BOY

Drooping with exhaustion.

I can't… In church… I was with her…

PORTIA and WACŁAW
                              And so,
She was with you. But now?

WACŁAW
                              What's happened? Speak!

BOY

As if in a trance.

The whole nave of the church was spread, in white,
White flowers…

WACŁAW
                    Do not be alarmed. He's been
Like this since birth. A slight convulsion merely.

BOY
The bishop came, a choir of priests processing behind;
The flowers on the tiles, in a tongue of such great range —
Just like Polish, for heart's speech is true, and doesn't change…
As you'll freely admit if you only toss away
Mental quotation marks, as if it were foreign speech —
'Glory!' the violets, 'Glory!' the lilies, and each
Flower in turn…

                    *   *   *

                    Where is mother? She was just beside
The priest, kneeling in prayer…

                    then a new friar arrived,
An investiture! That's the reason for all the fine
Flowers that decked the naves, the incense, and the bright shine
Of candles… Do you know who he was? And what his crimes?
You know his name? Zwolon. That gentleman that the cruel
Mob fell upon —

Pointing at Wacław with outstretched hand.

And whom, in your heart, you call a fool.

                  *   *   *

Where's mother, and… I don't know… Such great crowds…
        Where to search…

Pause.

A wall of bricks was taken down there behind the church,
Amidst so many yellow bricks, lime, and gravel, among…

Pause again.

They say 'He's dead,' — Yes, just like that, in their paper tongue;
That's what they'll tell you, but not in the language of blooms
That, like the Polish language, sense from fragrance construes,
Where are no vaults from which echoes might beat in reply;
For vaults are brittle things, vain…

Smiles.

                       Sometimes before my eye
I've seen them pierced, I've seen them crumble, I've seen them rent
As if I'd taken a spear and plunged it through a tent
To let the pure blue sky pour through the slits in torrents,
For vaults are brittle things, vain…

Rising, as if coming back to his senses.

                                  Hymns, flowers, and incense…
There is mother, at her missal, inclining her forehead,
But there, between the bricks there comes pouring a smoke, red,
And from that a red smoke to me he stretches forth his hand
As if a sheaf of wheat, yellowish, trembling like rays
That form words, writing strangely, and 'You!' is what he says
By that hand speaking (strange it is, but I understand,
And take it on trust from me, as truth, for I'm a child)
The hand is speaking — in Polish, but the tongue is wild,
Uncanny; 'Receive the name that is not of this world.
I need it no longer, its wings already unfurled;
Receive it, but add 'You all'[35] — and then he disappeared.

With an odd smile.

How quickly do they push aside the bricks!
And then they dump the lime — how fast and thick!

Pause.

At first, the stain upon the wall was wet
Like a tomb's shadow, then it began to dry
Side-inward, and the moist began to set,
Then, like the fleecy clouds up in the sky,
Or fleeting bird's shadow on a wall of white,
Or like a trembling spot upon one's eye
Which rests on no object, but is in flight…

He awakens.

Where's mother? I don't know. I looked for her
Throughout the church; I didn't want to say
Anything. I said nothing. What's to say?

---

35   The name, *Zwolon*, i.e. 'called, elected,' with the addition 'you all.' Thus 'You are all called.'

Enter Mother. She slows her steps and stretches out her hand.

MOTHER
Let him alone!

BOY
        I was asleep.

MOTHER
                    The sight
Of the funeral, the incense and candle light,
The stuffiness…

PORTIA
        And all the women's scent…

MOTHER
What is it, angel mine? Are you all right?

WACŁAW

Lifting the boy.

Ah, he was only joking. No harm meant.

BOY

To all present.

I beg your pardon…

ALL
        No need!

BOY
              I fell ill
Among you here, for sure.

WACŁAW

              Eh — not at all!

BOY
But Mama…

MOTHER

      What?

BOY

              Caesar… he had such spells
As mine, you told me once now, didn't you?

WACŁAW
Sweet, funny child…

PORTIA

Setting a cup at his lips.

              Come now, here you go —
Have a nice drink of water. But go slow…

WACŁAW
Not too much, boy!

ON THE MAIN SQUARE

Streets shaded by trees. To the rear, a view toward the castle and the more important structures. Many people in Sunday clothes, strolling about or seated on the green benches beneath the trees.

HAROLD
All in this microcosm here
Is so oddly in knots and tangles
That, should someone wish to unwrangle
Sense from it all, and disburse

This strand here, that there, make clear
The story, he'd just make it worse.
So dry — and so exhilarating;
So translucent — and so curtained;
Such silence — and so much prating;
So unsure — and yet so certain,
It's like there is no history
In this suit-of-clubs monarchy.
You know, whenever the cock crows
I start and gape about the place...
Where have I slept? And what are those
Walls, unfamiliar? A hotel?
I grab my clothing and ring the bell —
Where is my servant?

Taking a place on one of the benches.

                I had plans
For writing a stageplay, but spleen
Put paid to that — well, a romance?
What? Just have a glance about the scene
Uncovered to our eyes — so pale
And bloodless these faces, like sails
That bob about the lonely wastes!
Lord! It's so stuffy in this place...

He turns to his Cicerone.

CICERONE
The king has thought up for the nation
A new coat of arms — you see?

HAROLD
I tender my congratulations
(Aristocratic tyranny!)

CICERONE
It's been announced today. That, and —

HAROLD
What?

CICERONE
They're to execute some man
By knout.

HAROLD
Who?

CICERONE
Some conspirator.
By order of the ministers.

HAROLD
Ah, ministers!

SOMEONE
Bystroff's sentences
(The Count Bystroff) can be severe.

HAROLD
Indeed! Then, what can be done here?

Noting that a stranger has been gazing about, sadly.

Perhaps, sir, you'd like to sit down?

SOMEONE
I would… but in some other town.

STRANGER

Moving off with a sigh.

This land is nearing its collapse!

Drums are heard, then the guard appears, leading the disciplinary squad, with Wacław, the prisoner, in the centre.

HAROLD
As if we needed drums! Perhaps
There'll yet be fifes?

SOME
                    Poor man!

OTHERS
                                        His face
Drained of its blood so suddenly!

HAROLD

Looking around for a way out.

The streets are all blocked off, I see,
By bayonets. And such a wall
Of people! You'd need be a spy
To make the slightest move at all!

To Cicerone.

Is this where they will scourge him?

CICERONE
                                        Yes.
Three hundred lashes, not one less.
And then, if he survives the knout
He'll be transported to the mines.

HAROLD

Stopping a passerby.

Pardon me, can you help me out?
I need to leave the square betimes…

STRANGER
You'll have to pass through the platoon.

CICERONE
I don't think that's the safest way.

HAROLD
Why?

STRANGER
       Because they'll see you, and assume
That you like to go your own way.

HAROLD
It's an old habit of mine, alas.

STRANGER
And one more thing, before you pass…

Pushing through the crowd, to Harold.

HAROLD
What's that?

STRANGER
You'll miss the pretty girls who've come
To watch the execution!

HAROLD

Keeping up the conversation.

What?

STRANGER
What will they think, sir, when they see
You're squeamish at the penalty!

HAROLD
That never crossed my mind.

STRANGER
                    Well, then,
Come with me, I'll lead you away.

HAROLD
I'm in your debt.

STRANGER
            Oh no, I'd say
The pleasure is all mine.

They vanish in the crowd.

CHILD

In the crowd.

Where's the hangman? There's still no sign…

WOMAN
What does this mean, this long delay?

CLERK
Perhaps they need to add something
To the writ.

CITIZEN
            Or Count Bystroff, say
Has fallen asleep.

FIRST LADY
        That well may be —
All night long, on his balcony
One sees the lamp glow.

SECOND LADY
          Ah, poor man!

CLERK
Sometimes, he rests his head on hand,
And lets his eyes close.

VARIOUS WOMEN
         Ah!

SOMEONE
              That he should
Let his eyes close, and that for good!

CITIZEN
Ah well, he's so much work to do!

Drums; the crowd scatters in disorder. Movement to the rear of the square, cries.

CROWD
They're beating drums — the hangman's on the way…

MANY MIXED VOICES
Move! Get out of the way!!…

SOME
            What's going on?

OTHERS
A shot! They're firing! They're shooting cannon!

The chaos grows. Smoke to the rear of the square, constant cannon fire.

CROWD
What's going on? The street across the way
Is full of trumpeters on foaming steeds,
And archers, and these some young fellow leads
Astride the royal mount! And crowds of men
Milling about in circles, tangling, turning…

BOY

From the horse, with raised hand.

We've had enough! Look there! The castle's burning!

SOME
For all our tears!

OTHERS
   Our blood!

MATRONS
       Our children's groans,
Sent to Siberia, never returning,
And for those in torment for them here, at home!

OLD MAN
I'll gird my loins, and set out on my knees
In pilgrimage to Jerusalem today!

MIXED VOICES
Water!

CROWD
  No, sulphur!

OLD MAN
     The sky is set to fall!

PORTIA

In the crowd.

Wacław!

WACŁAW
Where are our men?

SOMEONE
They're on the way.

OTHERS
And what about the royal troops?

SOMEONE
Some, there
Are thrashing, while some others flail and drench
The burning thatch, beating sparks through the air…

MIXED VOICES

From the rear.

Hurrah!

SOME
They fire and fire…

OTHERS

Off stage.

They took the trench!

The stage empties.

VOICES

Off stage.

Hurrah…!

After a while the stage is completely empty Only Harold remains. Gazing around, he rises from his seat. An Old Man, nearly blind, is making his way from tree to tree by touch, seeking his path. The dusk grows thicker.

OLD MAN

Drawing near Harold.

What did I hear? The trench is overcome?

HAROLD
I know no more than you do, sir. But once,
Like good old Pliny, in an ancient land,
I entered a volcano, book in hand.

OLD MAN

Recognising Harold to be a foreigner.

Ah — then you're not one of ours?

HAROLD
                                         Well, as you will.

Harold offers his arm to the Old Man and they begin to walk off the stage.

OLD MAN
Ah, you young fellows! At your age, it's still
Good sometimes to mix it up a bit,
Sow the wild oats, hit someone and be hit;

Well, may God bless you and preserve your health,
And may your grandson not abandon you
To fight — but he'll do what he has to do...
Still, will I find the cottage by myself?

HAROLD

Attentively.

I'm at your service.

OLD MAN

                              God grant that no shell
Fall on the roof. If so, then, who can tell
My good, kind sir, what will become of me?

More smoke pours in, and shrapnel falls from burst shells.

While the castle was afire, I could see
A little better... It was a huge thing —
He spent a pile on it, the old, dead king...

They pass on.

CROWD

Rushing through the stage.

Hurrah!

HAROLD
Let's get out of the way. Give me your hands.

OLD MAN
Again they rush about with firebrands!

WANDA

A WORK FOR THE STAGE IN SIX IMAGES

1852

This play was composed several years ago, and submitted to the printer's, but the manuscript was lost. Despite this unfortunate event, it seemed good to someone to announce it in the press. Should anyone come across that lost manuscript, I would ask him to delete the notes and the prose introduction, and treat the work itself as a preliminary study — something rather general and lyrical. I think that the manuscript, should it ever be found, might be brought out together with the similarly lost manuscript of *Krakus*.[36]

   Since to twice CREATE the same thing in the same fashion is to DEGENERATE, the text offered below is something completely original, although the sense is generally the same as the earlier version.

Author's note

> *To Wanda's Mound near Kraków in testimony of his profound respect this work is dedicated by the Author.*

The Church holds that Jesus, just before He died,
Inclined His sacred head toward the NORTH side
Of Gethsemane;
In like fashion, He,
During His Passion, pointed with His hand
Toward — the PEOPLES OF SOME NORTHERN LAND.

---

36   *Translator's note:* A rather odd formulation, unless both manuscripts were 'lost' together. Norwid may be speaking sardonically about the 'loss' of the earlier versions of the plays.

From an old song, copied from a tome found in the monastery of the
Świętokrzyskie wilds.[37]

PERSONS

Wanda
Castle Keeper
Maiden
Trumpeter
Chorus of Villagers
Chorus of Folk Healers
Chorus of Village Headmen
Chorus of Piasts
Chorus of Sowers
Chorus of Shepherds
Chorus of Hunters
Skald
Jew
Boyan
Chaser
Chudes — Lechs — Bards — Old Men — Virgins — Children
Rytyger
Captain of Horse
Weiswort
Chorus of Runesmen
Rytyger's Army — his Bodyguard

---

37   Tadeusz Pini informs us that this is a 'somewhat altered strophe from
Wespazjan Kochowski's poem "Góra Łysa" [Bald Mountain].' Kochowski's dates
are 1633 – 1700.

CYPRIAN KAMIL NORWID

I
BEFORE THE PALACE

CHORAGOS
We've come before the porch here to inquire
After the health of our all-mighty Lady.
Send forth the Keeper! Her people desire
A word with him, as they stand, bowed and fading
Like daisies when clouds obscure the sun's sweet fire.

CHORUS
Let him come forth and speak to those who wait
Before the palace porch, before the gate.

CHORAGOS
The people want to know why it may be
That their sweet Lady, who wields supreme power,
Sits not enthroned, as wont, at this grey hour
(When every soul's inclined to piety),
To meet her folk returning from their tasks —
With upraised hand to cheer them, and to bless?

CHORUS
This is the reason why her people press
Before the palace — this is what we ask.

CHORAGOS
Good people, look — the Trumpeter appears
With his ox-horn; surely the Keeper nears!

TRUMPETER

Sounding blasts on his horn.

I bring you news — so listen, man and maid,
With meet attention, and with all your craft
To what I have the honour now to say:
Remember it — notch it upon your staff!

Our all-puissant Lady's in need of… tears.
Whatever herb, or song, or spell you know
To make her weep, now must you bring it here
To cause her heart with grief to overflow.

Your Lady must be purged of a grave illness —
Her heart washed clean, before it is too late;
This only can unbind her of her stillness,
That sickness mute that in her germinates!

Whoever, then, knows how to make one weep,
Whoever's skilled in bitter herbs, or spells,
Whoever through long practice or studies deep
Has fought his way to the arcanest wells
Of kenning, now's the time to bring your lore
Here to the palace, and bring it in store!

Sounds his horn.

Be he a churl, he'll get a silver plough;
Be he a stranger, then — a copper sleigh.
Be he a bard, he'll win widespread renown;
Be he a Lech — a blessing all his days.

CHORUS
Be thou a churl — a silver plough is thine;
Be thou a man — a benison divine…

*The Chorus exits to one side, murmuring; the Trumpeter to the other,
sounding his horn.*

II
AN INNER CHAMBER OF THE PALACE

MAIDEN
'Silence — my golden silence! — silence… my dear…'
My lady keeps repeating these few words.

You ask her something, and she doesn't hear.
Time was, as soon as that piper was heard
Out by the gate, she'd want him led in near,
She'd listen gladly… These days, no more word
Of such a thing. It seems that she's forgot
Quite everything — but, whatever takes place
Here, she notes well. Yes, it escapes her not —
Yet nothing brings a smile to her face.

KEEPER
One tear would be the charm to burst the spell
That seals her lips; one tear would make her well.

MAIDEN
But how? Meanwhile, our lady's silent, mute…
If only we could mount that horse with wings
And speed to that orchard of golden fruit
About which that old Greek grandfather sings —
Up to the skies to pluck her a blue rose…
Or else some prince, with cheeks as white as those
As Lady Wanda's…

KEEPER
                              But you don't propose
A prince like him we met the other day —
That red-haired German prince, with shield wrought
Of wood and belt of steel, whose soldiers stray
Into our lands at night, respecting not
Our border stones, nor sacred laws?

MAIDEN
                                                  The kind
You find in stories is what I have in mind.
O, if we only might get her to say
Something we could interpret! Anything
To signal what ails her. How we might bring
Her comfort…

KEEPER
        'To be moved' is all she said
Yesterday morning... 'but I'm already dead...'

Exit Keeper and Maiden. Enter Wanda. Seeing that she's alone, she speaks.

WANDA
O Łada, goddess of the lovely face!
So set am I, of your beauteous race
Amidst my ordered folk — in such a place
Where, as the sun's reflected from the lake,
From your reflection here, my people take
Refreshment, peace... Whatever their heart is wishing,
And missing nothing ... until something is missing...

She places her hand on her heart.

Ha! Like, for example, a silver ring
That fell when snapped my bodice-string
When my breast heaved with a sigh...

She slides her hand down her bosom.

Now you, her twin, burst forth too, like a star.
And you, muteness that binds me, snap! That the word
Might soar now, far,
Wide, through the pristine sky
And free! Like a snow white bird...

III
THE GERMAN CAMP

CAPTAIN OF HORSE
All of the runesmen, who with chisel blades
Skilled in the vatic craft
Groove spells in stone about the lonely glades

Alone, and rarely laugh,
All of their number, especially those
Who in deep cogitations have gone grey,
Kenning the future from random arrow throws,
Summon them with a whisper, here, that they
Might form a circle, ghostly, dim
Here on this meadow ringed with firs;
Here let them stand, where's spread the lion skin,
Where steam up from the winded horseflesh curls.

Enter Rytyger and his Bodyguard.

Hurrah!

RYTYGER

With a wave of his hand.

    At ease!

CAPTAIN OF HORSE
              At ease! Hurrah!

*The Soldiers withdraw into the darkness of the woods. When they have
made way, Rytyger seats himself upon the lion pelt. It begins to grow
dark. The Runesmen, in a long file, glide about the meadow, to encircle
Rytyger at last, his Bodyguard at his side.*

RYTYGER

Lifting a cup.

I raise this mead to Weiswort. Health, long life!

WEISWORT
May it rebound, and make you fortunate!

RYTYGER
Now — will I win both war, and royal wife?
Or not?

WEISWORT
　　My king, we must consult the fates.
Fling, lord, this cup — as far as you can throw.

Rytyger throws the cup into the dark forest. Some spooked eagles take wing.

CHORUS OF RUNESMEN
It is not ours to say: so, and not so;
People — the rede is woe.
The sooth is like a sword — until it flash…

Pause.

Until it flash, the sooth is like a sword.

WEISWORT
The queen shall fall in love, and with such might
Not seen since ages hoary.
Four eagles, at your throw, took flight.
Great shall be her glory.
She'll fall in love, and bathe her body white.

CHORUS OF RUNESMEN
She'll fall in love, and with such might!

RYTYGER
Oh, how you please me! Know, I shall not fail
In gratitude.

CHORUS OF RUNESMEN
The bard unsheathes the sooth unto the light —
The scabbard empty, now the bard is pale.

WEISWORT
What is begun without foresight,
Complete with prudence.

The Runesmen bow and withdraw. Rytyger lifts the mead again.

RYTYGER
              I'm pleased. Wassail!

*The Runesmen shuffle off whispering. Servants open the flaps of a tent,
from which a lamp suddenly flashes. Rytyger is alone; to the rear: the
tent and the servants.*

RYTYGER
Just as the faint sheet lightning first
Pales the horizon, ere thunderbolts flash,
So now, as prophesied, will I crash
Down, and take my queen, her folk dispersed…
Urging, with clever deeds, the prophecy.
The gods are good — but sometimes they're inept
Without man's daring… practicality.
They're just like swords and bucklers that are kept
Hanging on walls — a shining frippery.

Pause.

And she? He said: 'She'll bathe her body white.'

Pause.

So I'll seize whole Phoenician barges fraught
With amber for my queen's bathing delight;
From out the Orient I'll have spices brought
To scent her waters; conchs of pink and white,
Glass and ceramics from Sidonian masters —
She'll have a Roman tub of alabaster!
Such a nympheon she'll have! Unsurpassed, for

It shall be more costly than my own tomb!
And then I'll sip love like a honey-comb...

Pause. Then, clapping once.

Hey! Forefathers! Who in Valhalla rest!
When from my pyre to your ranks I shall mount,
Steel-belted, tempered armour on my breast,
You'll say: 'Behold our son! There is no doubt!'

Pause.

Wanda!... My love! The wife of Rytyger!
How they will love you! My army entire,
Each maiden with thick tresses of blonde hair,
Who plait our glory and our labours share,
All they who whistle at the lips of shields,
Each one who battle-axe and hammer wields;
Each elder who in vatic dreaming sees
Our wyrd; all visions, soughing woods, and little trees...

He withdraws slowly to the tent.

Ah, you! Emboldened by your sweet embrace
I'll rush in arms against the wolf Fenrir!
I'll smash an Alpine tunnel with my mace!
I'll burn down Rome! And holocausts of steer
Will fume upon the altars day by day,
With mounds of flesh to make the people gay...

Entering the tent.

Hey! Forefathers! Who in Valhalla rest!
When from my pyre to your ranks I shall mount,
Steel-belted, tempered armour on my breast,
You'll say: 'Behold our son! There is no doubt!'

Night falls.

CYPRIAN KAMIL NORWID

IV
AN INNER CHAMBER OF THE PALACE

WANDA

Pacing, slowly.

I do not know what's going on with me,
Or why this sadness grips me in its bind.
I love — and lovers often change their mind;
And Rytyger? Not necessarily
Do I desire him — or anyone
Since I'm the object of so many loves.
And yet it's hard to be alone in crowds
Of people — to be like the lonely sun
Beyond the reach of all the heaven's clouds,
Upon a summit — with nothing above…
O! If only I were stricken with some harm!
If God exchanged these robes for mourning weeds,
Tearing the gaudy plumage from these arms,
Banishing me to some hut sunk in reeds
With two doves cooing on the roof of moss…
Stone threshold… walls of wattle daubed across…

She crosses the stage.

KEEPER
See how she wrings her hands in her distress!

MAIDEN
Pacing about, she still seems motionless…

KEEPER
Like a sick child, we can't leave her alone.

MAIDEN
What time is it? D'you know?

KEEPER

                        It's long past one.

The Maiden exits to the rear, following Wanda. Enter the Skald. He halts at the main door.

KEEPER
Who might you be? And why is it you've come?

SKALD
I am a Skald.

KEEPER

        You sing?

SKALD

                          We are not dumb...
Sometimes I sing... But first the song appeals
To silence, that the ears of all should hear
When I begin, and then my singing wheels
Toward images, both colourful and clear,
And then to things sublime, sung to the soul
Upon which I draw forth from trembling heart
The purest, shimmering tone, and this I roll
In ever wider ambit with such art
As makes the echoes jealous; then I urge
The iris-bright song into a sheaf, bound
Till it resolves in dew; drops I asperge
Until I shake the earth with thunderous sounds
Like to a distant battle, while on high
There roar and rumble ghostly regiments
In vicious combat through the livid sky,
Where stars are pierced by lightning spears immense...

KEEPER
Indeed, a song exhaustive. Few are able,
I reckon, to fully unwind its thread...

SKALD
We Skalds are nourished on a holy bread
That falls from God's own opulent table,
Gathered for us by lithe, transparent maids
With spotless souls…

KEEPER
                    And do they have thick braids,
Those comely spirits?

SKALD
                    Long ones, like the switches
Of whippets.

KEEPER
          So their nature is of —

SKALD

Quickly.

Some, yes.

KEEPER

Lays his hand upon the Skald's shoulder.

          Below stairs, there's a warm larch fire
In a broad chamber, where two hundred spears
Glisten in sockets — there you may retire.

SKALD
Praised be your welcome.

Exit Skald, enter Jew.

KEEPER
               Who is it draws near?

JEW
I come from a far country in the east.
In Punic craft I sailed, four months at least,
And then it took me almost a full year
Of travel overland to get me here.
I come of a great nation, with the skills
To cure the shaking fever, the dry pain,
Wounds, palsy, dislocated limbs, chillblain,
The whitlow and the agnail and the ills
That cause blindness and loss of speech, all told…

KEEPER

Pointing to a bench.

Rest there.

JEW
        I also have some rings of gold —
Such talismans! (If I may be so bold),
Incised thereon by a wise man of Tyre.
No stronger spells be in the world entire!
I've ointments too, of aromas so strong,
One pinch will make odiferous a whole throng!

KEEPER
A wise man, surely…

To Jew.

        In the halls below
You'll meet with some soldiers near the entranceway.
Greet them from me — they'll tell you where to go.

JEW
May wealth and fortune fill your every day!

Exit Jew, enter Boyan, an old man supporting himself with a staff.

KEEPER
What is your name? And what is it you bring?

BOYAN
My name is Boyan. What I bring are songs.
A bard since birth.

KEEPER
                    And what is it you sing?

BOYAN
My song is like the eye that sees whole throngs
Of things, but not itself.

KEEPER
                              And before kings
Have you sung, ever?

BOYAN
                          To the bone, my lord.
Hungry, with ankles gripped in copper rings…

KEEPER
Can you make songs like rainbows, Iris-bright?

BOYAN
Yes, and freeze a bevy of swans mid-flight.

KEEPER
You can do all that, yet suffer the curse
Of poverty?

BOYAN
              It isn't from one's purse
That songs spill forth, but from the brimming heart.

KEEPER
And can you charm a maiden with your art?

BOYAN
I've seen them at my songs become so smitten,
They snuggle cheek to cheek, like purring kittens.

KEEPER
Then why are you so miserably poor?

BOYAN

To his staff.

You tell him, for I wish to speak no more
Of trifles.

KEEPER
    Every house flings wide its door
To such as you —

BOYAN
        That's true.

KEEPER
                  — a wandering bard.
At every house you find a willing lord
To greet you, whom men hold in high regard…

BOYAN
That's true. Especially before a war
Is undertaken. With our rhapsodies
They play as if with puppies at their feasts.

Pause.

O! There've been times when, past the Danube, far
To the south I've sung before a group
Of men — the Emperor of Rome
Stood right there — and with him, a horseback troop
Of body-guards…

KEEPER

Pointing to the bench.

> And what did you intone

For him?

BOYAN
  Glory.

KEEPER

> What were the steeds like?

BOYAN

> > Roans.

In scarlet-purple to the knees.

KEEPER

> His men?

BOYAN
There was a lad there — doughty — held a pole
Atop which was an eagle, wings outspread...
Like chiselled marble were the rest of them —
Clothed: half in armour, half in purple stoles.

KEEPER
Indeed?... Well... Come, old man, you must be fed
And heartened with some mead. There, down below,
Wait others in a cheery feasting hall,
Foreigners, magi, men from distant climes,
And one like you, who sense and metre twines,
And some who bucklers polish in the glow
Of the larch blaze... There you will find them all.

BOYAR

Exits.

Your health!

The Keeper strikes a copper plate, one of two hanging near the door.
Enter Chaser, who waits at the entrance.

KEEPER
Make everyone feel welcome, show respect,
And let no cost be spared in feasting them.
Women to one side, to the other, men.
The old men at their head. Take special reck
Of what the German runesmen do, your eye
Upon them, and the healing hags, for there's
No telling what a clever churl might try.
Avoid crowds. Get it?

CHASER
                                    Sir!

KEEPER
                                                Go. And take care!

V
THE PALACE ARCADE

WANDA
You've heard me. Now, stop chasing me, my lord!

RYTYGER
Wanda!

WANDA
        So I have spoken! My last word!

RYTYGER
And mine shall be — my name! They'll hear me cry,
Your Lechs, and rush upon me; I shall die
While you look on!

WANDA
                    These halls have never seen
Blood spilled!

RYTYGER
                    Indeed! Each here transparent strolls
About these peristyles, like bloodless souls!

WANDA
I tell you, prince, with all the hidden pain
I have within me — there's a time for all:
The sun sets, at next dawn to rise again;
The dew soaks the parched soil at nightfall,
But — there's no time for me. I have been set
Upon a summit like the virgin snow.
Beneath the sun, there to evaporate
Untouched — a sacrifice, the spotless glow
Of which — comely? — cheers all eyes but my own!
An orphan, taboo, perfectly alone!

RYTYGER
And so you stand upon that summit, white,
Evaporating into the thin blue,
Feeding the green vales to your folk's delight —
It may be what the people want, but you?

WANDA
O, prince, you've never seen a single tear
Of mine.

RYTYGER

Reaching toward her bosom with his hand.

        That's not true. I see two now, here —
They're sliding down the silver on your breasts
Like tiny petals fluttering to rest
Beneath an apple tree.

WANDA

Pointing to the window.

> You'll find a score
> Each evening there, where with my sprinkling cans
> I water the golden roots…

RYTYGER

Shading his eyes.

> Then take one more,
> Bestowed in parting — skimpy, for a man's!

WANDA
Go now!

RYTYGER

> You are a woman, without sword…
> I am a Skald… I go… but I shall wait
> Outside, at the gate!

WANDA

Halting him.

> You are a king… and I, Wanda… My lord,
> I beg you on my knees — go! And be glad,
> Be fortunate, be happy! In after years,
> O German eagle, should you come to know
> The bitter pain that comes of love, the tears
> Which flood the heart until it overflows,
> The love that clamours for a sacrifice,
> Then think on me — this queen of snow and ice!

She strikes a copper plate. Enter Keeper.

WANDA
Reward this Skald with silver for the road.

Exit. Pause.

KEEPER
Why do you stare, bard, at the floor like that?

RYTYGER
I have a song, but still it lacks a tune…

Pause.

O! I'll find it, somewhere… and I'll find it soon
Amidst the shrieks of battle, where swords clash
And, like those maidens who from Heaven flash
Down to the field to gather heroes' souls,
So shall I raise it, like thunder to roll
Above the blood-stained pennants; it shall rise
Like eagles stooping, when prey meets their eyes…

Exit.

KEEPER
A strange tribe are these Skalds, proud,
As poor as churchmice… yet so loud!

VI
A FIELD NEAR KRAKÓW

To the front, Wanda's tent, in the rear the Choruses pass. In the distance, the Vistula.

OLD WOMEN
We've gathered herbs from groves of the white birch,
Slim slips in baskets of green willow wrought,
And from decayed old barns: sift of dry-rot

Which ten times over fortifies the earth.
Gold grains of anthill incense, handfuls thick
Of spores, and water in jars as red as brick.

CHILDREN
We children and grandchildren, who can root
With tiny hands the treasures underground,
Behind Mother and Grandma bring tribute…

OLD WOMEN
Which, gods grant, peace might further, Wanda's crown
To flash above the mountains, woods and vale…

They pass on.

FOLK HEALERS
Words — words — the quiet ones by spirit pressed
As father's face on death-bed slowly pales
While sons watch; these we bring in caskets dressed
With metal crimps, of sycamore carved, hexed
With many a curious, arcane text…

HEADMEN
O Łada, may peace overflow the earth!

ALL
Peace, and songs praiseful of Wanda's great worth!

They pass on.

PIASTS
In pots we carry combs of honey white,
And moths that flutter round the hives at night,
Spell-bound with tallow, from which they'll take flight
At evening, when the candles shed their light.

SOWERS
Sowing-seed threshed from first-fruit harvest sheaves…

SHEPHERDS
Crafty concoctions from roots, herbs, and leaves.

HUNTSMEN
And creatures curious, from far-distant lands
Who, slipping their keys, fell into our hands.
Spectre-like things, and birds that have no name.

FOREIGNERS
While we, who from lands distant too, here came
Through seas of azure, bearing costly items
In jars of glass — the costlier in gems.

RUNESMEN
While we — soft spells and smiles, hammers and swords
Sharp, who can spark the clouds with words,
To flash at the blast of German horns,
Wreaths of laurel from Caesar's stirrups, urns,

Louder.

Strange words we bring, seed and root by turns!

They pass on. As the Choruses pass by Wanda's tent and take their places to the rear, they set themselves up in a semi-circle surrounding the tent, while in the far distance, the Vistula can still be seen.

MAIDENS
And now you bards with heads of grey,
Stand in our midst — what is to be?
Bring forth your words of power — speak!

LECHS

Raising shields aloft.

Who's fated life, new life shall take;
Who's meant to tremble, he shall quake.

The Bards step forth from the Choruses to stand before the tent. The Chorus Elder enters the tent. A moment of silence.

CHORUS ELDER

Emerging from the tent.

Our mighty lady, in prophetic sleep…

ALL
Aah!!

CHORUS ELDER
… Dreamt that you are to bring your gifts, her wealth,
And pile it all here in a mighty heap,
For this alone will restore her to health.

CHORUSES

Stepping to the front.

And this alone will restore her to health!

To the rear, the mound grows, to the accompaniment of song, in the same order as at the beginning of the scene, only — soft, and distant.

TRUMPETERS

From both sides of the tent.

Łada — Łada…

LECHS
          'Tis she!

CHORUSES
              Long live the Queen!

CHORUS ELDER
Like a feather of white
Through the air,
A peacock feather,
She goes, slender,
Sublime, great!

MAIDENS
Gripping her crown in her right
Hand…

CHORUS ELDER
    Like the wind, clear,
Immaculate.

CHORUSES
She passes — now she's standing at the mound!

WANDA
My good people — I've seen above our land
God's immense shadow, like a straight road, run;
It was but the shadow of His hand,
And that hand — pierced — for through the palm the sun
Shone unimpeded… Staring like a bird
Flying in darkness toward that chink of light,
Suddenly, something in my spirit stirred
To a sure knowledge of what I must do…

She takes a candle from the hand of Piast, and ascends the pile. Then, more quietly:

The knowledge that I must now… die for you…

ALL
What did she say? What?

WANDA

Great hearts, you brought such ware,
Each, what he could, in offering to me…
Enough for one life — one eternity!
My people, what strange warriors you shall be…
I shall entrust you into god-Prowe's care…
And as for me, I give you all…

OLD MAN

She burns!

CHORUSES

Two puffs of smoke, like wings of white, close, hide
Her from our sight, and now, they part to both sides…

OLD MAN

I see — blue sky! Bring water to the mound!

ALL

Bring the whole Vistula! It's burning down!

OLD MAN

I saw her crown flash once…

TRUMPETER

Rushing in.

People! Be still.
No water's needed here. I saw the queen
Her pure white body spill
Into the River Vistula's wide stream…

ALL

What's this?

LECHS

Germans!

Enter Rytyger on horseback, accompanied by his Runesmen, their capes tossed over their shoulders, revealing armour. A great army is seen behind Rytyger, as far as the eye can see.

RYTYGER

                       I'll tear them all to pieces!

LECH

Pushing before the horse with his spear.

Wait! You gaze upon a wound, fresh-torn and red!
A wound, you vulture! If it's a crown you want
I'll send you searching the deep river-bed!

RYTYGER
Where is the queen…?

RUNESMEN

               The queen… is not.

RYTYGER

Wheeling round, to his men.

Back then! This land is not given us by fate!
To Rome!
           For love is… helplessness… and late!

END

Written in 1851.

KRAKUS,

THE UNKNOWN PRINCE

A TRAGEDY

TO THE CRITICS

Critics today are something both rare and negligible. Rare, in that, in their role as tribunes and guarantors, they provide the public with an important service — especially that portion of the public who, on the one hand, feel the noble need to become familiar with matters literary, while on the other, have no interest in busying themselves with a study of present literary conditions themselves. Such critics are, therefore, resonant readers, public servants, transforming readers into listeners, and aiding said listeners to an assessment of what is read to them. In this role of theirs, as something of a public bond, they are very rare indeed. On the other hand, should someone demand of them a firm explanation of the *critical statement*, they themselves would uncover to our eyes how petty they are, how unsure of their own business! For example, that which they offer as a definition of ancient tragedy is nothing more than a simple display of their familiarity with the conditions of the layout[38] of tragedy, but by no means an answer to a question so respectable and unacademic as 'What is tragedy?'

As far as I am personally concerned, I believe tragedy to be *the making apparent of the fatal nature of history, society, the nation, or the age proper thereunto.* Consequent to this definition, it plays an auxiliary role in the progress of morality and truth. For this reason, it is no wonder at all that tragedy could, and indeed had to, be possessed of an almost ritual gravity.

---

38   Norwid uses the term *rozkład,* which can mean 'decomposition, decay' as well as 'layout.'

Today's critics, dispossessed of that simple, not to say Christian, informality, which permits a person to respond directly to direct questions, are very defective in that first great virtue of brokering[39] and mediating between works of literature and the readership. One might think that they preserve unto themselves a mandate of *casual and persistent review and censorship*, at the cost, indeed, of readers to whom the chief principles and truth of the literary art are unfamiliar — and who thus are presented merely with the particular works or reputations of such persons as said critics have permitted to exist!

How easy is it for authors to be elevated above such practices? A decisive answer to this question can be arrived at with a little patience. For criticisms of the same pen by the same pen, over the space of no more than two years, undermine themselves by constant contradictions. Time is lost, and nothing remains but the names won by the critics at the cost of the authors in question. Such *pandering*, for after all it is difficult to term their labour *criticism*, is mistaken in that it takes the mere *part for the whole*. It is similar to a man who supposes the whole of medicine to consist of gymnastics — something which cannot be accepted by all classes of society.

To these comments — which set forth *what concept of tragedy it is that I hold to* — I should still add this: I do not feel that it is the playwright's obligation or a necessary condition of his craft to reveal a *direct moral*, and that the falling out of siblings, presented in the following tragedy, is the inevitable outcome of the legend itself, and not the chief idea of the author, who originally intended to entitle the *Mysterium* in hand *Krakus, or Competition*.[40]

C.N.

---

39   Norwid uses the term *streczenie*. While it may have had a non-pejorative sense of 'brokering' or 'acting as a middleman' in the Polish of his period, today it has taken on the more specific colouration of sexual pandering, pimping. Later in this introduction, Norwid uses it with this very connotation.

40   Norwid here uses the term *wyścigi*, which is used primarily to designate a 'race', i.e a horse race.

KRAKUS

PERSONS

Old Man	Hermit
Lilian	His Disciple
Krakus	Prince, whose seat is Kraków
Rakuz	His Brother
Szołom	Royal scribe, or Runesman
Kiempe	A Scandinavian warlord
Keeper	of Krakus' Castle
Armourer	
Chorus	of Castle denizens and villagers

FANTASTICAL PERSONS

Fountain
Dawn
Threshold

I

The interior of a hermitage, near Kraków.

OLD MAN
The day shunts me aside. Hear the night call —
Soon will the hour be on me to depart.
To you I leave my herbs and lute, and all —
My candle, cunning, medicine, and art.
My *last words,* when at last I close these eyes,
I'll breathe upon your brow like butterflies.
Life is not given us, it's only lent:
A handsel merely, quickly burnt away;
Ours neither to begin, nor ours to end —
Our last words disappear with our last day!

If I've no longer breath, my Lilian,
I'll trace my *final words* upon this wall,
My last reserve of strength tensed in this hand.
At first, you won't quite puzzle out the scrawl,
But you will say, 'It was!' And then, efstoons,
Deep in your soul their meaning will distill
If, with your thumb, you will caress the runes
I trace upon your brow, and bend your will
Unto them, and become them, incarnate,
To speak aloud, what I'd no strength to state!

From time to time, those who search far and wide
For wisdom have reclined here at my side,
Where I have shared my board — though sparse and plain —
With them, who for her sake endure much pain.
One of these came from a far-distant land
Beyond a great sea, where no cloud disturbs
The heavens, and the stars by God's own hand
Are sifted — it's a land of paltry herbs
But lofty mountains… A sage, royal wight,
Sweet, wise, another one — from Asia hailed;
And then, one born on horseback: a stout knight
With limbs tree-thick, his barrel-chest fish-scaled

With armour; here a queen herself once stood:
Scarlet, as when the sun is going down,
Her hands were thickly covered in the blood
Which so befouled her brow and golden crown…
A page traipsed in her footsteps, carrying
An extra mantle — vain, that covering!

LILIAN
Father — two armed men are drawing near.
I heard them come — as you've taught me to hear;
Against their hips are clattering two swords…

OLD MAN
I've taught you to listen when there are no words.
Who listens well when soft the silence sings,
To him, the grave itself deep comfort brings.
Both day and night at times close counsel keep;
There's silence depthless, and silence merely deep.
The former's intricate, and wrapped in gloom.
This I cannot reveal, only the tomb…

LILIAN
Father! Should a spider steal
Along a forest of dry alder leaves,
With my spirit,
I hear it;
I scent the air he breathes.
And future happenings, not yet revealed,
Before they take tongue,
Before they shimmer in the pale sky,
These I descry —
The crackling air
Through which they flare
I draw deep into my lungs.

OLD MAN
A mind fresh and protected, O my son,
And wisely used since first it came to birth,

Is to be treasured above millions —
But who will know of this while he walks the earth
Unless such wisdom be to him revealed
By someone older, by life's tempests steeled?
And though the dead, the hosts who have passed on,
Are not such men as could have never been —
Such as they say the world has never seen,
Nor ever shall — be in their wisdom strong.
But this is intricate, and wrapped in gloom.
This I cannot reveal, only the tomb…

LILIAN
Master! Now I can descry
The men without recourse to inner eye
As you taught me… Princes they, brothers twain —
And as they come, they quarrel and complain.
Not after quarry speed they through the wood
Spurring their straining chargers' flanks to blood;
They gaze around them not, like men who've strayed;
They thirst not, seek not fountain, nor deep shade…

OLD MAN
Go intercept them on their way and learn
Their aims in coming — which I can't discern.
Sometimes, an old man's powers flag, and fall
Away like dry leaves. I hear the night call —
Soon will the hour be on me to depart.
To you I leave my herbs and lute, and all —
My candle, cunning, medicine, and art.

LILIAN
They've come — they're standing by.

OLD MAN
                                        Call the knights near.

LILIAN
Enter, good sirs. The hermit's lying here.

RAKUZ

Entering.

It's proper at a sling's distance to halt
Before a stranger's threshold, then to send
A boy with bugle forth, one's name to call,
Announcing one's arrival and intent.
And my lad's skilled. His clarion is like speech:
Striking with wonder all who hear his song!
Lords, maidens, whomever his trillings reach,
Stand gaping, while I nod to him: 'Play on!'
We've left him in the woods, like a lone pine
To which a horse is tethered — lost a shoe
Thanks to Prince Krakus here, this brother of mine —
While we all three were on our way to you…
It's a good thing you have no manor here!
I don't know how we'd trumpet, drawing near…
The roads are strewn with Prince Krakus's largesse:
Shoes, golden nails, harness bits great and small;
Now, I'd rather that the horse beneath me fall
Dead than trot up one shoe-nail the less…

KRAKUS
You shame me, brother.

RAKUZ

                Not at all! I'm just
Sending forth words as heralds to explain
To the most reverend father here, who must
Be startled at our advent: princes twain,
One horse between them!

OLD MAN

Interrupting.

> One's seen stranger things.
And stranger still, perhaps, tomorrow brings.

To Krakus.

Prince Krakus, before Heaven and Earth, now say
In your own words why you've come here today.

KRAKUS
Sons are we of that king who rules the land
Once held by Wanda the Magnificent,
Who Rytyger rejected out of hand
And him and his German armies homeward sent.
Now we are threatened by new peril there
In the very heart of the nation, for
Beneath the castle, a dragon's dug his lair —
With him our father's waging constant war.
As if storm-tossed in leaky craft, he bales
The fatal flood that washes over the gunwales
To capsize it. The drake spouts from his gills
Green spumes of poison, leaving noxious trails
Along the castle walls. This roots and grows:
Sometimes the tendrils breach the high windows.
You cut one down, another's at the door,
Spreading its venom over the stone floor.
This battle recommences every night.
Hundreds of men have perished in the fight,
And thus do we exist: like chicks who nest
Within a fowler's garret. No hope, no rest.

The castle's black with filth; befouled, the halls.
From every chink a fell contagion spreads
From decomposing limbs, unburied dead…
And of this snake there seems to be no end!
From constant hewing, the mightiest arm falls,
And still the dragon kills, and still he crawls.
We're witless how to mount a sure defence —
Talons lopped off… regrow! It never ends!

OLD MAN
Which of you counselled the trip here, to take
Advice of me?

RAKUZ
                I was first!

KRAKUS
                            And I — late.

RAKUZ
I had to urge him on. He made me wait!

OLD MAN
He shall not be a snake, who kills a snake;
No serpent he, who deals him the death-blow.
This matter was decided long ago
Past seven streams and mountains — far from here.
The breezes still waft near the perfumed air
From thence, where the first snake, by Virgin's foot
Was crushed; your dragon's merely an offshoot
Of that first evil. If the lopped-off limb
Rots, as you say, and does not generate
New reptiles, soon you'll see the end of him.

From time to time those who search far and wide
For wisdom have reclined here at my side,
And I have shared my board, though sparse and plain
With such as for her sake endure much pain.
One of these travellers came from distant parts —
He knew this matter of the snake by heart:
How he was conquered by the grace of God...
I listened long, and then fell deep in thought...

I listened long to that pilgrim's account.
He it was planted that gold apple tree
By which your archer now holds fast your mount.
He planted it, blessed it, now, annually

It bears fruit twice. Its fragrance fills the wood
To overflowing — an aromatic flood.
No pest or insect does it any harm.
It is respected by each flock and swarm…

He shall not be a snake who kills a snake;
No serpent he, who deals him the death-blow.
That first dragon by Virgin overthrown
Still spits his venom through your stubborn drake.

Princes — ride to the Tatras. Past seven hills,
Amidst the rocky summits capped with snows,
You'll find among the cliffs a tiny rill —
A clear thread, which into a river grows.
Whoever scoops its flood with copper helm
And drinks therefrom, infused with sacred might,
Never by dragon shall be overwhelmed;
He'll squelch the evil spawn in the bitter fight.

Those waters make one strong as well as clever,
And these two qualities are hardly ever
Met with in one man, able to employ
Them both in harmony. Often, one destroys
The other… I'd say more, but my strength falls
Away; spurned by the day, the night now calls…
Lilian, you host the princely brothers!
To you I leave my herbs, my lute, and all —
My candle, cunning… And I leave to others —

Weakly.

Princes, ride to the Tatras. Past seven hills,
Amidst the rocky summits capped with snows…

RAKUZ
How shall we find the stream? Who is it knows?

OLD MAN
Where the road ends the traveller fulfils
His pilgrimage; the spear ends in its stem,
The fabric of the cloak rests at the hem…
Man doesn't realise, when all's been heard
The borderline of words is still — the word.

LILIAN
Princes, ride to the Tatras. Past seven hills,
Amidst the rocky summits capped with snows…

The Princes exit. To Hermit.

The men have now departed. Quarrelling still.

OLD MAN
Well, let them go.
Where born brothers fall out in violence
Haste not to enter, third, into the fray.
It often happens that the third is — silence,
And then — a lackey, cringing after pay,
Subsuming in their fray himself entire
Till he becomes the touchstone of their ire.
If such a one be lacking, they shall curse
A tree, a roadside stone, a barren heath,
Until their swelling anger should outburst.
Anger — the noxious plague of dragon's breath —
A boil that must be lanced, as 'twas at first!

Pause.

Ha! I took their measure with those 'seven hills!'
A full week, far from home, so let them stray
Until what's nightmare seems a dream, until…
God aid whichever sees the seventh day!

II
The Deep Woods. Night.

RAKUZ
We leave the shoeless horse there in the wood
With bugle-boy to watch him, well and good.
We send the archer to his aid — with reason!
And now it's just as wise, I feel, my bay
To mount alone…

Mounts his horse.

       You have no horse, you stay,
Or walk — I fear brothers no less than… treason.

KRAKUS
Treason? O, brother! Whence comes such a thought?
How many times we've shared the selfsame cot,
One cape our common bed-clothing, while we
Sheltered when out hunting in some hollow tree —
And now! — a petty accident of fate,
We're down a horse, and you refuse to wait
A moment, merely? Stay! He'll soon be shod
And you'll be on your way at the first sound
Of horn announcing their arrival. Look round!
It's still dark… Come, dismount, and to the gods
We'll bow in prayer together. If we must,
We'll go after the horse has had a rest,
Recouping strength to carry both of us.
My presence will not cause you any grief!
I'll be as light behind you as a leaf
Fallen against your cloak — and just as small —
I'll hardly take up any space at all!
No more than your cloak gathered into folds…

RAKUZ
The nation trusts, as does our father old,
In me! You pray here to the gods and wait,

Or come on foot. Know: I reject you not,
It's just that we've been both outstripped by fate.
You remain here, my brother, and resign
Your will to humble sacrifice. Farewell —
The bile of the dragon continues to swell —
May the gods reverse our fate, restore the time!

He wheels about on the horse and strikes Krakus with his spur.

KRAKUS
Brother! What are you doing? — Blood!

RAKUZ

                            My spur
Caught you by chance. 'Tis nothing. I depart.

Exits.

KRAKUS
Your spur has torn my lips and rent my heart!

Solus.

Liken me to a trampled herb, now.
Without a crumb of bread here in the wilds.
A trampled herb — with shame stamped on my brow.
And dark — so dark in these secluded parts,
Nearly as dark as feuding brothers' hearts.
Un-brothered now — this breach, can it be healed?
Can such knots as bind us ever be untied?
So dark, what now? If only I could claim
At least one heart here at my side!
At least one friendly hand!
There's none. I stand
Alone, disdained.

He moves on.

I dare not make a sound while it's still night.
I dare not call the trumpeter by name.
The Nixes cherish silence — I won't slight
The woodland gods lest, straddling a moonbeam
The way a spider's diverted by a song
They stop my babbling tongue as punishment.
I shall not slight the gods, who through the mint
And ferns process — the woods are in their care —
Until the dawn breaks clear I do not dare
Summon the lad...

He halts suddenly.

              A shaggy rangale of deer
Like a long raft through the mist bobs and sinks;
A goat licks smooth his coat of spotty grey;
The eyelid of the bright moon opens, winks
As its beams upon the glistening ivy play.
The silence is so deep, I seem to hear
The sticky buds of trees burst with the spring.
I see by listening, as when Boyan sings,
With words transporting you to distant lands,
And yet — you're sitting still there, all the time,
Although it seems a sudden forest stands
Before you, or a cliff... and it's just rhyme
That — wounding not, still pierces you with pain.
Such is his might, to make you see, and feel
By hearing — it's no dream — it must be real...

He trips against a stone.

As real as this rock! That's realer yet —
It's raised a nice bump on my shin, I bet!
Stupid rock! Not to know
That I'm the errant son of a great king
Whose feet disdain to tread on such a thing
Unless it's planed and polished to a glow!

Pause.

That boulder… trembled! Cringed, as if it feared
A glancing slingshot bolt…

Pause.

It's risen! Past that larch… it's disappeared!
For the first time I feel my blood run cold,
My hackles rise in fear… Why? I don't know —

Pause.

Now I see it, as through the moonlight it goes…
It nears… It lies prone on the moss… I see,
Clearly, as if upon my outstretched palm
That boulder… No, that's shaped by hand… might be
A threshold, or a polished hitching post
Smoothed by a thousand thongs… Now it lies calm
While I… must err, struck by boulder and tree…

THRESHOLD
Your servant, prince. You don't recognise me?
Your humble servant Threshold. Gained a soul
After the old castle was torn down, and now
Whenever I get the chance, I like to roll
Beneath a traveller's foot. Is it not droll?
For many ages, long I held my peace
While gamblers used me for their shameless bouts —
A table for stacked decks and loaded dice.
I shivered once, when bandits whetted knives
Upon me, ere they skulked off to spill blood —
'Good God!' I rasped with each scrape of the blade
Against my flanks… But that's past. Now, I'm made
The threshold of another manse — unseen,
Yet broad — it comes to be wherever I
Happen to set me down — happen to lie —
Come, prince, your humble servant! Set your foot

On me again, and enter in, as you have done
Numberless times, Count Mieczysław's mansion!

KRAKUS
To believe this? Or not? That's the question!
My princely brother Rakuz, without thinking,
Would long before have done so; that, or spurned
The stone beneath his heel, and turned
It all into an anecdote, while drinking
With his practical chums. And this is why
He'll reach the charmed streamlet before I
Get past the second hill. He'll slay the snake
While I'm still moaning, erring through this brake.
I still suck at the blood from my torn lip
And already I'm tending to forgive…
Let him conquer, win the throne, and live
Long, King, since he knows how to rip
And wound so splendidly! I must confess:
Perhaps it's best I stay meek, and concealed —
If I can't set my shoulder to the wheel
Of weighty actions, at least I can… bless!
But now I'd laugh until my sides were split!
Is this all I can do then? Wave my hand
Through the thin air in benediction? Flit
About like some ghost over solid land
To him unreal, untouched? Is this my doom
To be borne on the wind to some threshold
To gaze upon a realm of phantoms cold,
Unrecognised of any — save the tomb?

THRESHOLD
My prince! You recognise me after all!

KRAKUS
That there be keeps invisible, I know well.
A certain knight such things to me confessed —
That he'd been hosted once by a princess
Who'd been cursed by just such a masking spell.

He feared no charms, and yet he was not made
For life; I saw the shield at which she'd stare
Long hours intent on her complexion fair,
Twining her tresses into comely braids…
And on the boss, the image still was there!
You see — I'm not some child who knows the ways
Of chivalry from song! This arm's been raised
For other things than blessing from afar.
My thoughts above the battlements have flown;
I know that there are different sorts of war
And wonder not at the courtesy of stone…
Yet I am one… whose heart is sorely pressed
With gloom… and long for nothing more… than rest!

He lies down next to the Threshold.

And so I'd rather on such moss to lie
Than be a guest in any splendid home…

THRESHOLD
In royal gardens, hidden from men's eyes
You rest, in grottos lain with costly stone.
In alabaster conch a fountain plays
And Stillness, friend of man, before him lays
Milk, fruit, and honeycomb, a sacrifice
Pure as her words… she's no intrusive liar —

Invisible walls enclose the scene.

You're resting in a grotto of sapphire!

III
*The first portcullis of the castle. Rakuz gallops up on his foaming steed.
He is met by the Keeper, at the head of the whole household.*

KEEPER / HOUSEHOLD
With heavy news we've waited by the road…

RAKUZ

Dismounting.

Let me hear it.

KEEPER
        His Majesty has died.

RAKUZ
I learnt this from the whispers of my goad…
Let all the keeners howl, the old men cry;
Have all the joiners raise a towering pyre;
Assemble all the troops and villagers…

Pause.

And what about the dragon?

KEEPER
                When it stirs,
The men… toy with it as before. It's dire.

RAKUZ
And of our brother Krakus? Any word?

KEEPER
We've heard nothing of the young prince, no, my lord.

RAKUZ

Aside.

So let him wander — all the way to Hell!
A boy like that won't bring a dragon down,
Nor should a stripling inherit a crown!
I found the streamlet, and I've brought the spell
To lay the dragon — how, and from which side…

But I must hurry! For you never know...
I must take care, like when one bends the bow
And aims, before he lets the arrow fly...

The dragon roars.

What? I quake?

Enter Szołom. Rakuz notices him, and calls.

        Szołom! Tell me how he died...
The old man...

SZOŁOM
        My lord! Being Runesman Royal,
I have the art — and 'tis a pleasant toil —
To write upon beech-bark — O, like this scroll,
With such a stylus — what the times dictate.
What you require, I gladly shall unfold...
Now, if it were a grave matter of state,
It would not be quite proper, baldly, here,
To speak; but these... sad tidings are of such import
To all people — both simple churls and court —
That, what I've written, simply, clearly, scorning
Embellishments indigestible by ears
Vulgar...

RAKUZ
   Get on with it!

SZOŁOM
         So... 'On the morning
Of the sixth day, King Krak, His Majesty,
With vatic presentiment, sent word
That it should be forth bruited from the high
Bastions of Kraków that he soon would die.
Many the Lechite then, sorrowfully
Gathered around the deathbed of their lord —

Around the royal couch, jet-black, of oak —
And then his majesty lifted his face
Pale, and, gazing at all there in the place
Gathered, to all there present, these words spoke:
"This castle shall be saved from dragon's tooth
By one, or by the other, princely youth —
I know not which... that speed here from... somewhere..."
He paused, and then: "There won't be many heirs,"
And he fell silent. All who were present
Broke into wails and sobbing. But then he,
Like a young hero, rose up on his bed
And cried: "I claim testimony
Of my forefathers! Rise, manes, and see:
Krak your descendant does not fear to die!"
Those were his final words. He sank down, dead,
And all the Lechites raised a thunderous cry:
"A worthy king, and bold!" Mournful, but proud,
They covered Krak's countenance with a shroud,
And left...'

RAKUZ
You'll no more touch those writings. Give them here.
For all times in his treasury they'll be lain,
Despite the fact his will was none too clear,
And failed to indicate an heir by name.

SZOŁOM
When all a man's strength is well-nigh consumed,
He's like a candle as it's burning down —
By this you'll know the man who knows the runes:
For he can clarify, explain, expound —
O, for example, look here: see what I'd
Inscribed with my own hand next to those words:
'By this, clearly, Rakuz is signified,'
Although he was awaiting both young lords...

RAKUZ
Such things, if anyone, the runesman can
Unravel — false appearances from truth —
I do not seek the praise of any man.
The truth is my concern alone.

SZOŁOM
                                        In sooth!

RAKUZ
And truth is…?

SZOŁOM
                    Ah, what is truth?

RAKUZ
                                Truth is a word.
Whatever you redact, don't hesitate
To bring to me…

They walk on. Rakuz gazes toward the outer courtyard.

                                Those people there, who wait
By the portcullis, huddling like a camp
Of gypsies — who are they?

SZOŁOM
                                    O, they have tramped
Many a mile, from bogs that no man sows;
A land that neither plough nor harrow knows.
They make their homes among tree-clumps, or *kemps*,
Hence our name for them: Kiempi. They're endowed
With skill for hunting drakes, besieging yales…
And if there's any credit to their tales,
There is a prince among that barefoot crowd.
They're good fighters — and can outdrink us all.
Whatever pours, they drink until they fall
Prone on their backs and sleep like toppled trees.

But they're a grateful people, and a kind.
They're known as Scandinavians, I find,
Perusing chronicles, and yesterday,
Upon hearing of the dragon, on their way
To somewhere else, they detoured here, to learn
More of it first-hand. One of them discerned
From the beast's roar, the thing — supposedly —
Is to be found in the onlooker's eye.
'Tis not a snake at all: a curse, a spell;
The roars are sent up by some sprites of Hell.
Myself, I've never heard so bold a lie!

RAKUZ
Such things are not for reason, but belief.

Sounds of a struggle, and howling.

If there are wounds, then surely there are teeth.
And since there are — and even now we hear
The battle raging at the porch, so near…

Pause.

A few days more, and I myself shall take
The fight — before the nation! — to the snake…

Pause.

Listen! Let them keep my horse caparisoned!
Listen! Before the sun three times stains red
The eastern sky, let all my people come
To watch the drake collapse to the dust, dead!
I know what I do — *fiat.* I have spoke.

Pause.

But now, the prince of that nomadic folk,
The Kiempi, why has he not been received

And feasted after coming this long way?
Our custom is to host without delay
Such travellers, as if to their own home
They'd come — make him welcome! This castle's known
For hospitality...

SZOŁOM

The very same
Words, good my lord, were on my lips, indeed,
As soon as they before the drawbridge came.
'Come on,' I said, 'These men must be received!'
And then, 'Who knows? Prince Krakus well may be
Begging some strangers' hospitality
As he errs, lost. And so we, just the same
Must shelter these!' That's what I said, my lord!

RAKUZ

Cutting him off.

I want these people given bed and board.

Exit Szołom.

And Krakus... has only himself to blame!

IV

The interior of the sapphire grotto. A spring to the rear; to the front, a table, set, and near it: a covered throne, like a couch.

KRAKUS

In his sleep.

I dreamed I dreamt — perhaps I'm dreaming still,
A painful parting-ways with my own brother
Which, from a grain of sand grew to a hill,

A wall that separates us from each other.
I have a quiet sapphire grotto, blue;
A table — laden so with fruit it groans;
And I am with someone who loves virtue.
I hear soft music — we are alone.
I'm lacking nothing, yet, alas
I thirst...

Starts suddenly.

And have no cup or glass!

He rises.

Asleep, I rise, and full of faith, I go
Toward the rocks — the babbling fountainhead —

Taking water from the fountain.

And from a bronze helm thus I soothe my throat
With cool water — though still I dream I'm dead.

He drinks from the helmet.

THE SPRING
In copper casque
The bright moon's flash
Tumbles, not without aim.
Like to my stream
Its pearly beam
Threads through the coral chain.

KRAKUS

Eating.

And still I dreamt — perhaps I'm dreaming yet —
The earth received me, with such welcoming!

Each creature greeted me; all present said
That I'd arrived at wisdom's holy spring.

THE SPRING
Past mountains seven
In cloudless Heaven
I'm born, though here I flow.
Do as you will:
Taste of my rill
In Heaven, or here below.

KRAKUS
And still I dream — but is it dream, or truth?
That no one wakeful notes, or dares assume
That through the warp of wakefulness, the woof
Of dream is led, as if on weaver's loom
Into one tapestry that never tears
Or separates into disparate strands.
Faster than light it flickers and it flares
Though he who looks on, never understands!

THE SPRING
Nothing am I,
Sans hand, sans eye:
Merely the fountain's daughter.
My last, and first,
Is to slake thirst —
What else can fountain water?

KRAKUS

Continuing with his meal.

Happy the man who, waking or asleep,
Desires nothing. Not even desire.
If only Rakuz saw the company I keep —
The threshold's given me all that I require.
I've never known such hospitality,

Such good will — from a stone! — such fraternity...
The humble threshold, prone there in the dirt
Would never slash my countenance with spur!

Raises the helmet.

I drink your health, Threshold, there in the dust...

He pours the drink and stretches out to sleep.

SPRING
The trek — difficult;
The advent — miracle,
It matters not: on foot, or horsed;
For one of the two
Time quickly flew
For the other, it edged out his course!

KRAKUS

In his sleep.

Something, like the hermit's words, I hear...
Water plashing, like a spring, it seems
As if I were resting somewhere near...
Past seven mountains, seven streams...
I crossed a threshold while we paused... we were...
Where is that stone? And Rakuz? And the spur?

Pause.

The castle? Father — Father! What's that they bear?
The dragon's body! Father! Can you hear?
The dragon... It's so deathly quiet here...

SPRING
Know now, young knight:
You've spent the night

Where men no thresholds lay;
But rather — God,
What they have thought,
Fulfils — another way.

KRAKUS
I still can't rub the sleep out of my eyes —

SPRING
Then no more sleep —
This wisdom keep
Ever present in your mind:
Poems can heal
And bite like steel.
Strike the dragon with such rhymes!

The walls of the sapphire grotto fall away. Krakus arises from his bed on the moss as before — the light of dawn begins to grow.

DAWN
Arise, Prince! Rise! Late is the hour!

KRAKUS
I rise, I rise! Able, and filled with power!

V
The Prince's chamber at Wawel Castle. Despite the fact that it's the middle of the day, a lamp is burning high up in the vault.

RAKUZ

Solus.

Day blends with night, and night and day are one,
And thus I wait for my great hour to toll.

He paces — stops.

Am I against myself this race to run?
To speed first to the square, in mind or soul,
Dragging my flesh behind, sick with lack of rest,
The weft unravelled to re-knot somewhere…?
To be where one is, that is to be blessed.
But such I am not. I've never been there
Where I was… am… my day is thick with mist
While somewhere… else… I know the sky is fair,
But never *here*. I'm like that lamp up there,
Always lit, sparking, be it day or night…
How many days already, sleep a stranger,
And everyone who's close to me — a danger.

SZOŁOM

Enters.

My lord — straight from the armourer's I've come.
The sword he hardened yesterday he took
Today to scrape against the royal tomb —
It burst —

He sets the pieces down before Rakuz.

       I, being a man skilled in book
And rune and augury, read this portent
Thus:
The sacred stone struck where the steel was weak.
In this, we hear your sire heroic speak:
'This sword is not the weapon that was meant
By destiny to run the monster through —
Son shall achieve what father could not do!'
By this the skill of runesman is revealed —

RAKUZ

Interrupting, taking a chain from his neck and a sword from the wall.

To you, this chain. To the armourer, this steel.

SZOŁOM
My lord, the people of the city teem
About the castle; all the roads are packed
With pilgrims and their tents. I've never seen
Such swarms of men — the old chronicles lack
Comparable accounts — and no one hears
Laughter or song; the folk are drenched in tears
Longing for absent princes, all forlorn…

RAKUZ

He lays his hand on his breast.

Who's absent? Who's not here?

SZOŁOM
                                        The people mourn
Your father Krak… And all the folk desire
To see his body lain upon the pyre;
Churl and halbardsman, from merest wight
To grandee… Many a foreign knight
I've seen among the waiting crowds, and some
In cowls, leaning on croziers, have come,
As gloomy as bricks fallen from battlement.
Some drape their visages in hoods, intent
On thus remaining till the pyre blazes;
Others have sworn to stay until all traces
Of the pyre disappear. Young maids and ladies
In sack-cloth sway, intoning threnodies…

RAKUZ
Let them all gather. Have the herald cry
That, ere the sun twice tincts the eastern sky
The dragon shall fall, slaughtered, to the dust
By Prince Rakuz, in single combat.

Szołom bows.

                                    Stay —
How fares the leader of the Kiempi? Pray,
We'd like to see him. Send him up to us.

SZOŁOM
He'd have paid his respects by now, my lord
But is abashed, shod merely in fish-skin
— A Scandinavian custom, so I've heard —
His people at the dragon's cave threw in
Some poisoned morsels, at which owls soared
Out of the cave mouth; huge they were, and all
Those present fell back, pale. Then roared
The beast down in the depths. At every howl
Pigeons fell from the crenellations, scorched
By fire or stunned with terror; even now
The servant-boys are clearing them from porch
And pavement…

RAKUZ
                    And my sword? Has it been honed?

SZOŁOM
I'm going there now —

RAKUZ
                              And what about the pyre?

SZOŁOM
All is prepared; you need but to make known
The hour the priests should light the holy fire…

RAKUZ
The hour, the hour… will come without delay.
It's always time for something… What's today?

He paces, stops, flustered.

Tomorrow — what's tomorrow? Yesterday?
What was I saying? Let them hone my sword.
As if for battle, have them bard my steed,
Caparisoned with gold cloth; furthermore…
And furthermore… What will happen, they'll see!

Pause.

When the pyre blazes, I'll stand to the clash.
I value the living thousands more than ash!

SZOŁOM
The king's voice like a mighty river roars…

Exits.

KEEPER
The Kiempan leader waits at Rakuz' doors!

RAKUZ
Gods frequently appear as guests disguised…

KIEMPE
Your guest I am, but of much humbler station.
I tender my respects. I'm of that nation
Whose shores sparkle with amber of the sea,
Like a child's crib, edged with gold filigree.
That's where God set us. Odin is his name
Amongst us — Adinoi amongst the Jews — the same
God of all, prince. From the Phoenicians
We learned the art of navigation…
And I know nothing more pleasing to the Lord
Than, mindful of His stars, to climb aboard
A skiff, and set out, trusting to the swell
And depthless currents of His holy will.

Pulling close a bench.

CYPRIAN KAMIL NORWID

I've said my piece and now —

RAKUZ

                                 Please, sit you down.
Quite different is the realm of Rakuz' crown —
Forests and farmland. But I know the sea
And where it lies; I've a runesman, and he
Is learned in the stars; how they comport
According to the seasons. Here at court
He bides. The chain that hangs upon his chest
I gave him — for he is learned, wise —
He knows the past, the present, and, what eyes
Can't yet make out — the future — he can guess.

KIEMPE
I shrink not before the wise, or before kings.
But what know I of birds and foretellings?

RAKUZ

Raising a toast.

Come — raise your cup. I drink your health, sir.

KIEMPE

                                     Skål!

RAKUZ
I'd like to ask you — can it be really true
The drake — is in the eye that him beholds?

KIEMPE
Dragons betray themselves by varied signs.
Here, in the eye, and there — in attitude;
Sometimes in both. I've often seen that kind.
And therefore, there are varied remedies:
Now trumpet blasts, now swords — sometimes the flat —
And some are exorcised by mockeries.

RAKUZ

I reckon that the one we've got is that
Which can be seen, and felt. A tactile thing.

KIEMPE

I had my lads into his cavern fling
A lamb chock-full of poison. Came a howl,
And then out-flew a few gigantic owls
And some unearthly spectres gibbering
On sticky outspread wing — a fearsome passel.
It thundered like a storm that can't give birth
To Heaven's fire — so shook the heaving earth,
I thought the pit would swallow the whole castle!

RAKUZ

Enough! — And far too little. I myself
Will grip with it alone, before the keep, while
You remain here, my guest, with all your people.
I like to talk with wise men like yourself.

KIEMPE

Past seven rivers from where I was born
I've wandered on a trek lasting four moons,
After a yale that pricked me with his horn.
Elusive, he — I dream each night that soon
I'll have him — Twice now he's escaped our snares;
Our horsemen overtake him, but he speeds
Away; and they return. I give them mead,
But no rest till they net him. So I swear
By Odin's hammer! We shall never rest
Until I take his horns, or he my life.
So, at the cold sea's edge, swore I to my wife:
Shamed I shall not return from this my quest.

He drinks.

And you — have you a wife?

He drinks.

Look at our girls,
Whose heads are flashing with thick golden curls;
Like the sea-shingle: eyes of blue and grey,
Quiet, and strong —

He drinks.

O, there's a lot to say
About our girls. Someday I will be homing,
I know, at night, when I gaze at the moon's
Crescent, and end this life of constant roaming,
As sad as ash and silent as carven runes.

The glow of a fire appears on the chamber wall.

RAKUZ

Covering his eyes.

My father's funeral pyre.

To Kiempe.

Be well, my lord.

KIEMPE

Rises to exit.

And you as well. Unvanquished be your sword!

RAKUZ

Immobile on his bench.

Remember us.

KIEMPE

At the threshold.

I shall. Wherever I go. For all my days.

KEEPER

At the threshold.

The stable-hands, black-liveried, have announced
The rider's death to all his weeping mounts,
And that his funeral pyre is now ablaze.

Exit. Rakuz, as before, sits motionless, resting his head on his hand.

VI

*The lower part of the castle: to the front, a vaulted chamber, to the rear:
an arcade leading to the courtyard. Through this arcade file funeral
Choruses: a number of people follow each chorus, some bearing banners.*

FIRST CHORUS
Pass over now to your new state
O great man — where pure the air, and free;
Where, subject no longer to fate,
You rule your destiny!

SECOND CHORUS
Take with you armour, battle-axe,
These loaves of bread, these sacks of gold;
Your chargers and swift-chasing packs
Once more behold.

BOTH CHORUSES
But why must it be, tell us why
Lord, you, who ruled this land so fair,

Must leave us now, who droop, and cry
In deep despair?

FIRST CHORUS
Pass over now to your new state
O great man — where pure the air, and free;
Where, subject no longer to fate,
You rule your destiny!

BOTH CHORUSES
But why must it be? Tell us why!

*The Choruses pass on. Rakuz, who had been following them, splits away
to the front and collapses on a great chair.*

RAKUZ
Why, tell us why?! I've heard oaks in the wood
Creak that lament as in the winds they sway —
'Tell us why we must crumble in decay!'

SZOŁOM

Toying with the gold chain at his neck.

I beg you grace's pardon, that I intrude —
But as a runesman skilled in books and learning,
I'd gladly lend my wisdom now, to soothe
Your battered heart, sunk now in gloom and yearning…

RAKUZ

Immobile.

Away! And follow those who croak with tears,
In place of us and our brother the prince,
Marching with shields of gold and upraised spears…

Immobile else, Rakuz makes a gesture with his hand. Szołom exits;
Rakuz sinks into meditation, slumped in the chair.

RAKUZ

Solus.

I've watched too long — these arms are not of flint,
These eyes not of the sun. I cannot stand
Without support of some kind… I'm a man…

Pause.

A man! From crown of head to soles of feet!
A mortal man! And meanwhile, every night
The castle walls tremble from pit to height
With roars — as if for blood, as if for meat —
Thin, starved, and rattling talons avaricious…

Pause.

And then those crowds of the… jealous and vicious!

More softly.

And him…

Softly.

       He's had a nice tramp through the wood,
Pale as a bone, in tattered cowl, slumped, sagging…
Fit for the task? I wonder if he could
Even raise up a spear against a dragon?
Too long I've watched — moments of rest — too few;
Both nature and the flesh must have their due…
So let them have it…

KEEPER

At the threshold.

                       Twice now from the walls
The trumpet's blared.

RAKUZ

            Sleep — sleep —

ARMOURER

Enters with the sword.

                          When thrice it calls,
This sword —

Seeing Rakuz asleep, he hangs the sword on the wall and exits.

RAKUZ

Dreaming.

         Sleep, only sleep, and nothing more.
I'm just a man — like you all — mortal, vile…

Pause.

Mere presence at the crucial hour — what dare
Man hazard without peace, conscience, and prayer?

Pause.

Three things, of which I've never had the pleasure
Of personal acquaintance…

Pause.

I hear — strange words — unknown, fall from my lips;
So let them fall, like dry leaves tumbling down
From tall trees that the breath of autumn strips,
Till at their feet are lain their withered crowns.

Dreaming.

Away with you! I turn my steed, am gone...
Go too! Or with this spur I'll mark your face...
The sun is rising — I rise with that dawn
As on a grand, foam-frothing steed I race.
The people — here and there, raise up a cheer:
Long live Włady-Tur Rakuz! Hurrah! Long life!
The people press in, vivats far and near,
While before me butchers put beasts to the knife —
The people crowd in, grab at stirrup, rein...
The earth is trembling with their songs of praise:
Glory!

Starting in his sleep.

But where is Krakus? Shamed, disgraced,
He turns away... There's blood upon his face...

Wildly, in his sleep.

Two such brothers I see there! On the moon!

VII

Krakus appears at the threshold, his face covered in a cowl. Noticing his brother asleep, he nears on tiptoe.

KRAKUS

Standing at Rakuz's chair.

He sleeps! And may the gods bring him Relief,
Who is a good maiden, with golden braids.
O, noble Rakuz! O, foundered in grief,
Half-dead with mourning at our father's grave!

Draws back on tiptoe.

Shall I reveal my face? Shame says 'Don't dare!'
Both quick and dead, misfortunate twice over!

Halting, he gazes at the sleeping Rakuz.

What worthy labour of yours have I shared?
And what might I do for you now, my brother?
What am I now? And was I ever other?
Before our father's death, and after?

From the threshold, where he pauses.

                                    There —
Sleep, prince, beneath your ancient fathers' shield,
And may the clouds that ring your brow now yield…
By his mere presence, what might a man dare,
Have he not peace, good conscience, and a prayer?

He withdraws.

VIII
*The market square. Here and there groups of people. To the front, a few
Villagers and Townsmen.*

FIRST
I say 'one,' he 'two,' and then a third
Cries out 'There were no princes there at all!'

SECOND

Taking note of Szołom, who has entered.

That one should know, in the golden chain there…
A courtier for sure. But dare we beg a word?

FIRST
That golden chain — some noble; who would dare?

SZOŁOM

Approaching the two, who seem to be arguing.

To see respect shine from such common faces
Is worth its weight in gold — that, I call wealth!

TOWNSMAN
It seems the toff'll accost us himself!

SZOŁOM
You are disputing — what?

FIRST
                              This one says both
Princes were there; this other, only one.
And he, that neither. Well then, whose truth
Is one to credit? That's beyond my ken!

SZOŁOM
If that's what you're discussing here, well then,
Let me clear it all up. Everyone! Come!

He arranges the people in an arc, and then draws near.

How many golden shields were there?

ALL

                                Two, sir!

And two spears!

SZOŁOM

With pathos.

           Since two shields of gold were there,
And two spears also, it is only fair
To assume that two princes were present.

He exits with stately tread.

FIRST
That's like — if there are two hands, there's ten fingers.
He said… something, and yet my doubt still lingers.

*The men go off, still arguing amongst themselves. Krakus passes over
the stage, Szołom following.*

SZOŁOM
Unless I'm mistaken? — We've good cause to sing…!

KRAKUS

Keeping his face hidden.

Avoiding mistakes is a blessing, I'm told.

SZOŁOM
You wouldn't be Krakus, son of our late king?

KRAKUS
The prince! If only I had a chain of gold!

SZOŁOM
Well, if you're not the prince, you're some old friend.
It's in your figure — your manner, your voice!

KRAKUS
No older friend here, where all to guile tends,
Where one arrives by hap, and not by choice —

SZOŁOM

Aside.

He's someone steeped in ancient, arcane truth —
Who knows the clan of Szołom from the roots!

To Krakus.

If only, gentle knight, you'd care to toss
Aside your cowl…

KRAKUS
                              I'm from beneath the moss,
Beneath the granite; from a nation laid
Beneath a heavy mountain, where grey ash
Warms the bare skull; where no one twines a braid;
Where when the moonbeams sift in through the cracks,
Through drops of dew,
If you're a knight there, you know what for, and you
Hide, like the moon, from these, the while you flash
To those, full. Where silence is recompense
For praise, and silence meets adulation.

SZOŁOM
Yours must be a magnificent nation.

KRAKUS
Its borders hold all borders in contempt.

IX

To the rear a gate, rounded by an arch of stone. A crowd of people press close — some clamber up the rough stones to look in. Groups to the front huddle in conversation.

FIRST

At the gate.

Why do you point like that? It can't be him!

SECOND
Would a prince dress up in such a queer habit,
Hooded, his face quite hidden deep within…

OTHER
With golden harp — he stands like carven granite.

MANY
They trumpet — thrice now — from the battlements…

SECOND
If that's the third trumpet, then that's the prince!

FIRST
His harp, just like the sun about to set,
Outflares the noon… He gives it a shake…

OTHER
And sings… approaching the lair of the drake,
Straight — ramrod straight — with steady, even tread…
Just like a statue, torn from its stone roots…
His cloak falls in still folds, like brazen flutes…
A strange bird!

MANY
        Whoever's near can hear the knight.

OTHER
I can —

TOWNSMAN
    He's singing now — you there, be quiet!

The crowds slowly grow still.

KRAKUS

Song.

Come forth! Now! By the faith of faiths
I conjure you, who gnaw the soul —
Your spell is gone with your last breaths;
My spell, it is no spell at all!

God knows how much sin, foul and black
Impels me here to sling this word
Into your face — my only sword
This lyre; this song — my only act —

My song is now no song at all!

FIRST
Forward he steps — his lyre he lifts and flings
Into the cave —

OTHER
        Whole clouds of winged things
Soar up, borne on the smoke, into the sky —

MANY
So dark it's grown! I can't make out a thing!

OTHER
Owls mangy-moulted, bats on leathery wing,
Whole colonies and panicked parliaments — fly!

TOWNSMAN
Go on, and tell us all that meets your eye!

SOMEONE AT THE GATE
What do you see? Can you see anything?!

FIRST
I see — a cloud… gigantic… everywhere
Or, like a kurhan, suddenly awake,
Rearing up from the soil in despair!
I see… might, in solid matter incarnate,
On tottering legs it reels, as if before
Upon a hundred thousand necks it crashes…

Pause.

And… darkness again — I can see nothing more…
Nothing at all, except for livid flashes.

DISTANT VOICES
The prince has won! Raise high the royal sword!

FIRST
I see the bank — trembling above the sward,
The castle ramparts — as if drunk, it sways!
The castle tottering atop the bank
Which is no bank at all, but dragon! Rank
And foul… it falls! And dead there now it splays!

SECOND
And now the pikemen leap upon the poll —
They swing broad axes; can you hear them chop?

VILLAGER
Like woodsmen in the forest hacking tall
Old-stand, they hew and will not stop!

TOWNSMAN
Like in the forge, when on the anvils ring
Hammers on red iron pinned in mighty tongs —

MANY
Still you can hear them — still those axes swing!

AT THE GATE
Long live the prince! Who leaves the battlefield
Victorious! The man who slew the drake!

FIRST
But where's he gone? I've lost him in the throng —

VARIOUS VOICES
Raise him aloft, the hero, on your shield!

*The applause swells and dies in waves. Then, from the front of the stage,
comes Rakuz, on foot, making his way through the crowds along with
Szołom and a group of courtiers. Following those on foot, horses are
led, all festively caparisoned.*

KEEPER

Pushing at the crowd with his arms.

Make way! Make way! The prince comes!

SZOŁOM

Loudly.

                               Rakuz takes
The fight to the dragon!

MANY AT THE GATE
              It's about time!

KEEPER
Make way!

The crowds are thick at the gate. Rakuz and his men halt.

FIRST AT THE GATE
The hooded saviour hides his face.

OTHER
Unmoved he stands, cloaked darkly cap-apée!

SECOND
Is he a god? Or Slava incarnate?

KEEPER
Part left, part right — make way!

SZOŁOM
                              O prince of mine!
The crowds are packed tight, like a wall of bricks!
We can't proceed…

RAKUZ

Tearing his hair.

                              Ha! A few hours' sleep,
And now I'm to ride down their stubborn necks!
Impossible… Once… Who'd credit the sight?

DISTANT VOICES
Raise him aloft! Hurrah, the saviour-knight!

AT THE GATE
The trumpeters form up in lines to clear
A path for him to us!

SZOŁOM
O fickle knaves!
You gaze at the moon while the sun is here!
Turn your eyes here! Rakuz, your prince, awaits!

FIRST AT THE GATE
The hooded man shies from the shouts of fame.
I see him — O, the crowd! Just like a stream
In flood that breaks its banks with mighty roar!

OTHER
Now I can see him also — free and clear!

RAKUZ

Leaping upon his steed.

All faithful thanes of Rakuz! Mount! All here!
Whomever nears your stirrups, strike with spur!

The Trumpeters appear at the gate.

CROWD
Long live the unknown saviour!

KEEPER
Hey! Long live
Prince Rakuz!

In two hosts, the trumpeters and the large crowd near the front. Between them comes Krakus, always covered in his hood.

SZOŁOM

Staggering among the crowd.

Hark! Rakuz will shortly give
An address from the saddle!

COURTIERS and KEEPER

Hush! Silence!
Let all the Poles now gather round — the raw
And learned, the spry and elders bent
Over their hobble-sticks!

A circle forms around Rakuz, on his horse. Krakus stands before him,
set to the front by the crowd, his face always hidden.

SOME VOICES

Long life! Hurrah!

KEEPER
Long life to whom?!

RAKUZ

From the saddle.

You, man! There in that hood
Standing, who hold in such contempt the crowd
As to refuse their reverence! I would
Appeal to your reason. Uncover your brow,
Hotspur! And bow to them who sing your praise!
They speak, God hears, but I bestow the wreath!

To Szołom, aside.

Szołom! You speak! I'm so wroth, I can't breathe!

SZOŁOM

Aside.

Speak on — they're listening now —

RAKUZ

Fluidly.

                                    What, dazed
Have I paused

Pointing to Krakus.

            speaking for a while? Why?
You, statue, have you the warm guts of a man?
Lift not your hooded head in scorn on high
Above the people, but —

Spurring the horse forward.

                        A firm, mailed hand
Is needed, where the tongue fails to convince —

To Szołom.

Have them now trumpet forth the new tourney!

The trumpeters blare a tournament call. Krakus raises his sword in defence.

MANY VOICES
He falls! The saviour!

RAKUZ

From the saddle.

                    Saviour? Where's your prince?!

KRAKUS

Uncovering his face.

It is finished…

RAKUZ – SZOŁOM – KEEPER

Throw themselves at the body to cover it from sight.

He's fallen — let him be!

RAKUZ
Now have the trumpets sound the tourney's end.

SZOŁOM

Pushing the crowds back, away from Krakus' body.

The will of the dead, however it may sound,
Is something holy; yes, a sacred thing.
Thus, like his hood, now let a dark, high mound
Cover the noble brow that dared to bring
Deliverance to us all… And now, good friends,
It's finished, as he said… Words that sincere
Are simple, short. Go, nothing more to do here…

The crowds begin to depart in an equivocal silence.

RAKUZ

From the saddle, to the throngs.

Hey! People! You who demanded great deeds —
Take now this token, this sword, that still bleeds!

He flings the sword afar.

It broke the knight that slaughtered the dragon.
Who is the champion now? Who's left? Who's won?
Whom should you praise? That merits some reflection…

OLD MAN

From the crowd.

I seem to see the dragon's resurrection…

OTHER
Both knights are worthy of chivalric praise…

Rakuz directs his horse to the gate, although here and there groups of the crowd remain, still. Rakuz' retainers begin to push near the gate.

KEEPER

To Szołom.

The crowd — like one man — binds together — stays!

SZOŁOM

To the crowds.

Good people! I, the runesman royal — look!
I spread my arms to you, wide, like a book,
My heart as well, to say: the spoken word
Is — not the prince's only — but the Lord
Himself speaks in it! I've many an example
That I might offer now, proofs old and ample,
For I've read through many an ancient tome…
I might, but now, good friends, go now — go home…

The prince's men press through the gate.

KEEPER
Make way — the prince's escort. Left, and right…

SZOŁOM
Go home, good folk.

SOLDIER

On all sides.

Whoever comes tonight
Before sunset, unto the palace hall,
Shall lift a cup with Rakuz — one and all!

OLD MAN

From the crowd.

Poles! Let not the saviour's body be forgot
Like offal tossed in roadside ditch to rot...

SOLDIER
Tonight — a cup of mead. But now, disperse!
Make way for the prince's men — the runesman first.

Szołom and Soldier enter through the gate.

X
Among the creepers and ivy near the city gate. Crowds of people are laying about the place, asleep. Enter Rakuz and Szołom, hooded, with shovels. Szołom also carries a lantern.

RAKUZ
The words of wisdom, with which I benumbed
Three hundred people — today, they are sore.
You are perplexed. But no other words come
To better fit the phrase I'm looking for:
My words... hurt. I am like an archer, who
Lets fly his dart into a gloomy wood
And strains to map its arc, while by some freak
Hap, it bends back and runs him through and through.
He feels it not, until he's wet with blood,
And from the loss of lymph gasps, and grows weak.

You who are expert in runes, as you have said,
Tell me: can empty breath, the spoken word,
Grow sore, as if 'twere run through with a blade,
Though, as you said then, within there dwells the Lord?

SZOŁOM
There is a type of writing — intricate,
Mysterious — kabbalah it is called,
Which but the wisest runesmen will admit
Into its arcane treasures, though not all —

Rakuz drops his shovel.

Careful!

RAKUZ
  Did I wake someone?

SZOŁOM

Lifting his lantern.

        Over there...
Here — pick up your spade.

RAKUZ

Gazing around at the sleepers.

         Like sheaves of rye
Sickled at harvest, the churls, drunken, lie.

SZOŁOM
Of pails of mead they dream with limbs outsplayed —
Dead to the world! You won't awaken them
With cannon fire, let alone a dropped spade...
Here — sling it on your shoulder. There! That figure!
No one could tell you now from a gravedigger!

RAKUZ
To hoist a spade... thing furthest from my thought.
Am I not the Prince? Rakuz? Touch me not!

SZOŁOM
To blend in everywhere is a good rule.
One needs to use the intellect like a tool.

RAKUZ

Pushing Szołom forward.

Go first! You've time enough to play the fool.

SZOŁOM

Quickly stepping to Rakuz' side in warning.

Quiet! Who goes there?

VOICE

Of a passing guard.

     Conscience!

RAKUZ

         What's that he said?

SZOŁOM
Tonight's password.

RAKUZ

      Are they gone?

SZOŁOM

Tapping Rakuz on the arm.

                                        Take your spade
And come.

RAKUZ

Looking around.

    O, wise one! Listen, in our haste,
Can it be that we've overstepped the place?

SZOŁOM

Lifting his lantern.

I saw a shield flash over by those stones,
Or some white clothing…

RAKUZ
                              No, those are some bones
Pulled from the dragon's hip by dog or crow;
Look — by the carcass there — some torchlights glow…
People? Or phantoms?

SZOŁOM
                              They have disappeared.

RAKUZ
My face just drained of blood — I sense it here
About the eyes, and on my cheeks.

SZOŁOM
                                        There loom
The dragon's ribs, see? Black against the moon
And huge — like to the spars of a wrecked ship.
A fox — see there? clambers between the bones;
Unkindnesses of ravens pluck and strip
The ivory of flesh… And now they've flown…
They flutter, and alight again.

RAKUZ

How long
Shall it last! Tell me — do the people know
That a great victory was won in this place?

Pause.

Here? It was here he fell?

SZOŁOM

There is no trace —
And the shield's gone…

Torches suddenly light up Krakus' mound.

RAKUZ

Look there — something's aglow!

SZOŁOM

Pulling Rakuz by the sleeve.

A procession — torches — pyre — funeral song…
Your majesty, uncover not your face!
Here, by the ditch, let's set aside our spades
And watch…

RAKUZ

Crouching near the wall with Szołom.

O, horrid night!

SZOŁOM

They're wending nigh!

RAKUZ
I shiver — who am I?

SZOŁOM

     My prince, you are a spy
Of mysteries in life and speech concealed.

RAKUZ

Threateningly.

Am I not Rakuz?

SZOŁOM

    Guardian of the field
Of pyre and gravemound! How long would you be,
If you announced yourself to more than me!

RAKUZ

You're right, you're wise — yes, follow now your own
Best counsel, as long as that man renowned
As saviour — let it be! — saviour unknown,
Were safely trowled and tamped into the ground!

*A bright glow — Krakus' Mound is ringed with fire. The Choruses
drawn near.*

OLD MAN

He who a bloody deed would blot away
Must spin the sun backwards, and reverse the day!

CHORUS

So let him spin — and the highroad of fame,
And the dead end of lust will once again
Face him a crossroads — honesty, or shame.
There are no more monsters, but monstrous men,
Alas! abound.

OLD MAN

    O lord and master true,
Who vanquished, and then vanished — where are you?!

CHORUS
Where are you, lord? The more conscious folk, and
Peaceful spirits, and the breeze now raise
This mound of mail to you, your glory's token,
And with an earthen sallet shield your face.

OLD MAN and CHORUS

Flinging jars.

We bring you shining jars of milk and mead —

CHORUS
With branches of the larch and wreaths of hops
And amber incense, we your pyre feed;
With soft and honest speech, heavy with sobs!

The blazing fire brightly lights up the plain on which Krakus' Mound stands. The Chorus, raising the last handfuls of sand, stand motionless, except for their arms.

SZOŁOM and RAKUZ

Cringe in the ditch, flat on their faces.

The body's consumed — the high mound has been raised!

OLD MAN and CHORUS

Tossing the sand, they make to depart.

Of ash and shattered weapons, may this earth
Of Kraków lie upon you, man of worth,
Lightly! Saviour unknown, Praise!

END

CLARIFICATIONS

The familiar tale of the Dragon, slain by *Krak* or *Krakus*, valid throughout history, as the traces of the hero's battle with the monster pass down the ages in unbroken succession, receives varied treatments in the popular imagination. With what success I have seized upon the whole, the Reader himself will determine. In any event, I add here a few words of clarification as to the content of the tragedy and the legendary elements of which it is constituted.

KRAK and KRAKUS were not, in my opinion, one and the same person. The former, I believe, was the father of the latter, just as the term *Lechites* is a diminutive of the name *Lech*, as Kochanowski justly notes:

'And thus it is the lesser Lechites seem to have descended from some great Lech, carrying on or revitalising the name of their antecedent.'

KRAKÓW is an adjectival noun deriving from the genitive — Whose? *Gród-Krakowy*, i.e. Kraków, or 'the city belonging to Krak.'

The name of RAKUZ, the brother of Krakus, is derived from an etymological root still to be found among the southern Slavs.

The name SZOŁOM derives from the verb *szołomić*, which in demotic use means 'to stun, to flabbergast.'

KIEMPE is the name of Scandinavian knights errant, one of whom thus addresses King Olaus:

'Know that I believe in no gods of stone or wood, and I mock demons. I have travelled through many a distant land, and have slain more than one monster and giant. In sobriety of mind and strength of arm I place my faith.'

NIXES are lesser spirits of field and wood among the southern Slavs.

The term WŁADY is an Old Slavic adjective meaning illustrious and heroic.[41]

---

41 Toward the end of Scene VI, Rakuz is hailed by the people as 'Włady-Tur.' This is an interesting title bestowed upon the prince in this very mythological drama; the *tur* refers to an extinct wild bull of the European forest, perhaps identical with the *auroch*. It is doubly applicable to Rakuz, in a poetic sense, as it both underscores Rakuz as a traditional leader, associated with the ancient pan-European worship of the bull, and with a tradition that is about to go extinct, replaced by the Christianity of which Krakus is the harbinger.

IN THE WINGS

A FANTASY

PROLOGUE

I

Traveller and Quidam, in hats, with walking sticks — Malcher in the middle of the room, struggling to close some baggage.

TRAVELLER
'Come on?' you say...? Where to...? It's good enough to stroll about here in place, drawing a proper ellipsoid with one's pacing — that saves the packing at least. Where's there to go to, anyway...? Malcher's bad mood would be constrained in a narrower space, and the radius he projects here on the floor will nowhere be longer or broader.

QUIDAM
I tell you, 'Come on!' Let's go! And so we're off...

They exit.

II

QUIDAM
And so you see that there are places in the world destined to be no one's goal: nobody from that great mob of people we elbowed our way through just now has come here...!

TRAVELLER
So you're telling me that all those people left home at midnight and wandered to this place, granting their servants the freedom of cursing bags that won't latch closed, and thrashing about? Freedom? space...?

So this is one more invention peculiar to big cities, to escape the interior of one's own lodgings…!

Far differently indeed did I bid farewell to my threshold in the country, my ancestral Omegi; a storm was raging and it so battered and spun the leaves — just as this crowd is spinning about here…

QUIDAM

That Malcher of yours must've been cursing a blue streak…!

TRAVELLER

O you, who examine column and statue with expert eye, tell me: have you ever trained the same sort of glance upon living people in our unstatued land…? Have you ever noticed how far distant the land of antiquity is from ours? Take, for example, the modern sort of servant — an Englishman or a Frenchman, or even a German; take, I say, these excellent servants whose entire living personalities seem to have been poured from a sublimely measured and masterful mould… Have you ever seen the like in Poland? Poles, you might say, aren't born to be servants: they're always pages, companions, easy-going fellows, a slightly debased order of knights who, although our feudal practices of cavalry have disappeared, hand you your hat and cane as once they did stirrup and sword. That's why they become great at great moments, but are lazy and careless in daily matters — more or less confidential story-tellers, who hold neither tear of emotion, nor dram of aught a bit stronger, in contempt.

QUIDAM

And so all the more was it right for us to step off the beaten path for a bit, here, where — of course — everything is modern… everything and nothing.

TRAVELLER

What do you mean, modern? Modern, how…? This multi-coloured African marble, the slim Lombard columns? They don't make any more marble like this…

CYPRIAN KAMIL NORWID

QUIDAM
Indeed they do. That's nothing but brick plastered over and painted.

TRAVELLER
That rectangular capital, carved with pious chisel by some master stonemason of the twelfth century?

QUIDAM
Was poured of zinc, one of a mass of factory-produced copies from the same mould, and subsequently gilded by a galvanising process. A structure such as what you look upon is built, these days, in the space of eight months.
  They call it a *café chantant*. But when they raise the curtain... A magical murmur sweeps through the crowds, who think that, just a moment more, and the most famous of singers will appear. And here she is... Thunderous applause... You hear what I'm saying?

.   .   .

It's not her! The programme, I see, has been changed... The audience grumbles with indignation, like Leviathan, after he lunges and misses his prey. Don't trust that marble balustrade — it's just wood with a thin metal sheath...

TRAVELLER
Something's going on, I see, at the side of the stage — those arms... What if the singer doesn't appear...?

QUIDAM
Be calm — You see that head and that half of an arm leaning out from the wings to the right?

TRAVELLER
I see someone constantly checking his watch, like a good photographer measuring the sunlight.

QUIDAM

That's the applause entrepreneur, the underwriter of the singer's value... As soon as the indignation of the audience reaches the apogee determined beforehand... But look! The time is nearing...! I hear something like that balustrade cracking under pressure — now, now! Here she is! The promoter puts his watch away. We can now safely exit the crowd and take in some fresh air...

TRAVELLER

What? What about the singer?

QUIDAM

Whatever and however she sings, she'll be greeted by a burst of applause all the greater for it having been carefully suppressed so long. The explosion will be such that you won't be able to evaluate the song — you won't even be able to hear it. A completely new art form, that...

Slip through here, use your elbows. I'm afraid that my album might get jostled and lost before you've had a chance to sign it before we part ways.

TRAVELLER

You've taught me about architecture, the mob, taste, style, and fame! Let's get out of here! Now is the time for me to write you a little dedication.

IN THE ALBUM

I

Not only first consuming mandragora, as
A ticket for crazed women into Hell...
Not only Dante and somber Pythagoras
But, I recall — alas! — being there as well!

                                               etc.

IN THE WINGS[42]

A FANTASY

Do you know Shrovetide in Venice?

Antoni Malczewski

PERSONS

OMEGITT	Lord of Omegi
LIA	His fiancée
EMMA	Her confidante
SOFISTOFF	A state referendary
MALCHER	Omegitt's servant
GLÜCKSCHNELL	Agent of a theatrical troupe
POLAK	A foreign official

Police commissars — officers — agents — conspirators — masks — etc…

DIOGENES (Mask)
FEUILLETON (Mask)
POET OF THE PEOPLE
CRITIC
MANDOLIN — CHORUS OF VIOLETS — ORCHESTRA
FLUTE — VIOLIN.

PAGE — HARLEQUIN — PIERROT — SULTAN (Mask)
DIANA — NIGHT
SECRETARY OF THE EMBASSY

---

42   From the foreword to this work nothing remains save an insignificant conclusion with the date: 'given 1869, *chez moi* — X.'

QUIDAM

FIFFRAQUE — A famous author.

I

A corridor leading from a theatre to a hall in which a masquerade is in progress. A few columns in the centre, beneath which some servants are standing; from the rear, one hears the strains of an orchestra. Where the hall meets the corridor one can see a few chairs, tastefully covered; between the columns, the corner of a buffet juts out.

COMMISSAR
Keep your eye on the servant who's just picked up a conversation with that guest.

OFFICER
The servant to the left of the guest is an agent in the fifteenth degree, twenty-seventh precinct.

COMMISSAR
To our left, but farther to the left of those... that one, I say, trailing a crimson scarf along the floor, as if he didn't know how to carry it.

OFFICER
Duly noted. A proper servant wouldn't drag a thing entrusted to him like that.

They move on.

MALCHER
The saying goes: Everywhere's fine to the peaceful in mind, but there's no place like home!... Cheers!

SERVANT FROM THE LEFT SIDE
If one has a home...

SERVANT FROM THE RIGHT SIDE
… and he who hasn't a home of his own, owns them all.

MALCHER
We had our share of them, I can tell you. Germany, France, and Italy, Algeria, beyond one sea, and beyond a still greater ocean — there too, where there's nothing but tents, no houses or cities, only people criss-crossing the trackless wastes of sand, schlepping along like gypsies! — I'm told we circumnavigated the whole world, but who could see anything, always in motion, always moving? Travelling for the sake of travel, and later on your head is spinning with the chirping of so many human tongues. But at the moment, how you're seized with a longing for your own people, your eyes fairly go dim!…

SERVANT WITH THE SCARF
They say a servant always longs the most for his fatherland…

SERVANT (AGENT IN THE FIFTEENTH DEGREE)
The toffs always find their own kind wherever they go. Here the leisured class, who do nothing, there the moneymakers, the writers of books, and then those that just can't stop talking politics… And — oh! — time flies!

Two Dominos pass over to the buffet.

FIRST DOMINO
Did you see the spy from the twenty-seventh precinct, standing next to that fellow?

SECOND DOMINO
Don't give it a second thought! The one on the other side, the one who was dragging that red shawl on the floor behind him, he's our sworn confidante.

They pass through.

GLÜCKSCHNELL

I'm starting to be very satisfied that we were wise enough not to make a separate venue of our production!…What a fine concoction might come of this! The only thing that holds me at arm's length is that the drama might not hold its own against so promising a masquerade, and that it might fade when we get to the slick comedy sketches, the ballets and songs.

POLAK (Foreign Official)

Unfortunately, Poles don't have the requisite intelligence for truly practical affairs.

GLÜCKSCHNELL

I'm looking for a certain writer here… I'll buy him a cup of punch and then let him gab. For the ancient philosopher was right when he said that truth lies at the bottom of the cup.

They pass through.

FIRST DOMINO

The anonymous author always reveals himself in the end. Usually before the production's over. As far as subject and background are concerned, I think you might extract much more from them than he has.

SECOND DOMINO

Me, I'd prefer something fuller, more packed with elements and tendencies. You might, for example, make a slight digression concerning yesterday's scuffle, and in a few monologues at least set out the main rationales of the partisans. At least an idea of the first, interim castramentation. Such propitious material for an author! It's a shame to pass it by.

FIRST DOMINO

The servant — that spy from the twenty-seventh precinct, is bringing round ices.

SECOND DOMINO
To take ices from the hand of a spy! That should boost his confidence, and yet — nothing more surely gives a person away.

FIRST DOMINO
Somebody from the Party might see us, and they've vowed never to buy a thing from a suspicious person.

They pass through. Enter Lia, fantastically dressed as Héloise, and Emma, in dominoes.

LIA
Come off to the side a bit. I'd like to rest. If those arcades above should suddenly split to let a whole sky of fresh air pour in, I'd still not have enough to breathe.

What do they want from me? Why are they leagued against me?… At least I'm right about one thing.

With a bitter smile.

One thing! And that is, if you looked through the whole cloud of masks and the whole weft of intrigues stood plainly before you, like the weave of Indian gauze seen against the sunlight, what you'd see there would be me, me and some other woman — you'd see us and nothing else but us!

Why this crowd? Why is it exactly different, than it is?…

EMMA
My dear — for God's sake, from the whole of this intrigue of yours, only two things are clear to me: the anxiety that glows upon your brow like a slight fever, and the little box in my pocket, so heavy, which — what am I doing with it, carrying it about? 'That is the question!'

LIA

Bending near the mirrored wall.

That's all I need, for printed letters to blush on my face, especially since I seem to be on the way to becoming a walking advertisement for what is surely the most unfortunate of all dramas anyway!

EMMA
That still explains nothing to me. I'd simply add that I would never admit anyone into a conspiracy without providing him with more information.

LIA
Forgive me, O forgive me, my dear Emma, but could I ever keep anything hidden from you?… Is it really necessary for me to go into excruciating detail about something that should already be patent to your eyes and almost palpable to your touch! A feeling similar to justified modesty and outraged *amour-propre* has constrained me to pass over in silence — not to conceal — the fact that my so-called engagement to the count of Omegi, or rather, the decision, and my word in the matter, have not yet taken on a concrete certainty…

EMMA
What? Can such a thing be?

LIA
The little box, which rightly you find so heavy, contains two rings, till now exchanged by no one.

EMMA
A person so proper, with such gravity! And more — at your age! Neither of you are children, you're all grown up… That such a proper person should be so frivolous, changing his mind without any real reason for doing so, and at a moment so serious, one anticipated with such longing?

LIA
My dear. He fell upon his knees before me, and begged for a delay of one day — this day — only; only until tomorrow morning, till the hour when the last star of this night should pale…
I repeat his words here, almost verbatim.

Did the self-respect proper to a woman not enjoin me to know how to receive such a little expected request? Of course, I didn't look him in the eye, nor did I deign touch the rings; I made a motion with my hand… And later, later, when I saw him nearing the threshold, it suddenly occurred to me that the delay he'd requested was the day of the masquerade… And so I tossed a few words in his direction as he was leaving… But he didn't waver for a moment, not at all…

EMMA
There's something peculiar in it all…

LIA
I've heard that, at moments when serious bonds are about to be formed, Providence sometimes thrusts in some unusual events which light up from tip to toe like flashes of lightning the characters involved. But, do confess, please, that in this case I had everything that reason and propriety dictate? His age, his birth, position, knowledge of the world and decent means; complementarity in humour and in height…. Certainly, I made my choice not like any lightheaded young thing, nor did I overlook anything that might guarantee domestic harmony.

So all the more, I'm right to feel hurt by his behaviour, which is both mysterious and suggestive of some baseless hesitation… Who are you waving at?

EMMA
Referendary Sofistoff. He was going to approach us but then some domino halted him on the way.

LIA
Are you quite certain that he hasn't recognised me?

EMMA
You were turned to the wall, although it is a wall of mirrors! He's gone away… He's gone… Go on now with what you were saying!

LIA

And so you can imagine that the one thing I simply couldn't bear not to do was not to come here, and that, moreover, with an expression of such calm as might be taken from afar as indifference.

EMMA

Suddenly.

Excellent! I don't see any reason why you should avoid your earlier adorers, either... In your place I'd have drawn Sofistoff himself near, when we had him within our reach.

LIA

Don't interrupt me at the very moment when I'm about to tell you the most irritating thing... Who are you waving at?

EMMA

Baron Glückschnell's arrived, along with the celebrated French author Annibal de Fiffraque. Did you know that de Fiffraque wears glasses?!
    But let's get back to that most irritating matter of yours...

LIA

You're interrupting me all the time!

EMMA

I'm listening!

LIA

Well, since I'd determined not to avoid the party at any cost, as ironic as it is for me to be here, I didn't come, deliberately, at the very end of the play and as the masquerade was winding down, but right at the start of the second act of that strange drama... And suddenly I notice that something peculiar was going on, and someone was circling, running about amongst our acquaintances...
    Some sort of joker — listen to this! — That wretched fool was spreading the rumour that the anonymous author was none other than Omegitt! The blood rushed to my head. Supposedly, the play

was jeered and whistled at in two places. I didn't know. But, just like when in a dark night a great flash of lightning lights a person up, revealing to his eyes the finest atoms of sand at his feet, so, suddenly, there was revealed to my eyes the truth of those mysterious delays and the history of the rings, with which I now burden your pocket, unable to touch them myself with hand unengaged. And so from the very first I believed the rumour and then — I couldn't even believe myself. Yet I began to lose the sense of the difference between the feeling of love for a woman and vanity, between seriousness and irony... And so now I know nothing more than this, that just as everyone seems to state, this drama now on stage must be much, much beneath any untimely comedy, of the sort that, who knows, I myself have been entangled in!

EMMA
Lia my dear, common sense demands a completely different explanation of all this. On the contrary! For, if he really did have a yen to test the waters of authorship, then for sure he wouldn't have hesitated to bring his personal plans to their proper conclusion. Because, however unrelated the two things may be, those personal matters risk becoming undone should one be buried under mockery and laughter.

GLÜCKSCHNELL
I won't apologise for interrupting you, mesdames — for shortly the bell will sound and summon us to enjoy the third act of our production, that is, our drama, our tragedy. I'd feel extraordinarily fortunate indeed if you, madame, would deign share your opinion of it with me...

LIA

To Emma.

'Extraordinarily fortunate' — that's beginning to be a proverb in the mouths of all those who speak with me!

To Glückschnell.

It would be more proper for me to seek the judgement of a member of the theatrical company — and one who just a moment before I saw in the company of a famous French writer — deep in conversation on some doubtlessly important issue.

GLÜCKSCHNELL

Ah, Madame! Am I to repeat the opinion of the celebrated de Fiffraque? Naturally, such gentlemen simply cannot be enamoured of works that have enjoyed a less than doubtful reception... I'm sure madame is familiar with the new stageplay of that genial, aforementioned author — *Saturnine, or The Devil's Eye*? What a furore that aroused! The eighteenth printing has just been exhausted. A contemporary masterpiece already translated into many languages, and famous nearly all over the world... A sublime fellow!

Yesterday I was shown two telegrams announcing that two medals were about to be pinned to that same breast: the Star of her Most Catholic Majesty Isabella, and the Star of the Mahometan Sultan...

ASTROLOGICAL MASK

Passing by.

For such conjunctions of heavenly bodies, truly, breasts as ample as the firmament itself are called for!

GLÜCKSCHNELL

Going on with his story.

Of course it does his career no good that he's so liberal... Ah, youth, youth! But here is de Fiffraque himself, with Sofistoff, and our countryman, a foreign dignitary —

A bell sounds, one hears the orchestra, the murmuring crowd, and protracted whistles.

EMMA
Lend our Juliet your arm, Referendary…

LIA
Shouldn't we wait until they stop… whistling?

SOFISTOFF

Offering his arm.

We needn't go in to see the play at all.

They disappear into the crowd, Emma and Glückschnell follow.

EMMA
The circumspection of your judgement — perhaps out of consideration for Lia who posed the question — has not enlightened me much concerning the value of the work…

GLÜCKSCHNELL
The business, the business interests of drama or tragedy — well, this is my capital complaint! It's an interesting work, Madame, something one can sense not only on stage or in the house. My years with the company have taught me that it's most often best to have a glance at the buffets in order to arrive at a healthy idea concerning a given work. A real, strong tragedy is a stimulus to the appetite. The audience eats more. I believe this is sound, hygienically speaking…

More peculiarly (from what I've noticed) – during long ballets, people drink more. A solid, well-played Vaudeville doesn't cross any lines, whereas works such as this by the otherwise respectable Count of Omegi…

EMMA
Let's keep our voices down.

GLÜCKSCHNELL
In complete confidence, I would not conceal this from an interested party like yourself: By nature of his long and far-distant travels, he's

lost the active native pulse that, on the one hand, lends a writer's language its peculiar strength, and on the other, incessantly fortifies his thought with the current needs of our society — and that is, I would say, what pleases… everyone.

EMMA
Now I understand perfectly. I'm much indebted to you, Baron.

II

Another part of the masquerade hall. Large windows, giving out onto an ambulatory, from which a heaven filled with stars can be seen; to the rear, dominos are strutting about, along with a small number of masks; the orchestra can be heard, now loudly, now softly.

OMEGITT
And so it's turned out just as I expected it would. They think the writing of a drama was my ultimate intention. Formal judges of all measure, who divide society into hosts of pedestrian minds and those astride winged steeds. In their opinion, these latter soar on pens with fluttering manes, like fantastic emissaries, while those former are busied with the prose of life — cripples hobbling along on crutches of lucre!

Can it be that I have encircled the world entire, revelling in the delight of a man-husband who has embraced the bosom of his world-wife, to arrive at nothing more than such dualism?

Was it all in vain that I gazed at stars that you have never seen, counting my evening hours while you were just awakening from your sleep?

And time and place and the whole corpus of history — lost from my eyes for nothing?

Is there no such being then, none, which, spread out everywhere, while yet not abandoning one specific place, that says to one individual mortal 'You are; you are, for you have embraced everything, everywhere, simultaneously, though ever here…'?

O you inebriated ones! You vain fellows! Can it be that amidst this crowd of vulgar jostlings the breath that cries to heaven, that pierces through the heavens, is stifled?

CYPRIAN KAMIL NORWID

Is there no longer man or woman here, but mere phenomena of coincidental custom and the technical balance of the senses…?

One moment more, and some of the stars will begin to fade. Just a few moments more, and the pale glow of dawn will begin to pierce the thick darknesses — what time is it? What day, year, month, age, and epoch? … And where?

Malcher, O Malcher, you walking compass and hourglass of mine, as long as I can see your drooping whiskers and those fresh, bright eyes beneath your heavy brows; as long as I can see the belt of your caftan, I can still come back to myself, even from the abyss!

CHORUS OF VIOLETS (Masks)
Let us sway around the melancholy traveller, we, half-graveyard blooms, quiet flowers! Let him recall where he respired the breath of our brothers and sisters, violets!

To Omegitt.

O melancholy traveller! Look here and breathe… a wreath of blooms — violets and greys, twining about you, a looming sorcerer's charm that would possess you…

OMEGITT
O fragrant and melancholy masks, how should I address you properly?

CHORUS OF VIOLETS
The first of us is called Violet, the second Violetta and the third, Vi.

And the second of us is also Violet, but only the first states that openly. However, if you wish…

And this is why, whereas in other places blushing maidens danced through the springtime of their years, we dragged behind ourselves funereal wreaths and crepe, which wound about every gesture of ours like strands of cobweb.

And none of us — as you wish! None of us knows a full-hearted smile.

I am a violet, and she says that she is a violet, and we are all of us... violets, and we ask you, if you have seen many graveyard springs...

OMEGITT
I've seen many violets clipped from violet satin and set on wires, O melancholy masks of mine.

FIRST VIOLET
And what did they say to you about us? Be sincere, now.

SECOND VIOLET
Was it in graveyards German and French, on the ruins of Rome and the broken marbles of Greece, in the south or in the north?... Speak!

VIOLETTA
Did you fall in love in Paris when you caught sight of my sister there? Trapped in thickly braided hair?

ALL VIOLETS
Ha, ha, ha! Intrigues!

FIRST VIOLET
He's never been to Paris! He's never been to Paris!

SECOND VIOLET
What is this France, this Paris? Tell the truth!

OMEGITT
France is a nation of great destinies, and Paris is nothing but the capital of European civilisation.

FIRST VIOLET
Since he's so smart, let him tell you what civilisation is.

SECOND VIOLET
Well, if you're so smart, tell us — what is it, then?

OMEGITT
Civilisation is a bastard thing…

ALL VIOLETS

Covering their ears with their velvet hoods.

Ah! How vulgar he is! And why?

OMEGITT
Because, all intellects are unchristian, practically speaking, and all Christian intellects are unpractical…

He withdraws.

POLAK (Foreign Official)
I was searching the floor for my cloakroom token, and I found a blessed medallion from Częstochowa.

DOMINO
You need to hand it over to a policeman on duty.

ASTRONOMER'S MASK
O Ursa major, whither shalt thou hasten when the sun strides through the sky?

To Omegitt.

See how those stars are sifting pale, and the others hardly glow, like embers trembling, dying…

OMEGITT

To Astronomer.

Wait…!

Looks around.

He's disappeared into the sea of masks, which has once more ebbed in a long half-circle, murmuring, leaving me alone here, like some wreck left on the sands by the retreating tide…

Sounds of the orchestra are heard from the connecting corridor, and a loud whistle, after which, the noise of the crowd hastening in.

Omegitt retreats to the frame of a large window.

GLÜCKSCHNELL

Wiping his brow.

I'll admit it — what a flop. Such a fiasco, the like of which I can't recall ever having seen!

EMMA
It's too bad that the author's name was made public.

GLÜCKSCHNELL
That'll fade slowly — once we move on to the sketches sensibly written. The thing I'm most sorry about is the disappointment felt by our lovely Heloise… Where is she now?

They pass through.

MASK OF DIOGENES
Don't thrust me aside, ungrateful ones! Am I not eager to please, as far as I may, so that you might show me the man who hesitated not before expressing himself straightforwardly, in a way our violets found so vulgar?

SOME VIOLETS
Are our ears so helpless? So often they bear the weight of earrings of gigantic pearl drops, the purest dew, and everything that is pure is heavy twice over…!

DIOGENES
O how light must be the crinoline weft of newsprint, in which that little mask comes rustling up…

To Mask.

Sit tibi crinolina levis!

FEUILLETON MASK
And yet every item of news lies heavy upon me, every rumour…! Beginning with the drama of that 'Tyrtaeus' of yours (which was just now whistled off the stage) and ending with this vision of Diogenes and the violets — in tender harmony!

OMEGITT

Half to the Mask, half to himself.

There's nothing new under the sun, nothing…! But how does it come about, that there's never anything new?

FEUILLETON
Now there's some news for you indeed! News flash!

OMEGITT
There's nothing new under the sun, for this reason: that everything we know now has been recognised before — either sensed, or by analogy, or comprehension, or the force of experience, or some strange inkling of foresight. Nor has there ever been such a reflection of the flat human eye that, gazing in the fall at an apple tree with few, or only one apple hanging on at its summit, saw only and exclusively that one apple, and more — merely that side of the apple facing it. Certainly, looking at an object, we don't see just one surface of the object, but through some mysterious and masterful sense of the whole, we see as if at the same time all other planes and sections of that object. The more comprehensible in its entirety the object of our sight is, the quicker we comprehend its multidimensionality at one glance. The same is true, especially — of Truth!

For she, being alone all one and indivisible, from the very first moment when she allowed herself to be apprehended, she gave herself over to people entire. And if not face to face, so to say, obviously, to the reason, then to the courser powers and means of comprehension.

For this reason we call new discoveries, at each moment, familiar or similar things, admitted once, doubtlessly, by the mind of man...

And so, for this one grand reason, there is nothing new under the sun...

DIOGENES
I thought he was a man — and he's a lantern!

FEUILLETON
I thought it was a news item — and it's the truth!

To Fiffraque.

If only I knew your opinion, O famous French author, still today after supper and some wine I'd have myself an article of impressive size.

FIFFRAQUE
I couldn't understand a single word of it...! We who deign not to learn foreign languages, only mock the burbling of their barbarian vocables — and that's good enough for us.

ALL VIOLETS
Ha, ha, ha, ha!

FIFFRAQUE

To the Violets.

But by the same token, we know how to speak such exact truths to ourselves, and about ourselves (as you hear) — and that is a power higher and quicker than linguistic exercises!

He passes through.

VIOLETS
This one was speaking of fruit!

OMEGITT

With melancholy.

A child sees an apple fall and stretches out his arms, as if toward his mother's breast. Yet the same phenomenon heralds something different to Newton and leads his thought elsewhere. A chemist lifts the apple from the ground and from its bruised side he reads the essence of the transformation of material which the philosopher immediately sends off to the very depths of the fiery sun, while the gardener passing by sees nothing, surely, but a fallen fruit and human hands reaching out for it.

DIOGENES
And if that 'Tyrtaeus' whistled off the stage should find himself here, after the passage of thousands of years, what should he see, or commence to do, with this masquerade of life?

OMEGITT
Certainly, he would speak the truth, believing in its power — something, truly, that I notice no one else is occupied with.

DOMINO-SPY
But whence comes the power of truth?

OMEGITT
It comes from the wholeness of truth, and thus from the fact that truth is an idea, constantly providing evidence of itself.

DOMINO-SPY
Is that to be evidence of my utter incomprehension?

DOMINO-CONSPIRATOR
That would be great evidence indeed if I had first guessed it…

CHORUS OF VIOLETS

To the graveyards! To the graveyards! To the graveyards! At dawn —
in the afternoon — in the evening — at night and as the stars begin
to pale!

POET OF THE PEOPLE

Hey-hop! Hey-hop, again! Up with the red caps! Up with the rattling
necklaces of coral and the skirts hitched up at the waist! Hey-hop!
Hey-hop!

And peacock feathers with their bright blue hearts, bobbing
above the brows on crimson caps! Hey-hop! Hey-hop!

POLAK (Foreign Official)

I know no national ballet that equals this, the Polish, and whenever
I'm at an evening entertainment at some governor or diplomat's
house where it is danced, I simply can't tear my eyes away.

DIOGENES

And our Tyrtaeus, whistled off the stage, if he were to find himself
here after the passage of thousands of years, here at this masquerade
of life, what would he hold above all things...?

OMEGITT

Seek your answer from the critic — who must surely be that character
dressed up in the robe with the printed pages stuck all over it. He's
on his way here now — the rustling betrays him — with a crowd of
masks scurrying before him, diving left and right, as if they wished
to escape his pursuit, his blows.

CHORUS OF THOSE ESCAPING

Don't ask, Mehercule, don't ask by what right the critic makes such
and such a judgement! For then you leave him two horrid weapons
in his hand: he'll either not allow you time enough to pose the
question to the end, or he'll do such violence to you with polemical
barrages that, taking on an appearance of umbrage, you'll transform
the discussion into a duel. Let him alone then, let him create on his
own. Let him give birth to something by himself, in the great peace
of his own cogitations!

CRITIC (Mask)

Here and there, glancing at the mirrored walls, I happened to see myself reflected tip to toe. Here and there — why do those walls dissolve into lakes of glass and light...? Here and there, at long last, I caught sight of the whole mystery of my inspiration. Eheu, I was not able to create anything, unless I had first been irritated, unless I had sunk my teeth into something, anything...! And for this reason sarcasm constitutes my entire wealth, security, and peace.

OMEGITT

Children at such times need to tussle and break things. Power falls in love with itself when it moves on from blind elemental force to act — it is the one thing most unlike criticism...

VIOLETS

That degenerate traveller, that man without a country, whatever he touches, he knocks down! And meanwhile have we not enwreathed ourselves into chaplets for that wise man, and for that poet over there, and for all that is bright and shining hereabout, bearing them the fragrant incense of dewy tears?

GLÜCKSCHNELL

Permit me to follow the critic for a few more paces yet, madame. Perhaps he'll still let fall a few words concerning how we are to judge and what we are to write about today's performance.

EMMA

Did you not notice our Heloise as she passed by, Baron? It was just a moment ago, but I hadn't the courage to halt her progress. Look — there behind that pilgrim dressed up in pearly shells! I see her yet, can you...?

Her arms of white... See how that arm of hers trembles from the outrage she's bottling up inside her! I've never seen such eyes — gazing into them, I shuddered; it was like gazing into an abyss, the magnetic force of which was pulling me in!

GLÜCKSCHNELL

I see her — she's nearing the large window that leads to the ambulatory, like someone in dire need of fresh air. And there through the crowd pushes and slides our unfortunate author.

EMMA

Oh look — you can see her profile against the backdrop of the heavens, which neither blush with the coming dawn, nor reflect the silver of the moon… And the last of the stars is tangled in her hair.

If only those guitars and mandolins would cease their strumming…! If only one could draw near her with one's ear!

MANDOLIN

I

And does she know, in mind or heart,
Awake or dreaming, has she heard
What happens to the lion's part
Of her so candidly sung words?

II

And does she know, can she surmise,
Herself fresh, ever new, and hale!
That all that lives so quickly dies
Though *her* youth never fail?

III

Does she know, at the very least,
As 'On!' and 'Onward!' still she raves,
Whose tears they are, by which her feet
Are laved, as if by lapping waves?

IV

And will — at least — she ever know
As on she'll blindly rush and race,
That poppies which on gravemounds grow
Some wear — instead of bays?

*   *   *

Emma, Glückschnell and a few other maskers lean to one side of the great columns at the large window to reveal Lia, leaning on the balustrade of the arcade. Omegitt draws near her, from the direction of the salon, through the crowd of masks.

OMEGITT
As Leander who, upon sighting the bonfire alit on the summit of the tower, across the glassy waves of Hellespont stretched forth his arms so as to reach the opposite shore in time, thus I, through the curtains of gauze and fluttering masks, catching sight of you and the last star hanging above your brow…

LIA

Deprecatingly.

Unless I'm mistaken, Leander drowned…

OMEGITT
Upon which the priestess Hero threw herself into the sea as well, and, she not being quite the mermaid, along with him met a tragic end. But… at first I didn't think it right to begin a conversation less freely, less in confidence…

LIA
Indeed, I marvel at your good humour. For I can't guess whence it springs. I will be brief with what I have to say.

OMEGITT
And thus — the last star vanishes!

LIA
One more reason for me to be jealous of her! Oh, how I envy that star! So many times, indeed, I've felt the need to erase my name from the list of the spectators of your tragedy — vanishing, if only I were able, just like that star.

OMEGITT

That star will rise again tomorrow, and certainly, someone's eyes will gaze upon it from this very spot. But this manner of weaving a conversation leaves much space between two persons, almost inviting a third from among this ghoulish crowd to rush in and fill it.

LIA

This manner of conversing, sir, is quite similar to the greetings and courtesies exchanged before a duel. And so I beg you not to think it improper if I cut off further words with a gesture, as I hasten to return your ring...

OMEGITT

Drawing back his hands.

Permit me to warn you... madame... that there are few more painful and persistent sorrows than the sense of having left behind oneself a heart that one has wounded. For this reason, refusing to accept the ring back again, I would yet like to receive from your dear hands something that I might retain as a souvenir testifying to your convictions.
[...][43]

III
The salon, seen from the outside courtyard.

MANDOLIN
From the parquet of the carnival arena
Where earlier had pirouetted masks
I watched, amid the now deserted scene, a
First ray of the dawning sunlight flash.
There, on the fresh-waxed floor, traces of heels
Marked every wheel and pas-de-deux they took:

---

43   Here the scene breaks off in manuscript.

It was like looking on sorcerer's wheels,
Sines and ellipses in some black-arts book.

There too — a petal fallen from a bloom
Breathed something to me with its papery lip
As it lay there, alone in the empty room —
Complaining of the dew it couldn't sip?

With force that shook the sparkling chandeliers
I prised a pane up through its stubborn tracks,
And from the hanging candles jostled tears —
However, they were merely tears of wax.

COMMISSAR
Keep your eyes on the backalley singers and guitarists. Aren't there
enough officially sanctioned musicians, that they have to hire these
buskers for their parties?

OFFICER ON DUTY
All of the alert and faithful have focussed their attention on the
cloakroom, where the guests are retrieving their greatcoats and
wraps. For now, as the saying goes, that's where the birds are chirping!

ORCHESTRAL FINALE

Together.

Just a few more sheets now, just a few more washed over by the pale
dawn, spattered by the wax of lights guttering above…
    They reckon we'll play some finale from an Italian opera, but our
sore eyes are unable to follow the feverishly leaping notes any more…
We can hardly stay in the same key.
    We're happy that only a few more sheets remain, a few more,
that's all, the edges of which are lit up by the rosy fingers of the dawn,
lit up from above by the flickering of the guttering lights.

FLUTE

Solo.

How nice it will be to recline in my case lined with white velvet! O how nice it will be to stretch myself out for a space…!

O, one more time only, just once more will those humid lips touch me, whispering something…

O, one more time only, just once more will those boney fingers run over my hips, and then, and then… O, won't I rest! My little casket is a long one, roomy on all sides and lined with white velvet!

VIOLIN

The flute has finished and hear how they're applauding!

Let their applause continue — let their applause be endless, deafening the barely noticeable movement of the bow! A few white horsehairs of the bow, as white as snow, have come detached from its mop of hair; they float away through the air!

ORCHESTRA

Together.

Only a few more sheets, just a few more now halfway lit up by the rosy glow of the dawn, spattered by the wax of the lights guttering above.

Just a few more sheets scribbled over with notes dancing in the net of the staffs, like the writhing and shuddering of unknown creatures drawn together in a trembling seine.

PAGE

With guitar.

I

I want no more sadnesses — no! For me, they are too small,
Although like the world's corruption they may be immense.

Have they not been suffered through now, one and all?
When I prick my ear, hear I not their laments?

II
And so I want no sadnesses — for none of them are new.
For all those cares and worries, I can't recall my own!
I lay down my head — they pierce me through and through —
Wherever I turn, I hear but moan and groan!

III
Someday footsoles will trample dust, that once was monuments;
Cities and fortresses impregnable — still rough stone —
Await their builders. But what hear I? Laments!
Wherever I turn, I hear but moan and groan!

IV
It's for this reason I like forget-me-nots, above all:
For they are most often plucked by perjured, faithless hands.
I like, exhausted, in sudden sleep to fall,
That seizes like death — before one understands.

It's for this reason I like forget-me-nots, above all:
Because they are only plucked by perjured, faithless hands.

*   *   *

EMMA
Melancholy page, deign withdraw… Sad page, permit my hand to
stretch out to Heloise, or please pass on to her this little box, desired
twice over this evening…

PAGE

Withdrawing.

Give me thy blue ribbon — I'll give it right back
Without delay…
Or give me the shadow of thy supple neck.

No, I want more than a shade!
For shadows change when thou stretch thy hand to me,
For they can't lie!
Beautiful maiden, I want nothing of thee;
I withdraw, I step aside.
It's happened that the Lord has awarded me
Time and again
Some slighter prize — a leaf fallen from a tree
Or some drizzle on a pane.

He passes through.

SOFISTOFF

Fantastically dressed as Abelard.

If not for the mutable nature of the crowds, and the wandering
guitarists drowning out the orchestra, I would promise myself, at
the end of the party, that for which others gathered here too soon
to garner.

DIOGENES
At last, a man!

He douses his lantern.

That's him, that's him without a doubt! Otherwise, he'd not mask
himself at the rising of the sun…

EMMA

In a whisper.

My dear Referendary, just one more word of confidential advice…
one more puff to blow away one last wispy cloud beyond the rosy
skies of dawn – – –
    Am I to hide from you, warn you, or present you with something
for your tact to deal with?

SOFISTOFF

Madame, a warning from you already determines my behaviour; your advice I take as a command. To appeal to my tact is to draught into your service yet another servant to aid the first two after the task has already been accomplished. For one sends a third only when the first two servants chosen had proven inept.

EMMA

I would leave to your tact no small matter — for it concerns your nationality. That is, the one and only obstacle that stands between you and Heloise... My dear Referendary, do you understand me?

SOFISTOFF

Madame! My one and only fatherland has ever been no other than tact! To point out the difficulties presented by my nationality and leave the same to my tact, why, that is to entrust my heart to my own breast. Such a thing not only does not terrify me; indeed, I would not even know how to justly thank you for it.

Madame, when all other peoples, in love with their own personal traits, were challenging all sorts of enemies of progress to the battle with varied weapons, seeking varied glory, my own fatherland was cultivating the reason proper to it: waiting upon the fruits of civilisation to ripen, which up until then had been unobtainable even by force. For this reason, now, in this present positive age, you see, Madame, that the wisdom proper to my fatherland, and the general wisdom of civilisation, are one and the same thing!

Can you understand, Madame, to what an extent my nationality thus simply cannot be an obstacle to anyone?

Beginning with the capital of my fatherland, founded upon a pattern derived elsewhere, and constructed, conquered, laborious age upon laborious age, to become at last the form and name of our state, to the very footwear and clothing of our chivalric caste who stand in defence of our fatherland, all of this is unnatural, foreign! And this indeed is the seal of the lofty and wide mission of my sacred fatherland — so how, O Madame, might it be that my nationality should constitute an obstacle? An obstacle such as Madame gives me to understand; an obstacle to my personal happiness?

EMMA
I leave you, Abelard, to your own genius. And if I vanish for a
moment, it is just as a good fairy disappears...

She vanishes into the crowd.

HARLEQUIN

Mimicking playing a guitar.

From roof's edge to green hedge
Leapt the cat;
My sweet song — not too long:
And that's that!

PIERROT

Seeming to take the invisible instrument from the Harlequin.

With loud woof on church roof
A bird grins;
The winds blow — watch him go:
How he spins!

HARLEQUIN

Seeming to take the invisible guitar back from Pierrot.

'No bird that!' said the cat
'It's a cur —
But he spins in the winds —
I concur.'

IV
The same. The cloakroom.

FIRST SERVANT
Your burnous, Princess. And Miss Hermenegilda's cotton hood…

SECOND SERVANT
Your cloak, Count… A carriage! Jakub! Jakub!

THIRD SERVANT
The carriages are drawn up in numerical order. Ours is number thirty-nine. Nepomuk! Hey, Nepomuk!

MASK OF SULTAN
Let's make a little detour and grab a glass of beer at Małgorzata's.

DIANA (Mask)
A little something to nibble on — game, that's what I've got a yen for, with a salad…

SECRETARY OF THE EMBASSY (To Diana)
I'd have a sip of champy myself, and a cigarette to bid the dawn hello…

NIGHT (Mask)
I caught my cloak of darkness, and my cape of stars, on the spur of a gendarme!

EMMA
Can you see them, Baron, there by the two columns? There they are, both of them — how beautiful! See? Heloise inclines her brow and sinks into the shadow of the window frame, while Abelard's arm leaps forth and flashes in the light of dawn… They're whispering something… As I look upon them it occurs to me that thus Canova must have gazed upon two of his sculptures nearing the finishing touches…

GLÜCKSCHNELL […][44]

---

44   Lines are missing in the manuscript.

OMEGITT …that I hear from one side and the other something like a litany, punctuated here and there with howls…

 Something like the clatter of weapons of an army on the march…
 My head, so heavy. I need to rest…

He lies down.

[…]

LEADER

Turning to his phalanx and cutting the air with his sword.

One more whistle of this iron, lads, one more swipe with the flat to push away the Lacedaemonian air…

 I can't sweep it all with my short sword… and you? and he?

FIRST IN THE RANKS

Sweeping the air.

I'll sweep that current over the threshold of my hearth, or I'll sprain my wrist trying.

LEADER
And if some balk or trave be smouldering, it shall burst into flame…

FIRST IN THE RANKS
For there were no fathers there, but only herdboys with their teams of oxen.

*

And our fathers had no wives.

*

When they were lacking blood for hecatombs, when the phalanxes were chipped beneath Messenian scythes, they sent the soldiers back to the widowed beds in their fatherland…

*

And here a woman, there another, sprang up and raced to the city gates to meet the envoy from the battlefield… Let this whistle of the breeze, this current of air, pushed on its way by the sweep of my sword, go in search of Spartan mothers and whistle curses through their grey hair.

ALL
For none of us had a mother, or a father, and none of us had a fatherland!

LEADERS
'Cos we're neither Spartan nor Lacedaemonian men — we're Parthenian bastards!
  And so we'll go where the granite repulses the sea, and we shall push the sea away with a hundred oars, and from our shoulders we shall shrug off the succubus of memory — for we've been hardened since our cradle, and we are able to bear all things — except this fatherland!

ALL
For none of us had a mother, or a father, and none of us had a fatherland!

They pass through.

MALCHER
They tried, sir, they gave it a go with the sword… But what they were saying among themselves, that I don't know, but it seems that those chaps were something like that Lejun Aytranjere we saw in Algeria.

OMEGITT

Grabbing him by the arm.

Call my boy — have him lead up my horse! We're off!

Omegitt and Malcher go off left, while from the right the Athenian Chorus enters, dividing into two half circles.

CHORUS TO THE RIGHT

In the life of man there are moments empty, moments hollow. But there are no such in the life of the truth, which is only one uninterrupted stream. And this is why the Athenian chorus is ever valid, ever present, like a continually watchful Aeropagus.

Who has never spoken with them? With them, who has never conversed? But they ever speak with the rhythm of truth.

They grasped the tone of harmony from the very start. The tone that leads the world, continually spinning, like the planet itself.

Have you ever seen them apoplectic, or laughing? Or have you ever seen surfeit or boredom lying athwart their path? Never. Thus the Athenian chorus.

CHORUS TO THE LEFT

Because in the life of man there are moments empty, moments hollow. But there have never been any such in the life of the truth.

EPODE

Blessed is the light; the darkness is not necessarily a curse; but he who seeks what has been lost is gladdened by both only in the discovery of what he searches for.

CHORUS

Here I see an Athenian approaching — he looks around with anxiety as if, crossing the borders of this Republic, and travelling its length and breadth, he'd come to inspect the fatherland in both diurnal phases.

LAON

On that day long ago, when I plunged from a listing ship after a drowning man, did I consider beforehand that I was to rescue a father for myself, and win my citizenship, my fatherland? Just the same even today I find myself occupied with the same thing — or is my identity that of a divine, constant concern for the orphaned?

On that day, memorable above all others, I was able to pull from the depths of the sea the silver-haired Cleocarpus. But who knows whether today I have not leapt too suddenly to my feet, giving all too ready an ear to rumours, following in the traces of the fled Eginea, even unto here?

CHORUS

O man, who embraces the core of truth with the exhalations of Asiatic slavery, but who has the figure and attire and gestures of an Athenian citizen — get to the point.

LAON

I am no metic, no foreigner new-settled in Athens, but something greater than an isoteles, having obtained civic rights, and my prostatos, my patron, is a man of the Aeropagus — he whom the gods gave me to rescue from the waves. I was born, it seems, on the distant shores of Phoenecia, but reborn in the foaming womb of the sea; my father was a black trireme with red sails, and I was made a citizen by the Athenians on the threshold of Theseus' porch.

Cleocarpus the Aeropagite is my father in the eyes of the law...

And law and justice come of the gods. I bear the signet ring of Cleocarpus on my finger not for outward show and glamour, to shine in the eyes of men. For tempests and whirlwinds occur not only on the sea, such as we look upon from our rooftops at a safe distance; no, there are also such as can even shake the very columns of this peristyle.

Now, the girl I seek is the worthy daughter of noble Cleocarpus, who vanished from home several days ago, and tongues unbridled have spread the news that her steps have been directed by the whispers of Tyrtaeus, ever since the great oracle spoke unto the Athenians, indicating that poet as the leader of the Lacedaemonian forces...

CHORUS TO THE RIGHT
The wisemen from the East say that at the edge of the world there spins an immense, boiling whirlwind of bodies and spirits.

CHORUS TO THE LEFT
Buffeted, swept to and fro as the planet whirls.

CHORUS TO THE RIGHT
There too gather great darknesses, which no heroic spirit has ever pierced.

CHORUS TO THE LEFT
And the horizons of the thought of man are ringed with silence and sadness.

EPODE
At this edge of two fatherlands, O citizen of Athens, amidst the ruins of that, which two bordering peoples dared not raise anew from the dust — and for that reason, they have sunk doubly deeper — it is here that you have come in search of someone? Why are you gripped by such anxiety?

LAON
Benignly glows the shining casque of Minerva, and the words of an intelligent man are never hasty. And such tragic intelligences as those of the chorus can more swiftly and surely predict tempests and judge of water spouts at sea by merely lifting a shell from the sand as they tread along the shore of life, than can the helmsman on the pitching deck, who seems to their eyes no larger than a shard of coral on the beach.

CHORUS TO THE RIGHT
How splendid is the democratic freedom of the Athenian polis, how sublime! And yet the currents of *vox populi* can be treacherous, and when their waves billow, they can bear a man away as easily as a pea. And for this reason it is unfounded rumour that spreads most quickly — the lighter it is, the farther it is borne.

CHORUS TO THE LEFT

And so in things that concern the gods, take yourself rather to the peaceful Aeropagus at nightfall! And like the heavenly spaces of the firmament in the full majesty of its constellations, so you too — becalm the emotions raging in your breast, so that all of your thoughts might shine forth like splendiferous stars, each of your words galactic in their composure.

CHORUS TO THE RIGHT

For this reason Solon of Salamis strove to fix the columns of the Aeropagus so that there, where the voice of the people is not restrained in the least, it might be measured as a reflection of the sea: in the depths of which heavy things settle beneath the flimsy chaff of the foam. The Aeropagus at night is as the sea beneath the starry firmament, deep and calm, whereas the clamour of the streets with their plashing rainbows and loud babble of popularity are nothing but the troubled membrane of its surface.

LAON

And yet it is much easier to hear news from Sparta at first hand than from the bowels of the earth, from the Delphic cavern, and then to interpret the words of Apollo rightly — and repeat them soundly!

EPODE

And for this reason, O citizen of Athens, this Chorus meets you here. For you have come in search of words of truth as may be wafted to you from this side or that. Just as when Jupiter, wishing to find the very centre of the earth, sent forth two eagles, one from the west and the other from the east — determining the trench of Delphi by marking where they met in flight.

LAON

O Rumour of one hundred mouths, who taught you to steal truths from the gods, and comfort and peace from the hearts of men? To blight the unborn future in the womb of time? You are like Moloch of the Ammonites, whose bronze idol terrorised my childhood dreams, as it stretched forth its hands glowing red with heat towards my wicker cradle in the darknesses of midnight. But here I see a man approaching from afar, who by his swift and nimble gait I reckon for a Lacedaemonian runner. He props his descent on bladed staff, shambling down the hillsides like a mountain goat gambolling. Certainly he has been sent with some reliable news entrusted to his memory, or to scroll inscribed by deft hand. He comes on and on, drawing ever nearer.

EPODE
Let us hear him too, and learn what truth there may be in what you first brought us. Such truths of victories are more numerous than the atoms of sand that cling to the lips of the sea.

Laon moves toward the rear, where the Chorus to the Right and the Chorus to the Left meet. He comes to a halt near the Epode.

After one final bound, Daim slows his pace and enters with special caution.

CHORUS TO THE RIGHT
He who bounded like the goat spry-footed now approaches with a priest's solemnity.

CHORUS TO THE LEFT
According to Lycurgus' testaments, still honoured among the Spartans, they are to discipline even the movements of the body.

EPODE
Indeed the man delivers his message before he even parts his lips.

CHORUS
To no one else the Athenian chorus approaches, to ring him with their planetary rhythm.

LAON
O man of Sparta! If indeed you be a courier, announce the news entrusted you beforehand. Or if the tidings you bear are written down in depth upon some tablets, tell us, pray, for whose eyes are they destined?

DAIM

The first word from Sparta is: 'Victory or death!' And the second is a query from the Lacedaemonians: 'Where is our leader?' And the third some Lycaonian folklore: Every man who bears an iron sword, stands as if rooted.

Round shields, sacks of bread, and the well-smeared undercarriages of battle-wagons all wait ready, trembling, to move out.

The chaplains at their sty of one hundred wild boars and fattened porkers wait, keeping their flames alit — they sit, and brood.

And other couriers like me have been sent out, their mission memorised the same as mine — to carry back the answer to the question: 'Where is our leader?'

For now, I am to wait here until I have some news worth reporting — and now I've said so much I lack even Laconian words!

CHORUS ON THE LEFT

These nationalist fellows lose their tongue by a sudden uprush of vitality!

CHORUS TO THE RIGHT

They've already lost a whole generation by the arbitrary exile of the Parthenians.

EPODE

You don't offer much in return for the information you seek, Spartan. Come, inform your inquirers candidly of everything that needs to be known at this pregnant moment.

DAIM

I am a slave, citizen. And thus watching and keeping my tongue in check is second nature.

LAON

An Athenian slave, on the other hand, is subject only to his master. Beyond the confines of his house he is every man's equal. Although it may be different in Sparta, for this reason I demand you tell us what you know!

CHORUS
Thus speaks a sober and alert citizen of the Republic, making use of
the laws incumbent upon him, not letting them just lie fallow.
    Spartan courier, we adjure you to tell us what you know.

Pause.

LAON
Tell us — what do the peers hold to?

DAIM
'Victory — or death!'

LAON
And the common people?

DAIM
'Death — or victory!'

A moment of silence as both sides weigh Daim's words.

*   *   *

CHORUS
Bold indeed in strength and content is that Lacedaemonian tongue!
Bold indeed! But the customs of people the world over are as varied
as is their speech and the sayings proper to them. For this reason the
Athenian wishes to embrace all the beautiful things found in every
dialect, for no one raises a temple on one column alone.

LAON

To Daim.

If there be such a distinction between the cry of the peers and the cry
of the people, then I see that there is no man in all of Laconia who
would take upon himself the office of Strategos?

DAIM

Offended.

Hieroplites the brave holds his own!

CHORUS
Citizen, who is this man named Hieroplites?

LAON
Who is this man whose name we know not?

DAIM

Upset, moved.

All the world from the Laconian Gulf to the Corinthian Bay knows of brave Hieroplites!
    Whoever has borne more thwacks of the bat than he — let him show himself!
    Whoever has stolen the bread from the altar and shared it among his friends, let him call me a liar!
    Did the Messenian girls not fall into a frenzy when he pastured his goats along the border of their land?
    Has he not sailed to Crete, the cradle of all wisdom?
    'Hieroplites!' — who pronounces that name has said a great deal, and may now rest, like an ox on a holy day.

CHORUS
You Laconian chap — can you tell us no more of Spartan matters?

DAIM
Hieroplites, hurrah! Death or victory!

CHORUS TO THE RIGHT
Hardly has the wind from Phocis blown, and still no one knows the prophecy. What behoves us to reply to this man? What can the belaboured Laconian learn from us, in short order?

LAON
The oracle gives, to those who understand: thought; to the violent and vigorous: a naked command, and for the former, waiting is merely a murky prologue.

EPODE
O Spartan courier, in but a few days the Strategos chosen by the gods will be on his way to the Lacedaemonians.

Athens will take the news upon her hands from the lap of the gods. But — whether by the peaceful meads of Arcadia, or through these ruins will he make his way, or whether fifty oars will pull him along the Cycladean shore to the Lycaonian Bay, this is neither needful nor proper to know on the eve of war.

DAIM
As a slave, citizen, watching and keeping my tongue in check is second nature.

LAON
As the son of a fatherland readied for battle, watch wisely and prudently.

II

Near one of the city gates of Athens. The outer courtyard of Cleocarpus' summer house. To either side: walks lined with laurels and marble benches. A loom stands before one of the benches, along with all that appertains to weaving. Early evening.

Dorilla glances around. Eginea enters from the rear.

EGINEA
O how quickly time flies, Dorilla, when its use depends now on our will, and now on other things.

DORILLA
When one is waiting on one's father, the head of the house, one's sister, and one's step-brother, nothing depends on one's free will…

EGINEA

Drawing near the loom.

This last weave of my shuttle...

DORILLA
Gazing at it, would you recall the conversation that you broke off so
abruptly, when you left home for so long?

EGINEA
I'm trying to see which colour fades most quickly in the thirsty sun,
when left outside so long.

DORILLA
Think not, Eginea, that this low trick was played on you by a sister
who loves you little. Think rather that she, who became mistress of
the house in the absence of three other persons, alone — ordered the
loom to be left where it was.

    Let our father and our lord, upon returning from the Aeropagus,
note the empty bench and abandoned loom, and let one of the slaves
respond to his questions, severe in all his authority... not Dorilla.

EGINEA
What priest of the Aeropagus knows not the preparations that
are made as the holidays approach? Or who, passing through the
Pnyx, will not come across the chorus masters and intuit how much
rehearsals the daughters of Athens are engaged in, especially when
new hymns are being readied?

DORILLA

Half-whisper.

By new poets...

EGINEA

Especially if they are to be new hymns and if the daughter of a certain Aeropagite is to be the choragos responsible for the whole chorus?

DORILLA

Should such (as you say) sacred tasks not be thought of beforehand, and not of a sudden…?

EGINEA

I suddenly recalled my dream, Dorilla!

DORILLA

Ah! And has it been interpreted propitiously?

Ah! Perhaps there was a real crowd of the curious in the humid forecourt of Phobetor?

FIRST SLAVE GIRL

Running in.

The gardener has caught sight of our lord your father beneath the great larch, at the parting of the copper paths…

SECOND SLAVE GIRL

The gardener long ago saw our master your father beneath the great larch. The bath attendant is to draw him water.

THIRD SLAVE GIRL

Our lord your father has set his foot upon his property. He is near at hand…

DORILLA

Your dream, Eginea, tell me your dream…

EGINEA

I will, my pigeon…

She sits at the loom. Enter Cleocarpus from the rear, preceded by slaves. He halts and gazes awhile at his daughters, and then makes a sign with his hand that they are to remain where they are, before passing through them like a man exhausted.

CLEOCARPUS

With a blissful smile.

Indeed, this is the courtyard of no Egyptian home, where men in backwaters busy themselves with women's matters, while the chirping and bustle of female voices are heard on all hands…

He moves aside toward the white columns of the courtyard.

DORILLA

Aside.

And… he gives her a pat on the head!

To Eginea.

I see, sister, that you've served the gods today.

EGINEA

Slowly winding her material.

In your name I hung a wreath of white roses, where they flame by themselves.

The First Slave Woman nears Dorilla with a message.

DORILLA

Rising, to Eginea.

Thank you, darling. I hasten off to make our father's bed.

EGINEA
However many times I see him as he returns from watch at the Aeropagus, it seems as if the pale moonshine were glowing from his hair and stars were spilling from the pupils of his eyes. Sister, let me go and prepare his bed.

DORILLA
You've already served the gods today.

She exits.

EGINEA

Watching her leave.

The daughters of the gods! The daughters of Jupiter, who engage the poets with inspiration.
The question is whether the gods are better and more often served by the slow and simple heart of a quiet girl, bustling about among the walls of her home, or by her, who plunges with all her being into the verdicts set beforehand by fate and, entering them and having to enter them and striving to enter them and unable to withdraw, withdraws from them by tearing herself away, in shivers?!

A stone falls, tossed in from the bay-lined pavements, wound about with a pomegranate stem bearing flowers.

EGINEA

Picking it up and rushing toward the shadowy bays.

Not one step forward! Did I not say no earlier than the first star?

TYRTAEUS

From the shadowy depths.

It seemed to me that it would burst forth as soon as I entered here, and that it would rise in the heavens as soon as I pointed with my finger…

EGINEA

Threateningly.

If you take one step forward I'll… I'll… It'll no longer be the first star, but the seventy seventh!

TYRTAEUS

Vanishing back in the shadows.

The milky way entire…

FIRST SLAVE GIRL
Laon, the son of the household and your brother, has handed his horse to the stable boy and is on his way to you.

EGINEA

Pointing to the loom.

I reckon that your lord my father will deign take his supper in a moment's time, before the first shadows of the night fall…

The First Slave Girl and two others begin bustling about, setting up furniture necessary for a meal.

LAON

Entering.

I see that I've plucked a twin blossom of your pomegranate, involuntarily. Perhaps from that same tree, the same branch? Whence have you yours, my noble sister?

EGINEA

Pinning her flower among her braids.

I'm using it as a pattern for a petty little project such as interest women; it bloomed right next to this loom. And yours, O noble brother — let yours rest in the thick tresses of Dorilla, so that both sisters will be equally garnished.

Without a pause, craftily.

At any rate, you oughtn't abandon your sisters, you oughtn't abandon that dear pigeon of ours, Dorilla, for so long!

DORILLA

Entering from that side of the courtyard where she directs those setting the table.

Laon!

EGINEA
Lean here you brows, dear. He wants to pin a flower in your hair…

At a slow pace, enter Cleocarpus from the courtyard to supper. Catching sight of Laon, he makes a friendly gesture with his hand, then he reclines on the bench spread for him. Laon and the women draw near.

LAON
To see you at rest, O my lord and my father, I don't know how fast I'd be able to urge my legs, but I was told at the Pnyx (something I might have surmised myself) that the debates at the Aeropagus on this pregnant night were to last long (as if they were ever any less weighty, any different). And so, in order not to be too far distant from your thoughts and wishes, I gladly accepted the call of my superiors to see to the men working at the port, to whom a free hand is proper, to the craftsmen who busy themselves with things which, if I may say so, are not completely unfamiliar to me. And there, like a fresh

nut which, perfect in its roundness, sloughs off its heavy green coat when it is golden and ripe, thus did we slide into the waters of the sea a skilfully constructed, new Corinthian galley — not without the usual libations and the first gay turn around the harbour.

CLEOCARPUS
Not in vain, not in vain am I used to repeat, O Laon, that the daughter of Jove, who gazes upon the Athenians with her sea-green eyes, never ceases to remind them of the blue expanses of the ocean. Let all of the nation's lads trust the flinty strength of their shoulders, in swiftness and nimbleness taking their example from the stag, to become the pride and joy of the applauding crowds and the men who apportion the boundaries of the fields Olympic! But let the mature citizen, the unfettered mind, harness the wild strength of the watery element, and increase the common good by commerce on the waves... What, truly, is more like the things of the gods than that skill of plotting the stars, the art which our sweet Thales excels in, that man, whose researches were once considered barren?

LAON
Less practical, father, than the labours of his own cook...

DORILLA
... who at least was helpful in her simplicity...

CLEOCARPUS

Again to Laon.

One might say that if one learnèd in heavenly things deign train his eyes anew upon the earth, he should take in hand government of the elements and thus wield all the power that the ocean affords — and that is the element, which first and most willingly subjects itself to man; but first, indeed, his mind must rise unto the heavens.

EGINEA

Looking aloft.

As flowers on the summit of a tree, so do the stars seem to me to be the blooms at the apex of this world.

One would think it time already for the first of them to blossom!

DORILLA

Her gaze trained lower.

I see a guest hastening near.

LAON
I recognise him — the polished son of Charikles!

GUEST

Nearing in haste, out of breath, addressing all immediately, in agitation.

No Koreb, no Koreb, the man most born to riding, has ever cast behind the hooves of his steed so much dust, so quickly and in so little time, as I have today, urging my foaming Thessalian charger around the ambit of the city walls!

Noticing the presence of the old man.

It is my honour to visit the noble dwelling of the third Aeropagite...

He takes the place indicated him, and continues with his story, pausing from time to time to catch his breath.

And so I am able to report that there is no longer any mystery... the rumour has been proven true...

Pausing once more, with a glance toward the Aeropagite.

Such being the case, I wished to break off and visit at least for a moment the family of the worthy pentakontarch, where they watch deep into the night. I was the first to bring the news, the unchanging and strange truth concerning the peculiar destiny of Tyrtaeus...

LAON

With an expression of disgust, he turns to the Aeropagite and then turns his gaze to the faces of the women.

'Twas not too many days ago — I remember it as if it were today — when I wrote that verse for the Lesser Bacchanalia, that poem (while the rhymes of Tyrtaeus were whistled off in mockery by all) — Who in the whole city would have dared to admit the thought, even as something most improbable, that that scribbler, who had been so recently jeered at, would stand at the porch of the great Theseus wreathed in the bays of Apollo!?

CLEOCARPUS

With a half-smile.

And so there does remain one mystery: how long has one to wait upon the day, marked with a white pebble, for the rhymes of the oracle of Delphi to be interpreted properly...

Cleocarpus gestures to the women to withdraw from the conversation of the men: Eginea and Dorilla join hands and withdraw into the shades of the laurels.

GUEST

As at first, speaking without regard to those present.

It was not long ago that here, nearby, before the dwelling-place of the worthy pentakontarch — I remember it like today — who did not speak of the hobbling Tyrtaeus, that he was a 'cripple,' a 'gimp?' Who, indeed, did not call him 'one-eye'? Today, when a cavalry of one hundred Spartans saddled up and plunged their long spears into the earth before the temple of the great Minerva, when the people have set forth from the Pnyx in order to gaze upon the foaming steeds, the red chlamydes and the silent figures of the bronze horsemen — today, when Tyrtaeus slowly ascended the marble steps and the chorus stood beneath the peristyle in rows, themselves so like unto columns, today it was noted that the shambling gait of the favourite of the gods is not without a certain grace — that this is the gait common to such men as are used to dominate the swaying waves of the sea, or those who are not over-eager to lunge at things that ought to be presented to them. Today, indeed, it has been noticed for the first time that such a narrowing of the left eyelid is the mark of a piercing glance, skilled in finding its mark. Today, the voice of the people is indeed the voice of the gods...

Long live the Strategos! But I hear my horse neighing impatiently...

He rises and leaves, so deep in thought as barely to make a gesture of farewell.

CLEOCARPUS
The fickle opinions and changing judgements of the generality, so like the waves of the sea, should hardly trouble those to whom the elements uncover their truth in their depths, and not by that which sparkles on their surface. But jealousy, when it shakes a man's heart, does not allow thought to enter there, where indeed the first truth is to be found; he who plunges within to discover it, is rewarded twice over with the strength expended in the effort.

Those who are discouraged at the injustice of their contemporaries are like a man sitting on a coachbox who stares at the movement of the wheels, which seem to turn backwards as well as forwards, and thus begins to doubt the possibility of progress. But those who are tormented by envy look only to their sides, and derive the strength to push onward only if they can see their rivals inching before them... Neither of these are able, really, to master the elements as the gods and virtue require. Their inner pain arises from the fact that, unaware that they are acting against themselves, they suffer from the sense of not being able to act at all.

Cleocarpus rises slowly and, resting his hand on Laon's arm, begins to move toward the exit.

CYPRIAN KAMIL NORWID

Can it be that even you, O Laon, felt a momentary twinge of envy upon learning of the peculiar destiny of Tyrtaeus?

LAON
As I support you with my arm, dear sir, there is only one thing I lack, for complete happiness, father!

CLEOCARP
Speak, my son! Speak, Laon!

LAON
As I support you with my arm, father, I'd like to be closer to you... in blood.

CLEOCARPUS
You have two sisters...

LAON
Two sisters...

CLEOPCARPUS
Do not both of them call you 'brother?'

*   *   *

They pass through the courtyard and enter the house. Dorilla first emerges from the shade of the laurels, while the slave girls enter from the other side. Dorilla directs them in clearing away the table.

DORILLA
Eginea my sister, look: the stars are reflected on the glassy surface of the wine in Laon's cup!

EGINEA

Distractedly.

Down it, my sister! I seem to hear the neighing of a steed...

DORILLA

The polished son of Charikles speeds round the city again, swifter than rumour.

EGINEA

Halting before the house.

I'll remain a bit to hear the nightingales begin their song.

DORILLA

I won't leave your side until you tell me your dream.

EGINEA

I won't tell you my dream unless you first allow me to listen to what the nightingales have to say about our dreams.

DORILLA

Passing over the threshold.

They'll churn your thoughts, and instead of dreams, you'll bring me bird-brain stories.

III

Another part of Cleocarpus' gardens. Night.

EGINEA

I thought a pomegranate flower fell at my feet — but I see it's nothing but a dry leaf…

    I thought I saw an impatient star flash by, but it was nothing but a lightning-bug.

    That which is in the heavens seems to be glowing before me on the earth, while the things of earth seem heavenly to me. Have both heaven and earth retreated from me, or do they possess me in a whirl of unfamiliar frenzy?

Now, unfortunately, I even cease to trust myself: is it a round stone against which my trembling foot now strikes?

Picking something up from the path.

A humid bud, and I shiver with a winged thrill that pierces me entire, pulsing so strongly, so fleetly and evenly, as if a chord were struck that resounds from the core of my person to the zenith of the skies...
I am become rhythm itself... I can err no more. It's... him!

TYRTAEUS
For a pebble that fell athwart your path today, you stopped the beating of my heart. It seemed to you the most vulgar thing in the universe. Would the divine Hercules have been able to toss a flimsy flower such a distance?... O spellbinding woman! That stone, wrapped in a blossom, is the secret of the world's reality. It is one of the richest gems of your sex; it is your world... and this is what offends you! Indeed, in your anger, you knocked against the world entire.

Pause.

'Thus are they all!' I used to say, blaspheming. Today I say: 'Thus are you, for the briefest moment...'
Thus, I say, are you as well...

EGINEA
And so, Tyrtaeus, for this I deceived my sister and my hoary-headed father, so that the first word of our meeting should be misunderstanding and a yearning, so similar to blame? Why does the waiting heart never attend in tune to the way that events progress and turn out at last?

TYRTAEUS
There you have the pit of that pebble, wrapped in the purple of the pomegranate flower, providing it with the necessary heft...
When the flower falls upon its target, the petals expand and the pebble rolls away...

Who of those strolling here tomorrow will come across its dense brows and decipher what that peaceful little pebble initiated the night before?

EGINEA
You are following your thought, Tyrtaeus. I chased my heart here.

TYRTAEUS

Offering his hand and his arm.

It led you not astray.

EGINEA
Tell me then what you've done today.

TYRTAEUS
I gave life, to take a lifetime, and received…what?

I gazed upon faces green with envy, and had to take the full measure of the entire society; guessing at that, I was impelled to see the future, and in grasping the future, I was destroyed by sadness. And I thought I should do something, anything, so that in the evening a sweet voice should ask 'What did you do today…?'

And I picked an amaranth pomegranate flower, winding it around a little pebble; I lifted my arm, gazing at the sky, and it seemed that I saw the flash of a star in the aether… And I threw the stone into the myrtle-clipped courtyard of Eginea's house, committing in so doing an unknown vulgarity: in other words, heavy, fleshly stumblings!

That's what I did… and a lot of other things as well, but all of them gloomy! For the great countenance of Athens entire, turning upon me for the first time in my life, has turned away again for the last. I am to bid farewell? Or hello? I've never been free to choose. And yet step by every step I must give greetings, greetings… At each of the thirteen gates I must remind myself beforehand that I will meet with thirteen acquaintances, who will greet me today with a confidential smile. A horseman pulls up near Kerameikos and, leaping down gracefully, embraces me with 'O divine, O sweet

Tyrtaeus!' This was the son of Charikles, who just a few days before was mocking me…

Among the shadows of the Nike peristyle worthy matrons and their daughters were standing. This one and that tosses white roses toward me, thinking not how hard it is for one born crippled to bend down and lift them from the dust… Although they know my handicap well, for they jeered at it but yesterday!

At the Prytaneum a grey-haired man thumps me on the shoulder as he goes along with a great number of other men (I'd never seen him in my life before), and as he passes on, without a word, he shoots in my direction an expression like that of an accomplice.

And near the lyceum! And by the theatre! By the theatre? Why is all this not occurring *in* the theatre?

At the final entrance to the temple of Bacchus a gigantic man falls at my feet and, darting his eyes around like a criminal, whispers 'Come with us, with us, O person foretold by the heavens! We, the giants, have been seeking just such a one!' This was some sort of Tsarohay — of the Scythian nation who scorned me as a blind cripple when I was tutoring his patron's children.

O, Athens is a lovely place! A holy place, strength-giving to her chosen sons; one who gives them strength the day after the voices of the gods are heard spilling decisively over a man who had been spurned by heels all his earlier life long… If one could only toss a pebble from here into the urn of the heavens, certainly this Athenian people would outvote Apollo himself in this matter concerning me…

They continue on together: Tyrtaues halts and sighs before beginning:

Why do these songs, weak and uncertain, whimper?
Limping bastardly?
Why is this lute of such dry-rotten timber
And not of ivory?
And yet, whence come these tears upon my face
My heart asks — from such clumsy odes?
Their banished queen, in all her vibrant grace
Goes hidden, in a juggler's motley clothes!

And he, whom the spirit of the ages draws
Upon his back, as Jove's great bird
The sun, why is he not torn by the claws
Of lions, but rather trampled by the herd?
Why did the larvae of black Erebus
Flush once more at the tuneful breath
Sung down to them by yearning Orpheus,
Who stinted not their tone, or strength?
He did not for the Furies twist his tongue
Into some screeching hecatomb of Hell
When he descended for his wife: sweet, young,
Alas! and mortal — he mortal as well.

*   *   *

Yes, you, who traipse your feet along the sand
Splendidly shod in brilliant gold cothurn
That shapes the dust of Hell like potter's hand
Into the smooth orbs of curvaceous urn,
No longer fierce, the god of Hell himself,
Charmed by your song, so did he respect you;
You, clad in purple (wretchedness, not wealth)
You — king — tell me: who are you subject to?

Pause. Then, somewhat frenzied.

In deserts, not in gardens, cedars thrive,
They flourish sole, beneath the baking sun;
And great poets? Eginea! They arrive
When there are none!

More softly.

So many pages in the book of Time —
This word is formed of breath, and that of spirit;
Such, sung from rooftops, settles into rhyme
For those with ears to hear it.

EGINEA
We've reached the end of the path. I didn't want to halt you as you strode along so energetically, and now look: you've tangled your hair in the boughs of the laurel.

She untangles the leaves from his hair.

Indeed, there's too long a distance between the great poets…

TYRTAEUS
That's how it's always been, Eginea. That's what my song's about:

In deserts, not in gardens, cedars thrive,
They flourish sole, beneath the baking sun;
And great poets? Ah, they only arrive
When there are none!

*   *   *

You spoilt the whole beauty of the rhyme and unpinned the bays from my hair, among which my sick eyes and the end of the path entangled me. Oh! It wasn't this I expected and desired from a woman…
     And yet I'll tell you that without you, nothing's worth…
     Nothing!
     Even the Delphic oracle itself is incomplete without a woman.
     Listen! What I'm telling you is important!

They seat themselves among the myrtles.

Today I saw one hundred Lacedaemonian men from the upper class (which they call the 'equals' or 'peers')… It's an understatement to say that I saw them: for it was for me and towards me, and I might even say after me that they gathered here. Did I speak with them? I'm not sure if the word of Spartans is a stage of human speech.
     Whatever the case may be, there are some idioms which are mutually untranslatable.

This I gathered in a flash at my first meeting with the Lacedae-monian envoys; and surmising nearly the entirety of what my mission was to be, my spirit spoke, praising in wonder the wisdom of the gods contained in that Delphic oracle!

And so I passed along their ranks, praying silently in my soul, striking this one and that on his arm of granite and having them understand without speech my entire determination by my engagement, my strength. But when I touched their breasts, however many times I lay my hand upon the region of their heart, behind that iron shield, my throat constricted to find — I tell you, Eginea — no human heart there beating!

More softly and subdued.

This is a great mystery. I'm shot through with a cold tremor as I try to explain this to you in confidential terms, but this I am enjoined to do by the heavens. Listen:

Leaning near her.

That entire race of people has turned to iron. The last word of Lycurgus's testament was born into the world with this generation created by its legislator... All is finished, and no god will create anything more there... Nor is there any place there for God, like some off-cast or deformed child, whom they expose to death according to the law before he is able to crawl out of his crib. And so the history of the Lacedaemonians has reached its limit, just like their language!

And so I am sent there, to prepare a place for the father of the gods...

Eginea makes a sign, and he pauses.

EGINEA

Noting that he has stopped speaking.

It was nothing... Just one great falling star. But though my eyes were lost in the heavens, I was listening to you all the while. Go on!

TYRTAEUS

This is a great mystery, Eginea, that no human descendants will come of besotted Pygmalion. You've heard of that sculptor from scripture, how he burned for the stone creation of his own hands so, that it came alive in his arms; that he took her to wife, and had a child of her. The son's name was Paphos...

Don't become terrified at my words, nor lift your eyes to the heavens to see if any star should begin to tremble, if I tell you that the people of Lacedaemon are the descendants of that very Paphos!

That Lycurgus was none other than old Pygmalion, who, embracing that ideal sculpture of his gave rise to a line of hard sons, whose shanks and brows and those most noble areas around the heart all shine like cut marble. This is a generation of the gymnasium, a republic of gladiators, the end of whom was foretold in Delphi. But they did not comprehend a single word of that prophecy, even though it spoke of them. Surely, Apollo said that 'Sparta shall remain as long as the law of Lycurgus is not exhausted...'

I want to laugh, O, I want to shriek with horrid laughter!

Truly, that's the way it is, the way things stand — and this is coming to be. A few tens of thousands of healthy stones, well chiseled with iron; a generality planned by one architect's foresight — they have their end at their beginning; and are monuments as long as the sketch is being plotted! Before, during, and after the construction — they are stone!

*   *   *

O, history! Has there ever been such a thing? O, history: behold — did the Athenian republic come about because of such elements? Kodrus the great, the last king... does he not rule still, ever-present in his very absence? He, seeking death at the point of the Doric spears against which the royal breast rested; he, clothing himself in peasant's homespun, he, falling with that artfully fragile scythe in his grip, when he cried out: 'This is the end of the Athenian kingdom!' — do you understand, Eginea? — he became the cornerstone of the transformation of his people, and thus Athens was moved to become a republic following his death.

He did not make apprentice-slaves of them like some dull and rigid craftsman, but, like a master artist, he created for eternity! His finger, soaked with blood during the Doric battles, traced his legacy in the sky. And this no one can efface with a cloak, rub how he will — thus Kodrus became immortal.

Such rule, O Eginea, is citizenship; and thus the citizenry became kings. It was otherwise with old Lycurgus, a military chief of children brought up to war since the cradle, the sculptor of marble youngsters, a man who was faithful to his own sketches, with all his strength, rather than to the divine power of transformation.

What was born of Kodrus shares in the divine, as do the offspring of those men who had their dalliance with the daughters of heaven. But the offspring of Lycurgus share in the stone of the earth — half-statuary herds descended upon the earth and, as long as stone can be victorious over flesh, so long will they be victorious...

But when they vanquish, wherever they do, not one stone remains upon another...

Suddenly.

Nevertheless, since I am to go there, some horrid truths have been discovered to my eyes.

How great a love will be necessary to me, how great — judge for yourself!

And this is why I ask you to rest your white shoulder against my bosom and give in to this so noble need of my heart entire. No one has ever called any of the daughters of Athens to love with such sacred violence. And if you do not understand me, if you still do not understand me and accept me, there will be no Athens any more, since there will have been in all of the city no woman!

EGINEA
Listen, Tyrtaeus! Let my aged father stand before me here, preceded by his servants as he sets out with torches to the general meeting; let those torches light up our eyes, lighting us up from tip to toe — as we are tangled in one another's arms; let all of the household surprise us here: and I shall say without hesitation and with the same tone of voice, that all of the Aeropagus, all of it, rests here upon the virgin

breast of this girl! For if the divine voice of Delphi has thundered out your name, this daughter of Athens will not give it the lie. Yes, I tell you truly, Tyrtaeus, no son of the great republic has been loved with a greater love than you. But not today, not now, not as this night ebbs away will you toss me across your steed for my locks to entwine with his mane in the wind. So violent a wind is not that which will cool my brow and dry my tears...

Tyrtaeus, you shall leave me in the city of your people, you leave me entwined about your thought and your heart, along with that power, with which I might confront today the Olympic gravitas of my father. The power that I take from you — and I shall call upon it myself before long — I know not how to call it this evening. With this power I shall await the moment proper to a decisive enterprise, at which time I will unfurl it before my father, along with all that I feel. And if my father will not understand me, the gods will; and if no one will understand me, your people will understand our orders, as will the horses you leave here, fleet of foot, sprinting over the dew of night — Oh, before us thunder the hooves of Victory!

Tyrtaeus, it seems to me that I have now grown to equal stature with you. Behold: are my shoulders now not as broad as your own? So broadly expands my breast, so full, so securely...

TYRTAEUS
I had a dream, Eginea, last night: I dreamt of this...

EGINEA

Placing her finger on his lips.

Have I not grown to your stature here in your embrace, becoming your equal, Tyrtaeus?

Say no more — say nothing more! I had a dream last night: I dreamt of this.

*   *   *

TYRTAEUS
Let us dream together! — Let us watch together! Let us live and die and fly away into the whirling heavens together!

EGINEA
God has wrapped us two round in the folds of his cloak of aether. How might the choragos of Ceres abandon you? Let slave girls and barbarian maidens sell their love for fields of grain, for a couple of golden trinkets, or what have you of earthly valuables. It was not on such trade that the history of this fatherland developed, which trod down the walls of Troy! There is no place beneath this sky upon which Helen gazed, or where the Aeropagus rises, for houses of such traffic…

TYRTAEUS
Such love, O choragos, is all of Greece — it is freedom, truth, and sanctity…
      And for this reason, when I shall ride into an unknown city…

EGINEA

Interrupting.

And when the Lacedaemonian maidens will strew the path before your charger with bay leaves, Tyrtaeus, remember: I am with you…

TYRTAEUS
And this is why, when I must struggle at the war within, and gaze from a hard chariot upon the breaking waves of bloody arms among the whirling eddies of sand…

EGINEA
I shall be with you.

TYRTAEUS
And for this reason when I grow lonely amidst the battle lost, and bending down, lap at a puddle to slake my thirst…

EGINEA
I shall be with you.

IV

A sycamore lined walk in Sparta. Here and there, seats beneath the trees; to the rear, a broad road leading to mountains; to the right, afar, one sees the Hippodrome. A blind Spartan invalid passes through. Boys are playing at war, and begging the old man to tell them stories of his exploits.

FIRST

Running up to the old man.

Just one little rhapsody, one more! We'll all sit in a circle at your feet like little goats beneath the branches of an oak when the moon is waxing...

CHORUS
We'll point out every living man that passes, and tell you his story. Just one more rhapsody — promise us!

FIRST
And we'll give you the bread we steal — nobody steals better than we do.

CHORUS
Look: a whirl of sand is approaching from afar. It's a Lacedaemonian courier with his staff.

OLD BLIND MAN

Sitting down beneath a sycamore.

That would be Daim, my boys, my barefoot dancing boys. That is Daim, son of a friend of mine, a martial courier. He will have a rhapsody for you, brought over the hills, pulsing with redder blood than mine…

Searching for his staff.

Let him approach, lads, call him over, tell him that I am one of the peers who twenty years ago lost his eyes in the Messenian swelter; he, who kicked away his one and only son, feeling a wetness on him and thinking it blood, not sweat — the blood of his child, on his neck, from behind!

BOYS
O righteous Spartan!

OLD MAN
He who first submitted the law that whoever tosses crumbs of bread to sparrows shall be pummelled with staffs, for encouraging the citizens to waste and encouraging birds to grow lazy!

BOYS
O righteous Spartan!

OLD MAN
Yes, the birds saw him from afar and flew away, tree to further tree as he progressed.

Boys, what do you see now on the broad road, such as my eyes will never again?

PRIMUS
We see, O righteous Lacedaemonian, Daim, as he proceeds along the sycamore lined road in orderly strides. He has softened his energetic leaps as he grows nearer, and takes on a humble mien as he approaches us, as is proper to a Spartan.

But behind him, where the paths branch off the great trunk of the road, we see, O righteous Lacedaemonian, O manly peer, here and there people falling away, like deserters or the wounded. Some of them (if my eyes do not deceive me) are making signs to the cavalry, who rush ahead; others lean aside and hobble.

OLD MAN
If it be catastrophe, my boys, my barefoot dancing boys; if it be a catastrophe, O disciplined boys exercised with the rod, red with welts and scrapes; if it be a catastrophe, then raise the choral chant! Victory or death!

CHORUS OF BOYS
Death or victory!

DAIM

Responding.

Victory or death!

Enter Tyrtaeus in long priestly robes, with a hood covering his head, hobbling like a wounded man. He enters from a side path, and then seeks a seat along the side.

TYRTAEUS
Death… or — victory?
    Ruffians of tussles, no war heroes — they know nothing but those two interrogatories; passion in their cry confirming what has changed; they know nothing…
    To die? To be victorious? these have taken root in their throats and have become the only speech they know…

He seats himself at one of the trees to the side.

OLD MAN
I'll find you with my rod, Daim. Come here and place yourself before one of the peers, the one who twenty years ago lost his eyesight in the Messenian scrape, alone, before this peer who summons you, say what you have to say!

DAIM
Your son, Hieroplites, is among the living…

OLD MAN

Raking his rod through the air.

Be therefore cursed and take my blows upon your shoulders, man, so like unto a traitor! No righteous Spartan asks you about one son — no!

Speak of what concerns us all, about our leader first, and not about anyone's son!

So customs corrupt blow in on me from all sides. I give the great Diana my sincere thanks that I shall never more behold the face of such dwarves!

What of the strategos? If you've seen that man with your own eyes, tell me!

DAIM
I saw that man, the leader, in the cavalry camp and among the ranks of the heavy hoplites, as with a tuneful voice he foresang the defeat...

He was a cripple, and one-eyed!

BOYS
Barathra! Bara-thra-rra-ra!

OLD MAN
The Barathra is unknown to the Athenians. Indeed, the most crippled or retarded citizen might be born there and hide himself away. Nevertheless, O healthy and beautiful boys, a peer is speaking to you, who advises you to ask first if that leader lost his eye by pursuing the craft of war.

DAIM
The man is an Athenian. The leader's craft is that of the poet.

OLD MAN
Barathra then, three times Barathra! O, treason of the Athenian people... or this is the end of prophecy from Delphi!

BOYS

To Barathra with the cripple! To Barathra with the one-eyed fellow!
To Barathra with all the silver-tongued! Barathra-rra-ra!

TYRTAEUS

Aside.

Vox populi!

OLD MAN

Step aside, boys, and you, courier, sit down here beside me; the peer
permits you. Seat yourself and whatever it is I will ask you, whisper
your answer into my ear.

BOYS

Going off.

Barathra!

CENSOR MORUM

To his suite.

These boys running about without a paidonom need some lashing!
How's that for a respect for holy places! And each foot of the
Lacedaemonian land is truly holy, something we owe to the divine
Lycurgus; but twice and three times sacred is the place where the
senate and kings and peers gather, and the land that receives the
Spartan soldiers returning from battle — however it ended.

They pass through.

CHORUS OF PEERS

Entering and seeking a place.

Let us confer amongst one another quietly, but with just words, deciding what the verdict ought to be concerning this misfortunate day.

CHORUS OF PRIESTS
The sacrifice to Jupiter the Conductor was offered, and the men set out from camp to the accompaniment of flutes, with the sacred fire, like a comet, blazing at their head. How might this have been fended off? How does one fend off a falling bolt of lightning?

CHORUS OF POLEMARCHS
What is it after all that carries the victory? And what returns covered in blood? Certainly not a song, nor the drawn-out words of exiled Lacedaemonians…

CHORUS OF PRIESTS
I saw him dismount from the saddle when he arrived; the people had prepared a feast for him in his tent. And I saw with my own eyes how he drank from the golden horn, singing fragments of the old hymn of the Argonauts.

CHORUS OF PEERS
Such a citizen-strategos the Athenian people send to heroic Sparta at a moment so critical!

CHORUS OF PRIESTS
And so let the senate and the kings of the senate, and the ephors themselves, and all the peers, polemarchs, censors and priests get a good sense of how the grass grows at their feet…

TYRTAEUS

Tossing off his cloak and steps forward.

The voice of the state!
    I've only to hear two more: the voice of God and that of my conscience!

Flutes are heard; enter the Royal Choruses.

HERALD
The senate is coming, and the ephors, and the aged senate kings.

POLEMARCHS
Truly untimely is he who arrives when spears raised aloft in thickets are swept from the hands of soldiers by the whistling currents of the air. Neither gesture, nor command, by single word quick or protracted, could be heard in the tempest of war. Whatever fate brings and whatever anyone might foretell, everything is lost, often, through untimeliness — and by the pronunciation of words according to mood, like to the songs girls sing.

PRIESTS
And that's the sort of citizen-strategos the Athenian people sent to Sparta — a leader untimely and who, retreating to his tents... as far as I can see did not accompany the broken Lacedaemonian choruses on their wretched return.

SENATE
The worthy senate does not oppose such complaints in the least: but judgement is what carries the day with us: the time at which the man of prophecy arrived in Lacedaemonia is not the affair of Tyrtaeus himself, who was sent; the blame lies with the Athenian people, who determined when to send him.

KINGS OF THE SENATE
We heard nothing said by the newly arrived man of prophecy that was foreign to us; on the contrary: he declared subjection to the government of Sparta a sacred thing; he recommended that the memory of the famed kings of the past be held in honour; nothing can be found that we might prematurely condemn in him.

HERALD
The Athenian citizen, the man of prophecy declared by Delphic Apollo, the strategos Tyrtaeus...

Tyrtaeus reveals himself to all.

FIRST EPHOR
Untimeliness is absence, and he whom absence declares innocent,
let him give broad access to him who comes to grip the wreath, even
that won in misfortunate struggles.

Tyrtaeus moves away with his suite to take a place along the side.

SECOND EPHOR
Come forth now, son of Hieroplites, since you will touch the wreath
with decided hand, let the polemarchs and knights give witness to you
and announce you; let the centurions thunder what they saw when
you were found on your place, before, in the glory of your fervour!

*The son of Hieroplites comes forth from the crowd and draws near the
chairs of the senators.*

CHORUS
It is enough if you receive the wreath of laurel, O youth, whose bold
deeds today no one has the strength to relate fully...

    If the countenance of heaven turned away from us during the
sacred battle

[...]⁴⁵

QUIDAM
... I recognised you in the crowd. I have something to show you, like
a visiting card — a little box, with some letters inscribed on the cover,
just a few minutes before, in pencil.
OMEGITT

Catches sight of Lia, takes the box and reads.

'Lia Sofistoff?' Madam!

---

45   Here occurs a lacuna in the manuscript. All that remains hereafter is a
fragment of the conclusion.

To the Referendary.

Scito te ipsum...[46]

QUIDAM

To Omegitt.

Don't halt so long — the crowd will tear us apart...

OMEGITT
To return to the subject of our conversation: here we have one more
gracenote, one more charm! This constant haste and rhythm, I say,
this inability to pause for a while under the penalty of being torn
apart and losing privacy or the thread of one's speech, which had
been so freely carried out; here and there that light, necessary quarrel
that mixes an unconsidered rhythm into a march... a quarrel that
dissolves into nothingness.

All of this is at the same time trivial and serious, forced and free,
garnished with withered (and unwithering, because never alive!)
flower petals sprinkled on the sides with a tear of white wax; all of
this taken together... Malcher!

MALCHER

Tossing a cloak over the shoulders of Omegitt.

Our horses are straining to leave the numbered place of our carriage.
I waited with your coat, looking left and right. For as the saying goes
(begging your pardon): 'Everywhere's fine to the peaceful in mind,
but there's no place like home!'

OMEGITT
Amen! I say to you...

---

46   Know thyself. Ironically, the title of a tract by Abelard (as whom Sofistoff
was dressed during the masquerade — matching Lia's Heloise).

PURE LOVE AT THE SEA BATHS

A COMEDY

My secret I entrusted to the night.
She passed it onward to the breeze, which blows
Where he lists; then the waves and the echoes
Inscribed it on the beach, where lissom bands
Of maidens passed by, dancing. In their flight,
My poems all they trampled in the sands.

From the Greek, C.N.

PERSONS

Julia
Marta
Feliks Skorybut
Erazm Count Flegmin
Male Servant

Scene 1
To the rear, the sea shore. To one side, nearer by, a sort of dairy with an arbour.

JULIA
You know, it's quite true what Erazm says
(Whose every word's an oracle of sense)
That human destiny is ruled by chance.
For otherwise, do you think that I would wish
To leave a letter like that one — my aunt's! —
Unanswered for so many days? A letter

From Aunt Irena, whom I so respect?
We know when we write letters, where they're sent,
But it's anyone's guess when they arrive,
And where! If only Auntie'd sent — last year! —
Such a… peculiar fellow as her charge,
I'd have had time enough to take in hand
This task (however strange and trifling it be),
But — just a few days before… the very eve of…
To take a letter from the bearer's hands,
Greeting the same with kin-like warmth, well, all
My duties are discharged, don't you agree?
But now I am at fault, not having answered
Auntie's letter — yes! Now I'm at fault!
And now there's no time left, the day before…
Why, I'm in such a tizzy lately, Marta,
I don't remember when we two last spoke!

MARTA
And thus the riddles keep accumulating.
What's Auntie after? And who is this charge?
And why do you keep calling this 'the eve of…'
The eve of what?

JULIA
                    Each of those questions, Marta,
Is of a different nature. You'd need logic
(Such as Erazm only possesses)
And memory, to avoid, in the end,
After too long a silence, when one would
Say everything — saying nothing at all.

MARTA

Significantly.

And is Erazm really so mindful?

JULIA

Another question!… Let's address the first.
Auntie Irena's still one of those matrons
Who hold the power of woman in high regard.
Their Queendom is of this world! Their influence
And rule omnipotent — and yet she can't
Handle this… gentleman! It's rather he
Who's got her wrapped around his little finger;
Whenever he pulls one trick too many, and clouds
Form crackling overhead, he pouts. He pouts!
And Auntie all but takes him on her lap
To cheer her blue-eyed boy. That he's in love
With some new girl each week is half the problem.
But now he's overstepped that line this time,
Where reputation is concerned — you see
Feliks, this time, went ga-ga for an actress!
And wants to be an actor now, himself!
So what does Auntie do, but pack him up
And send him off here, to the bathing beaches,
Trusting that constant commerce with Erazm
And my 'charms' (she writes it so — my 'charms')
Will have the needed corrective influence
On her scatter-brained ward. My 'charms' indeed!
How glad young Monsieur Feliks Skorybut
Will be to assess them publicly (theatrics!)
For three days after his arrival here,
He hastens with a box reserved — and look!
For tomorrow evening! For the very evening

Half-whispering, quickly.

Of my engagement… Now you know everything…

MARTA

I know enough to hug you, Julia,
But — engagement — to whom?

JULIA

                                    If you can't guess…
If you don't know already… but must ask…
To hear the mysterious final word…

Pause.

Remember that someday you'll be just like me
In this position — and I'll pay you back
With blushes on your startled rosy cheeks,
Asking you boldly and expressly: 'Who,
Pray, shall betroth you with a ring tomorrow?'

Pause.

Yet I shall be magnanimous today,
And just remind you that tomorrow night
Our little cénacle gathers, all of whom
Have missed you, dearly.

MARTA

                            If it's a chess party,
You know I can't play like you and Erazm.

JULIA
Erazm's good at other games as well.

Pause.

Do you feel hot? Do you know that fan of yours
Has won you a nickname here at the baths?
You're always waving it, always fingering it…

MARTA
One's hands must not be idle, be it pawn
Or fan one fingers… No one thinks it odd
To see your hands busy with chesspieces…
I… toy with a fan.

JULIA

        Listen — did you hear that?
Bells, and the tramp of donkeys. It's the hour
When they're drinking their milk. Marta, dear!
Goodbye for now! Remember me, always!

MARTA

Watching her as she goes off.

Tomorrow… is an important day for sure…

She exits in the opposite direction.

Scene 2

FELIKS

Approaching slowly, from the sea.

No! That would be a vulgar thing, a thing
Narrow and wretched, and impaired; it would be
(Let's speak frankly, shall we?) something stupid
Should one set boundaries to one's emotions;
Should one, beholding ONE enchanting profile
Brush all the rest into some murky background.
Medals and coins can have more than one profile
Set one upon the other — just as clouds
Gilt with the brilliant moonshine round their edges —
And this mars not the landscape; *au contraire*!
It's what enlivens nature…

Pathetically.

               For example,
That Diva (ah! with golden diadem
Upon her brow, as last I saw her!), say

I take her for the moon ALONE, exclusively,
Can others not float across her face like streams
Of gossamer mist? Fair nature is a book, no?
From which we've taken our lessons since ancient times?

Decisively.

No! Donna Klara's moon has been eclipsed,
And thereby she's more tragic still, since she —
Ah! She who poured with lissom hand my tea
Yesterday afternoon, the divine Julia!
Indeed! Since then the air's been silvered over...
I see her! And what matters that cold front
Of grumbling Erazms waddling from the north,
Swollen with sleety showers... It's getting cold.
You seek a parasol and think to lock
Your sad heart up at home.

Sighs.

                Yes! Leave, lock up...
These are but... words!

Liltingly.

In vain you'll curse yourself, and all
Your doggedness betray, decry;
Soon at her stoop again you'll call
But you won't find her there. And why?

One word that harms yourself, alone,
And then: to argue, mollify
In thought — You wander to her home
But — perhaps she's not there. And why?

And then — some happy guests drop by
To ring her round, draw up a chair,
And cut you off from her. Oh, why?

To chatter, sprawling everywhere!
Happy arrivals from infernal regions,
They crowd the house entire! Their name is Legion!

You wait them out, but still two stay,
With always 'one more thing' to say.
Then one gets up: 'Alas, I must
Be off; snaps watch shut, with a sigh…
But then he's back! 'Pardon, I just
Forgot my gloves…' Again he sits! Oh, why?

Perhaps it's better just to leave
Than be ignored and brushed aside,
And so you go, and still you grieve,
Stone-cold, yet broken hearted. Why?

The moon outside will be, as ever, dumb;
The constellations, as ever, shall roll
Along their paths, no living thing — not one! —
Will you find in those skies; no feeling soul
To weep before the CREATOR on high
The suffering of the earth-bound flesh, its dole,
That sparks in heaven no cry of shock; 'Lord, why?'

A servant enters with a letter. Feliks glances toward him.

That's Julia's servant… With a letter…

To the servant.

                                        Hey!
Who gave you this letter?

SERVANT
                        Miss Julia.

Feliks places his hand on the Servant's shoulder.

FELIKS
I'm sure you're happy with your service there,
But should you ever seek another place,
Remember me. Be well…

He tears open the letter and reads.

'My dear Feliks…'

With a quick flourish, he deposits the letter in his breast pocket. With strong feeling:

'My dear Feliks!' That is enough, already —
More than enough. No, that is… everything!
All that a man has ever dreamed about:
'My dear!' And written with her own sweet hand;
'My dear!' she writes — That opens the first line;
The most important words of the first line:
'My *dear* Feliks…' Oh, there we have enough:
Heaven and earth, and ocean, rock, and cliff,
And sand and wind — and this my walking stick,
My glove, my hand, my arm… my very heart…
Oh! everything is nothing in my eyes
Besides that 'Dear Feliks…'

He presses the letter to his heart and moves to leave. Blind to the world, he stumbles against Erazm, who is entering.

ERAZM
Feliks! Good day…

FELIKS
How would you know that it's a good day? No,
The very best of all days! You — cold man,
Hard and unfeeling creature…

Piteously.

Then again,
Perhaps it's not your fault; perhaps you can't
Be other than you are, who've never heard
The words 'MY DEAR ERAZM' on a woman's lips!

ERAZM
You needn't pity me overmuch, Feliks,
My entertaining friend, because tonight's
The eve of my engagement...

FELIKS
                              Eve? Why the eve?
Why not get married now — with whom you please?
Enriching mankind with one heart the more?
Farewell! I must seek out some lonely place,
Some beetling cliff above the ocean's harp
(The waves, you see, like fingers, on the cliffs...)
Where in my solitude I might savour
The missive that I wear upon my heart...

Exits, hand pressed upon his heart.

ERAZM
Like flannel trousers!

Scene 3

MARTA
How fortunate that our paths cross, dear sir!

ERAZM
For the first time in my life — I'm so happy
That nothing surprises me! I'd radiate
My joy upon whomever I should meet!

MARTA
Whomever you should meet?

ERAZM

                    Everyone, I mean.

MARTA

Well, that's deflating. I am no exception…

ERAZM

Exception! But you are exceptional,
Madame — to see you at this time of day,
When it's still cool, breeze blowing from the sea,
And you — exceptional indeed — stroll on the strand
Always with that beautiful fan in your hand…
So that, I've heard, the guests at the resort
Have taken to calling you — affectionately — the fan-palm.

MARTA

With melancholy.

This fan is the beautiful memento
Of such a magnanimously-minded person
That he forgets a gift as soon as given…
Or shades the memory with polite neglect…

ERAZM

Inspecting the fan a bit more closely.

That fan? Of course! Now I remember it…
But, such a trifle who might keep in mind?

MARTA

I keep this trifle always in my hand…

ERAZM

And so it glows with new meaning for me:
No longer just some petty token, that
A dancing partner once gave to a girl…

MARTA
All the more as one isn't always dancing…

Pause.

But no, you're right, sir. It is, in fact, a trifle…

She drops the fan on a bench.

A needless thing — a fan! At such a time
When the cool is blowing in from the sea;
Indeed, how cold it's gotten. Both the COLD
And common sense (which I know you esteem)
Urge my departure.

ERAZM
              I for one am dressed
As hour and season dictate. Here, I wander…
Thinking… Ah, Madame! thinking…

MARTA
                        Thinking what?

ERAZM
Thinking… today's the eve of my engagement.

MARTA
Is that thunder I hear? Did I just see
A lightning strike, afar? Or I'm mistaken…

ERAZM
I think you heard a wagon rolling down
The cobblestones, on the way to market.
This is that hour; today's a market day…

Casting a lazy glance at the bench.

Your fan — Madame…

MARTA

                    Thank you. And once again
It is your chivalrous hand, sir, gives it to me.

She exits hastily.

Scene 4
Julia's apartment. She is seated, writing. Enter Erazm with a little box in his hand.

JULIA

Tenderly.

Wait just a second — I'm writing to Auntie…
I'm almost done…

Writing.

                    You've got the rings, I see…
Hold on… I'm writing to my Aunt Irena…
I'm almost finished…

Writing.

ERAZM

Aside.

                  If a man might do
Everything at the hour appropriate,
He'd never be too soon, or ever late!
But when I'm made to wait, I use that time
To carry on my notes…

Extracting notebook and pencil.

                    So, in this way —
Never a wasted moment! Never too soon,
And never made to wait, in point of fact…

JULIA

With emphasis.

And yet I think, for now, it's all irrelevant:
Both haste and anticipation, after all.

ERAZM

Takes a seat close by.

One always has a right to one's exceptions
(Which all the same just prove the rule, you know!)
If we, in respect of the consequences,
Must pause our method's progress… what of that?
Method is method — rules are obligation.
I… can tolerate the infrequent exception,
And yet — the future generations of mankind?
Should my son, for example, set at nought
The method? Obligation? From his birth
I'd train him in a reverence for duty
— A piety for punctuality! —
Until he was the very incarnation
Of order… To everything its proper hour.

JULIA

Biting the pencil with her teeth.

As for my son, I'd ignite — from time to time —
A slight explosion of enthusiasm…!

ERASM

Suddenly.

Explosions can be fatal!

JULIA

Pathetically.

           … Which would make fall
The stones of system, and liberate the man!

ERAZM

Sweetly.

It would be hard, if not impossible,
To make such opposites agree in one
Nature…

JULIA

With irony.

    However, naturally, my son
Would be — close to you.

ERAZM

Bitingly.

        And my son, I reckon,
Would be no stranger to you.

JULIA
          You 'reckon'?
What's that supposed to mean?

ERAZM

Rising and glancing at his watch.

It's time to go.
The steam-boat's due to leave for England soon.

JULIA
And so, you're in a hurry all the same?

ERAZM
I'm very fond of British pragmatism.
And sometimes, when, here on the continent
One's made to wait for whole ages until…
Nothing quite soothes the nerves like visiting
Factories.

JULIA

With passion.

Ah? What sort of factories
Do you most gladly visit?

ERAZM

Unthinkingly.

Certainly
Not factories of gold! So far they've not
Been able to invent such things.

JULIA
Ah, if they did,
Then there'd be factories for wedding bands!

ERAZM

Ceremoniously.

I leave you to your letter. For the post,
Though it transport envelopes full of sighs
And tender heartbeats, is still a cold method,
Well-oiled machinery — a factory…
Subject to regulations… Madame, farewell!

Exits.

JULIA

Calling after him.

Farewell? Erazm — *au revoir!* I'm nearly done!

Alone, she gazes at the table, at which she had been writing, and then looks about the salon.

I'm nearly done… with what? My letter? Or…
What odd things happen in one's life! And now?
What did just happen here? And how? And why?
Did I offend him?… Or did he insult me?
Or have we both displaced some… vital atoms?…
Of unknown weight, and matter?… What is this?

She goes over to the place where he had been sitting. The box with the rings still lies there.

O! Misery! Wretched, disillusioned dreams…
All that a person plans — all that we plan —
Is of a sudden shattered. Why? Who knows?
Can it be that in this… traffic of hearts,
When soul and body at uneven steps
Draw close, all the while, destiny matures
Like some unpaid-off loan, and time, like Fate's

Usurer, treads at our heels, to suddenly
Lay hand upon one's shoulder and demand
Repayment, with exorbitant interest?
Or is it that, this moment of betrothal
Is like the conquering of some lofty hill.
And when one's eyes arise above the rim,
The whole horizon of her character,
And his, are seen in the bright, unobstructed air,
And all of Nature waits, hushed and revealed,
To ask here — Is this really what you want?
Sometimes, the mind suggests the oddest things...
But it's a bitter truth; so bitter sometimes,
That it may be best just to step away
Than gaze upon a landscape, from a mountain
That one might wish to leap from...

She gazes at the table.

O, that letter!
Let it remain unfinished, everything —
Unconsummated, separate, unknown...

Impetuously, she takes up her hat and shawl.

O sea! you ever-living cemetery!
You shall be my unique delight, your depths...
If they were to embrace me prematurely,
I'd fall in love with the faithful caresses
Of your waves, and the pale flash of your conchs
 I'd value more than human feelings. Come!
Let's go... and never more return to this!

Scene 5
*The seashore. The sea is troubled; a storm is coming on. Feliks, with the
letter in his hand.*

FELIKS

Darkly.

On that first line, on that first treacherous line,
Why did you not cease, eye, and with that eye,
My life?… Come, once again: Ha! 'My dear Feliks!
How kind of you to think of me, and send
Your offer of these box seats! Forgive me,
I so appreciate it, but tonight,
I just cannot accept them. For, you see,
Tonight I am to be engaged…' Again!
'I am to be engaged!' And then… and then!
'Julia.' *Basta*!

Approaching the waves.

                    Here now, sea, come on!
Jump at my throat now, like some wild beast
And scald my eyes with salt-foam venom! I am
Your prey, O sea! I call upon you! Listen!

Gazing at the waves.

It comes and goes… And mocks my broken heart!

MARTA

Looks around her, frenzied, searching.

Why did I not pick up that fan, and with
One fateful flourish, crush it in my hand
Before returning it to that… that betrothed moon-calf?
Or write upon it one or two last words
And fling it on the sand — yes, simply fling it!
That anyone might find it, read the words,
And spread the news to all the gossips here:
'Somebody threw herself into the sea

Today'— and when Erazm or Julia
Would hear that, maybe they'd think upon me,
Spare me one tender thought…

Catching sight of Felix walking into the waves.

                              Hey! You there! Man!
Is it deep there?

FELIKS

Darkly.

                    Too shallow for despair.

MARTA

With irony.

Sarcasm, everywhere.

FELIKS

Aside.

                    Hardly knee deep…

Pause, to Marta.

At times, even the chasms of the sea
Betray us…

MARTA
                    That man is no fisherman
Or rough bumpkin… but he's a pest!

FELIKS
                                That girl's
No local wench… But she's a lunatic…

MARTA
Listen, I'd like to find myself a boat
To go to sea today… I've got a task
I must get done with… But there's no boat here.

FELIKS

Aside.

O, let's be careful…

To Marta.

                        No one sails today.
The weather's rough.

MARTA
                        And yet you splash about…

FELIKS
Madame!
I'm searching for a pearl. It is my passion.
And passion — though you know it not — is blind,
And, being sightless, sees no consequence
That cool-headed folks — O, like that Erazm
Who's on his way here now I see, wrapped up
In prudent macintosh — clearly perceive,
Evaluating coldly…

MARTA
                        O, dear Heavens!

Straining her eyes.

Indeed — someone is coming… but toward the port
He's heading, turning round from time to time
As if he were expecting someone… Yes!
Erazm!

To Feliks.

  A second would suffice, I guess,
One moment — in the depths to toss oneself —
And those on the way here, would consider that
Oh, inappropriate! (Such a quandary
Crosses the mind — a mathematical
Problem…)

FELIKS
     The sea casts up, from time to time,
Deep thoughts from its trenches unplumbed, and yet
You are too charming, Madame, and too young
To furrow so your brows… (Please, pardon me
If I too freely speak)… That man you see,
His name is Erazm. He is common sense
Incarnate (and so dear in that aspect
To wondrous Julia!) And here he comes,
Right at the moment, when… If I were now
To throw myself into the deep, Madame,
You might complete the moral I leave undone
As I break off my q.e.d. (And this,
Is my conclusion… mathematical).

MARTA

Looking closely at Feliks.

Now, what would Julia — whom I love and admire —
Make of this? Could I not feel, and think for her?

FELIKS

With enthusiasm.

Madame, allow me to present my arm…

She takes it, and they go off, hand in hand.

JULIA

Offstage.

Erazm!

ERAZM

Enters, looking at his watch.

> The ship is late. The sea's too rough.
> And so, indeed, I'm made to wait again.
> (If a man who fills up each living moment
> Should wait, or must hurry — wait, do I see
> Julia, seeking out the morning zephyrs?

To Julia.

Madame…

JULIA

            Good morning, count.

ERAZM

                        You're out quite early.

JULIA
And you — are off to… somewhere?

ERAZM

                              There's no ship today.

JULIA
I… come to throw myself into the sea,
As I do every day… I'm just waiting
For my maid with the linen. After that,
I have a nice big glass of donkey milk…

                   Curtain.

THE RING OF THE GRANDE DAME,
OR *DUREJKO EX MACHINA*

A Tragedy in three acts
with a description of the dramatic progress
the gestures of the actors
and an introduction.

INTRODUCTION

Certain introductions awaken in me an involuntary memory of a certain event, to wit:

There once was a certain bookseller, in a certain town, who, hanging up Grandville's engravings illustrating the fables of LaFontaine, clarified the masterpieces with captions, as follows:

'The Lion — signifies might; the Rabbit — fear; the Partridge — simplicity; the Fox — cleverness; the Frog — self-conceit; and the Monkey — ??' Here, the explanatory texts came to an end.

I asked the citizen, not why he didn't merely add that the Monkey means a Monkey, but rather why he deprived the explicators of all their fun, by making everything legible in that way? The bright fellow enlightened me thus: 'The venomous bourgeois nature is so suspicious that, in reading LaFontaine's fables in which the lion, the ass, the parrot, or the frog take voice, people immediately assume that reference is being made to this or that citizen of the town, or their wives, their favourites, their sons, etc.'

However inappropriate it might be to describe one's own characters, still and all, according to the pattern outlined above, I wish to state that my Mac-X is by no means a parody of Ireland or Scotland, my Countess is not intended to be a notorious representative of countesses in general, and that in Durejko I do not take aim at Lithuania, or any other province, as he is nothing other than himself: *Durejko ex machina*! In a word, my intent was unutterably distant from any and all allusions to real persons.

In this present labour of mine, I have striven to supplement the tragic genre with a new type of tragedy, such as does not arrive at death and the spilling of blood. This I call by the name of White Tragedy.

I suppose that both as far as the comments in *Chowanna* or Trentowskiego's *Son of the Fatherland*, and no less the *poetry of Mickiewicz*,[47] are concerned, one mustn't approach scenic impressions in a personal way. Works which aim at, or attain, the ultimate summits of popularity, belong by that very fact to the region of *proverb;* they become *forms of speech.* The adjective to be used is the Italian *dantesco*, which means intricate, gloomy, *Dantean!...* So free (passing over Aristophanes[48] in our search for examples) are we to use the archly-popular greats in our speech without running the risk of having to fear such blows, which, if actors deal them out amongst themselves, are but thwacks feigned, on account of public safety.

It yet remains for me to say what, in the public aspect of art, I see as our obligatory task, in order for us to progress. And so I declare that,

as I see it, today we're in need of dramatic works, which would prove amenable to private reading as well as stage performance.

These days, it's not enough to distract for a few hours those who have nothing better to do of an evening, nor to compose so called *fantastico-philosophical* dramas, so often unfinished, rather than profound. I make this declaration for this reason, that if I were unable to answer the question *What is it that art demands?* I would show myself as being possessed of no broader competence than that of those who recline on the plush seats in the house or loges.

---

47 Norwid is making reference here, above all, to Part III of Adam Mickiewicz's *Dziady* [Forefathers' Eve] and two works by Bronisław Trentowski: *Chowanna, czyli System pedagogiki narodowej* [Chowanna, or a System of National Paedagogy, 1842], and *Wizerunki duszy narodowej z końca ostatniego szesnastolecia przez Ojczyźniaka* [Images of the National Spirit from the Last Sixteen Years, by the Son of the Fatherland, 1847]. In the play we refer to these as *The Educator* and *The Nationalist*, respectively.

48 A reference to Aristophanes' presentation of notable persons like Socrates in his play *Clouds*.

CYPRIAN KAMIL NORWID

As far as moral purpose is concerned, I am of the opinion that the *sacred, edifying, religious* aspect of ancient tragedy has not ceased to be present at all among us, nor can it disappear. However, it has found a chief place for itself somewhere else in today's dramatic works.

I believe that this genre, for which we do not have an adequate term in Polish (as the *thing itself* has not yet appeared amongst us) is — *la haute comédie*. It is that which lays open, mainly, the field to edifying drama in our Christian society. At least it seems that it should be so, since this is to be a period of *societal-self-reflection* as a whole, of self-examination, I say, from the top on down.

The whole of society!... I say, for it is here, and not in the comedies *buffo* (such as are masterfully sketched by the pen of Count Fredro),[49]

> **where one social caste** *examines another, discovers its ridiculousness, but such an act as a civilisational-societal whole*, as if a reflection of the universal conscience, examining itself.

This is an archly-difficult task for this reason, that the great, naked *Serious* here takes the place of those sensitive moments that tragedy is capable of drowning in blood — palpable and red. In accord with such a mood, all shadings must be indescribably subtle. But the language of exquisite conversational dialogue is surprisingly not as developed as it might seem from everyday use! If one may even name that dramatic genre *high-comedy*, it is because Dante named his great work a comedy, on account of its *happy*, not frightful, *conclusion*, as well as the even more subtle dramatic shading needed in the development of the matter. As it is only in the course of such a labour that one discovers the insufficiency of *punctuation*, as one makes use of such stresses in the text as would strengthen, or especially foreground, for the dramatic artist, the words he is to say, the phrases. From this we move on to remarking that the delivery of speech, on account of the lack of a social life, is clumsy; with the exception *described by propriety*, one might say, they know not how to read aloud. It is not difficult to rectify this vexing inadequacy. It is enough to set forth a few main, decided pieces of direction, such as:

---

49   Aleksander Fredro (1793 – 1876). The chief comedic dramatist of Polish Romanticism. His works may be generically compared to the comedies of humours of Molière and Ben Jonson.

The elocution of verse, in its delivery, depends on the skilful reading of *increments*.[50] Whoever does not know how to dread *increments* will be unable to express the beauty of the verse. One needs to take special care in the reading of blank verse, because its writing must be more correct than rhyme. And that for this reason: that one might say that unrhymed verse *rhymes all along the line, from the beginning to the end,* and not just with the final vocable of the given line!

Among the whole range of these technical difficulties, it is right to consider that this has been somehow completely forgotten, that on the day of rehearsal all renowned dramaturges, present at, so to speak, the trying on of a newly altered garment, do not allow a work to continue to pass on to the boards of the theatre without this or that final alteration, bettering it slightly, after having had to lengthen it there, or shorten it here, tightening it here or loosening it there. And finally, conscious everywhere of the original author's work, and the first actors who took it in hand, still, if I am allowed to continue with my metaphor,

> **one doesn't go about** overlong in clothes fitted for someone else!

Now the above-mentioned difficulties cannot be addressed by *one* work or one pen alone. Yet that one work, that one pen, can bring the matter into the clear, pointing it out, exemplifying a direction — this is not just possible, it is an obligation. Now, this sort of thing is most easily effected in such societies, which, accustomed to weighing and *employing the truth*, are able to distinguish at first glance the capital difference that exists between *imitation* and *self-creation*. The latter is an obligation, and something that becomes order-progress, and for this reason, it is desirable and helpful to him who begins; whereas the *former*, that is *imitation, mimicry*, being something even contrary to *spirit-nature*, weighs greatly upon both imitated and imitator, ending with the onset of madness.

From this we may note the following:

> **The less *lively* the society, that is, the less *vital*, *life-filled*,** the more murky its apprehension of the difference between *self-creativity* and *imitation!*

---

50   See note 57 to *Cleopatra and Caesar.*

And great detriment and damage arise from this… For, since those who make up such a society do not know how to *self-create*, every so often they must hunger after a phenomenal individual —

> *of whom they demand the institution of every and all sorts of things, and taking no advantage of this themselves,* in the end they befoul their very own springs.

Finally, for the dramaturg, it is a pretty challenge among us Poles that appears as a psychologically profound social question. Up until now, Polish *artisme* has not been able to recognise Woman!… Such as those grand profiles, like ideal stages, which (passing over the ancients) one finds among the women of Dante, Calderon, Shakespeare, Byron… With one exception (which I will not mention out of propriety) — they don't exist at all in Polish literature.

There are no, I say, essential and whole *women*:

Wanda, who 'wanted no German husband?' Well, do we know what she actually *did* want?? — she goes about on one leg, as beautiful a leg as it may be. *Telimena* (perhaps the fullest, speaking artistically!) is not transcendental enough. *Zosia* is a mere schoolgirl, and that gorgeous Maria of Malczewski was unable to develop into a rounded character, having been suffocated with a pillow so early on, that is, sunk into a marsh.

I felt it proper to sketch forth difficulties such as these in the introduction to my *White Tragedy*, so that, however widespread may be the competence reclining on the theatrical plush, it need not be met with such particular contempt, as may arise when it is produced.

Sincerely your servant,
C.N.

1872

THE RING OF THE GRANDE DAME,
OR *DUREJKO EX MACHINA*

PERSONS

Countess Maria Harrys	A widow
Mac-X	A distant relative of the Countess' late husband
Magdalena Tomir	The Countess' confidante
Graf Szeliga	
Judge Klemens Durejko	
Klementyna	The Judge's wife
Salome	Housekeeper
Master	Of fire-works
Police Commissioner	and Gendarmes
Old Servant	
New Servant	
Maid	
Schoolgirls	
Guests	

The action is set in the nineteenth century at the Harrys' Manor and its environs.

ACT I

A garret — filled with books — the windows give out onto green, but the shades are partially drawn. It is early morning.

Scene 1

MAC-X

Pausing his reading.

Here comes the first ray of the beams that scathe…

He adjusts the shade at the window.

As if they were familiars — some of them,
And others, unknown, rapping the window pane
Like strangers, or someone who would announce
A stranger calling…

He pauses at the window, tosses out some breadcrumbs.

But not you, winged friends,
Happy to peck at the last pinch of bread,
Happy to sing for crumbs, here to my sill
Always returning, flying off, then back,
And never taking more time, or more life
Than I would give you!

Returns to his reading.

With his ort, the bird
Flies off and leaves no tick of pain behind,
Hour of disgust, or day of suffering —
Or year of astonished disbelief in man!
He flies near, then flies off into the blue
Eye of the heavens, like the honest tear

Of good people... I once saw someone weep
Like that, but why she wept — I do not know.

Scene 2

SALOME

Entering cautiously.

With your leave, sir, at such an early hour —
I've come to let you know his Grace the judge,
Mr Durejko's coming by today
To visit his property. That's the cause
Of all this fluster... We must make quite sure
That all's in order, in its proper place.
And truth be told, it's our own places here
What's upmost in our minds...

Carefully, tenderly.

                              I know, good sir,
That you're a little, shall we say, behind
In this month's rent... But after all, your cousin,
An angel, truly! Countess Harrys, why
She's the real mistress of the manor, hey?

Cautiously.

Speaking of which, if you'll permit me, sir,
We simple folk speak straight from the shoulder,
I've never — quite — the reason — understood
Why, that being the case, you choose to live
Here in this garret, and not there, with her,
Your cousin, in the pavilion. Would it not
Be pleasant with that angel by your side?

Noting the effect these words have on Mac-X.

O, pay no mind to this old woman, sir!
I'm an old mother, who for so long now
Thinks so long on the son she hasn't seen
So long now, she sees him in every lad
And starts to mother him — pay me no mind...

Pause.

Speaking of which, I had thought to ask you
To intercede on his behalf with her —
With Countess Harrys — to put in a word
On his behalf... He's in Japan you know,
My only son... A letter takes two months!
From there to here, and he's my only son,
And she knows, oh, so many admirals
And more than one minister...

Catching herself.

                              But you know,
I'm speaking like a mother here, that's all...

Dabbing at her eyes.

And really, just to talk about her son...

MAC-X
This second thing you speak of, Salome,
Is first in my heart. I'll do what I can,
Gladly, quite grateful to be of service
To such a good woman as yourself. The first —
Why you see me here, and no other place,
Well, there's more than one explanation...

Emphatically.

The countess is an angel. Still and all,
Her woman's heart fears evil-minded tongues:

Young widow that she is, she wishes not
To have any young man under her roof.
As for our cousinship, it's rather more
Distant than you assume. She calls me cousin
Out of the goodness of her heart. In fact,
I'm nothing to her. I'm her husband's kin...
But as it is, I too have something small
To speak with her about, so, mother dear,
I'll gladly speak on your behalf as well.

Taking Salome's hand.

Don't thank me yet, Salome dear! I've not
Done anything at all yet...

Confidentially.

                There's one more thing:
The countess is so good, so generous,
She's done so many works of mercy, she
Gathers unto her so many, so quickly,
That she forgets — sometimes — a farthing here
Among so many millions piled about...
I'm only saying this so you should not
Place too much hope in my poor intercession.

Emphatically.

Now, I don't mean to say that she forgets
The people she would help...

Resoundingly.

                No, not at all!
But it so happens sometimes, with such people,
Who do so much good, to so very many...

Pause.

They say that cherubim themselves, speeding
From on high to succour the suffering,
Lose, now and then, a feather from their wings...
Haste is a good thing, but it goes awry
Sometimes...

SALOME
              Ah, learned men, sir, clergy too
Know everything without the asking. So!
That's why I made my suit to you, dear sir.
Old mothers know but clumsy words. And here
I've served long years, here in the manor, sir —
And you — I'd serve with my own life! But see:
The owner here, his Grace the judge Durejko,
Is going to change it all, so rumour runs;
He's going to give it all up, on behalf
Of someone — a friend of his — a gentleman
With whom he...

Moving to the window.

              Here they come, sir! Have a look!
They've turned toward the stairs — they're coming up...
I can slip by them yet, if I be quick...

Exit.

Scene 3

MAC-X

With a sincere sigh as he watches Salome depart.

If only that good woman was aware
Of what that bird knows, fluttering now away:
What news it brings to the other birds... That I've —
Tossed my last meagre crumbs out on the sill!

Distractedly.

And if She knew it, Ah, She! who right now
Distributes alms, perhaps, just like a saint
Stepped from some Gothic church's pointed arch,
Of pearly stained-glass, in robes of amethyst,
With golden nimbus encircling her bow,
The worthy lady!

Deeply.

          There's something profound
In this our daily bread — the last to be broken…
There's something there, to touch with errant hand;
Something, I say, that bids one to be still
Or at the very least, forbids the tongue
To speak of one's misfortune as fulfilled…
As if it were an easier thing to speak
Of some small lack, without wounding one's friends
Whom fortune favours more…

Mysteriously.

          And so there is
Something to handle there, touching upon
One's *amour-propre*, and… philanthropy.

Pause.

Why is it that the learned hold their tongue
About such things? And why do simple folk
Blush less at telling others of their pain
Than of the truth they learn through suffering?!

Looking about his quarters.

I've lots to keep my happy… O, this corner…

At the window.

There's Mary's shadow, clearly seen, afar…

Turning to face the interior.

The calm of hearts dead in these books of mine,
Communing with me, even when unread.

Mysteriously.

It sometimes happens that their outer shells
Tossed here and there are by coincidence
Enlightened suddenly by a chance ray
And, like a mummy-race in pyramids
Spread wide their mouths to speak, and when they do,
These walls entrap that breath — and it is mine.

Piteously.

Oh, let them call me idle if they wish!
We haven't yet summed up our labour, no!
The sun is shining brighter for all that.

Solemnly.

In Babylon, in Ezekiel's day,
The least inactive person indeed he was,
When standing with hands folded, and gazing
Lugubriously, and shaking his head,
He did no more than that… No, nothing!

Scene 4

JUDGE

Entering with Szeliga.

As my name is Klemens Durejko, sir,
A secret's safe with me. And anyway,
It's not about a secret — it's discretion!

Loudly.

What's it to anyone, if some lessee —

To both sides.

And as it's said, an honourable party,
A worthy man, precise, reliable,
No vagrant or do-nothing, no stray mutt...

Mac-X remains intent on what he has been doing, and does not rise.

Should he, I say, do this thing or another...

Doctrinaire.

Secrets, discretion — that's two different things.
To coax the spirit out of the dead letter,
That's the first thing the legal mind is taught;
The essence of the law — what makes a judge
A judge... and Judge Durejko's known to be
And is, an amicable arbiter.

To Szeliga.

You know astronomy, I know the law.
Once at the University of Dorpat
We had this German doctor. He lectured
At times with a remarkable *Ansatz*![51]

---

51   German: Approach. In his notes to the play, Tadeusz Pini translates the term
in Durejko's mouth as 'drive, momentum' [*zapęd, rozpęd*].

SZELIGA

Astronomy is neither a secret
Nor my sole occupation. I was merely
Explaining why these windows here, the high ones,
Are more suited to me than those down there...

Gazing through the window with interest.

What is that passage there between the walls?
Does it give out onto a street, or highway?

JUDGE

Neither. That is the driveway to the manor.
There to the left, among the maple branches,
Through those acacias — see those windows flash?
Those are the windows of the manor wing.
Countess Harrys owns it; on her properties
Which stretch here broadly, she fosters orphans
Of both genders, but mainly orphaned girls.
But the Durejko house stands as it's stood:
My missus' mansion, made for maidens.

SZELIGA

To self, at window.

In which the astronomical eye suspects
A perturbation gravitational
Among the planets... On that carriageway
The traffic to and fro, runs past the window
Of the salon in the orangerie...
I've seen no trace of her for two years now.

JUDGE

Quarrelling with Mac-X; their firm words can be clearly heard at times.

We need no words here, sir, but deeds! You see
All things are changing, all throughout the house!

MAC-X
And yet agreements must be honoured...

SZELIGA

To self.

Neither her carriage nor her dress's hem.

JUDGE

To Mac-X, loudly.

There are agreements and agreements...
The valid ones are upheld by both parties,
Or they are null and void.

SZELIGA

Equivocally, for soliloquising at the window.

Venus must rise in that quadrant of Heaven!

JUDGE

To Mac-X.

And there, you see? The astronomer's word
Will plot a new syzygia today,
Tomorrow, at the latest. Wait and see!

Turning to Szeliga, pathetically.

Venus and Mars and Saturn, and the rest
Of the planets are clearly seen from here,

My dear sir! Night and day you may observe
Their rising from that window where you stand,
As clearly as our Lithuanian
Marcin Poczobut, who descried their flight
Better than did Copernicus himself!

SZELIGA
I won't deny that my chief interest
Is the perspective from this very side…

Doctrinaire.

My astronomical experiments
Must be conducted from various points
Upon the globe with… a peculiar care.
My dear sir, surely I need not convince you
How valuable a science is astronomy,
And since that is my only interest here,
I've taken living quarters down below,
Intending to devote these upper floors
To observation. They'll further my research
Immeasurably…

JUDGE

To Mac-X, violently.

                 Up to the attic, Sir!
The matter's settled!

SZELIGA

Taking note of the quarrel.

I hope I've not infringed upon the rights
Of anyone in coming here, or even that
My advent should be an inconvenience?
If such should be the case, I will withdraw.

JUDGE

Threateningly, in Mac-X's ear.

Up to the attic… Now!…

MAC-X

Ferreting among the books.

                  I… need to find…
Something, first…

He extracts a pistol from behind the books, inspects it, pockets it.

 A relic of my father's. The last I own!

Exit.

JUDGE

To Szeliga.

That tenant had to vacate the premises
For reasons that I'd need long to explain.

SZELIGA
And so I ask no explanations.

JUDGE
He is a person… You know… In the head?
In case of any… serious paroxysm,
I need to keep all the people here in mind
Who live on my property… Is that not so?

Looking about the room.

It's the books what turned his head, I reckon…

Quickly.

I mean — the sort of books he reads! Not special ones
About astronomy…

Doctrinaire.

There's books, and books.
Good books and bad books, 'healthy,' so to say
'Content' and 'empty phrases.' The former ones
Educate, and the bookseller converts
Them into good round coin, whereas the latter,
They are — if you'll permit me — good for… what?
What, really? I'd like to know, those Greek fables?

Preacherly.

Has anyone learned a thing of duty
And civic obligations reading them?
To get up early, and take a cold bath,
Then sit down to the invoices, and tot up
The numbers accurately? To be a good servant,
A tender husband?

Caught up in his monologue.

Judge Durejko knows
How to evaluate his literature,
But he's against all empty fluff, conceits…
He'll take a book in hand when he's time for it…
When I was nineteen it might so happen,
I'd read a thing or two on my vacation
Back in our own woods…

With fervour.

A Lithuanian, sir,
Has inspiration at his beck and call!

To Szeliga.

You know, of course, the poems of Mickiewicz?
Who 'contemned wisemen and prophets inspired?'
With us a Radziwiłł's a Radziwiłł:
We don't need many — one man is a legion!

SZELIGA

Slowly.

Yes — but how much coal must there be in the mines
To make one homegrown diamond, which, when found,
One's sure is not just some stone lost, unloosed
From someone's ring?

JUDGE

Uncritically assenting.

         You speak so beautifully
Dear sir — You're right, just like the mines it is
Back where I'm from…

SZELIGA

Equivocally.

         Sometimes the miner's lamp
Lights up the darkest shaft… A handy thing
You can light a cigar with too, when bored…

Melancholically.

And yet the solitary obelisk's
A clumsy thing… You can't build houses from them,
And in the middle of a public place
They're meagre decoration…

JUDGE

                    Mrs Durejko
Keeps a fine boarding house for all the daughters
Of the best — wealthiest — families hereabout.
Ah, worthy maidens. And they're being taught
By lectors of both sexes such wisdom
Practical, now, all things a young girl ought
To know — but above all, morality!

Again off on a monologue.

'Knowledge' 'for' inner wisdom… Turn it round,
And you've 'foreknowledge,' as our national
Philosopher[52] once put it, whose wise words
Are now proverbs among our people; why,
He spoke in aphorisms that uncover
More learning than a month of Sundays spent
In libraries, providing patent knowledge
To all who are true sons of our nation,
The worthy landowner, the solid chap,
The pure patriot, and no false Arimanes…!

SZELIGA

Politely.

It would be pleasant to dispute philosophy
With an alumnus of the Dorpat School…
But let's return to our negotiations.
I'll take the lower floor apartment too.
Now, if I'd wish to try my telescope
Today, perchance, there would be no objection
For me to enter here again?

---

52   Bronisław Trentowski (1808 – 1869). Polish philosopher and messianist, propagating some awkward ideas concerning the gods of pagan Slavdom being emanations of the Judea-Christian deity.

Salome enters, but halts at the door.

These things
Are not the slightest inconvenience to me...
I'm interested in what is... beyond;
Where the eye's fixed, there soon follow one's thoughts,
And time and place cease to exist...

JUDGE

To Salome.

Hear that?
What this gentleman's said?

Severely.

Heed and obey!

SZELIGA
And so, I shall withdraw below. Au revoir.

Exit. As soon as the Graf departs, the judge begins to pace, rubbing his hands together.

Scene 5

JUDGE
The time for execution's come, and *vigour*...

To Salome.

I rang and rang for you. Where are your ears?

SALOME
Madame sent us all off in search of you.
She was concerned — and here she comes herself...

JUDGE
The time for execution's come, and *rigour!*

Looking around at the objects in the room.

It will take some time to clear all this away.
So, heap it up, as if to cart it hence,
So it can be tossed out the door with ease
Or shoved up in the attic...

Halting, listening.

                    I hear the tread
Of Madame Durejko rushing here to learn
What I've to say of our astronomer
And letting out the rooms. She's curious
Of how I've managed things. Well, she will see —
Her tender husband has good news for her.

MADAME DUREJKO
I've been looking for you everywhere, Durejko.
I need to confide in you today...
Not that I don't confide in you always!
But such occasions are so infrequent...

Pathetically.

Why is my Klemens so cold and unfeeling?

JUDGE

Sternly.

First, ask me if I've some important news.

Whispers in his wife's ear.

I've got the astronomer in the house.
You understand? The apartments are rented.

MADAME DUREJKO

Indifferently, coolly.

What news is that compared to what I bring?
Just listen: Countess Harrys sent this morning
Asking to see a roster of our boarders.

JUDGE

Condescendingly.

Well, that's not much!

MADAME DUREJKO
              No? Listen! Curious
As to the reasons of her request, I asked
The servant she sent over, and he said —
Listen! Durejko, all our girls, tonight,
Have been invited over there for tea!

JUDGE

With a laugh.

What you've brought me is but an *act*, my dear,
Whereas Durejko's news is *fact*, hard fact!

MADAME DUREJKO

Indifferently.

Act, fact, as long as all turns out all right...

JUDGE

Coolly.

Madame Durejko's not well-versed in logic.

MADAME DUREJKO

More lively.

Ah, but she's read more than anybody here…

JUDGE

Turning his back on her.

In Dorpat they read —

MADAME DUREJKO

Ironically.

> All of the *Educator*,
My Klimmy-Klemmy?

JUDGE

Over his shoulder.

> That and the *Nationalist*, my dear girl![53]

Turning around.

An act to a fact is like 'a fist to a nose.'
No academic disquisition, but

---

53   Both of these are works by the Judge's idol Trentowski, referenced by Norwid
in his introduction to the play.

The capital essence of a solid reason.
You'll find more healthy content in proverbs
Than in all of the books printed in Paris.
As our philosopher has demonstrated.

MADAME DUREJKO

Withdrawing, she stops on the other side of the door.

Les goûts sont différents, mon cher mari.

JUDGE

De gustibus disputandum non est.

SALOME
What goose and gander gabble through those gobs?

JUDGE

Monologue.

Durejko knows the value of business
And how to classify his interests.
Durejko's sensitive, but dangerous, too!
He won't be toyed with, not by anyone!
He knows his duties as a homeowner...

MADAME DUREJKO

Returning to her husband.

Madame Durejko's finishing the best
And most proper young girls the world has seen!
Future mothers, wives, and heroines!
The kind that share one's triumphs and one's woes!
Madame Durejko is sweet and severe —

With a firm grip upon the household reins.
Nobody's going to teach her anything!

JUDGE

Firmly.

Durejko was a judge and is a judge
With understanding and insight of things.
When he gives something a shake, it's well shaken!
He knows how to shut the mouths of others.

MADAME DUREJKO
Madame Durejko will not be drowned out
By groundless phrases and such clumsy style!
She values content, but requires graceful form.
What does my Klemensik know of synthesis?

JUDGE

With contempt as his wife exits.

Antithesis, and even some prosthesis!
More than once in his life has Durejko opened
Transactions to the mutual benefit
Of both parties, in varied matters. These days
We little need the profit of attestations
Of neighbour-folk to remain forever fit
To sit on all sorts of committees…

With a smile.

Then Klementynka will make a nice curtsey
To him, presenting this matter, or another —
But now the teacher will grow quiet… hush!

Taking snuff.

Rapping the finger lightly on the snuff-box
Once, twice... the president knocks —
What is it, Madame Durejko?

MADAME DUREJKO

Appearing again at the door.

No one forbids a monologue at all!

JUDGE

Calling after her.

'Self-speeches!' Speak clearly, and without shame
As your forefathers spoke![54]

MADAME DUREJKO

A portion of her head appearing at the door.

                              Wygiełłówna
Once, she knows well enough her native speech!

The Judge exits after his wife.

SALOME

Leaning on her broom.

And every day's the same. Whenever they meet
They stick their tongues out at one another —

---

54   Judge Durejko, the lover of everything 'national,' objects to the use of the
word *monolog*, as being a Greek loan-word. He prefers the odd Slavic calque
sobosłowień. This is not only clumsy, it is ironic, since both Durejko and his wife,
'née Wygiellówna' are of Lithuanian extraction, but locate their ethnic core not
in things Lithuanian — but Polish.

And who knows why or wherefore, when they gab
With German words… and then his Grace the judge
Goes off this way, and Madame that…
And then the servants are sent out in search
Of him or her just so they'd quarrel more
When met again, and at a higher volume.

Pausing to listen.

I hear the judge's met the astronomer…
Thank goodness that he's holding him back there
So he won't catch up with his wife! At least
The quarrels will die down a little…

Piles up the rest of the books and looks around.

There! Everything's almost in order. My!
Just like somebody died. Dear Lord in Heaven!
The world has no room for the quiet folk —
It rises round them like a flood, until,
One day, its waves are lapping at their brows.

SZELIGA

Entering with a telescope.

That's good enough. No need for more housekeeping —
For a few hours over here at the window
It's neither worthwhile, nor very proper
To disturb everything!

SALOME
                    Here in our house
We make a greater fuss for lesser reasons.

SZELIGA

To Salome.

The man who rents these rooms… However ill
In mind he may be, seems a nice, calm chap.

SALOME
The one who told your Grace such things must be
A bit more often off his rocker. We servants
Know better than anyone what the truth is.

She sighs.

The nice and calm are the orphans of the world.
They're pushed away and shunted to the side
Farther and farther, from each scrap of earth
They set their feet on, till at last they say
'They're crazy!' Now, when I was just a girl
And served as sempstress to Princess Orsi —
Your Grace may know her, she was on the stage —
Well, there I saw a world of freakish things!

Profoundly.

Not everyone who speaks his thoughts aloud
Is wandering in mind… Not everyone
Who leads a modest life is just some lump!

SZELIGA
There's a fine palace here too, at arm's length,
Where Countess Harrys lives…

SALOME
                              You're right, your Grace.
And what a gem she is — such a good woman!
I know only two such in the entire county:
The good Father Superior and the Countess!

SZELIGA
And what about the Count?

SALOME

                    Why, she's a widow.
Who doesn't know that?

SZELIGA

                    Ah yes, I'd forgotten.
I've been away so long on distant travels
That I was sure that she'd married again,
Like everybody else.

SALOME

Returning to her cleaning.

                    That would be good
I reckon, but what we think isn't the same
As what the lords think. Not always, anyway.

SZELIGA
Matrimony's the same for everyone.

SALOME
That's just what Father Provincial preaches,
And can he preach! Sometimes my specs are drenched
With tears, and yet — you hear one thing in church…

SZELIGA
The Countess, though, is pious, I believe,
And goes to Mass… She must know the good father?

SALOME

Loudly.

As I know these staircases and handrails!
You've never seen such a glow of wax candles,
As tall as your Grace! With your permission, sir…

With fervour.

And such a mass of flowers, plaited roses,
Lilies with silver petals… and such rare incense
And splendid chasubles of gold that flash —
Where will you find such pomp on Corpus Christi,
With ostrich feathers bowing like pious souls
Before the monstrance with the Sacrament!
And all because of Countesses like her!

Profoundly.

One owes the heavens at least a puff of smoke,
Since man can't give anything of himself,
Since all he owns is merely lent him, now…

Coming to.

Look at me running off at the mouth again!
I beg your Grace's pardon. An old woman…

Exits.

Scene 6

SZELIGA
She's made my own specs misty… How often
You dress yourself up fine from tip to toe
To make a distant pilgrimage, to hear
Nothing but cloying prattle, dull speech… here:
That old, bent woman puttering with the dust,
Strews flashing diamonds about her path!

Profoundly.

Only the real traveller knows how
To make a voyage around his own parts,

Uncovering the local monuments
To eyes that pass them blindly, every day.
And this is why, perhaps, the Englishman,
Who makes the farthest, and most frequent journeys,
Remains most true to his original.
The locals rest their backs against such things
As strike my eyes and ears with deepest meaning —
I'm always voyaging, as in Syria!

Catching sound of footfalls on the stairs.

Shh! Someone comes this way, mumbling to himself,
As if haranguing each and every step!

MAC-X

Deep in monologue.

And so, indeed, I come back to my place!

With double entendre.

And yet I've many more levels to climb,
Higher and higher, till I reach the place
Where Durejko and his possessions end…

With a crooked smile.

What a good thing it is that this globe hangs
In space yet untraversed by human foot —
Immense as the abyss — and solitary.

SZELIGA

Softly, to the side.

Whatever the old woman says, it's wise
To be on one's guard with such a fellow…

MAC-X

Entering slowly.

I see the place already shunts me aside!

Not even glancing in Szeliga's direction.

They've taken my measure, and my window —
So that I turn my back to it. No more
To see the light of the sun, or the moon.

To himself.

How many times have I been there, and elsewhere,
And all in vain! Yet one thing is for sure:
They don't even think of neglecting me…
Yes, one can be sure of the sunrise. No doubt
There, though it sometimes happens that the frost
Kills off the flowers before the breath of spring
Returns to revive them. I'll go again.
I must go, one more time! Salome's son —
I have to speak with her of him, not me.
The friction of ironic haps wipes clean
All personality — like it or not!

Sits down by a heap of books.

Misfortune sets the active will to spoil,
Transforming it to frenzy or atonia.
Nevertheless, good fortune infects
The feelings, making people dull and lazy…
Since both are able to ruin a man,
Are they then man's misfortune, or his fate?

Rising.

There comes a day at last lacking direction.
There comes a day to tread at a dull pace,
As if behind the coffin of one's heart,
Processing with an empty breast… and yet
A calm expression on one's face!

SZELIGA

Attentively.

                                He's raving?
No! That's love unrequited. Who more than I
Ought to have fellow feeling for that man!

Making his presence known.

Hello there, neighbour!

MAC-X
                        What? I didn't know
We were already neighbours. But, forgive me…

Gazing around.

All this, I see, has been made ready. Soon
There will be nothing here… Any day now…

Makes a sweeping gesture around himself then speaks to the side.

It seems I've already… removed the main thing…

SZELIGA
There are such parlours in America —
Salons, not little rooms like this, where all
Who rent a room are welcome to relax,
Receive guests… and it discommodes no one.

Seriously.

And that too is societal progress.

MAC-X
Europe tolerates no vacuums. Like
A chemical process…

SZELIGA

In a manly tone.

        So there are many too
Such beings who have not been broken down,
Nor taken their own lives, but undergo
Another death — a civic one — such as
Un-nations them, for all time. Such as those
New-resurrected ones, who set a sea
Between themselves and memory, creating
A new community. How many Irish
There travel, from their Emerald Isle…!

Snapping out of it.

But I beg your pardon. Your last name, sir,
It's Irish? Or Scottish?

MAC-X

Coolly.

        In every land
There are quite different names, especially
Those ancient ones, from the worn and foxed sheets
Of histories. Now, as for me, indeed
I'm one of those constitutive bodies
Of which we were just speaking, which can't bear
The chemical pressures of Europe.
I venture such details, because you ask.

SZELIGA
To venture further yet, I've become used
By travels long, from one place to the next,
From one theme to another, to kill time
By careful observation… So, I say —

Extending his hand.

I humbly offer you my firm support
If ever it should be your firm intent
To cross the ocean.

Morosely.

                   Not for this
Did I traverse the earth: to collect photos.
Wisdom obliges one to share with others
What one's accumulated; it's a duty
To oneself as well…

MAC-X

With feeling.

                   Only too rarely
Have I heard anyone speak like that… and yet,
It's bad to trust oneself unto the moment…
But there are such for whom one might renounce
Not only Europe, but the globe entire!

Taking Szeliga's hand.

Most heartily, therefore, do I accept
This proffered hand, sincere fraternal grace!

SZELIGA

Similarly.

This hand is yours whenever you call upon it.

Solemnly.

I've noticed that society's so ordered
That one might advance in learning and wealth
Together, only to a small extent,
For which reason there are constraints that stretch
Almost into the moral sphere.

MAC-X

With a peculiar smile, equivocally.

With some surprise I've noticed, up till now
You only make your studies by daylight.

SZELIGA

Quickly.

I get the joke. And yet the world deserves
Our contemplation in sunlight as well,
Without placing too much faith in the rays
Of that bright star…

Indifferently.

                    As for myself, you know,
I'm studying the layout of the windows
And cleaning my portable telescope —
Both of which things demand the light of day.

MAC-X

Frantically.

For me too, O good sir! those windows there
Have their own mystery…

SZELIGA

Lively.

Yes? Of what sort?

MAC-X
It's a small thing. A tiny detail.

SZELIGA
Tell me!

MAC-X
It's far too petty to mention.

SZELIGA

Aside.

Can he
Be such an astronomer as I am?!

To Mac-X, firmly.

Please speak in all frankness. Especially
As I'm to take your place here. Come now, tell
Me everything…

MAC-X

Peering closely at Szeliga.

Well then, if you'd…
But why are you so interested?

SZELIGA

Coolly.

> Because
> I just can't comprehend why such plain windows,
> Quite ordinary, save how large they be,
> Which are of interest to astronomers
> Alone, should have such meaning for… two persons.

MAC-X

Toward the window.

My friends… live there.

SZELIGA

Stunned.

> What, what?!

MAC-X

> They've plaited nests
There, in those trees.

SZELIGA

Relieved.

> Aha…!

MAC-X

In explanation.

> All kinds of birds,
> And I know all of them. They fly up here

To greet me in the morning. I've grown used
To breaking bread with them. And so, before
I stretch forth my own hand, considering
Abandoning Europe... Before I too
Become like them —

Modestly.

                  Let me first intercede
On their behalf... A mere handful of crumbs
Tossed here and there.

SZELIGA

Moving away from the window.

Indeed I'd like to take your place today,
But — now the hour approaches...

MAC-X
                  Ah, the hour
Of courtesy and visiting with folks
Not of this sphere, pleasant and undemanding...
Who often think on one...

SZELIGA
                  The social world
Has its own orbits, and eclipses...

Toward the window.

Look at the traffic on the carriageway —
It seems a new conjunction of the planets,
Or something quite extraordinary's happened,
And yet this gravitational pull is but
The hour when one receives one's visitors.

MAC-X

Skipping near the window.

With your permission, let me have a glance…

He leans out; Szeliga peers over his shoulder.

SZELIGA

Aside, with irritation.

What sort of bird is he looking to see!
That's Mary's carriage! I know the livery!

MAC-X

Hurrying away from the window, leaving.

Goodbye!

SZELIGA

Solus.

So there can be no doubt that someone else
Treads the same path as the astronomer!

Frantically.

And so it's proven again — discoveries
Are often known to others first, though one
Think otherwise… Here I've summited a mount
And find another's flag's aflutter there!

Paces, musing.

Yes! But — how can I be sure what I suspect
Is true, not hypersensitivity
Toying with my thoughts, and with my emotions?

Pause.

More than one carriage passed along the road...

Pause.

Not only hers is painted in such colours...
One bends through windows to catch sight of others...

Pause.

She's not the only woman in the world!

Pacing, then, suddenly.

And then — that youngster... How refined is he?
Can he frequent her circles? Can he know her?
That seems improbable, to say the least!

Pause.

No — over-agitated suspicion
Rattles my heart...

Pause.

        But that melancholy —
That wish to break away from Europe, that
Despair... His social graces... He's familiar
With our society's conventions... No!
He knows her! He enjoys her company!

With doubt.

This truly is an eclipse of the moral sphere!
Ah, you astronomer!

Profoundly.

To stretch one's ken beyond the eye's surface…
When it cannot perceive what lies within…
That's nothing but to peer through a pane of glass!

ACT II

One of the salons in Villa Harrys.

Scene 1
The Countess, Magdalena.

COUNTESS
So now I've told you well nigh everything;
Whatever's left, you'll find there in the note,
All listed in numerical order —
Just as my late husband was wont to do:
He'd laugh at me, you know, for being so
Disorderly, till he took me in hand
— Just like a child who's taught her ABCs —
He'd chuckle, above all, at two foibles
Of mine — my putative forgetfulness
And my putative superstition.
I'd term them thus, for I just seem to be
Forgetful, superstitious, though the latter —
It's hard to disbelieve in certain facts.

With melancholy.

This ring you see — a mere material trifle
To which I don't ascribe any great value —
I had an inkling of something when I lost it,
And when I found it, that presentiment
Was proven true. A ring is just a ring.

It has no power over anything
But in that inkling, well, something *exists*,
And I've enough philosophy, my dear,
To differentiate cause from mere chance.

Pause.

What has this ring to do with that acacia
Which yesterday's storm blasted to the dust,
Covering the path with petals white as snow?
And at that very moment, I received
A telegram… But let's get back to that
Arrangement of the tasks awaiting us,
Just as my poor late husband taught me once.

MAGDALENA

Taking note of something.

The slip you handed me is not a list:
It is a telegram. And so, let's speak
First of that point in your list of instructions
Touching upon Szeliga, whom I've seen
Once, maybe twice, although my ears are full
Of him since that time — and concerning you,
That he adores you, but — unhappily
As you don't share his feelings, and since then
(Since you discouraged him) he's been on travels
About the Dead Sea, moping around old ruins.
That's all I know. Will you not tell me more?

COUNTESS

Harshly.

I'll never cease to blame myself for once
Having committed something… like a lie…
But that terrestrial love of Szeliga's

Is somewhat similar to obstinacy.
And that's what prompted me to intimate
That I might soon be marrying again.
Since then I've just received one telegram
From him, from Smyrna, quite illegible…

Reading aloud.

'Returning to my land, I'll visit her.'

MAGDALENA
One must be terse when writing telegrams —
That's not hard to decipher: Here, his 'land'
Means his estate, and 'she' whom he'll visit
Is you — third person in polite address.
And so, in short, he's coming back; he wants
To visit you. So you should hurry up
With that 'putative' re-marriage of yours…
To turn our thoughts once more to prophecy,
I reckon that this love terrestrial
— As you term it — of Szeliga's would then
Transform itself — despite his obstinacy —
Into some other thing. For, after all,
There must be other feelings in the world,
If nothing else, then for variety!

COUNTESS

Coolly.

Let's leave that where it lies, and get back to
Our organising of our daily tasks!

MAGDALENA
So, if Szeliga should come by, while you
Are absent…

COUNTESS

        Greet him with all courtesy.
But in your conversation with that man,
Let slip nary a word to give him hope,
The slightest hope! Now, I rely upon
Your delicate discretion, your deft touch;
I do not wish to be by anything
Constrained or bound, since I've immersed myself
In duty, and discovered that great treasure
Called peace and quiet.

OLD SERVANT

Announcing.

        Your Grace, Laird Mac-X
Desires to be received.

COUNTESS

        I wish to see
No one before departing.

To Magdalena.

        O, Mac-X!
Have I forgot about him, too!

MAGDALENA

        And so,
What would you like to do with him, your cousin?

COUNTESS
I? Nothing. He'll do something with himself.
I've never had the time to ask his plans.
He's a good lad, who leads a hermit's life
Almost — I once saw him with unkempt beard
And thought: What a fine Capuchin he'd make
In solitary *ermitage* amidst

The green woods! But does it occur to him
To have a glance into the looking glass?
I'm certain that he'd be far happier
In some deep cell, in silence, tending blooms,
Where he would find that treasure: peace and quiet!

MAGDALENA
That what you say about the fate of men
Reminds me somewhat of those 'capuchins'
That serve instead of thermometers: you know,
That doff their cowls when the weather's warm.
Or those made out of paper — children's toys,
Folded, that tumble over on the floor
If you but flick your finger at them, thus.

COUNTESS
… Or I could marry him off, after all…
For matrimony is a sacrament.
But first we'd need to find some wealthy girl
Of the same age, same class, same love of peace
And quiet…

MAGDALENA
So many similarities to find:
Like apples twain hanging from the same bough…
And so I'd ask — have you very far to look?

More insistently.

Two swallows paired — so perfectly the same —
Are they not married, by that very fact?
And how are people different from them?

COUNTESS
You always pose such questions! I would fain
Send you off to the Father Provincial
For a nice talk!

Looks at her watch.

I've not much time left now…

To Magdalena.

What were we speaking of just now?

MAGDALENA
                                        Szeliga,
That should he come by —

COUNTESS
                              Not one word of hope,
My dear — that is the most important thing.

MAGDALENA
But I must greet him with all courtesy…

COUNTESS
How splendid! You remember everything!

Pause.

With every courtesy, yes, so to as to soften
The blow of his ultimate rejection.
For even love terrestrial, when it ends,
Is not a pleasant thing! At least I reckon
That must be true… no pleasant thing at all…

MAGDALENA
So now, what next?

COUNTESS
                        Read me what's written there.

MAGDALENA

Playfully.

I've made my own capuchin out of paper
That tumbles at the slightest puff of breath!

Reads.

'Point two: a couple dancers.' What's that mean?

COUNTESS
Read on…

MAGDALENA

Reads.

    Well then: 'I've invited the girls
From the pension, and a few little boys,
Along with Mrs Durejko, the caretaker,
And her husband.'

COUNTESS
               Some invitations
Already went out, with all *politesse*;
The rest are lying there. Please see to them!

MAGDALENA

Smiling.

Let me just look them over to make sure
You haven't shuffled in among them any
Of different contents…

COUNTESS
You take me to task for such bagatelles,
And yet, I reckon, there's not many women
Of my condition who are capable
Of organising and conducting matters
So varied and so many. Just because
You find a banknote in my Bible, where
An onion-paper ought to be, gives you
No right to jump to such conclusions, dear.
I can make a wrong turn, but I'll arrive,
At last, at my intended destination.
There are such days when every hour's full,
And every minute runs like clockwork, just
As they were planned on the evening before.
Right now, I'm off to a charity event…

Rising, she catches her dress, and it tears.

MAGDALENA
Not till you change your dress! To make a plea
For homeless people in a tattered frock
Would seem a farce…

COUNTESS
                    Accidents do happen.
It doesn't matter.

She rings, a maid enters.

Bring me my short violet coat. And quick.

OLD SERVANT

Entering, with Mac-X entering behind him.

Mac-X, Ma'am, once more begs to be received.

MAID

Handing her the short coat.

Madame, a little less haste…

COUNTESS

To Old Servant.

                      Have him enter.
He might need something.

MAGDALENA

                      He came in already,
But when he saw that you were getting dressed,
He went back out.

COUNTESS

              So much the worse for him.
What does he need?

MAGDALENA

                Would you get dressed before
The eyes of men?

COUNTESS

             Mac-X? He's not a *man*!
Hand me that pin.

MAC-X

Who hadn't completely gone out.

              You don't think me a man!
Well then, my lady. I do beg your pardon
For catching at these words of yours, when I
Let slip so many others that are tossed

My way — Yes, people such as I are not
As you say 'men,' we are merely creatures
Bound firmly to you, or better than most
Suited to value you aright; not *men*,
Not men at all! Before our eyes you may
Fasten a frock with sure fingers, not skipping
A single button in the row…

Cooling back down.

                              Forgive me,
Please, dear lady and dear cousin!
The words that fell from my lips stronger are
Than he who speaks them. Please, forgive me. But
I would add one thing more: It sometimes haps
That those who are not *men* today become men,
One day — it's all a matter of the background,
And when that changes, they stand out, at last.

COUNTESS

Forcefully.

Mac-X! Forgive me if my words have stung you —
Their hasty utterance outstripped the sense
Of what I had in mind…

MAC-X
                        It's I who rushed
My speech, which ought to have expressed
Some other content, slower… Ah, but now,
The chain of thought's been ruptured, and I have
Nothing more to add.

MAGDALENA
                        You're making a scene
For one slight word, or light manner of speech,
Accepted in the world, but — it's not hers —

It's not her way at all, I assure you, sir…
She spoke improperly, the gaucheness taking
From the improper atmosphere she breathes
As do we all, and shapes the way we speak
Despite our better will.

MAC-X
                    Madame! And I
Overpassed the boundaries of sincerity
In casting out unbridled words like that.
And if it is a weakness, still I must
Depart without finishing our conversation —
That weakness is my own, my personal
Fault, due to my flawed nature, not to any
'Improper atmosphere I breathe, that shapes
The way I speak.'

COUNTESS

Forcefully.

Mac-X! I'd like to… Come this evening, please!

MAC-X

Ceremoniously.

Madame — dear cousin — I'll be here without fail.

Exits.

COUNTESS
Hand me my camphor, and that pocket watch.

MAGDALENA
An unexpected event, unnoted
In your day-order list, has caught you out,
Off guard, off balance. For this world of ours

Is like a mediocre playwright, who
Sketching a few initial characters
Expects them to encompass the whole play,
Complete, intelligibly... and they moan
That Shakespeare's Caesar won't fit on the stage,
Being too tall by a whole head... Still, those who
Expect others to progress in some way
Ought to behave with like predictability.

COUNTESS

Impatiently.

I haven't time for this! You'll sermonise
Later... I've left you your whole list of tasks.

She gets up quickly to leave, then halts at the door and returns.

There's one more thing... I've left my missalette,
Taking last year's city calendar instead.

MAGDALENA
Here is your book of devotions. Goodbye!

Exit Countess.

MAGDALENA

Sola.

Ah you, with your last year's city calendar
And tattered dress and... eyes blue as the sky...
You are a saint! And I respect you, truly —

Profoundly.

Others might look sarcastically upon
Your faux-pas; for me they are something grand.

I peer through your tatters to see heaven
Like a prisoner who gazes through his bars
At the pure skies… Are there any people here
On earth who enjoy a greater freedom?

Scene 2

MAGDALENA

Gazing at the list, she rings.

So all that I'm to do is written down —
It's best to get it all done letter-perfect.

To Old Servant.

Draw back the table. Set chairs at the wall
To leave a space for dancing. And the same
In each salon adjoining. Should a guest
Arrive, show him to me.

NEW SERVANT

Entering.

Count Szeliga!

MAGDALENA
One moment.

She goes over to a mirror, checks her dress, takes her place. Then, to the Servant.

Send him in.

Scene 3

MAGDALENA

Taking the initiative.

                        Count Szeliga!
I'm Magdalena Tomir, the unworthy
Substitute that greets you in the name
Of Maria Harrys. I've already had
The pleasure of your acquaintance… But where? When?
I can't seem to recall the circumstances…

SZELIGA
Madame! It was but a few years ago,
In a locale that was far from poetic —
A railway station, in the company
Of a cousin of mine, you were…

MAGDALENA
                      Ah! Lesław!
I do remember it all now, quite clearly.
But since that time our paths have never crossed.

SZELIGA
For I was leaving Europe at the time
From that very station. I'm just now back
And here I meet you, once again.

MAGDALENA
                      Indeed,
A second time, and similar.

SZELIGA
                      Quite so.
Had some iota of the fatalism
So popular in the Orient fallen to me,
Tumbling from fakir's turban to my sleeve

While jostling through the casbah, I'd be fain
To see in this greeting the same farewell!

MAGDALENA

Equivocally.

Or in the farewell, a new greeting. Once again,
We'd be meeting for the first time.

Stridently.

                Alas,
But no one steps into the same stream twice!

SZELIGA
There's more comfort in that than sorrow.

MAGDALENA

                         True.

SZELIGA
We've not yet spoken of the lady of the house…

MAGDALENA

Sadly.

Of course… Who meditates on vanity
— The vanity of things — draws near her thought.
She… more than ever, is… aetherial.

SZELIGA

Lively.

And yet — they say — unless I am mistaken,
That she was soon… or is soon… to be wed?

MAGDALENA

Cunningly.

Those vows of hers are mystical… mystical…
And thus already pledged… but mystically
Speaking; indeed, what more is there to say?
And is it pleasant to speak overmuch?

SZELIGA
There are some things about which the less said
The better — the more merciful.

MAGDALENA
                              Often,
It's better to know clearly — yes, or no…

SZELIGA
Details are nothing more than anecdotes.

MAGDALENA
That's the main thing when someone's taken up
A firm decision that reforms her person
Entirely… Fixity, stability
Are virtues, as I see it. But these too
Can be fatal. What is fixity worth
In conjunction with a comet, whose orbit
Has changed?

SZELIGA

With a curious stress.

I'm in your debt… for something… I don't know…
How is the Countess' health?

MAGDALENA

Coolly.

                              Oh… she's quite well…

SZELIGA

Stands, moves over to the window.

We've had, this morning, something like a storm…

MAGDALENA
It's made the air grow cooler, that's for sure.

SZELIGA

Frantically.

Summer storms… lightning bolts and thunderclaps,
Even with downpours can be something pleasant…

MAGDALENA
I'm always grateful, for the flowers' sake…

Naively.

My window-sills are full of blooms, you see —
All thick with leaves and tendrils so, that when
The sun strokes them with its beams, the whole white room
Is filled with dancing shadows of their petals
That twine into the most delightful garlands…
I know them all — by name, you might say — so
That when a casual passer-by once plucked one,
And no uncommon one, a red geranium,
I noticed it… I sensed the loss.

CYPRIAN KAMIL NORWID

SZELIGA

Jocularly.

                    How's that?
You mean to say that if you came across
That pillaged flower, you'd recognise it?

MAGDALENA

Lively.

Ah, no! Not that — I merely meant to say
I noticed its absence — and right away…

SZELIGA

As Magdalena glances at her watch.

There are such people who only meet up
After their time predestined has run out.

MAGDALENA
And when such meet, they meet as intimates…
I apologise for glancing at my watch;
It's only because Maria's given me —

She rings, the Old Servant enters and takes the letters from her to post them.

So many chores. And her instructions are
Like military commands!

SZELIGA
                    Well. As I've said,
Some people meet only to see time's sands
Slip through their fingers, before their hands can meet.

MAGDALENA
Though when they meet, they meet as intimates.

SZELIGA
In Europe, that's something unusual.
But in the East, it's an accepted custom
Upheld by faith, or... social addiction:
The Arab considers him to be his brother,
Upon whomever his tent's shadow falls.

MAGDALENA
Such brotherhood in Europe is unknown.

SZELIGA

Jocularly.

And yet one sometimes finds such sisterhood...

MAGDALENA
I've never noticed up till now, how odd
It is — that word — brotherhood — peculiar
To the masculine gender.

SZELIGA
                              There's the proof
How little Europeans understand it.

MAGDALENA
And I'm an Oriental actually —
My mother is of an old Polish line
Originally from Armenia.

SZELIGA

Examining her closely.

That's true — there's something Eastern in your beauty...

MAGDALENA
Which sometimes has been to my detriment.

Wearily.

Today's world looks with murky eye upon
Girls who are… odd… And they call that upbringing!
One mustn't extend one's hand too openly;
When one is odd, one is misunderstood…
One must be chary of one's smile, lest
It be taken as something… conniving.

SZELIGA

Profoundly.

They think up philanthropic institutions
Out of self-interest, to keep at arm's length
Those they find different; and thus they cloak
The meanness of their souls in charity!
They fear a cannibal in crinoline…
Sidling backwards — right into the maw
Of the very dragon that's waiting to devour them!

MAGDALENA

With repugnance.

To sniff out rot on all hands, to enslave
Oneself, submitting to another's lie;
To crimp one's gait, lest others misconstrue
One's movements — is to limp toward Golgotha —
But that, the Golgotha of Antichrist!

She gets up and extends her hand. Szeliga does the same.

You know yourself — the Arab extends his hand
Oh — just like this, and trusts with perfect faith
That he who clasps it will not play him false!

While they remain thus, hands clasped, the Countess enters suddenly.
She halts at the threshold.

Scene 4

COUNTESS

Coolly.

I do apologise for entering
At such an inopportune moment…

Collecting herself, she blushes.

I mean — as in my absence Magdalena's
The lady of the house, I should have asked
To be announced before I dared to enter.

Casting aside rosary, book, and gloves.

I came too late to the charity event!

Offering Szeliga her fingertips.

Your telegram from Smyrna was illegible.

Nodding towards Magdalena.

Only just now she deciphered it for me.

SZELIGA

Aside.

Now there's a frigid front blown in!

A deep — magnetic — moment of silence.

MAGDALENA

Breaking the silence.

You haven't seen each other for quite some time?

COUNTESS
Am I supposed to recall such details?

SZELIGA

Cordially.

Two years it's been, my lady, since I've seen
Reflected in a lake the cloud your eyes
Deign rest upon…

COUNTESS

With revulsion.

     Such fleshly poetry!

MAGDALENA
A somewhat Oriental expression,
But not surprising in one just returned
From travels in the East — there's no reason
To be astonished…

To Szeliga.

     Soon, Sir, you'll recall
The tropes of Northern speech — as crisp as frost…

COUNTESS

With irony.

Again she's explicating telegrams!

To Szeliga, nodding towards Magdalena.

Is such a skilled translator to be found
In all of Palestine, sir...? A propos,
Why is it that you wear no rosary
Such as the pilgrims from Jerusalem
Are wont to bring back?

SZELIGA

Bitterly.

            I had one... of tears
That fell into the Dead Sea, surely by chance,
When thinking of friends distant; it was changed
Into dense grains of opal, crystalline,
Unutterably hard and bright... as ice.
Since that time I've dispensed with rosaries!

MAGDALENA

Stepping in.

One might dispense with anything at all
That slips so fatally through one's fingers.
Perhaps that's our great fortune.

COUNTESS

Stridently.

            I agree —

Entirely, whatever earthly things
One loses, teaches one blest resignation.

Pause.

But is a rosary an earthly thing?
This I must learn…

She takes out pencil and notebook, poised to write.

SZELIGA

      The kind I'm speaking of
Was threaded of a man's tears…

More forcefully.

       One man's tears,
Not those of all humanity, and so
It was an earthly thing, no doubt about it,
But priceless nonetheless! Now, I myself
Am just a man — a fosterling of Earth,
Where storms rage, and volcanos belch their fire,
Where lightnings flash through tempests in the skies…
But these are things that angels overlook
Just like — oh, citydwellers who appraise
The rain from underneath a parasol
Or through a carriage windowpane, without
The eye of those who work the land…

COUNTESS

Musing aloud.

       The angels know
Best, the best of all…

SZELIGA

Ceremoniously.

If you say so, Madame.

COUNTESS

Wearily.

One thing's for sure —they're never late for works
Of mercy — they always arrive on time
To their committee meetings. What they do,
They always do better than we.

To Szeliga.

Tonight
We've planned a little evening…

MAGDALENA

Which might be
Angelic, too. Girls from the boarding school
Will come to dance. How beautiful they are,
And full of goodness!

COUNTESS

Dance?! Oh, well. Perhaps…
But there'll be innocent entertainments too.
That's been determined.

Sternly, in general.

It's best to spurn the earth in everything.

About to exit, she once more presents Szeliga with her fingertips.

Until tonight.

SZELIGA

Bows.

> For sure…! This world, indeed,
Deforms men, inept potter! It kneads our clay,
But lacks the talent to shape us aright.

Scene 5

MAGDALENA

To Szeliga, who halts, hat in hand.

Must you be off so soon?

SZELIGA

>   I thought the hour
For paying visits was over.

MAGDALENA

>   Oh, those rules
Are not so hard and fast, judging from her —
I mean, how one can even miss the hour
Set for committee meetings…

SZELIGA

Toying with the objects tossed on the table.

>   This rosary…
Is not from Jerusalem.

MAGDALENA

>   You don't say?
We always thought it was.

SZELIGA

                    Venetian goldsmiths
Produce the like — but they are decorations
Made to be worn, with beads of varied colours
That match one's gender, or the gloves one wears.
The rosaries from Constantinople —
The ones the Muslims use — have a sweet scent,
And so are useful, too.

MAGDALENA

                    So then, there's fashion,
Perfume, and lastly, you can pray with them.

SZELIGA

Earnestly.

I've nothing against manufacturing
Wherever such arises rationally;
And piety's not incompatible
With happiness and pleasure, surely?

MAGDALENA

                                    Well,
When there was but one church in Jerusalem,
One only, and the whole nation set out
To fill it piously on holy days,
And the whole world waited, impatiently,
On the arrival of those holy days…

SZELIGA
When joyous songs of praise rang through the air
Above the paths fragrant with balsam scent…

MAGDALENA

Noticing him toying with a glove.

You'll soil Maria's glove!

SZELIGA

Equivocally and jocularly.

So small a thing,
What if I did… deflower it so?

MAGDALENA

Breaks out in laughter.

Ha, ha, ha, ha!

SZELIGA
What's so funny?

MAGDALENA
Small? Well, then it's my glove
You've got there!

She slips it on her hand.

See? Just look how small it is!
And you thought that it was Maria's glove —
And then it seemed to you…

SZELIGA

Rises and kisses her gloved hand.

I beg your pardon.

MAGDALENA

Rising.

You may leave now!

Pause.

But not for the late hour!

SZELIGA

Strongly.

If it's not time that shoos me hence, that power
That no man is able to overcome,
I would be blamed for leaving if I went.

MAGDALENA
Time passes on, until that hour comes
At which — I'd hope — to see you here again.

Staring him straight in the eye.

Especially as I find you much less sad
Then you were just fifteen minutes ago…
I sense less bitterness in the words you speak.

SZELIGA
To pay a visit… such a trifle it seems,
And yet it has a deep significance.
There are such people, in whose presence we
Are subtle, and naive, and there are such
Who'd put Raphael to work painting shingles,
Draughting each detail clearly, monstrously;
And it's for such that we become opposites
Of whom we are, and elevated feelings
And… style itself. And thus, turned inside-out,
We suffer violence, a paroxysm,
Convulsions — it's here bitterness arises,
When custom, which enjoins — quite properly —

Smoothness and flow, stifles us from the outside.
Just one impediment the more.

MAGDALENA

Very sadly.

To play Beethoven for such people must
Be an exceptionally pleasant business.

SZELIGA
Because it pleased you to assume the role
Of a physician for such sufferings,
I've uncovered this weakness to your eyes.

Deeply.

For it's weakness indeed — a real weakness…

MAGDALENA

Solemnly.

Since one knows it's a weakness…?

SZELIGA

Finally making to leave.

                              … One knows pain!

Exit.

Scene 6

MAGDALENA

Draws near the table, picks up her glove.

This glove is like a gauntlet thrown… My own!
Peculiar tournament!

She smiles.

                If only all
Maria's orders were so carefully
Fulfilled, by everyone…

OLD SERVANT

Enters, announces:

                The Supervisor
Of the Fireworks Display seeks admittance.
He's been sent by the Countess to retrieve
Some sketch…

MAGDALENA
                She's setting off some fireworks
In my head surely!

To Servant.

                All right, he may enter.
I've no idea what this is all about.

SUPERVISOR OF FIREWORKS

Enters, smooths his hair, and speaks: fluently, in one great rush.

I had the honour of demonstrating
On paper several modes of fireworks
To Countess Harrys, such as we've performed
If I may make a boast, to much applause;
Especially one like a peacock's fan
Transformed into a quiver of arrows
From Cupid's bow — ah, such delight we've wrought!
The spectators, my most worthy Madame,
Lifted me to their shoulders…

Pause.

                           Then twin fountains
Of hearts, I added, and each of the hearts
Burst off the stage, as if a martial scrimmage
Devolved into catastrophe, But! Down front,
A brilliant glory blazed, announcing triumph —
The… Countess wasn't too taken with that…
So I prepared a gigantic, rosy Cupid…

MAGDALENA

Suppressing laughter.

What did she think of that?

SUPERVISOR
                         She… wasn't ravished…
She preferred something lighter. Cupid, you see,
The whole, gigantic Cupid? that requires
Such a machine that cannot be set up
In just a couple hours. So I passed
On to some simpler thrills: suns, stars, and comets…

MAGDALENA

Growing tired of all this.

And in the end?

SUPERVISOR

> She sent me for the sketch.

MAGDALENA

With concealed irony.

Could you not, perhaps, manage to do… zero?

SUPERVISOR
We in these arts call that 'zero' a 'ring.'

MAGDALENA
Ah, what a splendid thought —

SUPERVISOR

With enthusiasm.

You understand! At last! For once in my life!
With your permission, Ma'am…

MAGDALENA

Aside.

> That's all I need,
For this one to court me too…

SUPERVISOR

Competently.

> Two rings… quite…
Pierced by an arrow… More than possible!
And we can add a parrot to each side,

And to the rear, a flaming, fiery tail
With lightning bolts to heighten the effect…
It can be done… It will have its own charm!

MAGDALENA

Bored.

And so, a simple matter. There's no need
To search any further. The artist's mind
Conceives it all, sketching it on his soul.

SUPERVISOR

With heated enthusiasm.

At last, someone has comprehended me!
For once in my life!… Your humble servant.

Exit.

MAGDALENA
I hear the light footsteps of the worthy Maria —
She needs a little dressing-down, I think!
So dear, so good, sometimes so entertaining…
I criticise her — yet I love her too.
She can be as naive as a small child
And then, as stately as a marble statue.
Now I look at her with a nurse's eye,
Now with that of a sculptor at the block…

As soon as the Countess enters, Maria confronts her.

You almost ruined everything, you know!
You almost played the traitor to yourself!
I received Szeliga as you bade me to,
With all politeness softening the blow
Of your final rejection of his suit;

I wafted all his gloomy thoughts away,
And spoke of the customs of generations
Which live, patriarch-like, in our own days,
Where ceremonials of suicide
Are not fulfilled on human hearts, and you,
When we were speaking of the sort of gestures
Used in society, with our hands clasped,
Then you rush in! With earthy bitterness,
Seeing our hands joined, you withdrew. How could you
Give him the hope of triumph thus? Indeed,
To heed your orders is to work the loom
Of Penelope!

Stronger.

       How I had to sweat
To spin your conversations true — just like
A sprocket in a factory machine!
How clumsily you betrayed yourself, madame!

COUNTESS

Severely.

I couldn't have betrayed myself at all!
Perhaps I spoke, or acted, like a child,
But I knew how to withdraw, immediately!

MAGDALENA

Lively.

And you did worse thereby!

COUNTESS

Sadly.

                    Perhaps, because
I once too had a crumb of earthly feeling
For him I pushed away today.

MAGDALENA
                    That's it!
That's where the harm lay…

COUNTESS
                    What? In a trifling atom?
A crumb, I say!

MAGDALENA
             Crumbs must be swept away
Too, angel mine! Or else you'll ruin it
Again — what's just repaired. You mustn't stint
In cooling him.

COUNTESS
             As if I'd time for that!
But — you are good; you are so patient, dear;
You've saved me once, today — save me again!
Yes! Keep on saving me! You'll be the saviour
Of your Maria. Magdalena, please,
I beg you! Be good to me!

MAGDALENA
                    It's not easy,
But we've made a good start, nipping the bud…

COUNTESS
Right? Seems to me he left just as he'd come.

MAGDALENA

Equivocally.

Well, not entirely. But somewhat, yes.

Pause.

All right, I'll take your salvation upon
These shoulders, whatever the cost, but — first
Your word: that whatever you say or do
Will be in line with, ruled by, my direction.

COUNTESS
I give you my most solemn word.

MAGDALENA
                              All right —
Sit down by me a while.

They sit down next to one another.

                              Have you considered
Who ought to fill the vacuum that you leave
In the heart of Szeliga?

Carefully.

                              There'll be much
To choose from with the girls who come tonight,
If it's a younger lass you've got in mind.

COUNTESS
The future mothers of the area;
Something, indeed, like our society's
Distant reflection… Only, they're so young!
No one among them, for example, is
Your age, your height…

MAGDALENA

In a decided tone.

                              Thanks for the clarity!

COUNTESS
They're only children, all of them —

MAGDALENA

With feigned surprise.

                              Ah! True!

Pause.

Yet you'll admit — the idea has its merits.
If it can but be set in motion, that is.
And — I have a falcon's eye, is that not so?
When I would be of use to you?

COUNTESS
                              My dear!
You've got a good head on your shoulders, yes!

MAGDALENA
You've got to cool him down — drench with ice water
Those earthy fires of your ardent votary.

Half trivially.

This way, we might arrive at a complete
Uprooting of his passion; in the end
He'll find peace…

COUNTESS

Frantically.

                    He's grown out his beard, and he's
Been to Jerusalem…

MAGDALENA

        …Loses rosaries
In the Dead Sea…

COUNTESS

        A murky parable
That even you have difficulty parsing
In human speech for me…

Kisses her forehead.

        Oh, Magdalena,
You've got a good head on your shoulders, yes!

        Curtain.

ACT III

The main salon of the villa. Broad doors give out onto a verandah; side doors give onto other salons.

Scene 1

COUNTESS

Milling among her guests.

Thank you for coming.

MAC-X

        …a little too early, perhaps…

COUNTESS
Oh, not at all. So many guests are here
Already.

MAC-X

Drawing near someone carrying a tray of pastries.

    And it was no easy thing,
For I've been suffering all day long.

COUNTESS
Don't eat that! It might not agree with you.
That's for the children with big appetites
From running around so much…

Taking note of Szeliga nearby with his relative.

Count Szeliga… Mac-X!

GUEST 1
                 This villa — ah!
It breathes the good taste of our charming countess…

GUEST 2
The ornament of our province, indeed!

COUNTESS
It's your politeness, sirs, augments its value.

GUEST 2
It's your politeness, ma'am, does us the honour
Of thinking so.

SZELIGA

To Magdalena.

          If I may be so bold —
Who's this Mac-X?

MAGDALENA
                    A distant relative
Of Maria's late husband.

MRS DUREJKO
                    The girls are all
So gay tonight — I cannot calm them down!

GUEST 1
No matter the age or gender, all of us
Share in the same rapture.

GUEST 2
                         Oh, that verandah!
I just can't tear my eyes away from it!

MAGDALENA

To Szeliga.

Sir — you who have seen so many wondrous things —
Have your eyes ever fallen on so much beauty
As this flock of maidens? See how they crowd
Around the countess — little girls, near-women…
Ah, what a splendid sight!

SZELIGA
                    I've seen my share
Of beauty, but I've never been so high-
Transported to behold the Virgin Mary
Smiling upon the cherubim…

COUNTESS
                         Stop there!
I will not listen to such sinful speech!

SZELIGA

Aside.

Palsied imagination! Frigid mind…

MAGDALENA

To Countess.

Excellent, excellent — keep it up like that!
You've got to freeze him!

SZELIGA

Sonorously.

          Can it be a sin,
What has inspired legions of artists
Of brush and chisel, singing litanies…

JUDGE
Ha! Fiction's not a sin, but that's a fiction.
The countess is a purist. Like Durejko.

SZELIGA

Aside, with distaste.

That, or some other thing…

MAGDALENA

To Szeliga.

          Why are you sad?

SZELIGA
Me? Not at all. But in comparison
With happy children, it might well seem so.

MAGDALENA

To Countess, with studied clumsiness.

Ask him — but wittily — why he's so sad.

COUNTESS

Approaching Szeliga directly.

If you are sad, you should eat some cold-cuts.

SZELIGA

Nearing the smorgasbord.

They say sad persons ought to eat something.

MAC-X
It's not so much about the appetite,
As how sad moods promote a good digestion.

SZELIGA
You don't say? Come then, let us sigh, and eat.

MAC-X

Eating.

One often eats at sea too, sailing out,
Away from the shore stretching out its arms
Toward us…

Some people enter through the middle doors.

GUEST 1
> That verandah is a wonder!
A real wonder — and that's that!

JUDGE
> An isle enchanted,
Hey?
Has anyone a better metaphor?
These cypresses, my good sir — how romantic!
And other bushes leaning this way, that…
So extra-moving…

COUNTESS
> One thing's still lacking —
But I've not yet come up with the right shape:
I'd like it if a tomb shone there among
Those cypresses…

GUEST 1
> Ah, no! Ah, no, your grace!
A tomb, in close proximity to the house?

COUNTESS
An empty tomb, a cenotaph merely,
A place to brood when evening falls.

SZELIGA
> In Egypt,
They've such familiarity with tombs
That people take their suppers in among them.

JUDGE
I must admit that in Durejko Village
I had a tombstone raised upon the grave
Of my dog, when he passed — Madame Durejko
Wrote a short verse that's carved thereon —

To Mrs Durejko.

                                        Come, dear,
How does your poem go? Recite it, please!

MAGDALENA and COUNTESS
How marvellous! You're a poet, madame?
Why have you kept that from us up till now?

GUEST 1 and GUEST 2
Ah, wonderful! You make verses!

MRS DUREJKO

To Judge.

                        For shame!
What sort of example are you setting
For the children?

To all.

                My Klemensulko's joking —
So jovial today!

MAC-X
                You surely don't
Mean to suggest that verses denigrate
The hands of their creator?

JUDGE

Violently.

                        Homer died
In poverty, my little lordling! But
In the rhymed proverbs of the folk are found
Much sense, if you but dig beneath the surface.

MAGDALENA

To Szeliga.

What do you think of that false tomb concept?

SZELIGA
That wasn't her invention, but Egypt's.
And they married their mummies, ate with them,
And danced…

MAGDALENA
                   Which must have looked a graceful twirl…

SZELIGA

With melancholy.

It's a sad concept. Here's the reason why:
Those it occurs to are often bereft
Of vital feelings… but I'd rather not
Initiate you into the gloomy details
Which are not very entertaining.

MAGDALENA
                              Please!
I beg you to, indeed!

SZELIGA

Seriously and slowly.

                    Death is a string
On life's harp, and it hums continually,
In every melody, and so it must.
Whoever would unstring it, must replace it
With something else to hold the bass, and such
Need graves to brood upon when evening falls —

This is the melancholy in it all,
Which has nothing to do with cenotaphs.

MAGDALENA
I understand exactly what you mean!

SZELIGA
That rarely happens…

COUNTESS

Approaching.

                            Of what are we speaking?
Some anecdote?

MAGDALENA
                    About your garden tomb.

COUNTESS
I've given it a lot of thought myself,
And still I don't know how I should set about
Designing such a tomb, which also should
Serve as a bower…

Catching sight of her cousin.

                    Mac-X, don't forget —
I am expecting you tomorrow morning.
We have some things to speak about that we've
Put off for far too long.

MAC-X

Ceremoniously.

                    My dear madame…

COUNTESS
Come, let's think up some game for the children,
Or two — appropriate to their age.

JUDGE
                              Or three!
I vote for two, or three.

YOUNG WOMEN and GIRLS

Running up.

                    On the verandah!
On the verandah! Everyone together —
There's so much space there, on the farthest lanes,
Just like in the salon! Yes, all, among
The boughs of fragrant trees, where the glass spheres
Are hanging like some unripe oranges
That flash with light when the sun is going down.

YOUNGER GIRLS
Out on the lawn's edge, by the verandah —
That's just the place to play 'slipper' and 'kitty'!
The older girls can stay in the salon
And talk with the old folks!

ELDER GIRLS
                    On the contrary —
Let all the children stay in the salons
So that adults might keep their eye on them!
While we go strolling through the shady lanes
Arm and arm, friend with friend, to have a glance
At everything all the way to the wall!

ALL
On the verandah! Everyone together!

MRS DUREJKO
The maidens who already have their wreaths
May go to the verandah —

COUNTESS
                              And meanwhile
We'll think up some proper entertainments…

MRS DUREJKO
We must ever keep distinctions in mind,
However all are well educated
According to the Durejko System,
If I may boast, which draws upon many
Schemes paedagogical, without mimicking
Or appropriating the essence thereof…

JUDGE

Leaping near from the verandah doors.

According to the natural thingkenning,
'Essence' is what we call 'allhighestness'!

MRS DUREJKO

Over her shoulder.

But that's not highness 'onallhandsity…'
Mon mari est puriste!

GUEST 1 and GUEST 2
                              As he should be!
As he should well be! Vivat the judge, his honour!
The time's come for our own terminology!

MAGDALENA

Taking care of one of the girls.

We'll swap all the young ladies' wreaths of bay
For ribbons of the colour that most suits
The wearer. How pretty she is in blue!

To the girl.

And Marta?

The girl runs off to find Marta.

        It's no trivial matter
To form a child's taste; if there are other
Things more important, still, it's good and proper,
That we rely on our own wits to suit
Our clothing to the season and occasion.

COUNTESS

Going off with another girl.

How pretty is she now, in amaranth!
And Anielka?

The girl runs off.

ALL THE GIRLS
All in a ring! A ring! All in a ring!
And let Anielka be the first to play
In the gay ring, turning round, and you, sir —

To Mac-X.

You will hold the tokens in the basket.
And then the judgement! Then the penalty!
ALL THE CHILDREN
All in a ring! A great ring! All in a ring!

MRS DUREJKO
The young ladies will stay on the verandah;
The girls will dance their ring in the salon.

COUNTESS
There's more than enough room there for the game!

ALL THE GIRLS
All in a ring! A ring! All in a ring!

COUNTESS
I will present the ribbon, and… this ring.

GUEST 1
The Grand Mogul would be proud to wear that
Stone in his turban! — O, madame, I say!

GUEST 2
It shines like braided lightning.

MAC-X
                                        Every stone
Is from the Mogul's turban — for they're dead,
Yet still they shine on and retain their value…

COUNTESS
It seems to me, today, that it's most proper
To use that shiny gewgaw in this wise —
It's so large, and so shiny, it seems made
For the occasion.

GUEST 1
                        Such a jewel preserves
Its value in itself, and pleases more
Than just the eyes of children.
GUEST 2 and OTHERS

Chorus-like.

Your ring, madame,
Pleases us all; it's a fine ring, madame.

SZELIGA

Who had been sitting to the side with Magdalena suddenly starts.

The countess offers her ring as a prize?
Then I shall try my luck…

COUNTESS

Sternly.

No — I take it back.
I withdraw it from the game.

MAGDALENA

With emphasis.

Good. That's right!

SZELIGA

Aside.

So cold, it makes me shiver!

COUNTESS

To Magdalena, seriously.

She'll wager hers…

SZELIGA
Madame, if that's to be the case, I too withdraw.
For then I'd have to be in the next room,
Basking in cold, reflected light.

MAGDALENA

Listening to the exchange.

                              Maria,
Come, give your ring.

COUNTESS

Obediently.

                    I'll put it on myself.

SZELIGA
I've grown used to adapting myself
To different climates, but now I feel… feverish.

MAGDALENA

Looking Szeliga straight in the eye.

That's nothing but a… solstice of the nerves
Which, though its causes are mysterious,
Some people, though they never change their clime
Are all the same, sensitive to its pull.
So disappointment pierces to the bone
Like shivers, and one's spirit can catch cold…
A clumsy expression that — his honour the judge
Might well replace it with some fitting mint;
But in its way it does describe a state
Well-known, though not fatal, more or less…

SZELIGA
When we bid farewell to certain people,
The earth ceases to be round. It grows flat
Remarkably; the sun takes on a glow
Queasy, like brass; the green takes on a hue

Like billiard felt — a fabric clean, and even,
And proper.

MAGDALENA
                And it's the others' fault?

SZELIGA
Yes. For there are other people, and from them
When we depart, the very stairs and porch
Take on a comely grandeur; yard and drive
Are bathed in an extraordinary light
As if the sun were an old master painter,
And even should a wind and tempest rage
We uncover ourselves to their black fury
Sensing in them something brisk and sublime.

They rise and begin to move toward the doors leading to a side salon.

MAGDALENA

With studied indifference.

How beautiful thresholds and stairs can be!

SZELIGA
In his *Odyssey*, Homer speaks at length
Of the threshold upon which Penelope's foot
Rested.

MAGDALENA
                Weighty evidence! And this threshold?

SZELIGA
Is not lacking a certain charm itself.

As they disappear into the side salon, Mac-X enters, sadly, and sits down at the table upon which the food is spread.

Scene 2

MAC-X

Solus.

And so it turns out that one moment merely
Of doubt, one mere impetuous, fleeting thought,
Can weigh upon one all day long, even if
One forgets it entirely.

Rapping the table.

                    This pistol
Rattles against the furniture, needless.

Eating.

I had an empty stomach, certainly.
My body thought to put an end to it…

To himself, with a smile.

Byron is right: the courage of the ancients
Depended on a proper digestion!

Sonorously.

That sounds like cynicism. Measured at…?
Them.
At those who look upon tragedy from afar,
Never approaching fate, nor ever touching
The idols with their fingers — and for this,
This very reason, they become idolaters.

MRS DUREJKO

Entering briskly.

For shame!
How can you be so materialistic?
They're in there having fun, and here you sit
Eating and drinking, and letting slip by
The most propitious of occasions! Come!
Go and collect the tokens in the basket!

Significantly.

Those maidens come from all over the province —
They're like a well-composed bouquet of flowers:
All future wives and mothers, doughty helpmeets
To share in your triumphs and challenges alike!
Go sir — and make your reputation known
As a pleasant young man who knows what's what —
And then for many years hence, hundred-mouthed
Rumour, if I may assume an Attic vein,
Will flit from house to house with the report:
'Mac-X knows what is what! A fine husband
That proper, pleasant, Mac-X would be!' Go!
Take the basket and collect the prizes —
Madame Durejko's giving you good advice,
Like your own mother — from her Christian heart!

MAC-X
Your humble servant. As to your advice,
It would be better spent on the more fortunate.

MRS DUREJKO
A man forges his own fortune!

MAC-X
                              Ah, no!
The wanderer covered from tip to toe
In the white dust of the byways he treads
Bears patiently the swelter, keeping cool
By staying focussed on his journey's end,
Made happy even by his plodding steps.

But what will you say of that roadside tree
Covered, each day, each leaf, and every blossom
With bitter lime-powder and sand kicked up
By passing feet and hooves and wheels? With what
Can it regale its green, so thickly choked,
In gazing at the passing wheels, that seem
Wheel after wheel of torture? Dust-to-dust,
Dust-to-dust those wheels creak by, each carriage,
Like a funeral conduct?

MRS DUREJKO
                    Why don't you
Translate some poems for the girls to declaim?

MAC-X
Later, perhaps. Now, let's go collect the prizes.

Scene 3

COUNTESS

Enters.

Come! Go collect the prizes! They've been at it
A long time now. Mac-X! Go to the children!

Mac-X exits; some guests enter through the verandah doors.

COUNTESS
The chief thing's taken care of now! One ring
Spins out on the verandah, another twirls
In the salon, and *basta*.

To the guests.

                    I was concerned
Lest they not be pleased, worried if I could

Host this *petit monde* of smiling, rosy faces…
Nor do I hold you free of blame, my friends;
For while those entertained my guests, you were
Merely assistants to the task at hand.

Mysteriously.

And yet, as my collaborators, I'll
Share a small secret kept from all the girls:
I was most worried with the evening's end,
With the finale to the entertainments;
Desiring that this world of youth depart
With memories of charming afterglow;
And so, there past the cypresses, where I
Am planning that garden tomb, I've arranged
A fireworks display.

GUEST 1
                        Ha, ha! That's brilliant!
Indeed, a bright idea!

GUEST 2
                        Each idea
Of yours, madame, is a real phoenix…

JUDGE
                                            Yes!
That rises from the flames, like fireworks!

GUEST 1 and GUEST 2
Good show, your honour!

MRS DUREJKO
My Klemensulko has an oriental
Imagination.

JUDGE

Skipping to the front.

        Ah — our Homelander
Would say that I'm 'easternish thoughtmakingwise.'

MURS DUREJKO
What's proper's proper...

MAGDALENA

To Szeliga.

           And what do you think
Of our little surprise?

SZELIGA
I'm feeling more and more incapable
Of carrying on a conversation, yet
In response to your kind question, I'll say
That I find fireworks a much more pleasant thing
Than tombs, even empty ones. For I feel
We have a duty not to sadden friends.
But there's enough room by those cypresses
For both, and a third thing as well, a bower
In which it might be pleasant, of an evening
To take a light snack.

MAGDALENA

Jocularly.

          Come, let's ask Anielka
And Róża... if they share your opinion!
They're fit for such exchanges; as for us,
The presence of children refreshes one's style!

A FEW PERSONS

Together, in surprise.

Something's happened in the salon!

MAGDALENA

                What? What's the matter?

SZELIGA
One of the cherubim was knocked over

MRS DUREJKO
When children dance, expect an accident.

MAC-X

Entering from the salon.

The ribbon snapped and the ring rolled away…
The game is over…

MAGDALENA

           And so soon!

COUNTESS

Dully.

                      Of course,
Of course — and now the ring is gone!

JUDGE

                How, gone?
We'll search it out…

MAGDALENA
                              Here, take my ring until
We find it.

COUNTESS

With odd emphasis.

                    Pardon me, I'd rather not.
Let it be found — it was lost once already!

MAGDALENA
Aha — You're right, of course.

Countess exits to the salon.

MAGDALENA

In a half-whisper.

                              She's superstitious —
Everyone's got their weakness…

SZELIGA
                              Who would think
That any weakness was to be found — there.

MAGDALENA
You seem to think of her as someone perfect,
And certainly — you're not far wrong.

SZELIGA

Coldly.

                              Ah, no.
It's just that everything should be kept
In its own proper place. O — for example,

Pineapples grow not on glaciers in Greenland;
They are too sensitive to cold.

MAGDALENA

                              Beware!
I'll stand to Maria's defence, and you
Don't want to grapple with me; when I fight,
I take no prisoners — it's mortal combat!

OLD SERVANT

Entering from the side, broom in hand.

I'm telling you, the ring is just not there:
Not in that room, each corner of which I've swept
For thirty years — unless that ring has wings
And floated upwards…

MAGDALENA

                              Once already lost —

OLD SERVANT
Always the same old story! I know that, ma'am,
As I'm the one who found it last time. Where?
In the salon? I know each nook and cranny,
I dust them every day. Why, in my sleep
I'd set my finger on anything there
At the mere recollection. Should something
Be out of place or missing, I'd feel it.
Old servants speak like old men. Don't we have
A new one, taken on just lately? Perhaps
He'd think up something new?

JUDGE

Violently.

'A new servant!'
Those words are meaningful…

Rising, to Magdalena.

What is it worth,
The countess' ring?

MAGDALENA
On it is set
That famous stone that everyone just now
Was admiring — like a comet flashing
Against the dark enamel — valuable
Enough, but what most people do not know
Is that it is Maria's… talisman,
If it be proper to refer to such
A thing pertaining to her… All the same,
She has a sort of faith attached to it,
So that she'd rather lose all her other gems
That that one ring she's lost.

JUDGE

Searching for his hat.

It shall be found!
All we need here are energetic steps!

Pulling on his gloves.

It shall be found! I'll be right back with it.

MAGDALENA
What are you thinking of doing, Mr Durejko?

JUDGE

Exiting.

The time for execution's come, and vigour!

Scene 4

GUEST 1
The judge has his own, legal, point of view.

GUEST 2
The judge's legal eye's descried something.

MRS DUREJKO
Klemens has a sharp eye, but sometimes his
Imagination carries him away.

GUEST 1

To Mrs Durejko.

If your husband has a poetic vein,
That might arise from his cohabitation
With a poet…

MRS DUREJKO
                Ah, the dog's epitaph!
A trifle of the moment.

GUEST 2
                        Which we've not heard
Declaimed…

MRS DUREJKO
                It's only an imitation
Of Lamartine…

GUEST 1 and GUEST 2

Together.

Then all the more it's just
To reveal the weft of your braided laurels!

GUEST 1

To Szeliga and Magdalena.

Sir! Add your entreaties to our own! Madame,
Please intercede! The poodle's epitaph!
The canine threnody of Dura Wola!
Along with the barrage of fireworks!

MAGDALENA
Perhaps a more fitting moment…

GUEST 1 and GUEST 2
                              Excellent!!

The judge is heard, offstage.

A FEW PERSONS

With surprise.

What's happened now?

MRS DUREJKO
                    That's his master's voice…

SZELIGA
The judge, yes, and the police chief, gendarmes…

MAGDALENA
What is it?

MRS DUREJKO
          Klemens has energetically
Set the ball rolling.

MAC-X

Entering from the salon.

He's called in the police!

GUEST 1
Since there's some basis to instigate
A search, such haste is not to be censured.
The gravity of the matter demands it,
For obvious reasons — not hard to guess!

MAGDALENA
But — poor Maria! The honour of the house!

MAC-X
The lack of honour is sometimes known
By some as energy, or even vigour.

MRS DUREJKO
The judge is an exceptional person
By title, and by his social position —
What he shakes up, is shaken well indeed.

MAGDALENA
But, poor Maria's nerves!

SZELIGA

Coldly.

Yes? You don't say?
She is as sensitive as all that? Hmm.

GUEST 1
Let's draw aside…

GUEST 2

                    And have the Countess come
Among us to hear the recitation —
And that is that!

MRS DUREJKO

Heading to the verandah.

               At times like these, I like
To send the girls outside to pluck some flowers,
So that the blasts of winter none too soon
Disturb the bloom of May...

VOICE

Offstage, from the direction of the salon.

                       Respect the law!

NEW SERVANT

At the threshold.

And just because I'm new in her employ
Am I to be a suspect? For that reason?
Your local laws are queer! In Hamburg once
Where I'd accompanied his Grace the Margrave,
There was a similar coincidence:
The Persian ambassador had lost a pearl,
And all those present, whether lord or servant,
Were patted down just as politely!

Equivocally.

And if one of the noble gents, in lifting
A napkin from the table, happened to knock

The ring into his pocket? Queer, queer laws;
But there's another Judge besides this one!

JUDGE

Leading the countess by the arm.

If you'd be pleased, madame, here to retire
For just a spell…

To his wife, over the countess' shoulder.

         O, Klementyna, please
I entrust Countess Harrys to your heart…

VOICES OFFSTAGE
If that is true, why must servants alone
Be subject to investigation?

SZELIGA

Rising.

         Quite!
That's true — Everyone who was present here
During the game…

COUNTESS

Sits, stunned.

         I never thought to see
Such an affront in my own hearth and home.
I feel… degraded. How can I, I beg you,
Tender my apologies to my guests…
What a misfortune!

SZELIGA
                    None whatsoever!
Durejko's hastiness, and the proper forms…

COUNTESS
Durejko, ah!

GIRL

Running in from the salon.

                    You should see all the men
Turning their pockets inside-out, and plopping
All that they have into a hat — like prizes!

MRS DUREJKO
It's not polite to joke at such a sight
That's so unpleasant to Madame Harrys.

Loudly, toward the door.

Come girls — let's see the sunset from the yard
And search for violets among the grass…

Scene 5

Enter Police Official, Gendarme and Judge from the Salon.

OFFICIAL
There's only Mr Mac-X, and then we're done.

MAC-X
I won't allow my person to be searched.

JUDGE
And yarn by yarn, the ball becomes untangled.

MAC-X
My word of honour should suffice! Besides,
I took no part in any children's game.

OFFICIAL
Except for taking care of the prizes.

MAC-X
I won't allow this!

JUDGE

Patting down Mac-X.

Careful! That's a pistol!

MAC-X
Loaded with but one bullet…

OFFICIAL
That's enough!
Call in the guard.

COUNTESS

Stretching out her hand from where she sits.

Mac-X is my cousin.

MAC-X

Coolly.

We're rather distant relatives.

JUDGE

Loudly.

Distant!

OFFICIAL
Such details are of no concern to us.
A loaded weapon, that's another thing,
And during a search, which he at first refused —
That is our business. Sir, you are arrested
In the name of the law.

COUNTESS
                                    I won't allow it!
It was my intention to lose the ring.

OFFICIAL
No shame comes to your house by this arrest.

JUDGE
Madame protests that there are children present,
From all throughout the region. A child's nature
Is to spread news, of things both great and small,
And thus the story will —

OFFICIAL

Indifferently sitting himself down to write.

                                    The story *is.*
Already those who've come here from the town
To watch the fireworks — which were prepared
Quite openly, a secret only kept
From the children — saw us arrive, gendarmes,
Police, and their surmises now
Swollen into rumours certainly have spread
The news of some unusual event —
The consequences of such happenstance
Are unpredictable — something we know
Quite well from long experience.

MRS DUREJKO
                              What's worse,
Although such rumours miss the mark
Often — so hatefully! — empty rumours
Leave real stains in passing…

Leaning near the Countess.

                              Heart to heart
I speak, madame, although I share your pain…

Pause.

Klementyna Durejko née Wygiełło
Knows how to value ancient heritage,
The good name of a house, and as for morals —
Well, after all, she does direct a school
For young maidens…

JUDGE
                              You needn't fear a blotch
On your escutcheon on account of this;
As has been said, officially, so to speak.
And yet, the judge feels duty-bound to state

Gesturing toward the Countess.

That the arrested man has displayed certain…
Signs of… irrational behaviour;
Such cases are foreseen by law…

COUNTESS

Automatically.

                              Yes, yes —
My cousin sometimes acts irrationally…

MAC-X

Angrily.

No! Never! Though the fates may slander me,
Let them allow me so much: I'm not crazy!
Whence come these machinations?

To Official.

                              Sir, I beg you,
Strike from your record all these vain aspersions,
Especially as I'm now being subjected
To violence — and it is not right or proper
To give weight to the words of my oppressor!

OFFICIAL
In that case I strike from the record this
Testimony just proffered.

To Judge.

                              I see no
Evidence of a wandering reason.

JUDGE
In that case, we must strike the evidence.

To all.

Who seeks destruction, always finds a way!
And this in itself is sufficient proof
Of addled reason.

MAC-X

To Judge.

And as I see it,
What you're up to, sugar it as you will
— And clumsily! — deserves a harsher name.
For so it seems that it has been forgotten
That there are evils, indescribable,
And yet, he who commits them is upright.

To all.

I will be brief...

With effort.

... having regained my strength...
Since morning I'd been on an empty stomach...

Sits down.

I've been buffeted all day long by blows
Of an extraordinary character.
I was evicted from my lodgings, then
In search of kin or friends, I found no one...

COUNTESS

Striving to interrupt.

Mac-X...

MAC-X
I am truly ashamed to admit it...

COUNTESS
Mac-X! I gave you the ring! Don't you remember?

MAC-X

To Countess.

If you would be so kind, Countess, I beg you
Don't interrupt me!

Continues.

                I'm truly ashamed,
Ashamed to admit to what had crossed my mind:
A vulgar thought. Most common of the common —
That is, to end it all with one bullet!
Since suicide is something people foil
When they know your intentions, for that reason
I tried to stop myself from being searched…

The guards draw near, he extracts the gun.

Here is the weapon —

From another pocket:

                And here are some crumbs
Swept from this table…

Loudly.

                Let these two things here
Explain the rest! I am a man. Tell me —
What business is it of yours, officers,
Should some weak wretch seek to destroy himself?

OFFICER

Tears up his report.

And so we must start over once again…

ANIELKA, OLD SERVANT, OTHERS

Running in.

We've found your ring! We've found the ring, Madame!
Indeed it did have wings, for it was hanging
On a bronze branch of the candelabra!
It hung there like a star.

OLD SERVANT

While they were dancing
And the ribbon snapped, it must have flown off.

GUEST 1
It snuffed the candle to shine there instead.

OLD SERVANT, NEW SERVANT
Come see how prettily! But it's so high
No hand can reach it.

MANY PERSONS
Let's go! Let's go! What a strange thing to happen!

JUDGE

Inspired.

Bring forth a ladder! Set it at the wall!

GUESTS
Ah! The judge is always right on top of things!

JUDGE

Skipping close.

The garden ladder! From the verandah!

OFFICER

To Mac-X.

Permit me to tender my apologies
To you, sir, first, and then to you, Madame
Although unnecessary, officially speaking...

To Gendarmes.

Let's go!

COUNTESS

Offering her hand to Official.

     Farewell.

OFFICIAL

To Mac-X.

        I wish you better health.

Exit.

Scene 6

SZELIGA

Coming over to Mac-X.

My dear sir! All of us, we...

Noticing how pale he is.

          My dear sir,
Everyone's so concerned about that bauble...
Allow me to concern myself with man.
Perhaps you'd like to see a doctor?

COUNTESS

Not rising from her seat.

                                    Yes!
My Mercy Hospital's next door. The doctor
Stays there by rule, and perhaps the Provincial.

Over her shoulder.

You're suffering — from what?!

The old Servant enters with the ring on a tray. He places this down on the table; the Countess does not look at it.

MAC-X

To Szeliga.

It's nothing. I'm just tired. Let me sit down.

Sitting down.

I was on an empty stomach... These crumbs... And then
I ate too fast... And felt too — much. Then all
This happened...

To Szeliga.

But — can I tell you something?
Quickly and in confidence...
I'll take your offer, and I'll go abroad!
Tomorrow I'll be just a laughingstock
In these parts... as the rumour's making rounds
Already, as even the policemen say...
I'm in my wits enough to be aware
Of that...

Pause.

And anyway, my heart is sick.
There's no joy in me now. My time, my health —
Both used up. All I've got now is my name
And you see what they'll make of that name now...

COUNTESS

Rising.

Mac-X! You'll come with me first to each house
Here in the region, and wherever folk
Are used to stroll, so that the people see you
Here at my side, as someone close to me,
Whom I respect. And then I'll submit your name
To the committees, and you'll be inscribed
A member of the board — a permanent one —
In our Society of Mercy!

MAC- X

Looking for his hat.

I'm one already.
I'm a Christian.

COUNTESS

In silence, she goes over to the ring, picks it up and gives it to her cousin.

Mac-X, this ring I take from my right hand,
Just as it is, I — yes — I give to you;
And that will put an end to all their talk!
You hear? How quiet they've grown?

MAGDALENA

All but genuflecting.

                                    O, Maria!
You're taller now by one whole womanhood!
I've had a feeling about you for so long…

COUNTESS
Mac-X! Say something!

MAC-X

With a bow.

Madame, the gem you'd 'grated' me just now,
Surmising that they'd find it on my person —

COUNTESS
I wasn't thinking! But now, it's not just a ring
I'm offering you… Say something!

MAC-X
                                    All right, then.
Under the pressure of a scandal,
Wherever your hand would incline, would it come
Along with that most precious thing — free will?
Would you have it that your husband owed you
To scandal, rather than your own free choice?

Pause.

No, Madame, I'd be leading you astray.
Perhaps I'd even become a liar, like
The fellow who claimed to be a great marksman,
Finding a hawk stretched dead upon the ground,
Felled by a lightning bolt, by chance, after he
Shot, and missed the mark! Ah no, my noble cousin!

You err sublimely, but even so, you err.
What we call the sublime is so for this reason:
Sublime, in that it is above all hap.
It spills forth from a heavenly fountainhead,
Everywhere self-inspired, and always free.
Can one be coerced to magnanimity
Without once playing false to one's own will —
Which, in revenge, will deceive one too, in time?
The sort of man who would accept so great,
So tempting an excess of such a heart
Would be a cunning fellow merely. I,
In this age, in this nineteenth century,
Would rather not be skilled in cleverness.
Of course I have been clumsy — more than once.
Clumsy? Well, maybe metaphorically.
Why? Let him understand, who is capable.

COUNTESS

Angrily.

Listen! It is a man's duty to transform
The sudden elevated moment to
A smoothly flowing level tract of life!
But if you are too weak yourself to do this,
If you're not man enough, unfit for that,
I'll take the duty onto my own shoulders.

MAGDALENA

Enthusiastically.

Maria! You are marvellous!

SZELIGA

To Countess.

> Madame,
> Permit me to go back upon my word
> Given your cousin. For I'd tendered him
> A promise to fund him a trip abroad,
> Across the ocean to America.
> I now withdraw the pledge.

To Mac-X.

>   To break my word
> Gives me great pain… As for the consequences,
> I accept them.

COUNTESS

Looking directly into Szeliga's eyes.

>   That's true, sir. It is hard,
> Extraordinarily, what you have done,
> And do now, for whosever benefit
> You do so; you are noble twice over
> Since, in breaking your word, it remains pure.
> Wait but a moment, Count, upon my thanks,
> For I must ask my cousin for his answer,
> Which now is crucial.

Approaches Mac-X and takes him by the arm.

Mac-X! Then, have you never loved me, ever?

MAC-X

Bowing deeply at her feet.

> From a great distance… and ever more,
> Ever more mercifully great, that I
> Really don't know now whether, all the same,
> With ocean underfoot, and when above

The masthead of some foreign ship shall glimmer
The Southern Cross, the same pure beam of light
That binds us now, will then. Essentially,
When distant I was always close to you.
But then the space between us disappeared
And time vanished soon after. True enough:
Those who so love are no longer to be found
On earth, or are from some other world…

COUNTESS
No…! It's they, it's they who truly are human!

Pointing to Mac-X with her finger.

He speaks of the mystery of the sacred bond,
Though what he says, he knows not.

To her cousin.

                                        You now speak
As the great men did before Christianity,
Or like people who suffer much, and proclaim
A Christian sageness with the lips of error!
You love me, really!

SZELIGA, MAGDALENA, ALL
                          Is this… really her?

Mac-X, at the Couintess' feet, takes both her hands in his own.

COUNTESS
Magdalena — take the count's hands in yours —
Mine are too busy now to do him honour.

ANIELKA AND THE GIRLS

Running in.

All in a ring, a ring! Or else, the presents!

COUNTESS
My ring is no longer mine.

MAGDALENA
                              And once again
Mine has been lost, but it's not worth the search…

Fireworks.

But look — two diamond rings flash in the skies!

MANY PERSONS

Running to the verandah.

Diamonds, like constellations!

MRS DUREJKO

Looking on through a lorgnette.

                              A splendid artifice!

JUDGE

Skipping over to his wife.

Who loves his nation doesn't use the word
'Artifice' — 'Skillcraft!'

GUEST 1
                              Ah, the flaming skillcraft!

GUEST 2
What more is there to say?

While the majority are facing the verandah to watch the fireworks, the Judge advances to the front to deliver a monologue.

JUDGE

Solus.

This all is like some comedy, which has
A moral sense, if one but search it through —
But who's the cause of it? Who set the thing
In motion? Who's the flywheel here, that is,
The energetic motor of it all?
That is, the axis? Who, in other words
Is beyond reproach? Or — that I finally
Revert to Attic speech: *Ex machina?*
Who's the *ex-machina?*

Pause.

Why, Durejko!

As Durejko tries a little gracelessly to bow, the curtain falls.

CLEOPATRA AND CAESAR

A historical tragedy,
written equally for scenic presentation
and dramatic reading
with the enhancement of dramatic gestures
and their succession in time, noted.

PERSONS

Cleopatra	*Ruler of Egypt*
Julius Caesar	*Roman Consul*
Marc Antony	*Triumvir, Spouse of Cleopatra*

Court of Cleopatra

Eucastus	*Marshal of her Court*
Kondor	*Grand Master of Game*
Knight	*Commander of her Armies*
Psymmachus	*Her Architect*
Olympos	*Her Physician*
Zechera	*Her Soothsayer*
Eroe	*Her Kanephoros*
Jackal	*Her Table Server*
Hero	*Her Table Server*
Karpon	*Her Servant*

Faleg-Mun	*Son of a Diver*
Abdala Ganymedion	*Son of a Reaper*
Achilles	*Envoy of Ptolemus*
First Priest	
Second Priest	
Harper	

Julius Caesar's Staff
Fortunius
Calligion
Aelius Cinna

Cornelia	*Widow of Pompeius*
Delius	*Roman Guest of Cleopatra*
Plancus	*Envoy of Octavian*
Dolabella	*Envoy of Octavian*
First Centurion	
Second Centurion	
Lictor	
Commander of the Guard	
Captive	
Centurion[55]	

Egyptian Choruses	*Chorus of Youths;*
	Chorus of Maidens
Courtiers	*of Cleopatra*
Soldiers	*of Julius Caesar*

The action is set in the city of Alexandria and its environs, during the years 48 – 30 BC.

INTRODUCTION
A FEW WORDS CONCERNING THE HISTORICAL TEXT

I: Concerning the *idea* of the tragedy. II: Concerning its *dramatic reading*. III: Concerning its *staging*. IV: Its obligatory contemporary progress.

I

Whoever makes use of the term *national-tragedy* makes clear a disseizing of certain tragical sublimities such as constitute the very

---

55   *Translator's note:* In Polish, *setnik*, which means the same thing as 'centurion.' What distinction Norwid is making here is unknown.

CYPRIAN KAMIL NORWID

nature of the tragic genre. A *play* might be described as national, a tragedy — extremely infrequently, or not at all. *Calderon* and *Shakespeare* were aware of this, for they did not derive the material for their tragedies exclusively from national sources.[56] Not because engaging with this or that tragic subject cannot be national in nature — in a manner of speaking, it always is. First, because the *anecdotal* aspect of the characters can be considered from various perspectives and variously divined by the particular researcher, and second, because his point of view itself betrays various peculiar historical aspects of his reading.

II

Voiced reading, the performance of poetry, depends chiefly and firmly on the intelligent reading of *increments*.[57] Whoever is unable to do this, is not able to read verse aloud. For this reason, blank verse, deprived of rhymed couplets, is a much more difficult thing to write than traditional verse linked by rhymes. This is because such verse is linked not only at the end of the lines, but all along its length. Unrhymed, unlinked verse, requires much more exactitude and correctness in its composition than rhymed verse.

III

[*Here the manuscript ends*]

---

56 Among the ancients, *Greek* tragedies were *heavenly* tragedies!… Only for us did they become national, that is, 'Greek.'

57 *Translator's note.* 'Czytanie krementów.' Janusz W. Gomulicki, who edited the text of the play from which we are translating, defines this unusual term as 'probably the syllabic derailment which occurs from time to time in his unrhymed (but rhythmic) verse line (before or after the caesura); or also in reference to nouns, the syllabic nature of which changes according to their grammatical declination, which causes a change in the accentuation of the syllables.' This remark has nothing to do with the play as it appears in English. Modern English verse is stress-based, while Polish is basically syllabic; Modern English is not inflected to the degree in which Polish is, the nouns of which change their form depending on the grammatical role they perform in a given sentence. What is more, the stress-accentuation of Polish is almost entirely uniform, with the stress coming on the penultimate syllable of every word.

ACT I
RECIPROCITY

Scene 1

Cleopatra's palace near Alexandria. Two inner doors to the sides; one grand door to the rear. The interior is decorated with sphinxes.

EUCASTUS

As if they'd gossiped with the chancellor
Or him who wags the fan on the left side
Of the throne royal — everybody thinks
They've sniffed the secrets of the times. So glad
They are to preach to others; better yet,
To everyone. The Romans have a god
For it, I've heard; it's name: *Forum Romanum,*
Whose priests don't shave their chins, are dirty-minded,
And sham *sapientia…*

KNIGHT

               There is no such thing —
That is a thin tale, spoken without forethought,
Or if so, then with such thought as to deceive.
The Romans' gods are mighty; Roman chins —
Kempt, though they not be scraped every third day
Like those of your Egyptian priests. As for
The Roman Forum, true, at times it floods
Like the Nile Delta, with its citizens,
When moved by impulse of the pregnant hour —
The waters of the Roman Commonwealth,
Which make the whole world fertile. (And that's more
Than the mere stuff of ceremonial).
And these times that we live in? Disprize them
At your own peril. Yes — for we're at war,
And war is more than theory, though it have
An order of its own…

KONDOR
                    Just like the hunt!
When I hear the crisp bugle sound, the pulse,
O how it quickens! Then, astride my horse,
With beaters, light-footed, surrounding me,
Supple as sandals of fresh papyrus,
Then doth the panther tremble, while above me
A whole bazaar of sacred falcons wheel,
Calling out lustily: *dih dih, dih diihh…*

KNIGHT
Something like that, but war's much more than spunk
(Though boldness has its role to play, of course);
There's prudence in the drawing up of ranks
— You daren't be hasty — castramentation, and
The art of routing the opposing camp,
And discipline — in these three things excels
The Roman soldier, brooking no comparison.

EUCASTUS
Ah?

KONDOR
    Ah!

EUCASTUS
            As if there were nought to be said
Of the Egyptian warriors, our hosts
Led by such giants as cannot be found
In any Roman legion, bred to sow
Panic with halberds, whole generations
Syriac-Cretan-Philistine, and then:
Our noble chieftains, scions of such stirps
Soldierly, of estates enfeoffed of valour,
Titles and pedigrees on demand, dear sir.
All gentlemen — no base auxiliaries…

He lays his hands upon the arms of the Knight and Master of Game Kondor.

But let's withdraw a while, until the hour
For audience and interrogation call;
It's good to be, while such is in our power,
Until — it's proper not to be at all.

To himself.

As if they'd gossiped with the chancellor
Or him who wags the fan on the left side
Of the throne royal — everybody thinks
They've sniffed the secrets of the times…

Eucastus, Knight and Kondor withdraw, Cleopatra enters at a slow tread.

CLEOPATRA

To herself.

This palace is no palace, but a tent.
This monarch is no queen…

Passing, she halts by the sphinx.

                    This sphinx… a sphinx.
Someone who smiles at its own bland reflection,
Expressing no more than… a bland reflection.

Touches the head of the sphinx with her finger.

Inside: its own self. Honest stone. No more!

She takes a small dart in hand, and strikes a shield with it.

Servants, 'our' servants… Do they still serve us?

Eucastus and Kondor reveal themselves at both sides of the rear doors;
the Knight approaches from the rear to the centre stage.

What news, hey? Where will we be found tomorrow?

KNIGHT
Your Majesty! Before whose feet I fall,
If in word only, I merely fulfil
Your Majesty's command forbidding me,
A man in armour, from abasing brow
To lowly dust... Where will tomorrow find us?
Where shall we be today? Say but the word —
Today — is no more. Say 'at this moment,' then...

CLEOPATRA
My fifty galleons, have they reached Pompey?

KNIGHT
When Pompey was...

CLEOPATRA
                    What would you say?

KNIGHT
                                        The news,
And as it seems, reliable, reports
His headless trunk is bobbing on the waves;
His head, no longer his, strikes dust before
Your Majesty's husband, brother, and king...
Whose fingers fondle the consular ring.

CLEOPATRA
I pardon your words, soldier.

Pause.

                    My brother
Was raised by me from clumsy boyhood on.

No king hath Cleopatra! Her husband —
That little boy — slept in the wicker nest
Of her gazelle…

She stops her speech. To the Knight.

Wait — let me finish speaking…

To Master of Game at the door.

Kondor! Go see how my gazelle is faring.
I would not have her suffer from neglect
While men are busied with their wars. For she,
The queen's gazelle, is a sacred symbol.

To Knight.

Pompey is… gone, you say? Where, when and how?

KNIGHT
According to the painted scroll, as soon
As he'd set out with wife Cornelia
And their son Sixtus, he wrote to the king,
Whose father he'd once hosted while in Rome,
Begging like refuge. But the people in ire
Pounded the sacred ear with their dissent
Until he gave in to them. He sent men,
Smiling, with wide-spread arms, who cozened Pompey
To come ashore. Those same arms struck him down
There in the sucking shallows, from the back;
His head they lopped off, and his ring they slipped
From his limp digit. Both of which they sent
To the Egyptian monarch.

Pause.

There's something else beside.
The mob then bore their heroes on their shoulders

Into the temple precincts, but the priests
Bolted the doors before them, mindful of
The Roman Prefect Gabinius, who sent
Wheat here, when Egypt was pinched thin with famine.

CLEOPATRA
By the Sphinx! Those lackeys — are they mad?

To Knight.

Batter these ears of mine with every scrap
Of news as it arrives, without delay.
You may withdraw.

She looks down and sighs.

        Egyptians! Spawned, and bred
Between Sphinx and mummy! Woe! to their kings...

To Eucastus.

I'd like to break my fast, alone... with Zechera...

Noticing that the Knight has not withdrawn.

Deaf art thou when queens speak? Begone, I said!
Or hast thou some petition to the throne?

KNIGHT

Genuflects on one knee.

Your Majesty, this man of many wars —
Thirty years' worth of battles, who's been known
To spurn his helmet in the hail of blows
That he might be recognised from afar,
This man dared never think before his queen
To utter such things as he's now begun...

CLEOPATRA
Arise and speak your mind.

KNIGHT

With sudden violence.

                 Your army chiefs
Hold me and my strategies in contempt.
For one, that Romans are unknown to them,
Second, that I know Romans, being one,
A Roman, and thus not born of their caste,
The caste of chieftains. By the lord Bacchus!
Amongst your Majesty's most faithful hosts,
Full twenty thousand Romans such as I
Might have been counted — and not long ago! —
Who in your father's day came here to Egypt
Under Gabinius, married local girls,
And served in Egypt's armies, stout as cedars!
So that whatever military yet remains
Now in your armies, are the Roman eagles!
Alas, but they come not of chieftain-caste…

Pause.

Your Majesty! Your chiefs trust in three things:
Strength of numbers, battlements, and distance.
A strategy that's carved in stone. But Caesar?
Even today, my queen, you may be lost,
Before sunset — before the evening star!
Yes! Where is Caesar? Tell me where's the speck,
So tiny in the heavens, which the eye
Of the gazelle can barely register
Before its talons pierce her weak calf's throat
And bear it to the nest high in the cliffs
From which it broke unnoticed as a rock
Split by erosion… Caesar's just such an eagle.
He has eight hundred horse, three thousand foot,

No walls of stone where we might hem him in,
And know — it's happened more than once, that those
Besieging Caesar became the besieged!
No style determines Caesar's battle-order;
It happens, that a handful of his men
Cut off much greater forces, forcing them
Into a narrow bottle-neck, and then,
Falling upon the weaker flank, close ranks,
And as the lightning, at a short-sword's distance,
Engulf the enemy like a simoom!
Swarms, javelins, horse-hooves — *victoria!*

Pause.

I'm out of breath…

CLEOPATRA

At the throne, to herself.

                    How great he's grown, that man,
In speaking of great things…!

To the Knight.

                    I'm listening…

KNIGHT
When speaking of your Majesty's safety
— Which God preserve — when I set forth my thoughts
My words were stifled by uproarious laughter
From those whose pedigree's beyond reproach:
'What? Listen — an untouchable like him,
Would speak of kings as if they were mere clay!'
They roared, and thumped their sword-butts on the board
Until the Punic crystal danced. And so,
I held my tongue.

CLEOPATRA
        What was your plan?

KNIGHT
                      My queen!
What kings discuss amongst themselves, what rests
Upon the laps of gods — not mine to know.
But as a soldier, and a sober man,
Reflecting on your situation, grave,
It's clear — you must withdraw from here at night,
In such a way, it should appear the court
Remains where it had been, a screening force
Of troops advancing here, while you withdraw
With your palace guard — one movement of troops
Cloaking the other. In this way, you'll win
Both time and safety. How much time? Who knows,
After the death of Pompey, whom your fleet
Had aided, what direction now events
Will take... No single sailor has returned
From that mission — we know nothing at all!

CLEOPATRA
Your words are sensible.

KNIGHT
              As for your safety,
Dare I speak of the queen, whose sure support
Is with the gods, upon whose shoulders strong
She rests...? Nor of the army's good I speak,
Who know danger well... Or of generals,
'Good' generals of pristine lineage,
Who come of generations of 'good' generals,
And thus cut stylish figures on parade
And say the proper things...

Pause.

                    ... Who talk and talk
The while they do nothing, because they can't!

CLEOPATRA
Having considered well your words, the queen
Entrusts you with her signet — for three days.

She slips it from her finger, but holds it in her hand yet.

Whomever you should curse, shall die. Your words
Become deed with their utterance. As far
As the Nile stretches, on both banks, so wide
Your power... But one thing it cannot do,
This ring — protect you from man's Jealousy.

She strikes the shield with her dart.

Eucastus! Bring me my fillets of Isis,
My sceptre, and the two Hermetic tomes.

*Cleopatra sits down on the throne. Eucastus hands her the fillets, which
she binds on her brow; she takes up the sceptre and the Hermetic books.
The Knight kneels.*

To the Knight.

Approach, and hear:

She opens a book at random and reads.

                    ... and then a caste was set
For everything that lives — the little bird,
The crocodile, both just as beautiful.
And when the latter has eaten his fill
Along the sands reclining, with his maw
Half-open, then the little bird hops near
To pick his teeth clean. For the plover's caste
Is one, the crooked-beaked Ibis' another,

And still another is the crocodile's,
So, rarely doth envy erupt amongst them.
But let the sacred crocodile behold
Another bull of his own caste, a stork
Another stork, and rivalry ensues.
So is it among men.
They look not to themselves for excellence,
But imitate what others have begun,
To ape their glory. Just like the gardener
Who creeps into his neighbour's plot to steal
The fruit that grows there, careful to efface
With his own foot the traces that he's left
In the soft dust, his presence there to hide…
For this reason, the castes have been established,
So that one man might gird his jealousy
Upon the broader envy of his caste…

*She closes the book, taps the Knight with her sceptre, and drapes a
golden chain around his neck.*

Thus I now raise you to the chieftain-caste.

KNIGHT
Great is Hermes! Great, the Egyptian queen!

CLEOPATRA
Touch the sphinx, and withdraw.

*He touches the sphinx and withdraws, bowing. Eucastus bows to him.
To Eucastus.*

      I'll break my fast,
With Zechera.

*Cleopatra goes off, disappearing through one of the porches at a slow
pace.*

Scene 2

EUCASTUS

Moves to the large door in the back and calls.

Kondor! Servants!

KONDOR

Offstage.

Jackal! Hero!

Those who were summoned enter — one after another, at a ceremonial pace. Kondor, the Master of Game, Jackal and Hero — table servants. A table is then carried in, along with a Mummy, in a casket with lid uncovered, on wheels. It is placed at table. Different servants busy themselves at setting up, aided from time to time by those characters engaged in dialogue.

EUCASTUS

In thought, to himself.

Egypt!
O Nile, O sun, O how all things do change!
Kings take their breakfast in the afternoon —
The world spins backward, so it seems. Before,
Nothing so measured time as a king's stomach.
Up with the sun, pressed to table.

KONDOR

We've a lack
Of table-lackeys in the palace, so
I've brought these whelps — they're litter-bearers.

EUCASTUS
Let those at least who've touched the mummy stand
There at the back — They're all of different heights...
It seems that doesn't matter any more
These days...

To himself, in thought.

          It's not like how it used to be.
Today a temple servant takes to wife
The daughter of a fisherman. Pah! At least
He'll have good use of incense... The scribe's son
Marries the daughter of the gardener,
Taking his stiff pen to the ploughing. Castes
Confused, no more regard for ritual;
I blame it on the spread of literacy.
They learn to read; they think they understand,
And push their way in here now, even here,
To teach their betters... In the good old days,
The castes were like the temple-steps: granite
Or porphyry — both impermeable.
And borders were fixed — impassible.
Priest with priestess, scribe's son with scribe's daughter...

KONDOR
I know a mummifier took to wife
The granddaughter of a casket-joiner.

EUCASTUS
... A farmer's son became — what? Why, a farmer!
From order springs the birth of demi-gods.
I myself knew a matron — princely caste —
Married to a priest, who brought forth a child
That looked just like a cat. Another girl
Was born resembling the sacred crocodile.
Manifest grace, that was...

KONDOR

         I'll tell you what —
It's all the fault of this new music here!
They've brought in syncopation. You change music,
You change morality, by Isis!

EUCASTUS

         Right!
The sun-king, Auletes, the princess' sire —
How did he spend his time? Playing the bagpipes!
All day, all night! Now there's a king for you!
Tradition! Bagpipes! Virtue! Monarchy!
How I remember when he passed away...
He called me to his fragrant bed of pain,
Like this he crooked his finger... I crawled near,
Kissing the earth, my heart was beating wild,
All trembling, and again the finger — 'Come!'
He mouthed some words to me. I bent my ear
To his pale lips... 'Pipers! A mob of 'em!
And bring my own pipes here!' They were of gold,
The chanters, mind you, and I brought them near,
But he could blow no more. He huffed, he puffed,
He squeezed the bellows — gods! I still can hear
The tuneless rush of wind — his breath divine
Expired...

KONDOR

         If he'd done nothing more than that,
He still was worthy of a pyramid!

EUCASTUS

Catching sight of Zechera, hobbling near on a cane.

Ah! Here she comes — a proper Egyptian dame,
Our ancient Zechera. She knows all things,
Whatever happens anywhere. Her smile,
Wise as the sphinx, and just as deep, watchful, still,

But not afraid to speak… The old king said
Of her such words worthy of hieroglyphs —
'The purpose of owls is to see at night.'
Zechera! Gods grant you good fortune!

ZECHERA

In a half-whisper.

                              Fortune?
I've just parted from two lads — common-casters,
There at the inner sphinxes, where the queen
Promised them good fortune.

EUCASTUS
                    Ah, when they come,
See that they use the underground passage…

JACKAL

Entering quickly.

The sunlight falls now on the nineteenth column
Of the peristyle, speeding with golden sandal…
Soon we shall shield our eyes…

HERO
                              And now the queen's
Paused at the eleventh column, where she wavers;
She speaks to herself softly, wipes a tear
Away with filmy veil, which then she throws
Behind her, past the shadow of her steps.

EUCASTUS

To all the servants, grouped in a semi-circle.

She comes! The daughter of the Ptolemies!

Scene 3

Enter Cleopatra, reading a small papyrus scroll.

CLEOPATRA
My people! There is an old Egyptian saying
That teaches that the palaces of kings
Are nothing more than stations on the way
That leads to our true home, which is the grave.
This palace is a hostelry, if grand;
It is not Cleopatra. She — is Egypt,
And shall endure as long as flows the Nile.
She is the law, and she is in your hearts;
As long as your love lasts, she will abide.
Let not your hearts be troubled, then; give ear
To no ill rumours or appearances.
Hear this from my own lips: When the first column
Of the court peristyle casts its shadow down
Upon the stairs, we shall depart from here
— But leaving signs as if we yet remained —
Nor we, nor you, withdrawing a single inch.
So, when that shadow, prone athwart the step,
Has crept up to this porch, my maids shall unpin
These royal cloaks, and bind round my slim waist
A heavy soldier's belt, setting on my head
Instead of a tiara, a rough helmet.
Then shall my lightest dromedary kneel
— The white one I've named Ostrich Feather, she
Who skips along the sand obedient
To a child's whisper on the reins (which words
Incised are on my obelisk) — and take
Me on her back.

She lifts a chalice, flicks some drops toward the mummy, and then touches the liquor to her lips.

       O thing, once man or woman,
I greet you in the fellowship of the void.

She eats.

I want no Syrian crooners — they are soft.
Nor quandaries hermitic — ponderous.
I want life — and have you as my companion!

To the mummy.

O silent nothingness! Which of the maids
Subject to thee breaks fast like Cleopatra?
Far from this palace, under wattled thatch,
In cities and in castles far distant,
They think of her... what they would like to think,
Whose ears drink, eagerly, embroidered tales.

She eats. With irony.

Manek the Arab expedites a train
Of camels and horse, just to carry here
A looking-glass encrusted with rubies
And ribboned love-notes... Herod, the red-haired
Lord of Judea, sends a fragrant leaf
— No more! — in a chest, with the inscription
'Heart of all women.' More than one emir,
Petty or grand, to the very Pontic chiefs
Who wear their locks uncut, chivvy their envoys
To bear to me greetings equivocal.
Even rough lads from the lowest of castes,
Empty, but willing, clamber up the cliffs
Leading to Cleopatra's flimsy heart!...

To mummy.

Laugh at them with me, a girl already dead,
Who's never known a real husband's embrace,
As if she could be touched by mortal arms!

She pauses eating.

Is my heart such a thing as to be cozened
Into belief of everlasting love?
Or is this some titanic rebellion
Directed at the gods — to sense an ideal
Not cut from granite, but of pulsing flesh?

*   *   *

Betrothed unto a child, who shared my bed
But as a pet gazelle — I'm now deprived
Of brotherly support, now that he's grown —
I've never had a husband or a brother!
To say nothing of my father, an exile,
A guest of Pompey's, who came here to die;
Nor mother — who has sunk deep in the mists
Of memory, that is, oblivion;
Nor sister — who became — so soon! — my rival;
Nor friends — for I, daughter of the Ptolemies,
Cannot brook maidens equal me in rank.
Never — nowhere — no one beside my heart!

To mummy.

Except for you, dumb husk… of whom? No matter!

Lifts chalice toward mummy.

So, to the judges of the underworld
I spill libation, as a recompense,
For you, the dead, and peer into your skull,
Dead man — or woman — I, who've never lived,
Might greet you with a hug, who live no more,
Like old friends meeting — both of whom belong
To that same heartless caste… though of you, perhaps,
The wordsmiths might concoct the oddest tales
As they do of me. And that old gossip
That they call History, half decrepit, who
Forgets her yarns before she's finished the telling…

But praiseworthy she is, and for the age
Peculiar in her affections.
                                        Zechera!
I'm gloomy now, like some freshly hewn tomb
Awaiting its tardy innards. Come! I thirst!

She extends the chalice, which a servant fills.

No, no! — I want no wine transported here
Over the seas, for what it gains in strength
It loses in bouquet. Wild strawberries!
Just one, plucked from its stalk, fresh with the dew,
I rate above all suchlike sluggish nectar.
It's water I thirst for, from granite wells
Reflecting back the sky as in a mirror!
Or, what is it I thirst for? — I know not…

                        *   *   *

Closer, Zechera, slide your rug in close.
Here at the royal table-legs set down
Your bowl, your golden bowl… You'll carry it
Back home, a gift, if you reveal to me
All that I ask… Zechera!…

ZECHERA

Taking her place at the queen's feet.

                                        Deep in the depths
Of every bowl lies truth.

CLEOPATRA
                                        Yes? Tell me then —
What omen did I meet up with today?

ZECHERA

Gazing before herself, slowly.

The queen went out, but not in queenly guise;
Dressed as a woman of the merchant caste.
She went along the marge of the cornfields
And there was recognised — the acres full
Of bearded wheat bent low their gravid heads.

CLEOPATRA
Not all the crowds there recognised their queen.

ZECHERA
One stalk there was upon whom, butterflies,
Two, had alit, and with their playful wings
They blocked her from his view…

CLEOPATRA

              …And nothing more?

ZECHERA
And one youth — Abdala Ganimedion,
A reaper's son, of Belzer's generation,
Of extraordinarily smooth cheeks,
Who gave a girl who skipped near a cool draught
Of water from a clay jug…

CLEOPATRA

Aside.

        Upon his cheeks there flashed
Something my eyes have never seen, nor heart:
A flash of mystery…

To Zechera.

As to the queen,
Was there none else who recognised her not?

ZECHERA
There was one other commoner, who bore
All of his earthly goods bound in a rag,
Who, with a dancer's step, like a white camel's,
Sped through the queen's shadow upon the dust…
He is a diver's son, named Feleg-Mun,
And with Abdala he now waits, pacing
Between the sphinxes of the inner courtyard.

CLEOPATRA

Aside.

In those eyes, that mouth, in those sun-bronzed cheeks,
Wind-tousled hair and swelling chest, I saw
Some unknown movements… of the soul… Eucastus!

To servants.

Have both of them who wait stand here, before
The countenance of the queen. Zechera! Thoth
Granted you such sight as is rarely found
In palaces…

ZECHERA
　　　　　For palaces are cliffs
Sheer-plummeting, which cedars barely grip
With their strong roots, the while the meagre scrub
And other paltry growth shrivel in the sun.

CLEOPATRA

To servant.

Bring here the golden vase on which my face
Is newly etched; I'd have it within reach.

EUCASTUS

From the depths.

Mun-Faleg enters, elder of the two.

Mun-Faleg approaches Cleopatra and bows.

CLEOPATRA

To Zechera.

Ask him why he did not perceive his queen.

ZECHERA
Even the prophet's eye, boy, cannot see
All things. Respond then, Mun-Faleg! At dawn
When on thou hastened with thy tiny bundle,
Where the queen's shadow lay athwart thy path,
Thou spurned the same with tripping tread, as light
As a white camel's... How was it that thou
Sawest not the shade was cast by Egypt's queen?

MUN-FALEG
O wise Zechera, to whom such things are known
As mortal tongues speak rarely, I'll tell you:
Today, at long last, I redeemed the chest
In which my father's arm — a diver's — rests.
Upon the lid the legend is inscribed
Of how the sole prop of his family
Was seized amidst the waves by a great shark,
Which tore that arm, and I, true son of bed
Unsullied, hurled myself in, knife in hand,
To rescue the old man. Yes, this I did!
And yet, soon after, Father's wound worsened:

He lost both arm and way of life — no longer
Able to pull the oar through the burly water.
I had the arm preserved by the embalmers
— For on such things eternal life depends:
How might he enter the next world, a gimp! —
And long was I in debt to them, the spicers,
Until today, when I redeemed the limb!
This was the day I crossed Her Majesty's
Path, all-unknowing, as I flew back home,
The sacred casket in my bundle, joyful
To bring the hand which blessed me when I married
And moved my wife beneath my humble thatch
Back to its owner... Shadows, Zechera,
Are cast by all things. When the sun is strong
And level at its rising, a queen's shadow
Stretches as far as doth a pyramid's.
And in his joy, he noticed not, whence this,
The royal shadow, fell... that son rejoicing.

CLEOPATRA

Aside, gazing at the young man's face.

Yes, yes, that same mysterious beam of feeling...

Pushing a handful of gold in his direction.

Depart. Your queen rejoices that you have
A father... and a peaceful hut...

EUCASTUS

To Cleopatra.

                              My queen,
The column casts its shadow on the stairs...

Mun-Faleg withdraws and Abdala enters.

EUCASTUS
Abdala Ganimedion.

CLEOPATRA

To Zechera.

                  Ask of him
Whatever you wish, Zechera…

ZECHERA
                  Abdala!
Son of Ganymede, this morning,
When thou placed thy amphora at the lips
Of the young reaper-girl, Her Majesty
The queen passed by that way, and thou
Neglected to fall to the dust in homage.
Is this not true? Speak openly!

ABDALA
                  Zechera,
By Apis, yes, it's true. Against the rose
Of the sky dawning, there amidst the corn,
Melmeia, my betrothed, swayed near, and purred
'Give me something to drink!' And this I did,
Resting the cool amphora on my shoulder,
I kissed her lips with the jar's wet clay mouth.
She closed her eyes. And gazing at her lashes…
So black they are, although her braids are pale…
As golden as the corn… Her Majesty,
The queen passed by, you say? It may be so…

CLEOPATRA
It may be so? It was! How might it be
That thou sawest not the monarch of the world
As she passed by? Nor didst thou recognise
Her shadow as it fell across her face —
Thy… What was it? Melmeia… nor the tinge

Of her breast that the sun lay on thy shoulder?
This shadow, boy, that falls here at her feet —
Look down! Look! Thou wast born to hang, thou scoundrel!
Nor walks thy Melmeia in proper paths,
Seeing she's hair of gold and ebon lashes —
Unsuited to each other, conflicting — false!
Thy queen shall give thee nothing!

Aside.

                                          For what
Might she give thee now, more than what thou hast?

To the boy.

No, take this coin — Look there: it bears my likeness.
Go, pin it to Melmeia's breast, so that
From now on thou shalt recognise thy queen…

ZECHERA
Bow nicely and withdraw…

Abdala does so.

CLEOPATRA

Rising.

And so, I have subjects who have fathers,
And sons, and sweethearts! Peaceful cottages…

To Eucastus.

You say a column's shadow's shoving me
Out of the palace of my fathers? Come!

Enter servant girls.

The belt, the helm, the lance! And my white camel:
Let her now kneel before me like a swan.

The servant girls bustle about Cleopatra's table.

By now that boy, and that comely young man,
Flashing their gold amidst the babbling mobs,
Are spreading through the crowds new parables
Of Cleopatra; from city to city
Like tramps they'll travel, their cloaks spattered with
The distant roads they wander. Yet the heart
Of Cleopatra, like the Nile, sweeps clean
All dung of love away…

To Eucastus.

                I thirst!… Give me
One pearl of the vine.

To servant girls.

                Buckle my sandal!

She rises, begins to move toward the great doors, then raises the short travelling spear aloft.

The blessings of the Royal Will be with you!

ALL

Both on-stage and off.

Great is the name of the Ptolemies! Great
Is Cleopatra!… Egypt's only queen…

Scene 4

EUCASTUS
So what now?

JACKAL and SERVANT BOYS
     What now?

EUCASTUS
               All wise Zechera —
Now have we need of your prophetic mind.

ALL
What is to happen?

EUCASTUS
        What will happen now?

Zechera is silent.

KONDOR

Approaches the table.

My mind is fixed on matters horizontal,
But all the same obligatory. *Primo* —
Let's feed the body to make strong the soul…

MOST VOICES
Praised be the wisdom of the Master of Hounds!

KONDOR
Secundo, as dictates the stratagem
Enunciated by Her Majesty
To keep appearances unchanged, to wit:
To eat one's cake and seem to have it too,
I — for example — take this paté in hand,
Baked like a peacock, from which I subtract

                                                     CYPRIAN KAMIL NORWID

The inner stuffing, leaving thus untouched
The proud outward appearance. Strategy's
A clever gambit.

To the table boy.

Let me have some wine
To make the mind sharp for my next manoeuvre.

ZECHERA

Wrapping up the golden bowl in her shawl.

Well, as for me,
I've got to think up my own stratagem
To port the queen's gift safely to my house
Without some rowdy rank-and-file deserter
Or Roman spy getting too curious.
That's all I have to say. The gods be with you!

Exit.

HERO

Approaching again through the main doors.

You should have seen our Ptolomeian lass
When up her camel straightened, raising her —
Why, to the heavens! In her shining helm,
With that short spear — the soldiers all aquiver
Before, behind, and all there present cheering,
Beating their shields — Caesar himself would pale!
The Romans will high-tail it, mark my words,
Crawling away, those who can't run, bled-white
With terror, like the clouds of dust that fall
Behind our troops as they march off to war!
This civil strife is at an end… Look, here:
You still can see them from the porch, the crowds,

You still can hear them cheering… See yourselves
With your own eyes!

KONDOR

From the table.

                    Bearer of such good news,
Come eat!

EUCASTUS

To Jackal and the servants.

                    And yet Zechera's vatic words
Must not be taken lightly. Hide the plate,
And basket all the valuables. My head
Lies on the other dish of the queen's scales…

While some go about packing the valuables, others finish the food spread on the table. Thus, two conversations are going on simultaneously.

HERO

At the table.

Thus Egypt will be, as she always has been:
Great and immortal.

KONDOR, OTHERS
                    For all ages, vivat!

HERO
We'll spread across the sea, straddling the Tiber —
For that's the river, mind you, that splits Rome…

KONDOR
River! A streamlet that one crocodile
Might drink and piss out…

HERO
     … And though I am not
Of warrior-caste, I wouldn't be surprised
If I was to meet, hand to hand, let's say,
With one of their grandees — O, like Pompeius,
That great and headless trunk…

EUCASTUS

To the boys.

We'll leave a few… What you've got there in your hands,
And that vaisselle there — for appearance's sake.
But take away the Mummy — that's taboo.
The sacred custom of ancient Egyptians
Which all don't understand… The times change so…

Servants take the Mummy away, and continue to bustle about.

HERO

At the table.

We are the oldest of all the world's peoples,
Descended from the gods themselves. It's natural
For us to take these ruffians in hand…

KONDOR
You know, it seems to me that there are castes,
And there are *castes*, and with the nations too,
The same applies: There's Ethiopia,
There's Rome and Pontus, and then there is Egypt!

EUCASTUS

Withdrawing along with the last boys and baskets of valuables.

The gods be with you!

HERO
                    Speaking of the gods…
This one thought has been nagging me a while…
On a far distant island, where I landed
When sold by my Phoenician master — and not cheaply! —
This was the springtime of my strange beauty —
Well, I met many foreign peoples there
And came to know some… theological truths.
This thought, or, rather, memory that nags me…
Blurred by the mists of sleep, you might say…

KONDOR
                                        What?
Here, wet your whistle, man, and spit it out!

HERO
There was a group of men there… Through a mist
You know, this memory… Who took me for…
Who took me for a god…

He falls asleep at table.

KONDOR
                    Is he asleep?
It would be impolite to wake him. Now,
Seeing as Eucastus has done his duty,
Rescuing those things that might tempt the eye
And itchy fingers… I should help him out
With these few knick-knacks — it would be a shame
If they were lost to… Cleopatra… Quick then —

He pockets a few of the more costly items of tableware.

Diligent Jackal, I must now be off,
Leaving my blessing with you…

Exits.

HERO

With nodding head propped on his fist.

                            … Through a mist…
Or smoke… or steam, perhaps…

JACKAL

To the remaining two table boys.

                         The Master of Hounds
Seems to have forgotten this here chalice,
Studded with gold, and that flat silver flask…
And those trifles of lesser worth… Come, boys,
Brush up the crumbs!

He exits with the valuables.

HERO

Continuing to mumble.

Or through a thin, thin sheet of papyrus…

FIRST BOY

Drawing near to Hero.

Perhaps we shouldn't leave that cup behind
That he's got in his hand…

SECOND BOY
> … the saucer, too…

BOTH
Leaving our double blessing on him… Come!

They exit quietly and swiftly.

Scene 5

Hero is asleep with his face resting on the cleared table. Through the open doors, from both sides, two Roman soldiers come rushing, swords drawn: from the left, then from the right. Then, enter two Roman Centurions from either side.

FIRST CENTURION

Looking around.

Nobody here either!…

SECOND CENTURION
> Indeed, the spy

Had to have given him extensive plans —
This is a fortress, such as might have withstood
The pressure of our crew entire with but
A few men, resolute. Such piles of granite
Are not to be contemned! They had to tell him,
What their own eyes knew…

FIRST CENTURION
> Yes, but when? And who?

If up until now there had been no time
For royal envoys to be introduced…
Ha! Royal envoys! Ere I dragged them close
Under my guard, Caesar had not the time
To dismount and to speak; he wheeled about,
Still in the saddle, with his finger, thus:

Those here, those there, splitting the crew in halves,
And sending us to take the place, falling
Upon it from both sides at once... I here
With Fortunius, as you can see, and he
With but one lictor... Ah, but you know better...
What? And where did he begin?...

SECOND CENTURION
                              It was as if
He'd trotted up before his own front door,
Dismounting at the porch, resting his hands
Like this — upon his hips — relaxed, and then,
Torax, the lictor, going on before him,
He, step by step, between the pair of sphinxes,
With even tread passing through the arcade,
The hall, the inner arcade — all the way
To where the water plashes as it falls
Into the tub of porphyry. The baths —
And then he went no farther. There he is,
Taking a bath, and listening, perhaps,
As Calligion reads to him!

FIRST CENTURION
                              Meanwhile,
Some chance deserter, or a couple of tramps
Might, in this place unknown, fall upon him,
Assassinating Rome!

Shouts from off-stage.

VOICE
Hurrah the Sixth Italian! Hurrah the Consul!

HERO

Startled.

By all the gods of hell!... What's going on!?

FIRST CENTURION
At last, an inmate!

Grabbing Hero by the shoulder.

    You, man — what's your name?

SECOND CENTURION

Looking around.

A mummy, maybe?

HERO

Pointing to the mummy at the rear.

    Not me, but my date.
We'd had a tête-à-tête in this refuge
Far from the prying eyes of… vulgar men…
My name is Hero. And I am, in short,
That which the Greeks call Sophos. Seven years
Entire I've held my tongue…

FIRST CENTURION
        Relax it then,
And let it pour forth seven years of wit
Stifled till now… 'tis Rome entreating you.
What is your party? That of Arsinoe?
The king's? Or Cleopatra's? Lepidus'?
Or maybe you served Pompey?

HERO
        I serve wisdom!

SECOND CENTURION
And so let's hand him over to Intelligence.

FIRST CENTURION
They know how to get men to play their parts.

HERO
That isn't what I mean when I say 'smarts.'
Parties arise from verbal imprecision —
From people who don't know quite how to speak.

FIRST CENTURION

Aside.

One thing I'll give the chap — he knows his Greek.

To Hero.

This edifice of the Ptolemies — why
Stands it deserted?

HERO
                        O, it's inhabited,
By spirit. Accidents are… illusion…
But that's a commonplace. Our wisdom says
There is no such thing as a dwelling place,
There's only stops along the road. But graves —
There are as many palaces as graves.

FORTUNIUS

Entering, sheathing his sword.

The consular insignias are rammed
Into each socket. Soon the delegates
From the Ptolemies will be here… Who's this?

CENTURION
An unarmed captive.

FORTUNIUS
                    Take him to the back.

*One of the centurions leads Hero out. Enter soldiers bearing small
bundles of military gear. One sets up a camp chair and spreads a lion
skin on the floor; another sets some smaller objects on the table. Enter
Calligion with a sword under his arm and a scroll in his hand.*

CALLIGION

To Fortunius.

Salve!

FORTUNIUS
    Your health.

CALLIGION
                        You know, I must admit —
If they have palaces like this in their backwaters…
What must Serapium be like?!

FORTUNIUS
                        No wonder
Pompey the Great sought out a pillow here
To rest his travel-weary head on…

CALLIGION
                            For men
Worthy the name of men, even Misfortune
Is but a countermarch, or a repose.

FORTUNIUS
You don't say? That's not always true.
For if it were, there'd be no tragedies.

CALLIGION
Ah, tragedy divine! The ritual stage —
But, as it was in the old days, you know.
Yes, it's an exception! Thunderbolts, gods…
But even tragedy must have a thread…

FORTUNIUS
Some day, in Tusculum, on pebbled paths
Between the boxwood hedges, we'll stroll and talk
Of things like tragedy… But not today.

To Centurion.

You — seat the Ptolemaean windbags there,
Upon the benches at the entranceway,
With all the tiresome loot they've scrounged for Caesar.

To Calligion.

It isn't often that a battlefield
Can be so quickly jerked to other use —
A granite socle fit for a tribune…

*The centurion leads in two delegates and seats them at the door.
Fortunius and Calligion pay no attention to them. Calligion sits down
at the table and begins setting his scrolls in order. The centurion who
had led in the delegates begins setting up the lion skin, and camp chairs,
draping one of the headrests in purple.*

LICTOR

From the inner doors of the chamber.

The Consul comes!

*The delegates all rise. Caesar enters, dressed informally. He approaches
the chair, takes one corner of the purple wrap in hand, and drapes it*

over one shoulder. He remains thus, neither finishing to dress nor sitting down, so that half of the purple garment flows down upon the seat.

CALLIGION

Nearing Caesar.

        … The chief delegate
Calls himself Achilles.

CAESAR

With a half smile.

        O mighty delegate!
At least he got here quickly? Swift-of-foot?

ACHILLES
'… Ptolemy, the King legitimate,
Successor of Auletes the Egyptian,
Almighty Ruler, Lord, and the true friend
Of Rome and Romans, and the Republic's
Admirer most fervent, sends the Consul
Victorious — his guest — words of welcome.

After a short pause.

However opulent Egypt may be,
However warm the Pharaoh's feelings are
Towards his brother monarchs, on account
Of minor broils and dustups in the land,
He finds it difficult to safely send
The gifts he would exchange. Yet there is this:
Aware that Caesar is in hot pursuit
Of fugitive Pompey, a criminal,
He hereby sends his ring to you, and head,
That it might strike the ground before your feet
In penitence…' Such words my monarch sends.

        CYPRIAN KAMIL NORWID

He unwinds a cloth in which the head had been bound, and sets both the head and the ring at Caesar's feet.

CALLIGON – FORTUNIUS – CENTURION – LICTOR
Eheu! Pompey the Great! 'Tis he indeed!

CAESAR
You roach — You vultures! Be gone! Out of my sight!
Upon such gifts Caesar shan't soil the beam
Of one eye! Nor would any citizen
Of Rome! Your King, and all his generals,
And you as well, perhaps, will shortly learn
That Rome wreaks no revenge — she punishes!
Caesar's a soldier, not some base assassin!
A Roman consul's vengeance is the law.
The fact that you shall leave here with your heads
Gives ample witness to my words!

Turning away and covering his head with the purple.

                    As great
As Pompey was, my sorrow is.

ACHILLES and SUB-DELEGATE

As Caesar remains silent.

                  The... envoys
Who... are but go-betweens... delivered now
Of their great monarch's... message, beg to know
If they are to bear some reply...

CAESAR

Remaining in profile to them, without turning his face.

                  Tell him
That Rome recoils — her soldier frowns — and Caesar weeps.

Holding his stare motionless, he exits through the inner doors. The
delegates retire backwards with their gifts.

CALLIGION
And this is the Pompey whom I recall,
As if it were today, when he played host
To that Egyptian monarch's father, once.
I saw him there, banished to Rome he was…

FORTUNIUS
The very same, who when he was at war
With Mithridates, learned from a scoundrel
A quicker route to victory, and villainy…
The man proposing treason was the one
He did away with…

CALLIGION
                    Pompey, late our foe,
Our great antagonist, whom we chased here,
To the last marge of his, and Rome's, protection…
O Tragedy! And War! Like ritual dancers,
Who linking arms, lead on the prancing rout
To destiny…

The Lictor enters again through the inner doors.

                What is the Consul's wish?

LICTOR
We are to purify with holy water
These boards befouled, and spread the lion's skin
Over…

Hesitating, he begins to arrange things for the cleansing.

    He will receive no one today
Save messengers from both camps with reports.
It's silence he desires.

CALLIGION

With lowered voice, unrolling a scroll. To the Lictor.

We need more light.

Rolling it up again, to Fortunius.

            What will Rome say, when word
Of this abomination stains the Tiber?

FORTUNIUS
Perhaps she knows already. News, like stench
Is borne afar by winds no one controls.

CALLIGION
It's odd. Peculiar.

FORTUNIUS
            Just the night before
When we still slept behind leather tent-flaps
Bedded on sand, I had the strangest dream.
I was on foot, there was a heavy wind —
A blizzard, but of stars, and on we pushed,
I and the Consul, amidst the howling sparks,
And then we heard a cry… The wind was strong.
It bent the palms, like keening mourners, flat
Spreading their hair dishevelled on the sand…
And then the Consul turned to me — 'So close,'
He said, 'the end, and yet we but commence!'
Then I awoke. I was awakened by
A jackal barking, and soft, halting pads
Of some hyena skulking near…

The Lictor is setting up lamps. To the Lictor.

              And you?
Do you have dreams?

LICTOR

                  Me? I sleep like a log.
Last night fled swiftly by. Like all the rest.

Exit.

FORTUNIUS

To Calligion.

I'd wish that for myself. And you, no less,
Though you'll watch on.

He puts on his cloak and moves to go.

                      Vale!

CALLIGION

Alone.

                    Peculiar times!
The whole Empire is — swelling, on all hands,
From Spain to Pontus, from the British Isles
To this chair, swelling, as broad as it's long…
The sense of the state… Powers are grappling
In bouts mysterious. Sometimes, it's death
That hitches up her kirtle, sets to work,
Out-labouring life, and life — life equals death…
Sometimes one thread unspools through centuries,
Ages of deeds, and we stand with one end
Between two digits, like old Theseus…

Nodding in the direction of Fortunius.

My friend has dreams, and I… Why, I have visions.

Scene 6

Enter Caesar, at a slow pace, as if he were strolling about the palace. He passes through the entire chamber, taking no note of the presence of Calligion. He stops at the lion pelt covering the place where the head of Pompey had rested, and raising his hand, speaks:

CAESAR
Fortuna!… Called by some an Avenging Spirit!…

He resumes his stroll, nears the table, and makes a sign for Calligion to take up his pen.

CAESAR

Sprawling on one of the chairs.

We paused at chapter two, it seems to me.

CALLIGION

Reads.

On the Egyptian Crisis. Book One,
Section Eleven.

CAESAR

Dictates.

      With ten ships of Rhodes,
The Asian legions in reserves, Caesar led
Three thousand and two hundred infantry,
Eight hundred cavalry. In three days' time
He came to Alexandria…
        … Knowing well the nature,
Corrupt, of the Egyptian populace,
And how little those men are to be trusted,
He set up here and there the Roman eagles…

CENTURION

Rushing in from the main doors, out of breath.

Calligion! Fortunius! Whoever's here at hand,
Come with me, fast! I know not what to do,
Without the Consul…

CAESAR

Turning his face to him.

But the Consul's here.
What's wrong? What is it that needs his attention?

CENTURION
Something extraordinary! At moonrise,
A bauble of a boat slid in near shore.
The coast-guards let it pass, having exchanged
The proper call-sign and response. When shingled,
A mighty fellow — and a trusted one,
Apparent this, from his bold carriage — leapt
Into the shallows, burdened with someone
Secure in canvas swaddled. This he bore
As lightly as Anchises Troy's penates,
Or any demi-god a slender nymph,
Or a pearl-diver, treasure… Anyway,
He strode so quickly to the palace stairs
The flash of his calceus buckles streaked
Like meteors. And when she was unwrapped,
The nymph — the gods excuse my levity —
Was Cleopatra! Egypt's queen herself!
I saw no more, racing to find Your Grace,
And barely them outpacing…

CAESAR

Rising lazily, he takes a step toward the main doors, addressing the Centurion with a smile.

When we were crossing Rubicon, my child,
You still were galloping on broomsticks.

The main doorway in the depths is now filled with camp guards. Their officers step aside and Cleopatra enters, passing between them. She takes a few steps forward. Arriving at the lion pelt, she kneels.

CLEOPATRA
Consul…!

CAESAR
           The queen kneels. Your Majesty —
And not in name alone, I've not assumed
Quite all the power in Egypt. Under arms,
There's neither place nor time now for tribunes.

He takes her hand and helps her to rise. Indicating Calligion.

Pardon me, ma'am. I'd have my words witnessed —
The fate that's placed you on this lion pelt
So crouched, I've long desired.

CLEOPATRA
                What does it cover?

CAESAR
A spot which I have sanctified to Fortune,
Who is a vengeful goddess, I her priest.
Later, you shall become initiate
Of her stark mysteries. Let's say a vase,
A marvellous and costly one, was smashed
Here. I being a superstitious man,

Had the shards covered to entrap the luck.
A vase, perhaps, that I'd prepared for you.

CLEOPATRA
And I've come empty-handed! I have nought
To match your just deserts — and yet,
These two pearls in my earlobes are world-famed;
I name them 'Indivisible.' Take one,
And wear it in the fibula that pins
Your purple cloak, that everyone might know
That Cleopatra, bending near her head
To catch your words let drop this heavy, white
Tear of the sea!

CAESAR
                    My queen, this tear, and all
The others you deign drop upon the folds
Of my cloak, I shall treasure in my breast.

CLEOPATRA
Then let the first deposit be the tear
I shed upon the news of Pompey's death.
He was your foe; he was my father's friend.
He'd hosted him in Roman exile. Yes,
He was my father, an unfeeling one,
But still my father, and my king as well,
Who wore this crown before me. When I knelt,
I did so as a penitent, since you
Are Fortune's priest, to make my confession,
For having sent Pompey full fifty galleons
For his safe passage with Cornelia.
But what are fifty galleons worth, my lord,
When breasted, Caesar, by your Victoria?

CAESAR
Especially as there were ten with me.

CLEOPATRA
With you!

CAESAR

Not permitting her to finish her thought.

Please, deign continue…

CLEOPATRA
I set not the whole
Might of my army and navy to war…

CAESAR
As for your other tear, O queen and daughter
Of him who wore the crown before you? Whom
Pompey housed at his exile to Rome?

CLEOPATRA
My other tear?… Allow me to collect
My wits… This very morning, a soldier,
I know not whether mine or yours, although
It's said that all my soldiers now are yours,
Slew my gazelle and breakfasted on her!
The monstrous man!

CAESAR
Eheu!

CLEOPATRA
Perhaps you'd say
That I've over a million other calves
Prinking my deserts? Ah, but that gazelle
Would gaze into my eyes with eyes so soft,
Their pupils large as paving stones. She'd lay
Atremble at my feet… But not from fear,
So delicate her members. Caesar, she

Was as a flower open to the sun,
From which it drinks its only sustenance…

Short pause.

… From which the cruel eagles stoop to fall
Upon their blinded prey like lightning… Why
Did your man kill my pet? The one gazelle
That symbolises the Egyptian people
As yours — those bloody claws?

CAESAR
                              Queen of the Sphinx,
Who speaks nine tongues, they say — Speak like a Roman,
Or call to mind Hellenic vocables.

CLEOPATRA
The Egyptians are good people — when
They're left alone, as they leave others, too,
Having no lust of wars of subjugation;
Accustomed to their life along the Nile,
They'd fain repose where lucky fate has fixed
Their birthplace, simple as a river reed,
Supple and rooted in its native mire.
They come of gods — and that's an ancient clan —
And unto gods at death do they return,
According to an order as well known
As seasons in their yearly revolution.
Is there a thing more beautiful? More proud?
The patient man is truly great; he grins
A temperate smile although your headsman flash
His poleaxe overhead — just like the Sphinx.
Your caligae may tread him underfoot
Like so much sand, and there he'll lie, prostrate —
And yet his pyramids… They scrape the stars!

CAESAR
Pride is the fruit of years of patient toil.
It blooms no quicker for the dung of boasting.
Your people have no pride; they're merely smug.
An ancient clan? Of ash and brittle bone —
A free man's lungs swell not in ossuaries.
It isn't good to be *more* than the first,
Or think it's bad to be first in anything.

Short pause.

You're not the first to ask, 'What's Rome to our
Ancient establishments?' Hear it from me:
They're no concern of ours. For this very reason
It's Roman custom to respect the rites
And mores it defends with her own breast —
The breasts and bloody claws of Roman eagles.
But it's another matter, when some clique
Of braggarts in the wilderness swells bold,
Swaggering as though their will were supreme judge
Of right and wrong, respecting nothing more
Than licence and intrigue… When Rome steps in,
She levels out the law and smooths privilege
To justice… In this way she protects them,
The people, bettering their laws, their life,
Leaving untouched their rites innocuous.

Short pause.

But teach me, please, Your Highness! By what paths
Must honest Roman citizens pick their way,
There, where the monarch slays men by deceit?
Ah, but he's innocent! It was the rede
Of some advisor, indispensable, while he,
That counsellor? His ear was filled
With whispers from his wife, who swore to help
Her eunuch to some goal for which *it* longed!
And you, my noble lady, tread on earth

Made slick before your feet. And on you slip,
Snatching at crutch-like words that fall from mouths,
Of blind men groping in the dark: 'What's Rome
To our ancient establishments?' Caesar —
I ask Your Majesty — would he agree
To serve as consul to any nation
But one with such ideals? He'd rather cast
Himself upon the mercy of the waves,
A new Leander, searching for that isle
Dreamt up by poets in their nobler trances,
That ideal, lovely rock, than stoop to haggle
With practical villains.

Pause.

              It's not that easy,
Apotheosis — it too is a chore,
Years-long, of patient labour, day by day.
How much simpler a thing, and easier,
To don the archpriest's fillets once a year,
And slay some wretched cattle, in return
To reap the gratitude of the dark mobs.
Well, madame? Shall we say that Caesar seeks
Plush comfort? See his gear — the rough camp chair —
That's his judicial bench; a lion pelt,
A purple cloak… and then there is his sword,
Though even it's an orator that some
Still refuse to heed.

              *

           The Roman is a planet
Of hefty mass and gravity, that sways
Other stars, errant, by magnetic pull,
Not thunderbolts. Ah no, those rather strike
The planet, from its envelope of cloud,
Leaving such scars upon its face, a comely treasure,
And fitting, as well-wrought hexametric measure.

You know, I've written verse too, Cleopatra.
I know how to make myself understood.
I'm certain no deceased gazelle of yours
Has ever grown wide-eyed on Goat-Olympus
Hearing such elegies as I've delivered.

CLEOPATRA
O Caesar — you no longer seek my tears,
But they seek you! See how they press in waves,
Eager all to reflect a real man,
The first essential man their eyes have seen!

She covers her eyes with her hands.

O what a poor thing was wretched Cleopatra!

CAESAR
Look, my Queen — the new sun flickers on the ground.
The dawn has come.

CLEOPATRA
                    Already?

CAESAR
                              I hear my horse
Snuffle the air, and neigh — The legionnaires
Awaken — it's a hard thing to be rushed,
But time will have its due.

CLEOPATRA
I've never heard that supposition.

CAESAR
                    No?
No one's in such a rush as children are,
And those whose hour seems never to arrive.

He extends his arm to Cleopatra.

Allow the cool to bestow on me the right
To wrap your limbs in purple, and my arm
To lead you through my camp, Your Majesty!

CLEOPATRA

Permitting this.

I rest upon your arm. For the first time
I feel as if I had the world's support.

CAESAR
'Tis not the arm of Caesar that you feel,
Madame, but that of a Roman consul.

CLEOPATRA

Artfully retarding her pace.

The dawning light skips nimbly at our feet
Like playful waves. I think I've never seen
So beautiful a sunrise. Is it Sunday?
And can you feel the tips of Eos' fingers
Play on your eyelids?

CAESAR
                        Gazing at your pearls,
 I see reflected there the dawning light;
The world entire.

CLEOPATRA
                There's only two of them,
Caesar, remember that.

CURTAIN

ACT II
A ROYAL MARRIAGE

Scene 1

The portico of Cleopatra's palace at Serapium, giving onto the shore, and the harbour canal. Now and then, vessels can be seen sailing past the arcade opposite the stage. On both sides: two rows of columns. Marble tables, flowers in vases. Eucastus, and a boy, the latter watering the flowers at Eucastus' commands (delivered by gesture, while the former is conversing).

EUCASTUS
By Hermes, sir, there once was a wise priest,
Born of a priestess, whose grandfather (a priest)
I well remember — who once thus declared:

Into the Knight's ear, half-whispering.

'The genius of Time itself arrives
In Egypt at the coming of Caesar,
To hasten on the wheels of destiny.
Many a zodiac will spin that day.'
And so you see how things elude our grasp,
Rushing away from slippery fingers; why
I myself just yesterday — you hear? —
I broke two vases, they so twirled away
When I would grip them. Vases! Two!
And I, an old experienced table hand!

KNIGHT
They say that, one night, right into the bed
Of that old Roman king Hostilius
Fortuna crept herself! Right through the window!
And Caesar's worth more than a Hostilius...
The sentries swear they've seen someone like that
Flutter about his tent-flaps by the moonlight,
While he was watching... Why, not long ago,
Besieged, he lay siege to his own besiegers —

Through narrow alleyways, near the lighthouse, too,
Though well defended! Seventy-five ships
He smote to smithereens himself with — nothing!
Leaping from deck to deck, breasting the waves,
Book in one hand, beating the foamy surf
With the other — like a diver so he swam.
Meanwhile, the king, pressed tight against the Nile,
Smothered in yellow water.

EUCASTUS

He shall rest,
Swaddled in whole necropolises of balsam.
Saw it with my own eyes. Piety pays.

KNIGHT
He'd but accomplished that when I beheld
The wagons enter, groaning under loads
Of bows, quivers and spears, then: foaming mounts,
None with a saddle, from the battlefield,
Where fighting lasted all of four hours!
But he who's never seen the Parthian horsemen,
He ought to hold his tongue.

EUCASTUS

And in the end
(I reckon it's the end) two legions came
Marching along the Nile banks from the desert…
But you know better; I speak out of place
Even to mention it.

Proceeding with their tasks, Eucastus and the boy retreat by degrees into the depths of the arcade. Enter Calligion and Aelius Cinna, arm in arm.

CALLIGION

To the Knight.

Salve!

KNIGHT
                    Your health!

AELIUS CINNA
And yours!

Looking around.

            It seemed to me, I'd just
Of music drank my fill, and here — the scent
Of incense... What have we here, *theoria*?[58]
Or the realm of forms itself?

KNIGHT
                    So often think
Those new-arrivals to this land.

EUCASTUS

From the rear, from the side.

                    This Egypt
Of ours is one great theorem. Forever!

CINNA

Aside.

And Rome — is Praxis.

KNIGHT
                    The Queen's galleon
Slides through the harbour from those lines of masts,
Drenched in aromas, sails bellying with wind —

---

58   In Polish: 'Czy to dzień THEORYJ...?' A confusing reference, which can
either suggest (rather anachronistically) mystical meditation (*contemplatio*) or
philosophical theory.

Hey? Catch that scent? Three rows of oars,
Carved to resemble musical instruments,
Hang over the chuckling waves, and then they strum
One chord that ripples here upon the breeze...

CINNA
In my eyes, none of these queer things surpasses
This portico. A fine place 'tis indeed
For homage piled at the Republic's feet
Such as is due her, from all the world's lands...
Or Pompey's funeral repast. Yet I would
Waste no more time and get away from here
With the pouch diplomatic, taking nothing
Except, perhaps, a crocodile or two
For water sports...

*Enter Caesar and Cleopatra from opposite sides of the inner arcade,
simultaneously. They cross to each other and the Knight withdraws.*

CAESAR
My lady!

CLEOPATRA
    Caesar! So it seems, we have
At least one common moment in the range
Of daily offices...

CAESAR
      When and wherever
I chance to meet Your Majesty, it adds
One harmony more to the music of the spheres.
I thought about you on the battlefield,
Yesterday —

CLEOPATRA
      I carry in my bosom
The letter you sent thence. Can it be true
The battle was so quickly dispatched? Please,

I beg you, Consul, describe it to me,
Whose stylus, sturdy, sharp, and elegant
Is like a well-wrought sword.

CAESAR
                    In other words,
The missive scratched out while the battle cooled
Has not quite slaked your curiosity?
It's quite a simple thing, really. Well then:
I came there, had a look, carried the day.

CLEOPATRA
So speaks the thunderbolt.

CAESAR
                    God's messenger
Speaks to the point, in the service of Heaven.

*Calligion and Cinna approach and bow. Caesar and Cleopatra
acknowledge their greeting, but continue with their conversation.*

CAESAR
These times of ours suffer no hesitation.
And all that moves hastens to its completion.

To all.

We must honour the manes, send messages to Rome;
We must…

CLEOPATRA
            … repose a space…

CINNA
                            Indeed, time presses…

Calligion extracts some scrolls from the folds of his toga, Cinna, tablets, and both move off to one of the marble tables. Caesar and Cleopatra stroll about the portico leisurely.

CAESAR

To Cleopatra.

Ah! To repose…

To Calligion.

       By my bedside, within
The shallow vase, you'll find my letters ready.
I had some time last night…

Calligion exits, Cinna remains at the table.

CAESAR

To Cleopatra.

Allow me to dictate some words, my Queen,
The sense of which, if fugitive, perhaps
To untrained ears, ought to concern our Senate.

Cleopatra draws off somewhat and busies herself with a vase of flowers. Caesar dictates.

The area — immense — of our empire,
The wide variety of its inhabitants,
The distant postings of her citizens,
Sometimes — for many years, it's hard to say —
Require a… widening… of the marriage laws.

Cleopatra sends a knowing glance in his direction.

The legate, or plenipotentiary,
The law's custodian — and its hostage, too —
Is he to die in… certain… attributes
Because of the law, in its present state,
Which up till now forbids him to take a wife
In that province entrusted to his care,
According to the laws of that people
Whose civil unions Rome won't recognise?

Pause.

For it might seem, since each province is free
To practise its own customs, every man
Or woman, regardless of their civil state
Contracted in the circuit of Roman law,
Should be allowed to enter into marriage
Anew, in said provinces, according to
The local laws in force there. In the case
Of, say, a legate in Gaul, or Germany,
Who has a wife according to Roman law,
Is he to be considered by the Gauls
Or Germans as unmarried, in the eyes
Of laws pertaining there? And vice versa,
If he be unaccompanied by wife
To his posting, must he remain beyond
The bounds of that society, as if
He were just passing through? This is a blot,
I say, upon the Republic, which seems
Lacking in gravity in such matters…

CINNA

Interrupting.

I'd stand in opposition to such a law
As you're proposing —

CAESAR

                  And you'd stand alone,
I reckon, Cinna, or with few supporters…

CLEOPATRA
Of all the Roman legions who came here
To aid my father, some twenty thousand
Took twenty thousand of Egypt's fair daughters
To wife. But if the Queen, true friend of Rome,
Is to take voice in this matter, Caesar —
Please, let me have that parchment…

Caesar hands her the scroll, which she, lightly yet ostentatiously, casts aside. It falls on one of the nearby vases filled with flowers. She, smiling to Caesar and Cinna.

If these were flowers from Gaul, or the Rhine,
They'd reckon that a sudden snow had fallen!
But blooms Egyptian trust the sun…

Calligion enters and hands the letters to Caesar, who passes them to Cinna in turn. Calligion remains in the depths of the portico.

CAESAR

To Cleopatra.

                       That was
Merely a post-script.

CINNA

                  Consul! I take my leave
Of you and, begging Her Majesty's permission,
Of her as well.

CLEOPATRA
        I wish you a safe journey.
I've had a lion, with collar of gold,
Prepared for you —

Plucking some petals from a rose.

        Take this rose petal, too…
May these tokens of power and weakness
Keep you in mind of Egypt…

CAESAR
        … and mortality.

Vale!

Caesar accompanies Cinna a few steps toward the exit, then whispers something in Calligion's ear, at which the latter immediately withdraws. After Cinna leaves, Cleopatra pauses at the vase upon which the parchment lies, then speaks.

CLEOPATRA
O Caesar! Between those who understand
Each another, they say, only one thing
Is horrible — the shadow of untruth!
Besides that, nothing's to be feared. Now you
Should know this better than I do, as I
Have been, merely, the wife of little boys —
Misunderstood rather than indifferent —
To speak on behalf of the provinces,
For keeping them in mind (and here I speak
Of that parchment, which I tossed upon the flowers).
I did not wish to thank you with the lips
Of woman. For a woman's heart is such —
Women have this terrible advantage,
That they cast themselves into life's brisk current
Before they might be expected to know
What it is that they do. A man, it seems,

Is always a statesman. A woman, though,
Is like a statue which, when tottering
Cannot always be steadied by the hands
Of man, however loving, however strong.
Show me the man who, having glimpsed the ray
Of light from heart beaming, ever followed it
To the end? Trusting that it cannot be
Anything but divine — for God is love.
Yourself so godlike, can you think the gods
Love with a love not light-filled? Or, perhaps
The most important work of hands divine
Comes forth from them defective, incomplete?
Something unworthy the supreme sacrifice
Like that once offered by the poetess
On the Leucadian cliffs, pressing her lyre
Against her panicked heart? Well, Julius?
Tell me, O you who crossed the Rubicon
Without the approbation of the Senate,
Fording the stream, boldly, against the tablets
On which curses had been inscribed to turn
The over-bold from daring enterprise…
Is it not just the same in war, and often,
When the victorious mind settles to rest?
In such great moments, Caesar, people totter,
They always do. But women, O, consul,
Above all things, a woman is an instant.

CAESAR
The only true repose is heroism,
And it — the progeny of will and thought.

CLEOPATRA
I hear a cry — and feet upon the stairs…

*A shout, and in the depths of the portico leading to the shore, one sees
the Roman army.*

CAESAR
I set the legions marching. Whither? How
Are we to know, we, so often without maps?

CRY

From off stage:

Hurrah, Capitolines! Hurrah, Caesar!

CAESAR
I set the legions marching in the morning.
Whither? How shall I name the untracked sands
Where foot has never trod yet? I know not
Where soars the Roman eagle, I but know
That he's awing, and neither primary
Nor covert plume is trembling — one might think
He rests aloft with wings outspread. To know?
How might one know so many things? His roads?
Who's lain a statumen and paving stones
Through the blue air? Why, we know not
The Nile headwaters, nor the treasury
Where Ocean weighs the carat of her swells.
Petty sparks have set puny men ablaze
With boldness, but without the splendid soul
Beloved of God, because it comes of him.
Egyptian wisemen search the Milky Way;
I, of Europe, the depth of deeds to come.

CLEOPATRA
Come, Caesar, let me lay bare to your eyes
Some fitter regions to explore, a mound
On which to rest your bosom and your head.

They make their way toward the exit.

Come — this plank leads aboard a galleon
Of which our purple robes shall be the sails,

And they shall billow with the evening's breath,
Propelling us amongst the stars. To gaze
At them in peace as the warm breezes play,
Flapping their pleats of amaranth, is to gaze
Into the heavens, and into the heart…

CAESAR

Moves over to one of the colonnades and calls with commanding voice.

Calligion! Bring my tablets. And you, Torax,
My helm and sword. We sail! I'll take you where
The Empire of the world ends. You will gasp
At how close is the edge.

CLEOPATRA
                                    So let us sail!

*Simultaneous with the following cries, we hear the music of Cleopatra's oars
as the galleon approaches. All of the arcades below fill with people. Caesar
and Cleopatra pass through the crowd to the ship, accompanied by shouts:*

CRY
Great is the daughter of the Ptolemies!

SECOND CRY
Hail, Caesar!

Scene 2
*A crowd of gapers fills the depth of the stage, and continually
grows. From time to time, people wander to the front and engage in
conversation.*

FORTUNIUS
Two legions only, in the end, remain!…
In the whole city!… Such a rout of troops
Can't even man the lighthouse…

CENTURION

                              Fortune herself
Serves as the Consul's cohort.

FORTUNIUS

                            Cinna gone
With letters at high tide (letters that say
Nothing of Pompey, or any great Manes)…
Now Caesar's premature departure — these
Are two events, I'd say, un-fortunate.

CENTURION
Rumour has it that when the legion left
They tramped off grumbling.

FORTUNIUS

                         Whence come such rumours?

CENTURION
Flying, on the wings of Fate!

Catching sight of the Knight, who nears them from the rear.

                          O, here he comes:
A foot soldier under Gabinius,
The new-spurred Knight…

FORTUNIUS

                    What is the news?

KNIGHT

                        The folk
Are feasting through the city, wherever
The Queen's foot fell… And all the same, a pyre
Is being piled up on the square.

FORTUNIUS

                        Cornelia
Pompea waits upon Caesar's return
With arms crossed…

KNIGHT

                   Sphinx-like? We're in Egypt,
And we shall have Egyptian funerals:
Cremation and a feast with pipes and beer.

People begin to mill about the tables to the rear.

CENTURION
The tables groan with piles of food, and drink…

Fortunius, Centurion and Knight withdraw somewhat.

EUCASTUS
Such were the queen's own words: 'Wherever my foot
Has touched the earth, let there be gaiety!
Let the Exchequer count the costs.' And then.
Turning her eyes past Caesar's head she cried:
'Eucastus! Make many in Alexandria
Happy — when I return, I'll query you
On this myself. Now, do you understand?'
That last word still rings in my ears…

Gazing at the bustle to the rear.

                        And yet,
You must confess, the folk are being served
With more alacrity than are the priests…

KONDOR
'Understand?' Yes, indeed, that's meaningful.
It's as if someone said, 'Get to your task —
Largesse on all sides, front and rear, from barrels!'
And yet, it has a second meaning too —

'Within reason,' you know, 'with understanding.'
Good food, good wine…

ZECHERA

Strolling about, to Eucastus, with a half whisper.

                    Melmeia leads the choir
Of new-betrothed harvest girls; the boys
Are led by Ganemedion — shall they start?

EUCASTUS
It might be edifying too, I think,
To mummify with all due elegance
All those expiring in this night of grace…

KONDOR

Attempting to withdraw to the tables in the rear.

It's a good maxim: Filch a little bit
From each and every table; just a taste
To savour the cook's talents — 'sine qua non,'
As Caesar's secretary would put it…

EUCASTUS

Taking both Kondor and Zechera by the arm.

Let us sit down and watch the people play.
It gladdens the heart, O Zechera the Wise,
And you, Kondor the Temperate; later on,
We'll put our heads together — all three, mind you —
And regulate everything, everywhere.
For it's not here alone, the rout of joy,
Nor only on the sacred palace stairs,
But as when lightning strikes, all in the pale
Of its irruption bristle with the charge!

KARPON

Pushing his way through the crowd to the front of the stage.

And like that lightning bolt, your sage dictum
Has hit the mark, O silver-tongued Eucastus!
All Alexandria's aflame! At last —
I've looked everywhere for you. Let me rest
Amongst you for a bit...

He sits down.

                I've been racing
Hither and thither, curiosity
Unsated, Crowds, ever greater, people
Everywhere, but Men? Such as you, Eucastus?
Or you? Master of Hounds? To say nothing
Of Profound Zechera... You know all things;
Tell me — the rumour is that the young king
Is soon to wed our monarch Cleopatra...
All eyes are trained upon the terraces
Where lounges the young prince, beneath the fans
Of ostrich feathers that his nurses twirl
Above him. Is it so?

EUCASTUS – KONDOR – ZECHERA
             The testament
Of King Auletes — may he rest in glory —
States clearly, 'After one son, the Cadet
Shall take his place on Cleopatra's bosom.'
Thus, just as words eternal, writ upon
The leaves of aloe wrapping a cold heart,
Awaiting their re-incarnation. Vivat...
So does it run...

KARPON
             But others say that Caesar
Is kidnapping Cleopatra to Rome!

My modest ears recoil in shame from words
Like that... While others say the city fetes a wonder —
A miracle that happened in the palace;
That Cleopatra rides triumphantly
Upon a milk-white camel, while all Rome
Horripilating, flees across the sands
— Caesar included — after some great fright —
Ghosts in the palace shrieking... I have this
From someone well informed. A palace servant
Who at one time the Romans had held captive...

EUCASUTS
A servant of the court?!

KARPON
His name is Hero...

EUCASTUS – KONDOR – ZECHERA
That says it all!

KARPON
Hero, that wide-famed man,
Who's drawn two poets to his side; one Greek
At work upon a long heroic poem,
A Heroiad, singing the exploits
Heroic of Hero. The other one,
Egyptian, skilled in versifying thought
In suitably archaic dialects
Is glorifying Ptolemy's ancient realm,
Live! To the delight of ravished throngs!

KONDOR
By Crocodile Divine! I always knew
Our Hero had more hidden in the pleats
Of his kirtle than we gave him credit for!

EUCASTUS
And I had thought that he was lost for good —
Transmigrating into some happier form
Of scarab-beetle, or a crane, perhaps.

KONDOR

Itching to leave.

As I see it, Eucastus, and I've come
To this conclusion only after much
Deliberation: the flesh must be fed
No less than must the soul. Ergo, we eat!
And let the rest be, in the 'status quo'
— If I may use my Latin — after all,
Since as we see, our good people fulfil
Their Queen's instructions even before they quite
Leave her almighty lips, inspired, I say,
A folk 'prophetic' (that's a Judaean term)
But fitting, so I'll add in Greek — by Bacchus!
Let's join them!

ZECHERA

Solemnly, mysteriously.

       As long as living water
Spurts from the bosom's fountainhead, one need
Not place a cloth upon the spring to filter
The humours into purer droplets. Thus, ripe thoughts
Expressed in any tongue prove blameless
Their oracle…

EUCASTUS
       Zechera, by Hermes,
I've never been struck in the brow more squarely.
Egypt has yet her Sybil! And her peers?
Where might they be? Among the bearded Greeks?

The pale and chapped who call themselves philosophers?
For me, I doubt they've scrambled to the rung
On which the owl sits, on life's scaffolding!
Whatever they know, why, they have of us!

KONDOR
Tandem, it's settled, Eucastus, Zechera,
And Karpon — it is the Queen of Egypt's bidding:
We must be gay and set a good example
To others, in accomplishment of this,
This sacred mission we're entrusted with!
From square to square we must advance, eyes peeled,
On every table in strict discipline
Culinary until the trumpets sound;
Which, if I set especial weight on this,
It's that the trumpets do belong to me.
My trumpets, and I've taken care to see
That they won't spare the brass.

Harps resound, the crowd to the rear rushes toward the sound.

CRY

The lyre of Egypt!

KARPON
One choir arrives, the second on their heels,
And with them, Hero, in mail, cap-a-pe,
Clad thus in token of his captivity…

HARPER

At the front of the stage, sings:

1.
Let other nations lash their slaves
Along the sweat-drenched furrow;
Egypt is served by one true thrall
Who serves her as she's always served,

The gardener of old Egypt:
    The holy river Nile!

CENTURION

At a side table.

And Egypt only, all that while!

CROWD
All hail, the lyre of Egypt!
By Hermes, hail the harper!
Vivat!

HARPER

Sings.

2.
Let other nations carry off
The marble limbs of sculpted maid
As plunder for Pygmalions.
Behold the sure Nilotic lass:
The looming Pyramid that broods!

CENTURION
With shape befitting vestal prudes.
Pygmalion gives her a pass!

MANY VOICES
Praise to the patriotic bard!
Quiet you, there!

HARPER

Sings.

Egypt's eye pierces the heavens.
She knows the world and plumbs the wit
Of others — shallow and untrained!
She's balsamed thought — a boon indeed! —
    Inventing script!

KNIGHT

At the Centurions' table.

Aye! Such as only she can read!

VOICES
The singer stops — for there would be no end
To singing, had he sought to list the sum
Of Egypt's wonders…

CENTURIONS

From their table.

Onward, Legions glorious!
From British Isle
To Egypt's Nile!
Long live the godlike Julius!

HERO

Near the front of the stage.

The bard who has proclaimed such truths
Unto the crowds, has stilled his tongue,
Stifled by overabundance. Yet
Not only he imbibes of Helicon…

To the Greek.

Disciple of Psymmachus! Thrum your lyre
To dithyrambs that rival those of Homer!

LYRIST
I'll cut a snippet from my epic poem,
The *Heroiad*... Ahem...
I sing of Hero... of Hero is my Song...
I beg your pardon... neither niggard muse
Nor skimpy subject is at fault... My throat...
I've caught a cold... Ahem... *Incipiam de novo*
Of Hero is my song, who pent long years
In Roman prisons, devoted his mind
To wisdom, growing wise... I beg your pardon,
I simply can't go on. My throat... scratched raw...

HERO
Sing not of Hero then, Psymmachus' son —
Rest thou thy throat, exhausted with the toil
Of epic epithet and metaphor.
Long hast thou laboured, out-gutting whole pounds
Of glowing tallow...

KARPON

Rushing up to Hero with the others.

                    Look, it's him! Hero!
Our Hero! Hero in the flesh! *Salve!*

HERO

In a half-whisper.

No triumphs, please! Raise me not on your backs!
Let us remain incognito for now...
Come, let us draw aside...

VOICES

To the rear.

Hurrah, the shepherds' choir!

VOICES HERE AND THERE
The shepherds' choir! The best there's ever been!
Here come the bagpipers! And now, in ranks
The harvest-boys, the maidens with their scythes
Upon their shoulders brown, like crescent moons
In constellations…

YOUTHS IN THE CROWDS
The blades of those scythes
Will dull by pushing through thick curls of hair…

VOICES
Listen! They sing!

Just as throughout this scene, with some advancing to the front of the stage while others withdraw, so here — the choir of country-people advances.

CHOIR OF YOUTHS

Sing.

For all the apples thrown at us
From hiding places, and for all
The giggles, winks, and every blush,
Before the bench you must be hauled
To face Diana's sentence
With hearts full of repentance.

So come now, offer honey cakes
And comely reparations make.

CHOIR OF MAIDENS

Sing.

Whose fault is it? What drew their eyes
To chaplets that maiden hands spin?
Who says we threw those apples, lies —
They were blown at you on the wind!

We'll settle up Diana's score
When we are wed — and not before!

EPODE
Soon shall the rooster with his comb
Of coral wake the newlyweds
To common sweat and toil and groans
And then, at evening, back to bed.

CHOIR OF MAIDENS
There is no rooster on our sill —
Just turtle doves, who bill and coo.

EPODE
But hark — the rooster's calling you
To change your life — for good or ill.

CHOIR OF MAIDENS
Rains come, the sunshine dries them still.

BOTH CHOIRS
Each pigeon finds his turtle dove;
The only rhyme for this is… love.

HERO
In the springtime of my life, on a distant isle,
When I was sold — I was a comely lad —
By my Phoenician master, there among
The Cyclades, I knew a certain bard

Himself an exile there, who crafted iambs
Quite eloquently in well-turned bucolics.
But I always preferred the martial strains.

KONDOR
You speak for me!

EUCASTUS
                    Eheu! The theoria,
The classical theoria are vanished…
The pure Egyptian ones — oh, for example:
'The Crocodile who Drowned in Tears of Love:
In Twenty-Seven Strophes, with Chorus
And Gesture —' What, today, can equal that?

CENTURION 1

At the centurions' table.

Hey, brother — what's that propping up your skirt?
A staff of office? You there, peeping at
The harvest maidens through your fingers!

CENTURION 2
                              Me?
I ain't looking at nobody. Something
Flew in my eye, like once along the Tiber
Before a cottage door, when veterans
Like us were granted tracts of land!

CENTURION 1
                         I see!
The chatter of their scythes it is that set
You to bucolic reminiscing, eh?

CENTURION 2
There's sommat in that… Tell me that I'm wrong:
Something a shield can't beat away, something

You can't drown out with wine or dice-clatter.
Mehurcle!

A trumpet sounds.

CRYER
               Hark! The feast is over now —
The second trumpet sounds in the palace square.

VOICES
The second? Which of us even heard the first?

OTHER VOICES
The singing and the music drowned it out…

CRYER
Silence must reign at the third trumpet peal,
As deep as in the true Egyptian's home,
The grave…

Large portions of the crowd exit the stage through the arcades.

FORTUNIUS
       I've just heard tell from the suburbs
That Legions, cheering, have been overheard.
The merchants sliding from their kneeling camels
Report that, even down the sands, the scent
Of balsam reached them, still leagues out of town,
And strange music was wafted on the breeze,
Which signified for sure the royal galleon,
The Thalam. Here in Alexandria,
Whether it's vice or virtue, nothing happens
Before the vatic gossips start their babble…

CENTURION 1

Rising quickly.

But no such rumour's reached our ears of Pompey's
Funeral pyre lit, and burning to ashes!
Look!

CENTURION 2
    Mehurcle!

FORTUNIUS
                    There at the column —
Another flap of flame revealed her face —
Did you see? It's Cornelia! She turns!
It's her!

CENTURION 1
    She's coming back this way...

All the Centurions arise. Cornelia passes through.

FORTUNIUS, CENTURIONS

                            Salve!

CORNELIA

Raising her hand.

Your greeting I accept in Pompey's name;
If but one eagle bows, so Rome entire
Pays her respects to one truly Great man...

FORTUNIUS
I wish you strength, madame, to bear your sorrow.

CORNELIA
Should Cornelia swoon, Pompea will steady her.

Cornelia passes over the stage slowly.

KARPON

From the crowd departing.

A perfumed breeze has passed through the near suburbs
And those who heard those who heard the shouting
Have come — reporting mutinies among
The Legions...

FORTUNIUS
                Was that witnessed by someone?
If so, he should approach the tribunal
To testify!

KONDOR
        He'd be the last such called...
Hark! the third trumpet blares!

Trumpets. The front of the stage is occupied by two small groups: The one — Romans and Centurions following Cornelia's departure in silence; the other — Egyptian courtiers. The rear of the stage empties entirely. The low voices of both of these groups are like two tragic choruses.

FORTUNIUS and the ROMAN GROUP
These people flare their nostrils for the stink
Of perfumed galleons, while that widow
Fills her lungs full with wisps of tarry smoke
That bear aloft her husband's flesh, consumed.

EUCASTUS and the EGYPTIAN GROUP
There's going to be a wedding, that's for sure!
The queen approaches the gay thalamos
Where waits her brother-spouse bedecked in baubles;
The ladies of the court practice dance-steps.

ROMAN GROUP
The great men leave this dowry to the people:
Their aura, like a shadow tincturing
The thoughts of all; a shadow sensitive
That darkens, or grows brighter, stretching tall
According to events, proceeding death-wards.
And the events themselves in mindful care
Of the great men deceased stretch wispy arms
Toward the wife forlorn.

EGYPTIAN GROUP
                        Auletes' will,
That stipulates his daughter's hand be given
Into her brother's, this, second time round,
Shall be so celebrated as never before
With joyous glamour. For our royal line
Preserves ancient traditions like the hands
That wrap the dead in spices everlasting!

ROMAN GROUP
Ah, death is strong. Diana's darts are quick,
But the Republic keeps the memory
Of great men ever green by hewing to
Their legislation, and their manly deeds'
Example! Which better than cedar or balsam
Immortalises the apotheosed!

EGYPTIAN GROUP
I seem to hear the crooning of the oars,
The happy chants of the returning crews,
Muddied by echoes of tramping Roman boots…

ROMAN GROUP
I hear the thunder of the Legions marching —
Laying a basso continuo to some thin
Effeminate chirping…

CRIES OFF-STAGE
                    Thalam! Thalam!

ONE OF THE EGYPTIANS

Rushing forward from the rear.

Indeed, I see a stain of purple sails
Like to the setting sun afar at sea,
And there — the masts and tackle; O! The anchors
Are dropped, and now the cries grow louder. Look!
It's Cleopatra leading Caesar here!

ONE OF THE ROMANS
Caesar approaches, leading Cleopatra!

CRIES OFF-STAGE
Hurrah the eagles of the Capitoline!
Hurrah Caesar! Hurrah for Egypt's queen!

EUCASTUS
Quick — two ranks, both sides — thus ceremonial
And circumstance dictate.

ALL
                    Then, all to home
As galleons to harbour!

Scene 3
To the rear the prow of a ship appears. Caesar and Cleopatra, arm in arm, chatting as if in confidence, approach the front through the ranks, whom they greet with a slight gesture. New arrivals occupy the front of the stage; the two groups that had unfolded into the ranks withdraw completely.

CLEOPATRA
Once only, though supported by your arm,
I felt a sudden fright (though calmed at once) —
When the Legions refused to progress farther.

CAESAR
In that they merely marked the edge of our world.

CLEOPATRA
Brave Alexander went no farther that way,
Save once, when the phalanxes mutinied.

CAESAR
And this is why, in leaping from the boat,
I called Your Majesty to mind — I kept
My word, that you'd never lack the support
Of Caesar's arm, until the eagles bucked,
Baulking farther flight; until the rivers
Of the world's waters steamed away in sand;
Until we'd reached the bounds of history.
You cried 'Go!' and I went. Are we not men?
Brave Alexander flattered himself to think
Him of god's blood — a youngster! — someone's son...
Ah, Cleopatra! 'Tis an honour too
To be mere man. It is to set one's neck,
Bejewelled, to the yoke — more than enough!
O, Madame! Queen and woman! To be a man
In your presence is both to fall prostrate
And grasp the wreath of victory.

Taking both her hands in his.

                    Clasp once more
The hands of Julius... Before too long
The Consul, having completed his task here,
Shall be recalled unto the Capitol
Twice over — by the people and the Senate.

CLEOPATRA
Caesar — a napkin, please — the woman asks.

She rises and moves to exit.

The Queen of Egypt now presents herself
To her expectant people, who await
The news of her marriage to... her brother-spouse,
The king... and that the plenipotentiary
Of the Roman Republic should announce
The testament of the monarch deceased.

Eucastus enters, with an empty shallow bowl of gold.

EUCASTUS
I took the pineapples unto the king,
And told him that the Queen kisses his brow.

CLEOPATRA

To Eucastus, as she is about to leave.

How many were gladdened during my absence?
I want to see it all here, written down.
And take the king this camel made of paper...

She moves off.

CAESAR

Calling after her.

It is not my will that you marry him!...

CLEOPATRA
It's Rome's.

CAESAR
                No, it's not on account of Rome!
Along with you, he would be sent to hell
Were it not for Dynastic reasons. Ha!
You'd be a Roman slave, and not your people's
Mediatrix… The dead king's impotence,
The plotting of your own sister, your brother-
Spouse's vacuity… It's on account
Of these — and furthermore, it's on account
Of your Egyptian people! Bred between
Sphinx and Mummy!

CLEOPATRA
                    Consul! Egypt's queen
Has not time for such speech to be prolonged.

She goes on farther.

Farewell!

Pause.

    And once again, farewell. Tonight,
On that spot which you once did consecrate
To Fortune the Avenger… Julius!
There, at the same hour…

Caesar bows his head.

                        I say no more.

Returning a few spaces, halting.

Except for this — that love is always happy,
And fortunate… simply because it is!

She covers her eyes and hastens her steps.

Farewell!

She turns her head over her shoulder.

    Write! What you once confessed in script,
Initiating a response.

She stops again at the arcade porch.

              I've placed
A scarlet eastern anemone in your room…
Deep red… purple! I'll go there sometimes…
Perhaps the sun will use its leaves to write
In shadows on the wall… before it wilts.

She disappears through the arcades.

CAESAR

Alone, as if wandering in thought.

… The embers of the sun now glow beneath
The heavy vaulting of the pyramids
That stretch their granite ribs across the skies…
An angry comet thrusts aside the drapes
Of darkness, in disdain…

Calligion enters, bearing helmet and scroll in hand, a cloak draped over his arm.

CALLIGION
The emissaries of the priestly caste
Bearing the testament of King Auletes!

CAESAR

Coolly.

The people and the senate of Rome
Have known his will for ages. The whole thing —
Drenched as it is with embalming fluid…
Its stench of mummy permeates the court! —
Befouling like a mist the air of Egypt
So that the very eagles' pinnae gum
With spices of the tomb, and they sit fixed,
Bewildered mummies on their sticky perches!
Holier than Ptah, if less exalted here…
Should the envoys of the arch-priestly caste
Now wish to enter, sniff, and smudge themselves
With King Auletes' will, well, show them in!

PRIEST 1
O, mighty one! In us, the deathless bow…

CAESAR
O, likewise, likewise, deathless, et cetera…

PRIEST 1
We, who through whole millennia guard
The sacred tombs, whose hands receive the trust
Of earthly shells that once were Egypt's kings,
Of which no knuckle has been lost! So lovely…
Preserved together with the mortal innards
— If any portion of the kings be mortal —
In alabaster jars; emboldened by
Our service and our caste, and being called
The will of King Auletes to present…
So do we now, so that the marriage day
Of Egypt's queen take place not, sans the touch
Of Roman Consul's hand…

CAESAR

Taking the scroll in hand.

Thus doth he touch it,
And… push it back to you.

Priest 1 begins to wind the scroll, ceremoniously.

PRIEST 2

We have prepared
A spacious chamber for the earthly shells
Of both the Queen and her young husband. Years
May they remain empty! With sweet incense
Each day we keep them pure… Two empty slots
In the long row… Such is our skill… Our patience…

While the two Priests are busied winding the scroll, the Knight enters.

CAESAR
What news is worth our hearing?

KNIGHT

Egypt's queen
Has set two provinces on full alert —
Pelusia and Kanopa — throngs of men
Readied as couriers, and piles of wood
Pitch-smeared, await the torch as signal fires…
Galleons are asea as far as the Cyclades!

CAESAR
Keep a close watch. *Vale!*

Calligion hands Caesar his helmet, and drapes the travelling cloak on his shoulders.

CAESAR
Tonight I wish to visit the palace
Where first I rested when we came to Egypt;
Where the pale brow of Pompey, at my feet,
Blocked farther progress.

Exiting.

> Have the Legions meet
> Caesar on the way, tomorrow morning!

The Priests and the Knight bow low to Caesar, and then see him to the porch.

Scene 4

PRIEST 1
And as it was in the beginning, so
It is now — Peace on all hands — Queen
And King ever the same. Ha! Only Egypt —
Egyptian wisdom — can accomplish that!
Hermetic precepts the causative force...
A man — a great man, given — now departs
Her threshold, but it's the accumulation
Of petty things that makes that man so great.

KNIGHT
He came — he saw — he conquered —

PRIEST 1

> One thing yet
> Remains, O knight — a weighty thing, at that:
> For which here, there, and now — we are... concerned.

PRIEST 2
The conjunction of the heavenly bodies!

PRIEST 1
Indeed! It never has occurred before
That royal nuptials should have taken place
Without the stars fortuitously aligned!

PRIEST 2
A sudden, astral flash — afar, and dubious…
Quite worrisome, although…

Enter Psymmachus and Olympos, without interrupting the dialogue.

PRIEST 1
                                        … Although it boots
It not to call it dubious or worrisome
Until some Arch-astrologer, or Zechera,
After long fasting, probes the murky skies.
The true syzygia, worthy of horoscopes
Like theirs, portends other things than that splotch.

Turning round to Psymmachus and Olympos.

Although in saecular wisdom (if such
We may term it) there are some learned men
Who plot their zodiacs from bursts and spurtings.

PSYMMACHUS
How different the eye, heavenly blue,
From the blue heavens…

OLYMPOS
                                  All men are young in spring.

Enter Cleopatra, clad in elaborate wedding robes, accompanied on the one hand by Eucastus, and on the other by Eroe.

CLEOPATRA
Here too we come across true, happy souls.

PRIESTS
Everywhere! Always!

CYPRIAN KAMIL NORWID

CLEOPATRA

Seats herself unceremoniously.

            I'm tired. And it's true —
I've reason!

To Eroe.

          Relieve me of as much of this
Wedding stuff, as you can. I need to breathe…

*Cleopatra's outer garments pass through Eroe's hands and pile onto
the floor.*

CLEOPATRA

Taking note of the Knight.

Aha! And is it you on guard tonight
In Serapium, following the feast?
That's very prudent…

To those assembled.

            This man's my army's star —
He is the one who first warned Cleopatra
How dangerous is Caesar… A fighter
At moment's notice! He redeemed the queen,
Leading her troops once, at a nearby fortress…
'Tis true…

KNIGHT
    My queen?!

CLEOPATRA
          Let pure humility
Suffer this once to serve as an example.

KNIGHT
Ma'am?!

PRIESTS

Taking measure of the Knight.

As if he were sprung of the warrior caste!
A scion born unto pure-blooded chiefs!

CLEOPATRA

More softly, with a sigh.

'Twas he who first announced Caesar's arrival…

To the Knight.

To have her part in your labours tonight,
The queen would change the password: 'Dawn and Pearls.'
O — from my ears to yours, these hangers-on…

To Eroe.

The cloth of words that drapes official thought
Is sometimes just as heavy as the folds
Of that of which you have unburdened me.
Can nothing more be stripped away? Come, all!

To Olympos, stretching herself out on a chair, tossing the bands from her hair.

Physician! Folk-medicine says that leaves
Are good for cooling down the fevered brow…
And this is how it came to be we wear
Chaplets while feasting. Of what sort? Would you say
There's reason in this gossip? Can leaves truly
Bring soothing to the heavy head abused?

OLYMPOS
Laurel, because it's slightly venomous…
And ivy too, for it retains its cool…
Thyme, fragrant… And some say the eastern
Scarlet anemone…

CLEOPATRA

Strangely moved.

Anemone?!
The near-purple scarlet anemone?!

OLYMPOS
But inner peace — contemplating the stars…
The firmament's cooled more than one fever.

PRIEST 1
The divine aether… from the heights of heaven…

PRIEST 2
Which only rarely mortal man has sipped…

CLEOPATRA
And so perhaps I'll toss some oilskin
Upon these shoulders, and set out in a skiff
To gawk at stars. You think I'm capable?
I'm so exhausted…

Pause.

Wise Psymmachus! You,
Scrabbling together books for my library
In Alexandria, whose stoa, from the dawn
Are crammed with eager youths hungry for knowledge,
Tell me — I'd partake of your wisdom now.
But first — how comes it that you've jumped the grooves
Of pure philosophy to rattle here?

Those schoolmen of such excellent renown
Possessed the power to transform emotions
Into such ghostly might, unknown before...
Take for example Plato the divine
— That I pass over the old Pre-Socratics —
The present age is... Please, enlighten me:
If, for example, good Eroe here
Was pierced, unwary, by bold Cupid's dart,
Could any of you, like the ancient masters,
Take that head, as lovely as an amphora,
Spill out its old contents, and pour in new?

Stretching out on her chair and drawing her eyelids closed.

I put the question to you as a queen
Duly concerned for her subjects' welfare...

PSYMMACHUS
Like the old masters, Ma'am, I'd beg a day
To think the matter through.

CLEOPATRA
                                                Only one day?
My goodness! What about an age entire?

She stretches her body on the chair, her eyes closed.

EUCASTUS

To all, in a soft voice.

The queen, if I may be so bold, is tired.

KNIGHT

In a half-whisper.

Passwords delivered, now I shall take up...

OLYMPOS

In a half-whisper.

                                    Mere shadows
Of slumber sometimes bear authentic fruit.

EROE
The queen permits her court to speak aloud
While she is dreaming…

*Cleopatra makes a slight movement with her hand. The priests, who are
determined to leave, approach her with their papyrus scroll on a golden
plate. Cleopatra, noticing their gesture, reaches out a hand to the object.*

PRIEST 1
The Consul's touched it…

CLEOPATRA

Starting.

                              Julius?! Caesar?
Touched this? What is it?

PRIEST 2
                              The king's testament.

CLEOPATRA

Rising from her chair.

The memories… too painful… Eucastus!
Have someone bake a sweet shaped like this scroll
And bear it to the Monarch. My husband
Likes touching things like that with his wee hands.

Exiting.

The Queen wishes you health!

Eroe and Olympos, following Eucastus, accompany her out.

PRIEST 1
How beautiful the love of the crowned heads
Of Egypt! Of whom every one we guard
Mummified — not a single knuckle missing!

PRIEST 2
In frames well censed, sarcophagi of wood
Sweet-scented… Not in vain do they await
The noble herd!

To Knight.

Good knight, receive our bow…

KNIGHT
Likewise.

Exit priests.

Scene 5
Night falls appreciably. Some light to the rear.

PSYMMACHUS
That woman, fluent in nine languages,
Learned in Greek wisdom, no less adept
At mysteries Egyptian, clever, then,
In riddles of all sorts, astonishes
With words no less — ah, more so! — than with sceptre.
Often after a royal audience
Will I return dumbstruck, lost in thought
Amidst the huge images of the Sphinx
That sun themselves spread out upon the sand.

To transform — love? — into some higher power?
Some strength unknown? Which of the old minds ever
Prescribed something like that? What would you say,
My warlike knight? Let's say that Chloe spurned
Your amorous advances. Would you then
Betake yourself unto Pythagoras?
Could those who blabber in the stoa relieve you
Of unrequited passion's suffering?
Or would you hasten to those mummy-quacks
For a prescription astrological?

KNIGHT
There have been times when, at nocturnal pickets,
Resting my chin on spear-butt, I would gaze
Rapt at the constellation Virgo,
Or at the stars of Leo, as he raced
Through the clear skies. But, as there were lions
— Real ones — in the near desert, I'd no time
For profound musing on the zodiac.
Nor have I much time now. And yet I reckon
The surest antidote for melancholy
Is gambling with the dice, or drinking wine,
Or the sure knowledge that there's more than one
Virgo — or Chloe — in arm's reach…

PSYMMACHUS
More than one Chloe?
More than one Venus too, as epic poets
Teach us by varied metaphor, apostrophe…
There are as many Venuses as rhapsodes.
From this arises doubt, from doubt — philosophy.
The prettier girls are fain to such philosophy
As are their relatives, and those that peddle rouge;
Who'd call that into doubt would be locked up
Or laughed to scorn for denying the sun!
Further, the slightest Chloe-Aphrodite
Would raise a lump on his nut with her shoe!
And so we do philosophy a service

In serving well the girls, which furthers too
The concord of the state!

KNIGHT
                        Here comes the watch.

He goes to meet them, Psymmachus following.

PSYMMACHUS
'Pearls and the dawn!' You heard it from me too —
Let those passwords protect my learned hide
Like syllogism or iron-clad *sic probo*!

The Watch halts before the Knight.

But what do I see? One of my disciples?

KNIGHT
Who is this man? And why is he under guard?

WATCH LEADER
For spilling libations to the god his belly…

PRISONER

Interrupting.

Drowning regret… a broken heart… you see
A victim here, no criminal! She!
Harinoe! Who spurned my verse and feelings
Although I gushed forth the one and the other
Into her ears like… like…

WATCH LEADER
                        Gush forth nothing here!

PRISONER
Unfeeling people... No one heeds my pain,
As deep and wide as world-encircling Ocean!
And I'm arrested for a little jug?
And then, they want a password? From a lover?
A password, from a poet? Such cold logic
Is for our masters...

PSYMMACHUS

To Knight.

                    And as I am his,
I beg you, let me lead him home with me...

PRISONER

Recognising him.

Psymmachus the Wise! The Temperate! The Sober!

PSYMMACHUS

Taking him by the arm.

Let me support this teetering... intelligence
With crutches of axioms, lead him home,
And I'll return him a philosopher.

*Psymmachus leads the Prisoner off, the Watch exit, while the Knight
and the Centurion remain.*

KNIGHT
Night-watchmen are your true philosophers.
They and the crews that sweep the streets at night
Know what life really is.

CENTURION

Rattling some dice in his hand.

It's quiet now.
What say we roll the bones?

Tosses.

Ten!

KNIGHT

Tosses.

Ten again!

CENTURION
And one!

KNIGHT
And one again! Symmetrical
Our fate is? Where is a philosopher
When you need one? I'd have him answer that.

CENTURION
My head spins at the very thought of it.

KNIGHT
Caesar alone knows how to wield such arms.

CENTURION
What do you mean?

KNIGHT

Alea iacta est!

CENTURION
Splendid!

KNIGHT

With finger to his lips.

     Shh! I hear some tiny steps brushing
The flags there — like the rustling of small leaves.

CENTURION

Peering toward the sound.

A woman!… And such a figure — Mehurcle!
The tissues that she wears reveal more
Than had they not been shouldered! Such a girl
Who cannot hide her charms even if she tried
Is lying, when she does!

Enter Cleopatra in a long cloak.

KNIGHT
                    You see the queen!

CENTURION
A boat is waiting for her…

KINGHT
                It's our duty,
And prudence, to show her that we're on guard.

He approaches the queen.

CLEOPATRA
You see the passwords dangling from my ears.

She disappears to the rear.

KNIGHT

Returning to the Centurion.

You see, it's true: they only know real life
Who keep the watch at night. On this side here:
A practical philosophy is born,
On that, a queen trips out to gawk at stars.

CENTURION
She is a priestess of Isis, her veins
With ichor pulse.

KNIGHT
                The soul of Isis' soul…

They return to the dice.

CENTURION
Ten!
I wonder what is going on in Rome?

KNIGHT
There are two men there, waiting on a third.

CENTURION

Adding up his score.

Forty for me… The one is Mark Antony,
The one awaited: Caesar. But the third?

KNIGHT
Who else? Lepidus.

CENTURION
                    Alongside those two
Lepidus is the shadow of a man.
We saw him darken, slightly, Egypt's sands.

KNIGHT
He is a wary fellow, tries each rung
Before he presses foot on it too firmly.

CENTURION
With your indulgence, you'll find no such one
Among the Legions… Antony, now, gambles
Va banque… He rolls the dice —

KNIGHT
                              — And loses all…

CENTURION
Sometimes, sometimes…

Pause; he rattles the dice.

                    Point is, the Legions have
Men in them from the days of Pompey's exploits.
Soldiers who've seen the end of the world, lands
Where frozen seas bite into frozen shores,
Where Roman boot first trod, between Colchis
And eastern Phrygia; where Hyperboreans
Lumber about in leathern hoods. Broad steppes,
Dark seas and gloomy forests without sun,
Where sluggish flocks of birds stumble about,
Too weighted down with cold to tempt the sky.
And where the salt is culled from the sea foam,
And but one warlike tribe rumbles the tundra
With mail-shirts sewn of shaven horses' hooves…

KNIGHT
Caesar brought one of those back home from Parthia.

CENTURION
No, no, another.

KNIGHT
What? Saw it myself.
The scales transparent as a fingernail.

CENTURION
Parthians! Sure — there are such things as Parthians,
But I am speaking of a horrid tribe,
With whiskers twisted on their upper lips
Like to a hawk, when in its beak there writhes
A serpent… Restless are they; indolence
They hold in strict repugnance. This tribe tills
No fields, and little recks the gods. They race
About on stallions, skimp-shanked, but eager!
They drink the milk of mares, which they ferment,
And fear nothing but witches.

KNIGHT

Starting, again placing a finger to his lips.

Hush! I hear
A chaos of trampling feet… and calls for help!
What can this mean?

CENTURION
Indeed, they hasten here!

PRIEST 2

Rushing up from the rear, crying.

Help! Help! Where is the knight?

CENTURION

                Who rushes here
Without the password?

PRIEST 2

            Pearls and dawn! It was
Set in my presence. Otherwise, I should
Never have passed your pickets…

KNIGHT

              True enough.
And I remember you. What's going on?

PRIEST 2
Allow me… catch my breath…

KNIGHT

             What's happened, man?
Something important?

PRIEST 2

         Something violent!

KNIGHT
He's sweating like a pig…

PRIEST 2

Beginning.

            For many nights…

KNIGHT
Speak boldly!

PRIEST 2

       For many nights now, Zechera
Has watched atop the Zodiacal tower,

Along with other priests, searching the skies
For that syzygia foretold, expected…
In vain. Until tonight. At last, alone,
And scanning with more diligence than ever,
Her eye-beams burning deep into one vector,
I, weak myself with fasting, heard her cry…
Like harp-string snapped, or costly krater smashed,
It was the scream of a blind woman…

CENTURION, KNIGHT

                              Ah!

PRIEST 2
… Following light and ending up in darkness;
Reading another's fate, losing her own!
O, ironies of destiny! I ran
Toward that scream, and she, howling, confused,
Bewailing what had happened, filled the womb
Of that hollow plinth with echoes of doom,
Her shrieks of terror mixed with prophecies
Funeste… Perhaps she lost her mind as well
As her twinned daylight when the jellies burst,
And on she howled, spewing forth prophecies
Unsanctioned by the archpriests, far and wide!
A scandal! Extraordinary!
I scrambled up the higher ladders, grabbed
Her arm, but she jerked it away from me,
And as a spider scuttles over the net
That she herself has woven, she crawled away,
Fingers and toes for eyes, her silhouette
Blotted the moonshine briefly, disappearing
As she leapt to the granite scaffolding;
Nothing remained of her then, save the echo
Of her shrieks vatic, howling of the realm,
Its destiny, and its heroic shades,
And all of this, sans priestly approbation!

KNIGHT
She lost her sight without petition, too!

PRIEST 2
Of course… And even that is scandalous.
You haven't seen her pass this way, brave knights?
On her way to the tombs to chat with those
Who lie in the Necropolis?

KNIGHT
                    No maid
Nor matron passed this way save one alone,
A coryphe of the goddess Isis
And she — I say — a pretty one at that!

PRIEST 2
That won't be her…

Pause, deep in thought.

                    Yes, the Necropolis.
There would her frenzy draw her, like a magnet,
The wretched woman… and 'tis there I haste.

Exits hurriedly.

KNIGHT
Which of the two is of sounder mind, hey?

CENTURION
It's not proper, I reckon, to reprise
Our game?

KNIGHT
The auguries are less than propitious.

CENTURION
Each night has some odd power of its own.

KNIGHT

Suddenly.

Comrade — rush to the graves before
Zechera or that other reaches them.
Stand guard there at the entrance. I'll wait here
To makes sure no priest meets with prophetess.
For if this should go sour, what shall we,
Two simple soldiers, say in our defence?

CENTURION
I go!

Turns on his heel and exits quickly.

Scene 6

KNIGHT
It's God's own truth — each night's a sorceress
Unto itself. The day is nothing like it,
Although we split the rolling earth in twain:
Day — night, as if they were two equal halves!
No, those of us who watch through the dark hours,
All seasons of the year, in varied climes,
Know the respect that's due the night's shadows!
So many learned men — I won't say *wise* —
Stunned into silence by a nocturnal riddle
Greet the new day like helpless children, whom
A nurse must take in hand, and lead, where they
Would never think of toddling by themselves...
Returning from my nocturnal pickets
I've chanced to meet more than one face, wan, blank
And thought: *I might just let a word drop here,*
Such as would make him jump — Revealing something
They'd tucked between their ribs... *How did he know?*
Each place sounds its own symphony at night —

Curious thing! The first movement is gay,
With laughter and applause that sifts upon
The cobblestones in bright, major accords,
But then a modulation — birds of night
Whirr through the air; dogs bark by the canal,
And then — like a brass cymbal comes a splash,
A cry of doubtful nature… and a pause.
Then, ha! — the tattoo of a woman's heels,
A flute sounds and breaks off, the minor scale
Hangs in the air like some melancholy ghost,
Resolving in the whispered scrape of leaf
Against the pavement. Coda! Camels bellow,
And asses bray; wheels clatter on the stones
As swells the chorale of the swearing teamsters,
And whispered morning litanies…

He strains his eyes toward the rear.

Zechera!

ZECHERA

Finding her way, arms outstretched.

Thus the blind woman reels, from column to column,
As if among the charitable few!…

Aloud.

Guard… Who is it keeps watch at the portico?

KNIGHT
The same who honoured you when you were sighted,
Lamenting that his own eyes see you thus!

ZECHERA
Ah, son… Mists cover all the earth in dusk,
And the world ends in darkness…

The dawn slowly begins to break as she speaks.

                                    Thunderous within!
The priest mumbles his calculations high
Up in the tower, plotting a syzygy
That never shall emerge; the stars disdain
To clasp their beams across unfriendly skies,
Where cosmic nuptials never shall be seen.
This land, this Egypt, shall become a river —
And nothing more! The Nile, and nothing else!
A ditch and not a kingdom, a sewer, not a realm!

*A gondola is seen to the rear. Enter Cleopatra, dressed in the long
cape she wore in Scene 5. The dawn grows slowly brighter. Hearing the
prophecy, Cleopatra draws near. Pointing to his eyes, the Knight informs
her of the misfortune that has befallen Zechera. Cleopatra halts, silent
and attentive. The front of the stage is still quite dark. Zechera continues
with her prophecy.*

The priests unlatch the kennels of the stars
And one bounds off with paws spurning the dust!
Across Egypt he runs, overleaps the sea,
To pant at last above Rome, bristling red…!
High above one of her seven hills, the Capitol
As humans term it — there the comet pauses:
Will it take the city by the scruff and shake it,
The whole litter of palaces and temples?
It wags its head aflame above the city —
There, a great man, whom you all know…

To the Knight.

                                    Good sir,

Is any here beside you?

Cleopatra signs him to lie.

KNIGHT

No, there's not!

ZECHERA
That man, who grips the world in his pure hand,
His right hand — mighty — but not for himself;
That manhood ripe, who rules by necessity,
That pillar! shall be chipped until it shatters
By short stiletto bites — treason! — Three and twenty
Quick stabs that pierce his breast... He'll hide his face,
As if beneath a purple cascade tumbling,
Behind the blood-stained drapes of his toga...
And thus he falls! And thus shall Rome fall, too!
And thus the world shall crumple to its knees!
The man's name...

In a changed voice, searching out the knight with her hands.

Hey! My son! Your word of honour —
The queen — she is not here?

KNIGHT

Looks toward Cleopatra in silence.

CLEOPATRA

Again signs him to lie.

KNIGHT

I told you once...

ZECHERA
But — on your word of honour?

KNIGHT

Looks toward Cleopatra, who again signs him impatiently. He extracts his sword from its sheath, breaks it over his knee and lays the pieces at the queen's feet.

My word of honour!

ZECHERA
My son... The great man's name... is Julius Caesar!

CLEOPATRA

Stumbles, fainting.

Such is the great man's name? If so, let Rome
Be known henceforth as... Abomination!

The darkness at the front of the stage is suddenly split by the glare of a comet.

CURTAIN

ACT III
LONELINESS AND DEATH

Prologue to Act III[59]

OLYMPOS
It's one thing to give ear to words, another

---

59   This scene, which was to open Act III, was left unfinished by Norwid. Juliusz W. Gomulicki does not include it in the version of the play printed in the *Selected Works*. It is, however, included in the play as collected in that number of *Chimera* (1904) dedicated to Norwid, and the play as edited by Tadeusz Pini. We include it here, as, even incomplete, it fills a notable lacuna between the end of Act II and Scene 1 of Act III. We call it a 'Prologue to Act III' so as not to disturb the numeration of the scenes.

To do what must be done. The doctor now,
Who has a sick man in his care, will call
The household all together and direct
His prayers to Hygieia, or at most,
Send up his pleas to Apollo the Healer…
That said, it's hard to overlook the gossip
That's bandied round the city, that the queen…
That ever since the comet snagged its tail
To hang above the world — has held her tongue,
Foregoing speech entirely… That the tombs
Of the Necropolis have gained in depth
One more degree by this her silence. Still,
The word repeated second-hand is oft
Twisted in repetition. Thus, it's good
To follow back the tangled thread unto
The fingers that still pinch the end…?

EUCASTUS

                              Of course…
Is it not true that no food is unclean
To the Egyptian monarch? That the rules
That bind us mortal men do not apply
To her? That if today she have a yen
For Nile-snipe, it's prepared! By special edict…
Has this not held true through millennia?
And yet exceptions royal abrogate
The universal law — not! The same's true
For the horarium, and even — even! —
The ceremonial!

Pause.

                    But, speechlessness?
Those rumours lie. Or else misrepresent
The solemn gravity of Egypt's sceptre.
When the news came from Rome of Caesar's death,
The palace protocol might have been arranged
By those who hold a ceremonial rank:

A person sage — like you, for example!
Or else some priest, with meetly shaven crown,
In robes immaculate from tip to toe
Might sound the proper incantation, *but!* —
Let all those fingers soiled on market stall
And alley brick be placed — thus! — cross the lips
That reek of garlic, by the holy name
And power of Osiris!

OLYMPOS
                    Oh, my dear
And reverend Eucastus! By the name
Of sweet Pythagoras, rare is the man —
The rarest! — who speaks to another man
So that one hears exactly what he means.
For there are some who, speaking to the prince
Of the spur at his heel will swell and blow
That it outshines the sun's own blinding boss,
And so — they say nothing at all, they just
Jabber *at* someone empty vocables.
And there are others who converse alone
With their own selves. It matters not with whom
They seem to be in conversation,
Neither receiving nor advancing truth
Or any sort of content, really — these
Are mute as well. And yet, a great silence,
A vacuum, fills the world, such as the wise
Don't always mark… or opt not to betray.

EUCASTUS

In a whisper.

Clever Olympos! If such were the case…
And so, indeed it is… It's true: the Queen
Has not uttered a word since Caesar's death.
You hear it for yourself — that great silence
That, hearing, Eucastus dares not betray…

OLYMPOS
But her last word? The last word that she spoke?
Might you repeat it, faithfully? Come now,
I'm asking you as the Royal Physician…
And so, there's no infraction of the rules,
No blemish to the ceremonial…

EUCASTUS
It was… It was, yes, when Calpurnia's envoys,
In secret, brought great treasures to the Queen,
Gifts from the widow of Caesar! So grand,
Indeed, in caskets of Italian walnut…
The caravans of mules and camels passed
Under the deep vault of the gate; Eroe,
Her kanephoros, brought the news to her
(In words well-chosen)… It was evening then…
The Queen flicked off the waxen seal with finger
Indifferent… But as she read the letter,
Her eyes flashed suddenly, like two bright stars
That fill their lungs with air before they race…
She dropped the letter from her hands and clapped
Once, uttering two words, no more:
'Roman Tribute!' — nothing more, just those two:
'Roman Tribute.'

OLYMPOS
                    Nothing more…

EUCASTUS
                              And yet,
However few, those words were uttered so,
That all the guards throughout the long arcades
Leapt to attention, and one hundred halberds
Thundered against the floor, their butt-ends striking
A crashing echo through the chambers, like…
Lightning… The first thought that came to my mind
Was that a basalt sphinx struck with her paw
The granite flags, and howled… I turned my head

And saw — a golden sandal flash in passing
Through thunderheads of gauze… It was the queen
Who passed by… So sound sphinxes when they roar…
[…]

Scene 1
A chamber with the appearance of a tomb. Two Doric-like columns to
the very rear; two entrances nearer the front, on either side. At the front
of the stage a throne, and benches; the entire area between the columns
and the throne is covered with drapes of a dark colour. The windows
are small and also draped. There are risers, shaped like small seats,
leading to the throne. Cleopatra lounges on one of these, carelessly, her
feet resting on a lion pelt.

CLEOPATRA
When first I gazed upon that comet's mane,
My soul grew bright, as then in Amenti,
Those hellish caverns… I see everything
With perfect clarity: each bit of straw,
Each circumstance I read! Just like a book,
Read through and through! The whole sad volume — it's
As if the stream of words formed whirlpools
That grip and pull me down into the depths.

Pause.

As long as these two hands, eyes, memories
Could find support on Julius's breast,
I gave no thought to Rome — For what Rome is,
That great man, with a word, or in the still
Majesty of his being kept from me,
Blocking my sight by gesture, or a nod —
Just like when someone sits down at a sill
Beyond which lies a city, and with elbow
Or fabric softly falling from a shoulder
Cuts off the view of millions of townsmen,
One finger blotting out a battlement,

Eclipsing a huge temple with an arm…
But now that noble man's been pushed away
By three and twenty thrusts. And should my eyes
Peer through those three and twenty slits, I'd see
But three and twenty curses!

Fainting.

                              O yes! Rome
Has something great in it — I've often sensed it
When, on my barque, resting on Caesar's arm,
I listened to the chanting of the oars,
Lulled by his words… Even today I see
— Not only hear, I see — all that he said…
And yet this Great Rome is now but one great crime!
And Egypt? Shall she fall in the same way?
Two worlds darkened beneath two setting suns,
Two hearts submerged in these two worlds' demise —
While Julius and Cleopatra yet remained
Together, they were like two living beings.
But with a woman, Caesar is a stone
That casts its shadow broadly on the sand,
The greatness that was Rome obliterating
All commonality… Men come to know
But slowly that they have nothing to share
But their own weakness with a woman, while
Women have nothing to give in return
But one more *Bravo!* as the triumph passes.
Rome is great — but such greatness cannot bear
A man! My father-king was torn by Rome
From out this heart of mine… From Egypt, too,
When he was made into a prostrate slave.
My virgin breasts — twice! — playthings for two boys,
Were tossed before my brother-whelps by Rome…
At last Rome stood before the living heart
Of that great man — did she tremble, perhaps?
And bow the head…? If so, 'twas like a bull
About to pierce his innards on its horns

And fling the flesh aloft. Yes, such is Rome!
Caesar! I shall not traipse behind your troops
With lint and bandages to bind the wounds
Of Roman veterans. I'd rather sail
With hundreds of galleons to the Capitol
To cast my eyes upon your bloodied breast,
Interrogating three and twenty times
Each gash…
        Eroe! Come, blot out the light
Of heaven — drape the windows — at these skies
No longer can I gaze, since I have stared
Into that comet's eyes… Poor, blind Zechera!
How well I understand — Alas! — your darkness.

Pause, then, suddenly.

How fares the good and frightful prophetess?

EROE
She props herself upon a cane and thinks
But rarely of her blindness. She does say
From time to time that, since her eyes were burst,
She is no longer two-sighted, but sees
Like any other man…

CLEOPATRA
        Those words are hard.
Harder by far than blindness…

Pause.

        I've a spasm,
Eroe; set the lion-skin beneath
My feet here… Is this the same lion pelt
That had been in the Palace??

EROE
                        Yes, bartered
From Caesar's lictor for six better skins
And a smile.

CLEOPATRA

Stretching forth a finger.

              Come and kiss with that same smile
This hand of mine.

Gazing at her feet.

                    Only once in my life
Did I kneel on this mane…

To Eroe.

                    What of our guest?
What says he after spending his first night
There in the royal palace?

EROE
                    I can say
Only what I have heard from Antony's friend
(A Roman knight named Delius). That is all.
What he himself thinks, this I do not know.
But Delius repeats that, when they beheld
Your Majesty in Ephesus with your train,
They reckoned there might be no grander sight,
And that Your Majesty surely never took
Such care to dazzle anybody's eyes…
That all were ravished by your charms…

CLEOPATRA

With sincere laughter.

                                        Ha, ha, ha!
Of course, my aim was to seduce Antony,
And thus I had them trick us out in all
The spangled things of my forefathers. Well,
It seems they're good for something. Such a dress
As yours — I wore for Caesar, and the pearls
At my earlobes… Eheu! What else have you?

EROE
They were quite startled at your choice of quarters
And reckon that Egyptian superstition
Prompted Your Majesty to depart the palace
Leaving… life… to your guests, while for yourself
Choosing the grave — they say, 'and thus, the shades
Are to be envied over life itself!'

CLEOPATRA
That's rather smooth. But should Mark Antony
Desire to see me — where? And when? How often?
There's nothing simpler. I shall ride with him,
And laugh — like a madwoman! I don't look half-bad
I reckon… What's there left to long for? Well,
I'm quite in love with Antony… What more?

                        *

Now, strictly speaking such a love as he
Desires and comprehends — I have such love
Essentially at his command. And true!
I know Mark Antony's needs, and my own:
An occupation, worries, furthermore —
Absolute loneliness… Being alone,
To be at one! To be oneself…

                        *

                        And furthermore
A babel of voices, a swirl of life,

A joyous chaos, frenzy — opulence!
And gay companions like Mark Antony
And like him, people made happy…

*

                   And more!
I need — a trusty guide. I have no army.
Egypt has none, besides those draughts from Rome,
Those legions… Mine grow weakened at a march,
Unskilled, and I have plans… Give me some wine…

Touching the cup to her lips.

I feel a spasm… This lion pelt — the same
That once was in the palace?

EROE
                Yes, the same.

CLEOPATRA
There's nothing like a lion's mane, to wipe
One's feet upon, so smooth…

Pause.

            Mark Antony
Can count on my love… No, not him! But Brutus
Himself might… me…

She sobs and covers her eyes.

        … Yes, Brutus might be sweet…
Although he saw his ghost at Philippi!

To Eroe.

But why do you weep?

EROE
                            These are the Queen's tears.
I weep despite myself.

CLEOPATRA
                            You big baby!
You big and silly babe! At times like these —
Listen! — At such times I need you in love,
You understand? You don't know how I need it,
That you should be in love with someone. Anyone!
As long as it be madly! I've run out
Of stratagems. I'm tired of thinking up
Seductive entertainments to entice
Mark Antony… But loving hearts, it's true,
Are hearts creative. They are capable
Of ambushing their loved one with delight
That fairly drowns them! One of my servant girls
Advised me thus: To have a diver latch
A salted fish upon Mark's fishing line —
A brilliant concept, that posterity,
Who never gives credit where credit's due,
Will credit Cleopatra with, not her!

EROE
Set me a man to love, Your Majesty,
And I shall love him well. At your command.

CLEOPATRA
No, that's the sort of love that can produce
Nothing but twins, at best. Give me more wine.

EROE

Presenting her with the cup, which Cleopatra touches to her lips.

These gloomy curtains are Your Majesty's…
Invention?

CLEOPATRA

Rises, approaches the drapes and stares at them intently before returning.

       Curtains! Curtains! Drapes and shades
Are my invention! They're the only things
The mind of man is capable of spinning.

KONDOR

Enters.

Your Majesty! Efforts unparalleled
And good-will galvanised to satisfy
Your Majesty's commands, adjudicate
Diversio — to use the Roman term —
In our ceremonial palatine.
Florid Psymmachus, pious Eucastus,
And myriads of Your Majesty's subjects
Are faithfully employed upon each task
Outlined by the mere waggle of the finger
Royal.
      That such hath always been the case,
The obelisks that pierce the firmament
Uniting Egypt to the realms divine,
The zodiacal regions; and the vaults
Where the remains of Ptolemaic lords
Brood in their sandalwood sarcophagi
(Necropolises that outshadow realms
In their extent and splendour), offer meet,
And ample testimony thereunto.
The skills of all your subjects are engaged
Where they do best fit to advance the fame
Of your immortal Egypt — architect,
Astrologer, and priest are at your beck
And call — No less your Kondor, labouring
In joy as your doorkeeper.
               Majesty —

Pause.

It is my sacred honour to announce
The advent of Delius, Roman *eques,*
And the Knight of the Golden Chain. My lady,
Which of the two is to advance the first?
Whom will you beck? Whom first shall Kondor call?

CLEOPATRA

Mimicking his grandiloquence.

It shall be our delight that Delius
Advance the second; it is only right
That first his suit presents our subject-knight.

KONDOR
Such words should be inscribed in hieroglyphs
For mortal eyes; will Kondor's tongue suffice?

CLEOPATRA
I know no other tongue so hieroglyphic.

Kondor backs out of the presence and the Knight enters.

CLEOPATRA
Whatever news you bring me, sir, be quick.

KNIGHT
I know, my queen, the value of your time,
And thus I'll get right to the point. The news
I bring has been urged on by signal flame
And provinces of runners. Of such weight
It seems, that its delivery outstrips
Its calm interpretation. The Cyclades
— And ergo, Rome — forecast a growing storm.
The several thousands of Italic troops
Who serve Your Majesty, here tied by blood…

The armed camps from the desert to the sea
Await but one word from Serapium
To fix their spear-points in Italy's flank.

Pause.

The coming war is — common knowledge. Mouths
Are full of it more often than with food…
I am a mere soldier, so I spend
No time in questions. I would only say
That, in a time of war — should we attack,
Or prepare attackers to repulse, great care
Must be expended to ensure success,
Insofar as success may be ensured.

CLEOPATRA
Have we a leader to grip firm the reins?

Pause.

I'm satisfied, who know Mark Antony…
But as I'm fond to recall it, 'twas you
Who first brought Caesar to my attention.
And so, with this in mind, I'd like to know
Your thoughts on the Triumvir?

KNIGHT
                                He's one of three,
My queen, as the very title indicates.
Mark Antony himself certainly knows
That, if during his earthly life, Caesar
Was offered the crown royal from his hands,
And after his… translation, holocausts…
These are sufficient reasons to compare
Him not with the divine…

CLEOPATRA

Extending a finger.

                         Come, kiss my hand
In token of forgiveness, that you speak
Thus of Mark Antony…

KNIGHT
                         Justice, at times,
Speaks roughly. Military aptitude
Mark Antony has in abundance. Still,
He lacks Fortune. And as the ancients claim
That she would slip over Hostilius' sash
By moonlight… Once inside, 'twas Victory
He clasped within his arms' embrace.

CLEOPATRA
                                   Ha, ha!
The strumpet! And a bold one too, I reckon,
To interrupt a warrior-chief's slumber!
Say on — say on —

KNIGHT
                    The Triumvir worked up
A pretty strategy at Modena, yet
He was forced to withdraw to Gaul… He fought
The Parthians with undeniable valour,
And yet — the outcome?

CLEOPATRA
                    And at Philippi?

KNIGHT
By all the gods! I'll be first to admit
Myself unworthy to unloose the strap
Of the Triumvir's sandal! All the same,
Did he not cry out 'At long last, I've won!'

When he slew Cassius? Yet even this
No judgement rare would deem a blot upon
Antony's glory! Of course, what I say
Is aimed at something altogether different.
Despite the rumours, rampant as they be,
That, for the increase of his proper fame
There's no expense in regimental blood
That is too dear a price for him... While you
Alone, my queen, your prudence can restrain
— And prod, when necessary — his impetus...
Such is the common barracks-reckoning,
That, if it come to war, without the will
Expressis verbis of Ptolemy's daughter,
The newly-draughted Italic legions
Would follow Mark Antony, but the rest...
It's somewhat doubtful...

CLEOPATRA
                            Has it come to war?
Will it? Tomorrow? Or ever, at all?
Three questions, in an even row, a state
Indeed peculiar, dark, to the people;
Familiar to monarchs, eerie to priests;
Not only Egypt, but the world's Empire
Stands thus... Not monarchs by themselves, nor people,
But time! When the gods gather at the gates
Of Janus, whatever might be their will
Shall come to pass! Shall come to pass, indeed!
Today, the Triumvir, now one of two
Lords of all Rome and friend of Egypt's queen,
Mark Antony, shall wield the power supreme
Over the Egyptian forces. Let those men
— Of Rome and Egypt — who so hang upon
The word — *expressis verbis* — of the queen
Hear this and heed it. And bow down... before him!
Just as they laid their spears before my throne,
He too has dedicated me his sword
With just as exemplary a flourish!

Pause.

KNIGHT
Hail to Mark Antony!

CLEOPATRA
                    If thousand-mouthed
Rumour so quickly speeds to Serapium
From distant Rome, why shan't Victoria
Fly with so light a sandal here, as well?
I've little more to say than… Go with God.

Knight bows.

The queen well knows Mark Antony's intent
In sending here his envoy, whom I greet
On his behalf, and in no other wise,
Than as a guest. And so, good sir, farewell.

The Knight withdraws.

*Delius barely enters but Cleopatra forestalls him; stretching out her hand,
she indicates a seat on the lower degrees approaching the throne — one
of the seats reserved for guests.*

Citizen of Rome! Good Delius,
Cleopatra awaits you. Nearer, please —
I shall rehearse to you what you're to say;
The words Mark Antony spilled in your ear
And you have drummed by rote along the way.
So then, 'Good day.' A greeting which, despite
Adverse experience, we stubbornly
Repeat, as if we jammed thus a white stone
Into the calendar; and we shall do,
We bleating fools, three thousand years from now:
'Good day!' our children's children still shall bray,
So simple and so… timely. So naive.
And with just such naiveté you come,

Good Delius! To scold me too, perhaps?
'Mark Antony is displeased,' you shall assert,
At my ineptitude in welcoming
The envoys of the Roman people; a charge
Indeed, that piques the interest...

Delius makes a gesture of protest; Cleopatra forestalls him.

Eroe!

To Delius.

A plaint, in fact, beyond all measure, sir...

To Eroe, pointing to Delius.

This Roman knight would gladly learn of you
How I'll be clad for today's tournament.
Such is the substance of the embassy
Entrusted him by the Roman Triumvir...

To Delius.

Mark Antony shall take his seat upon
The golden chair next mine. I shall be clad
In misty gauze...

EROE

                    Gathered with Isis' belt
Criss-crossing here and there...

CLEOPATRA

To Delius.

                    Well? There we are.
And one more thing. Pray tell the Triumvir
That I shall not receive such messengers

As pass between him and Octavia
With household trifles or low-whispered gossip.
In overlooking to invite such guests
To today's tournament, I'm... being kind.
For they'll return to Rome to make report
Of Egypt to Octavia, chattering
At one ear and the other...

To Eroe.

                              ... And my shoes?
How shall I be shod?

EROE
                    In Egyptian cothurni,
With thongs of pearls spilling down their gold
Piping and shafts like drops of sea-spray gathered
By Zephyr's skimming hands from the warm waves...

CLEOPATRA

To Eroe.

Enough for now. Withdraw and wait for me.

To Delius, with a strange smile.

See?
If ever I ascend the Capitol,
The Senate and the whole People of Rome
Shall think that Caesar's granddam had arrived,
Feet frothed with sea-foam to ask after Julius...

She extends a finger to Delius.

Go now, farewell. And tell Mark Antony...
Whatever comes to mind.

DELIUS

With a deep bow.

That shall be more
Than what you've now permitted me to say,
Outstripped, always, by Your Majesty's words
And graces…

CLEOPATRA
You may add that I perceive
Each feeling harboured by Mark Antony
For my person even half a mile away,
Over the heads of intervening mobs
As if from camel's back, the hieroglyphs
On obelisk out-riddling. If, therefore,
His wait today is somewhat melancholy,
Have him think upon the queen the while he paces,
Now pensive, now impatient, back and forth
Through the arcades.

About to exit.

The palace of the tombs
Is broad as any metropolis…

She makes a pleasant sign of farewell. Delius withdraws. Cleopatra calls:

Kondor!

KONDOR

Enters.

CLEOPATRA
Eucastus, Psymmachus, Olympos, the Knight…
Let them all know, according to their station,

What is their duty, what to carry out…
My audiences now are at an end.

Pause.

Is there any other person on this earth
Who speaks with mortals less? Is more lonely?
Or muses more calmly, in deeper stillnesses?
But, Eroe, tell me — Why are you not gay?
Your heart should be naive — a child's heart, but wise…
Man is the infant of things… ineffable!

*

Gather some sand there — from beneath the censer.
Let's play! Here, spill it into seven hills…
That's right, and now — make way! The queen withdraws
From the audience chamber…

Treading over the handfuls of sand.

These seven clods
Portray the seven hills of Rome. I've spoken!

Exit Cleopatra followed by Eroe.

Scene 2

PSYMMACHUS
The schema, draughted by the Queen herself,
Who like few others understands Greek style,
Transmitted from on high, is realised
Here on the dusty earth, fulfilling all
— If not exceeding — expectations, quite.
The amphitheatre — no hippodrome
Exceeds it, stretching out towards the harbour,
Open to all the hoi polloi — who'd guess it?

Curtained at this end by thick hafted drapes,
Thus reconciling Attic harmony
With the vulgar chaos of the arena, there.

OLYMPOS
It's only just that Egypt hold the keys
To all gnosis, for Alexandria,
Not Rome, was founded by the son of Ammon,
That child of the ages, Alexander,
Who, sifting flour from his troops' mess-wagons
Here on this spot, traced in the white his plan
For his metropolis — was it not an omen?
Did he not sense the spirit of the place?

KONDOR
Fresh air, flesh and fish in abundance!

OLYMPOS
All sorts of herbs, creatures of every tribe!

PSYMMACHUS
A mind harmonic with the genius loci —
That is the main thing.

OLYMPOS
                    The Alexandrian,
Combining in one man Greek aptitude
And Oriental spirit, in each craft
Becomes a master.

PSYMMACHUS
                    Ah, speaking of which,
I know no better mynahs then the tribe
Of Wendo-Scythians. In Athens, once,
While I was studying geometry,
I had a slave of that far distant nation,
A northern tribe… His name was Imitalski —
And so protean was his mimesis

That — sell him to a cobbler, and behold:
The finest cothurn was stitched on his anvil.
Pass him on to a tailor: in a trice
Garments flow through his hands with weft out-spinning
Rhapso or Ariadne. A looking-glass
The fellow was — empty when left alone,
But should a man come near, becoming him.
He could do anything except invent.
And for that reason he remained a slave.
He needed a master just to exist.
Once, two masters vied for his industry,
And left the matter of whom he should serve
To his own arbitration, the poor chap —
That did him in. He simply couldn't choose
Between this and that, both worthy men.

OLYMPOS
So, like the fabled ass, he died of hunger,
Between two bushels of cracked oats?

PSYMMACHUS
                                    Not quite;
The poor man tore himself in two halves
In straining so, now east, now west.

With a nostalgic sigh.

                                    'Twas a knave
Worth having! Taking others' crafts in hand
He made them his own, naturally. It's true,
At times he needed rough encouragement…
Ah! would I had him with me still! What might
A man not achieve with so slick a churl?

KONDOR
But you have nothing to regret, Psymmachus,
You master-builder! This amphitheatre,
So splendid, wondrous, ah — nothing at all!

OLYMPOS
The city's never seen such a construction!

PSYMMACHUS
O, there's no lack of critics, but the learned?
The competent ones? It's like aboard ship:
Those without sea-legs tumble to the rail
To bark into the waves… their morning meal.
So much for critics. They know how to clap
Or piss at one's foundations. Spasmatics
With bladders full… The artist has no need
To court their favour or blush at their bile;
One needs a reasonable dose of —

KONDOR
                    Caste!
The surest guardian of —

PSYMMACHUS
                    Egyptian taste!

OLYMPOS
People are bad, not on account of bile,
Or not merely; they're like marble: they're sound
Or flawed. And when the marble's flawed, no leaf
Or mystic fluid can repair the rot.

PSYMMACHUS
Happy are those, who make their sole appeal
To future ages; we though seek the praise
Of our contemporaries, more's the pity.
The amphitheatre must welcome all
The deputies of foreign lands, in hopes
That when they go back home, they'll wax poetic
And spread the fame of Egypt… today's Egypt,
Which never stood before as it stands now —

KONDOR

Interrupting.

That's just the point! And yet, there are others
Who croak of wars threatening on all hands…

OLYMPOS
Ha? Cleopatra rules the world entire!

PSYMMACHUS

Unrolling his parchment plan.

More worth our time to weigh our monuments
Than heed vacuous gossip. Ah, someday…
The battles waged against material
By master-artist will be quite forgot…

Scanning the plan.

The thing was — like a midwife to extract
The amphitheatre, like newborn babe
From the womb of the necropolitan
Mass… Here: the tomb doors open the façade…
See? Where my hand is?

OLYMPOS

Leaning in.

                    It's clear from the plan.
But, who will see it, he shall understand!

PSYMMACHUS
God willing…

A worker's arm emerges through the drapes.

WORKER

        Master! You're still needed here!

PSYMMACHUS

Exiting in that direction.

Perhaps some day I'll disappear forever —
Becoming one with my work…

KONDOR

To Olympos.

              See? There's proof
Of all I say. Our Egypt stands secure!

OLYMPOS
There may be something to these war-fraught rumours.
For what a Monarch wishes, she may do,
Unfettered power wielding on all hands!
The kings send envoys forth time and again —
What matters that? And if there should be war?
War's always going on, somewhere or other…

HERO

Rushing in from the side.

Kondor, my dear friend! Happy, happy Hero
Greets you with radiant cheeks! They're shining, no?

KONDOR
Somewhat… a wine-red blush, a Bacchic tinge…

HERO
No Orpheus, with wife redeemed from Hell,
Has ever been inebriated so
With her recovered charms than I am now.

KONDOR
Spare further breath… It far outstrips your news.

HERO
I've always dreamed of meeting a Great Man!
I've always known that demi-god exists,
And always sensed his spirit in the air…

KONDOR
Spirits, indeed, are sensible about you…

HERO
And finally — the incarnation comes!
Kondor, let me embrace you! And you too,
Worthy physician! Oh, these lips of mine
Would dabble at the cheeks of all the world!
O, happy day I've spent like shadow flitting
Around the Great Man! Do you catch my drift?

KONDOR
Not quite…

OLYMPOS
            Me, not at all.

HERO
                            I have traversed
All the arcades of this necropolis,
All of the inner courts, walks, peristyles,
Gazing unseen with rapture from afar
Upon him… like a shadow…

Meanwhile, Mark Antony enters, at a stroll. He is dressed elegantly, in Roman fashion, and carries a rose. He halts, but does not interrupt the conversation. Olympos and Kondor gesture to Hero, trying to convey the fact that they are no longer alone, but Hero takes no note of this.

Quite unseen,

Although, once, he did pause, to pluck a rose,
And spun round, quick as lightning, sighing deep…
His sigh, just like a lion's roar! With eyes
Sparkling toward the queen's pavilion…
I thought he saw me! But, so quick of foot
Am I, so deftly did I spin upon
My toes — quicker than spooked bird! — the Great Man
Caught sight of me not… Thus my thirsty eyes
I sated on his person, barrels-deep!
A whole half-day. The rest you know…

KONDOR

To Olympos.

Perhaps…

Or not at all…

HERO
Must I spill out the truth
Here at your feet? The Great Man of my dreams
Is Mark Antony! Are you made of wood?
Or unfired bricks of mud? Well, next to him,
Who isn't? Listen here: Should that Great Man
Point to one hundred legions facing me
And bark out: 'Fight them, to the bitter dregs!'
By Hercules! I'd slay them, every one,
Or fall myself in slashing…

Pause.

So say I!

MARK ANTONY

Approaching at the same slow tread, He places his hand on Hero's shoulder.

Perhaps you'd be a lictor?

HERO
                    Anything!
As long as I felt your right hand above me!

MARK ANTONY
Enthusiasm is not to be scorned.

To Olympos.

I'd like to think the people at my side
Are bolts of lightning, dry, and crackling
For me to fling down from the smoky clouds...
Aeneas had his Pallas — I'll have him.
I hate no men more than those who drag their feet.

Toying with the rose, to Hero.

Do you speak... soberly?

Not waiting for an answer.

                    As I see it,
A brave man likes his wine. Thin-blooded knaves
Alone drink water.

To Olympos.

                    Drinkers, and the drunken —
There is a difference between the two!
Melancholy's far worse than... exaltation.

OLYMPOS
Inebriation doth enthral the soul.

MARK ANTONY
I'd like to have all of my body guard
In love… Ah, what a general was Bacchus!
I'll have none of your desiccated guards
Of obelisk and tomb, no sacristans…

Eroe passes over the stage, carrying perfume in golden vessels.

MARK ANTONY

Tossing the rose before her feet.

Lovely Eroe! No, no, bow not — you're laden.
That rose shall wilt before your fingers touch it.
My lictor shall retrieve the bloom instead.

Hero throws himself at the rose.

I merely wished to halt the march, before
Commencing the assault…

Comes near Eroe.

               And first of all,
Your haste, Eroe, is a needless fever
If — not feigned. Can it be that blooms need scent?
Does anyone perfume the full-burst rose?
Doctor Olympos, say — am I mistaken?

Drawing near the chairs.

Second, come, sit with me upon these steps…

As if carelessly.

Now, should the queen ask why you've lagged behind —

KONDOR

Wishing to take the golden vessels from Eroe.

Say it was Kondor's fault, belatedly
Relieving you of these burdens...

EROE

                    Relieving me?

MARK ANTONY

Flirtily.

You tell the queen that her guest — that same one,
Who promised not to snoop at works commenced
Before gala unveiling, here and there
And everywhere lifting a hem, unbuttoning a placket
To peek within, was caught out, *in flagranti*,
By you, who seized him by his scabrous hands,
Which deed heroic caused you to be late.

EROE
So many doubtful words to memorise...

She exits.

MARK ANOTNY
Hero! Announce my coming to the queen!

HERO

Skipping in front of Mark Antony.

The Triumvir Antony, Egypt's guest,
Approaches!

KONDOR and OLYMPOS

Bowing deeply.

Our lord and our guest!

MARK ANTONY

Familiarly.

Our chum!

KONDOR

Watching them as they go out.

Well, I've always thought that clever lad Hero
Had something up his sleeve! And here I was,
Racking my brains to see him to a place,
Of which there are so few, now that with strides
So brisk, the tournament approaches!

OLYMPOS

Catching sight of Eucastus, who enters.

Look!
Here comes a one who never fails to bring
His talents — and a train — to the tasks at hand.

Richly dressed, Eucastus enters with a group of servants, laden with things.

EUCASTUS
There is one rule that must be borne in mind
My boys, one supreme canon, handed down
From King Auletes — one, familiar, precept:
The table must be laid, and cleared again,

With the same pomp! When serving at the court
It makes no difference the golden bowl
To carry in, or carry off; the full carafe,
Or empty…

Approaching the throne and lifting the veil with a pathetic gesture.

Peeling back the cloth of gold
From throne or golden chair — how is it done?
With the same *gratia* (to speak Hellene)
As if one touched the very throne itself.

The boys whirl about with their paraphernalia, imitating Eucastus.

You see… What could be simpler than that?

KONDOR

Indicating Eucastus.

Yes, lads! Heed well your master, whom long years
Of practice have made nimble in the swank
Of pharaonic elegance! One thing
Kondor makes bold to add: More light! More light!
The sun divine aid you!

Exit.

OLYMPOS
I shall be brief,
By Hygieia — be well!

EUCASTUS

Watching the boys at work.

In days of old,
When sending forth her progeny beloved
To serve at court, a tender mother would place
One hundred river-reeds, from which to plait
A sleeping-mat, into their travelling bag:
So that the incense of the Nile would be
Always with them — a reminder of home.
And with each reed, a saw ancient and sage,
Which, as they slept upon the fragrant rushes,
Would seep into their ears — Such boys, my lads
Have grown into the flower of Egypt!
Beneath the warm Egyptian sun — more light,
As Kondor said — will make you strong and hale,
Which wise Olympos wishes you, while I
Train you in ceremonial, that you
Might worthily serve Isis, and your land
In splendour!

BOYS

Together.

      Vivat!

During the foregoing speeches, the boys had set up two tables at the lower seating places, at the foot of the throne. These they now commence to cover.

EUCASTUS
        And the last precept:
When all is in its place, the serving team
Retires, to wait, in patience.

The sound of a clap is heard. Psymmachus enters with the Knight, through the side curtains. He is dressed in splendid robes, and the Knight in brilliant armour. Through the parted curtains, a portion of the amphitheatre can be seen. Gazing in that direction, Psymmachus rubs his hands together.

PSYMMACHUS
                              Thus to vanish
In executing one's creation! That's art!
I know no chiefer precept, and I reckon
It is the same for any honest craftsman.
The work ensures our immortality,
They say — but that's a metaphor of Hell
If what we make were to lengthen the span
Of misery, backbiting, and jealousy
That make up this life — 'twere a better thing
If our creations were ephemeral.

EUCASTUS
There's a great press of people at the gates.

PSYMMACHUS
It's not the edifice that's drawn them here.
They've come to gape at silken tress and trinket —
A stable of clothes-horses canters near.
But those who see my blueprints, they can judge
The outcome of my plans…

EUCASTUS
                              To them, I bow.

PSYMMACHUS
Blessings…

EUCASTUS
                    We know that the Necropolis
Looks out upon the stadium, but like a sage
In silence gazing — like the Sphinx herself —
Opens… and closes… both comprehensible
And yet mysterious.

PSYMMACHUS
                          And, in an eye-blink!

Enter Priest 1, Priest 2, Lector and Chorus. The first is bearing a tripod for the incense, carried by the second.

[...]

A trumpet sounds, a Herald appears.

[...]

Scene 3

To the rear, the curtains part and reveal the interior of an amphitheatre. At the same time, through rows of courtiers at an inner entrance, enter Cleopatra and Mark Antony. She is led by a Page bearing a short spear, a little shield, a basinet with crown, and martial crackowes. Mark Antony is preceded by his Lictor, bearing a helm with beaver and diadem, and sword. The stage lights come up full, and from the arena cries and the shouts of competition are heard. A small group of princes, ladies, and people follow in behind the queen. Delius follows Mark Antony, dressed in rich Roman garb.

PRIEST 1

Lifting the censer before the queen.

Great things are set in motion by the hands
Of demi-gods — toss in the first sweet grains
Of incense that the fragrant smoke may rise
Unto the realms divine above our heads.

CLEOPATRA

Spooning in myrrh.

What we commence, may the gods accomplish.

To her guests.

Be gay! I would behold but joyful faces!

To Mark Antony, aside.

Foh! What a stench. Does incense smoke not choke you?

MARK ANTONY
Not when it rises from your hands…

CLEOPATRA

Aside, to Mark Antony, mysteriously.

                                        O, there!
Did you note that?

MARK ANTONY
                    I did.

CLEOPATRA

Aside, to Mark Antony.

                        Therefore, I shan't
Ascend the throne — nor shall you take your seat
Beside me, till your envoys…

MARK ANTONY
                        My envoys…??

CLEOPATRA
Until those envoys enter.

MARK ANTONY
                    May it be
According to your will, Omnipotent,
Although…

CLEOPATRA

Interrupting him, and setting the matter at an end.

        Although, if you had your own way,
They would not enter here at all.

MARK ANTONY

Sharply.

               At all!

DELIUS

To Cleopatra.

In executing your plans, Psymmachus
Succeeded, and worshipfully!

MARK ANTONY
             Permit me
To set before your feet my library —
Two hundred thousand scrolls.

CLEOPATRA
             You'd have me tread
Upon the breath of poets?

MARK ANTONY
            Through the clouds.

CLEOPATRA

Aloud, to all.

Mark Antony, I fear, would set me up
A candidate for apotheosis!

And yet I fear I'm far from the ideal
Established by your Roman goddesses…

MARK ANTONY

Contemptuously.

That pack of vulpine bitches?

CLEOPATRA
                              Delius,
To arms! We must now stand allied in Rome's
Defence, who's threatened with vulgar assault!

DELIUS

With a light smile.

The gods make it their business, Majesty,
To come to Rome's defence. I am no Titan.
But you — do as your will divine directs.

MARK ANTONY
And if the gods have spurned the seven hills
Out of sheer boredom?

CLEOPATRA
                      I have heard it said
That gods grow bored, sometimes. Homer himself
Asserts as much, with one colossal yawn
Somewhere in his *Iliad.*

DELIUS

Bowing.

                      Such being the case,
Although it makes one shiver, I'll entrust

Rome to the hands of Fate, and this my ring
Equestrian...

CLEOPATRA

To Mark Antony.

The envoys should be here —

MARK ANTONY
To hear the speech of the last Roman knight!

DELIUS

With a slight sigh.

The very last...

PSYMMACHUS
Right now, they're visiting
The battlements of Alexandria,
According to the plans of the Divine —

CLEOPATRA

Aloud, to all.

Caesar? If it is that which makes them late
To greet Cleopatra, because they trace
The steps of Caesar, then, they are forgiven!
The shadow of a Great Man on the earth
Can be more vivid than a maiden's cheeks
Ablush.

MARK ANTONY

Touching a goblet on a nearby table.

I dedicate those words unto
The divine Manes… O, your Majesty,
Allow me to spill libation from this cup
That, like Phoenician looking-glass, reflects
Those blushing cheeks, those lips of coral hue,
The flash of your two eyes!

He sips from the cup. Then:

                         Let the thin shades
Evaluate the pale; let them adore
All monumental necrosis… I bow,
And deeply, before death, and yet I raise
A toast to living blushes. Am I vulgar?

He sips. Then:

'Tis why I smote Brutus — for he was pale.
He ached to be a shade. Or he was pushed
By Uncle Cato who taught him fasting,
Mortifications… Hah! Conspirators
Bloodless, yet bloodthirsty! And when they lie,
They lie to the immortal gods! I spit
Upon all lies… I drink the health
Of all here present! For it's health,
Red, pulsing, that I value!

OLYMPOS
                   Mens sana,
In corpore sano!

CLEOPATRA
            But Cassius?
He was attracted to — what style of life?

MARK ANTONY
He was a greengrocer, hawking the garlic
Of your Egyptian mud, but with aplomb —

Outshrewding Mercury! But garlic's pale
As well — for meatless Fridays. Even Cato
Wouldn't touch garlic…

PRIEST 1

> And Pythagoras…

MARK ANTONY

Jocularly.

Who knows what old Pythagoras gnawed on?
What does he sip in Hades? Lemonade?

Seriously.

They call them Stoics, who practise such things,
Praiseworthy, maybe — but if they spoil
One organ, say the stomach, in so doing,
I ask you — do they well?

Enter the Roman envoys, rather casually.

CLEOPATRA

Sonorously.

> And should a nation
Slaughter a Great Man so — on principle?
Should Cassius and Brutus — modest men! —
Befoul the Senate floor with blood, to prove
A point of doctrine! Delius! Roman!
Among the spells and curses of the skies,
Is there one such to conjure Destiny
The Vengeful?

DELIUS

Aside.

> Still the holiest revenge
> Is the deed self-determined!

EUCASTUS

Who had been in conversation with the envoys, sonorously.

> Majesty,
> Egypt's guests, Roman travellers, the envoys!

CLEOPATRA

To Mark Antony.

Hear what they call themselves?

MARK ANTONY

To Cleopatra, taking no note of Eucastus' announcement.

> Let us hear more.

CLEOPATRA
You understand me, Mark, sometimes.

MARK ANTONY

> Sometimes?

CLEOPATRA
Sometimes you understand me, but — always
Your feelings are trained on me…

MARK ANTONY

                              All the same,
Not always comprehending?

CLEOPATRA

                              No, not always.

MARK ANTONY
A small matter that, perhaps. My library
Of scrolls two hundred thousand, set at your feet —
What more is there to understand?

CLEOPATRA

                              To act, and will
Before thought, is an attribute divine.

MARK ANTONY
The brows of both centaur and Phrygian dwarf
(So we are told) are furrowed deep with thought,
And broad with swelling brains. And yet Apollo —
Why, his proportions are harmonious.

CLEOPATRA

Spontaneously.

Words… such as Julius might have uttered!

MARK ANTONY
You glimpse his shadow everywhere, my lady!

CLEOPATRA

With melancholy.

The shades of Limbo darken half my bosom,
And this is why I love the dawn's penumbra,
The Hermetic half-light…!

EUCASTUS

Sonorously.

                       The guests of Egypt,
The Roman travellers…

CLEOPATRA

Interrupting.

              O, countrymen
Of Caesar!

To envoys.

          Guests in Egypt are not made
To wait on their reception overlong,
Whether the threshold be of wattle-daub,
Or granite, like this royal palace. But
If honoured guests such as yourselves arrive
Before the presence of the world's Queen,
It is the leaves of Cleopatra's heart
That swing wide to admit you to the places
Prepared against your advent, long ago!

PLANCUS

With emphasis.

My lady, the world's Queen indeed you are,
By your immortal graces. The world's wonder,
Which, to admire, we travellers of the world
Now turn our back upon the globe. We, envoys
Of the Roman Empire, pause here in Egypt…

DOLABELLA
Grateful to gaze upon you…

CLEOPATRA

Coldly, to Eroe.

> Compliments
Deserving recompense. Lovely Eroe,
Present the Roman knights with my gratitude.

Eroe presents the envoys with cups.

DOLABELLA
The togas that we wear do not permit
Us graceful motion in such elegant
A company — yet thus we must be clad,
So formally, out of the respect due
The ashes of all Caesar's veterans
Who first fell to the sands we tread upon
In this tributary province...

EROE

Reading from Cleopatra's eyes how she is to respond.

> We know quite well
This suit of honour...

PLANCUS

Glancing in the direction of Mark Antony.

> Which derives its value
From the shoulders it drapes.

Cleopatra makes a gesture to Eucastus. Trumpets sound, the whole court takes its place.

MARK ANTONY

Tosses his purple toga to Hero. To Cleopatra.

This cloak… it overburdens me whenever
I am to offer Isis my support —

CLEOPATRA

Tosses her veil from her shoulders.

Mark Antony! Isis is but a woman;
Even this gauzy veil is a fardel
Oppressive to her, when you toss aside
The purple — Come, permit me to rest upon
The scaly armour that you bear; it seems
I rest upon a gentle dolphin's back…

ALL
Long live the daughter of the Ptolemies!
The world's Queen!

CLEOPATRA

Ascending the throne.

          Come, Triumvir, take the chair
Next to me.

MARK ANTONY

Accepting his exalted place.

Outside, the lesser tourney has commenced.

CLEOPATRA

To Eucastus.

I'd hear first from the master-builder. Then,
I wish to recognise and commend my Knight.

PSYMMACHUS
It was the Queen's idea to extend
The circus through the city from this place,
Without, however, changing anything
In this construction of her forefathers,
The stones cyclopean of which lean upon
One another like slumbering colossi,
And that the whole complex combine in one
Refinement, grace, and rough athletic tumble,
Both attic beauty and cinders, all the while
Conserving the imposing unicity
Of this fair, ancient palace. And thus it stands.
It has no peer in Rome…

CLEOPATRA

Interrupting, loudly, to Mark Antony.

                    No peer in Rome!

PSYMMACHUS
And the result is such, that the palace
Necropolitan, opens to the life
Of bustling Alexandria, the while
It can close ranks immediately, becoming
A fortress quite impregnable.

MARK ANTONY
                              A thousand
Such redoubts in one!

CLEOPATRA
                    Nay, more!
Immeasurably more!

DOLABELLA

To Plancus.

A tourney-grounds of rather large extent.

PLANCUS
And eloquence…

CLEOPATRA

To Psymmachus.

                      The cup that now I touch
With my lips, receive — a gift of gratitude.

Psymmachus ascends to receive the cup.

MARK ANTONY

Greeting him.

In gratitude I clasp your hand as well.

Psymmachus withdraws, the Knight advances to his place.

KNIGHT
It was the Queen's idea that, today,
While all the world is presenting their tribute
Here at her footstool, we should get a sense
Of her armed might, by a parade of troops
Three days a-marching to Alexandria.

DOLABELLA

To Plancus.

That is, from where the galleons stand at anchor!

KNIGHT
One hundred thousand heavy infantry
Italic, Roman…

PLANCUS

Aside.

Vagabonds!

KNIGHT
And horse:
Twenty-two thousand, all forming a chain
That stretches from the Queen's gold-sandalled toe
To the horizon of the world — more distant
Than where Neptune has dredged with his trident
The limit of the land, for that chain snakes
Across five hundred galleys at anchor:
Two hundred men at arms aboard each ship.

MARK ANTONY

Leaning on the back of the throne.

And thus, my Queen, if you but shake your foot
Like this, a charge harmonic would shoot forth
And undulate through all the golden links
Like to a bolt that falls from Mount Olympus
To thunder out upon the sea!

CLEOPATRA

To Knight.

Good sir,
I give you nothing, which is more than all
That Cleopatra gives her faithful thralls.
The Queen of all the world's in need of such

Capable hands that grasp at naught, and thus
Are envied by no man. For there's no boon
I might bestow that would equal your merit.

[...]

Scene 6[60]

[...]

MARK ANTONY
I bent the Fates, although I was myself
A toy in Fate's hand! I fixed it so
That were anything evil to befall
The Monarch's purple barge, or if the ring
Of spiked men bristling round her tent was breached,
Here! Here she was to be led! If but one man
Remained armed with a shattered oar, then, here!
Here she was to be delivered! I fixed it...
And shall be fixed hereafter on men's tongues
As Antony the general inept,
Who blindly lost her realm by clumsy plans!
Hero! Two cups — and that Phoenician jug
With script illegible... Let's see your sword —
We must lop off the wax...

Taking Hero's sword, he bends it, tests it.

                              No, this won't do.
Here, take my blade... Yes, you've got a firm grip
For close combat... How well do you know Homer?

HERO
He says the sight of naked iron firms
The wrist, and makes it supple...

---

60   This concluding scene takes place after Actium.

MARK ANTONY

                    And nepenthes?
What might that mean?

HERO

               Nepenthes, O my lord
And leader, is a philtre that the maids
Of Thessaly brew — 'tis an aged liquor,
Distilled at the new moon, when conjuring
Hecate… There are different sorts of philtre…

MARK ANTONY
Fill full the cups… Speak on… Pour steadily!

HERO
Each philtre has its properties… Nepenthes
Emboldens the heroic thew, and spreads
It warmth throughout the heart.

MARK ANTONY

                  So, drink up, man!
With Mark Antony, flattened Triumvir!
With him who counselled the Divine Caesar
To strike out on the road to Rome; who gave
Him… greatness… and who offered him a crown;
Who firmed his flank there at Pharsalus,
Who was a friend to him — beyond the grave!
Remember that, Hero! Drink up! Back then,
How he addressed the city of assassins
With his harangue, and then, at Philippi,
Prepared Augustus' glory, shattering
Full three and twenty swords! For Augustus:
Glory… There and here… For Her — a tragedy.
I took no measure of Phoenician purple
In ells like some Sidonian draper!
He? He is great? Tell me — or if you'd rather,
Tell me what greatness is.

HERO

Indeed, the humour of this flask now firms
My will to any speech, or any deed!
A strange thing, liquor — this right hand, once frail,
Now Herculean it seems! As for this left,
O, I could wag it now among the learned,
And spank the theologians in dispute!
Greatness, you ask? Great is the man who grips
An obelisk at midpoint, which uprooting,
He hurls at Rome — another, and another!
Like so many dry bottles… And now I seem
To see as through a mist, or a thin sheet
Of moist papyrus — shattered basilicas!
Was it not you, my lord Mark Antony,
Who dared this? *Ergo*, however strangely
Fortune spins on her toe, the deed remains
Great, though falling short, and the Triumvir
Great, though assailed by pygmies!

MARK ANTONY

                                        Hero, listen:
I have dispensed greatness and liberty
And fame, like a patrician's largesse…
Take you this gem from me: I here bestow
Knighthood upon you, with this sinking hand…
But you must be trained in arts equestrian…

He pulls his armour off, as if it were weighing him down. Hero places it to the side.

There must be two cups left in that flagon?
Pour then, and be of good cheer!

Writing.

                        I set down
Your patent properly, creating you

Sir Herius Nepenthius, cavalier,
Attesting this with consular signet…

He does so.

I, magister equitum… It is done!
I've a patrician's nose that scents the wind,
An eye that scans the times! Men like Caesar —
Like Julius… like Pompey, like Antony
These days — are nothing. Once, when I was young,
Fighting the Jews, I saved a Hebrew prophet
Dragged by his beard by a centurion,
And he, in gratitude, taught me that time…
Revealed to me that, though we speak of time,
There is not one unique time… there are times!
Sir Herius Nepenthius! Your blade
Grip with hand Herculean… yes, that's it!
And test it out — there — on the fish-scale armour.
There: thrust it at the breast, on the left hand —
Slip it between the threads that underweave it,
The blade; can you slide it in there, unerring?
See how the scales reflect the flashing metal!
Again! Can your hand thrust unerringly?
Here — take your patent. When I tap your arm…
Come on — I must see you strike home, two times —
I'd leave nothing to chance…

Hero does so.

        Yes! Excellent!
Now, when I give the sign, can you strike hard,
The target indicated, wavering not?

HERO
Ten times, without one sheathing of the blade!

MARK ANTONY
One thrust, if true, suffices… Drink, Sir Hero!
Now, when I give the signal, strike home, hard!
People like you… are the Empire's future.
I've got a nose patrician, and I scent
From whence the wind is blowing. I see clear
When times are gravid, and nearing their term.
Julius, Pompey — Brutus the plumb-line,
Cato, and I, who dreamed a world of epics,
Have seen the binding rot, the pages fly
And scatter — these times are in need of knights
New-fashioned, practical…

HERO
                        What is that noise?
I seem to hear hooves thudding, bugles blaring…

MARK ANTONY
You hear your time approaching at a gallop.
Give here that armour. Have a glance around:
All must be quite in order. Set aside
Your goblet and your patent… The new time
Is practical! Yes, I would even wager
That should some god descend from high Olympus
To walk incarnate among these new men
And seek to teach them, they'd lay hands on him
And sell him to a joiner as a slave,
Or hack the wretch apart…! Make tight your spurs
And wipe away that purple stain… My cup,
Please… Now, unsheathe your sword, and plunge it home!
Come, try your luck… Strike! Stab!

HERO
                        What do I hear!

MARK ANTONY
You hear time racing off into the past!
I'll kill you like a dog, you new-fledged knight!

Withdraw not one step more! Come, and thrust home!

HERO

Drains his cup and rushes at him with his sword.

In self-defence!

Runs Mark Antony through.

MARK ANTONY

Dying, he strikes Hero on the shoulder.

Be well... You... Roman... knight...

[End of the Manuscript]

BIBLIOGRAPHY

SOURCE TEXTS

NORWID, Cyprian. *Pisma wybrane* [Selected Writings], ed. Juliusz W. Gomulicki, Vol. 3 *Dramaty* [Plays]. Warsaw: Państwowy Instytut Wydawniczy, 1968.

NORWID, Cyprian. *Dzieła Cyprjana Norwida* [The Works of Cyprian Norwid], ed. Tadeusz Pini. Warsaw: 'Parnas Polski,' 1934.

SECONDARY SOURCES

BABUCHOWSKI, Szymon. 'Cyprain Kamil Norwid' [Brochure]. Kraków: Instytut Książki, 2021.

BEAUCLERK, Charles. *Shakespeare's Lost Kingdom. The True History of Shakespeare and Elizabeth*. New York: Grove Press, 2010.

BŁACHNIO, Jan Ryszard. *Polskie inspiracje i wartości w nauczaniu Jana Pawła II* [Polish Inspirations and Values in the Teaching of John Paul II]. Bydgość: WSP, 1995.

BRAUN, Kazimierz. 'Poetycki teatr Norwid' [Norwid's Poetical Theatre], in Inglot: 359-375.

CUMMINGS, E.E. *Eimi*. New York: William Sloan, 1933.

GARDNER, William Henry. *Gerard Manley Hopkins, 1844 – 1889: A Study of Poetic Idiosyncrasy in Relation to Poetic Tradition*. London: Secker and Warburg, 1948.

GOMBROWICZ, Witold. *Dziennik (1953 – 1956)* [Journal]. Paris: Instytut literacki, 1984.

GRABOWSKI, Mateusz. 'Historiozofia zagłady. Uwagi do *Kleopatry i Cezara* Norwida' [Historiosophical Destruction. Some Comments on Norwid's *Cleopatra and Caesar*]. *Acta Universitatis Lodziensis, Folia Litteraria Polonica*, Vol. 1, No. 27, 2015: 79-91.

GRABOWSKI, Mateusz. 'Dialektyka przemocy w ofiarniczych tragediach Cypriana Norwida' [The Dialectics of Violence in the Sacrificial Tragedies of Cyprian Norwid]. *Czytanie Literatury. Łódzkie Studia Literaturoznawcze*, Issue 5, 2016: 139-160.

INGLOT, Mieczysław. *Cyprian Norwid*. Warszawa: Wydawnictwo Szkolne i Pedagocizny, 1991.

INGLOT, Mieczysław. 'Ogólna charakterystyka twórczości dramatycznej Cypriana Norwida' [The General Characteristics of the Dramatic Oeuvre of Cyprian Norwid], in Inglot: 134-169.

KRUSZEWSKA, Albina I. and COLEMAN, Marion M. 'The Wanda Theme in Polish Literature and Life,' *The American Slavic and East European Review*, Vol. 6, No. 1/2, May, 1947: 19-35.

ŁUCZAK-WILD, J. 'Polnische Norwidiana 1945 – 1969: Teil II' [Polish Norwidiana 1945 – 1969: Part II], *Zeitschrift für Slavische Philologie*, Vol. 36, No. 1, 1971: 153-226.

POUND, Ezra. *Selected Letters, 1907 – 1941*. New York: New Directions, 1971.

SŁAWIŃSKA, Irena. 'Metafora w dramatach Norwida' [Metaphor in Norwid's Plays], in Inglot: 347-376.

WITKOWSKA, Alina. *Literatura romantyzmu* [The Literature of Romanticism]. Warsaw: Państwowe Wydawnictwo Naukowe, 1987.

WYKA, Kazimerz. *Norwid w Krakowie* [Norwid in Kraków]. Kraków: Wydawnictwo Literackie, 1967.

ABOUT THE AUTHOR

Cyprian Kamil Norwid (1821 – 1883) is known as the 'fourth bard' of Polish Romanticism (along with Adam Mickiewicz, Juliusz Słowacki and Zygmunt Krasiński), a title he was accorded only in the twentieth century when, after the manner of Gerard Manley Hopkins and William Blake in England, he was discovered by a new literary generation. Previous to the 'Young Poland' period of the early twentieth century, Norwid's penchant for coinages and dense philosophical verse was received less enthusiastically, although he did have his admirers, such as the novelist Józef Ignacy Kraszewski, who called him a 'dislocated genius' [*zwichnięty geniusz*]. Norwid was born in Warsaw. On his mother's side, he is descended from one of the greatest Kings of Poland — Jan III Sobieski, who delivered Vienna from the Ottoman siege of 1683. Norwid was a multi-talented artist. Some of his lyrics, such as 'Fortepian Szopena' [Chopin's grand piano] and 'Bema pamięci żałobny rapsod' [A rhapsodic lament in memory of General Bem] are among the best known works of modern Polish verse. Besides his poetry, he authored works of prose fiction and short aesthetic sketches, as well as eleven works for the stage and six minor dramatic pieces — all of which are found in the present volume. Norwid was a talented graphic artist. Following his emigration from Poland, he supported himself in France and Great Britain, as well as during a short stay in the United States, as an illustrator. He died in Paris, in virtual poverty.

ABOUT THE TRANSLATOR

Charles S. Kraszewski is a poet and translator, creative in both English and Polish. He is the author of three volumes of original verse in English (*Diet of Nails; Beast; Chanameed*), and one in Polish (*Hallo, Sztokholm*). He also authored a satirical novel *Accomplices, You Ask?* (San Francisco: Montag, 2021). He translates from Polish, Czech and Slovak into English, and from English and Spanish into Polish, including classics such as Adam Mickiewicz's *Forefathers' Eve* and experimental poets of the modern period like Tytus Czyżewski's *A Burglar of the Better Sort: Poems, Dramatic Works, and Theoretical Writings*, both published by Glagoslav. He is a member of the Union of Polish Writers Abroad (London) and of the Association of Polish Writers (SPP, Kraków).

A BURGLAR OF THE BETTER SORT

by Tytus Czyżewski

The history of Poland, since the eighteenth century, has been marked by an almost unending struggle for survival. From 1795 through 1945, she was partitioned four times by her stronger neighbours, most of whom were intent on suppressing if not eradicating Polish culture. It is not surprising, then, that much of the great literature written in modern Poland has been politically and patriotically engaged. Yet there is a second current as well, that of authors devoted above all to the craft of literary expression, creating 'art for art's sake,' and not as a didactic national service. Such a poet is Tytus Czyżewski, one of the chief, and most interesting, literary figures of the twentieth century. Growing to maturity in the benign Austrian partition of Poland, and creating most of his works in the twenty-year window of authentic Polish independence stretching between the two world wars, Czyżewski is an avant-garde poet, dramatist and painter who popularised the new approach to poetry established in France by Guillaume Apollinaire, and was to exert a marked influence on such multi-faceted artists as Tadeusz Kantor.

Buy it > www.glagoslav.com

The Mouseiad and other Mock Epics

by Ignacy Krasicki

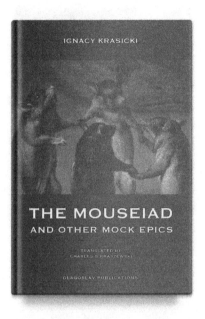

International brigades of mice and rats join forces to defend the rodents of Poland, threatened with extermination at the paws of cats favoured by the ancient ruler King Popiel, a sybaritic, cowardly ruler... The Hag of Discord incites a vicious rivalry between monastic orders, which only the good monks' common devotion to... fortified spirits... is able to allay... The present translation of the mock epics of Poland's greatest figure of the Enlightenment, Ignacy Krasicki, brings together the Mouseiad, the Monachomachia, and the Anti-monachomachia — a tongue-in-cheek 'retraction' of the former work by the author, criticised for so roundly (and effectively) satirising the faults of the Church, of which he himself was a prince. Krasicki towers over all forms of eighteenth-century literature in Poland like Voltaire, Swift, Pope, and LaFontaine all rolled into one. While his fables constitute his most well-known works of poetry, in the words of American comparatist Harold Segel, 'the good bishop's mock-epic poems [...] are the most impressive examples of his literary gifts.' This English translation by Charles S. Kraszewski is rounded off by one of Krasicki's lesser-known works, The Chocim War, the poet's only foray into the genre of the serious, Vergilian epic.

Buy it > www.glagoslav.com

The Sonnets

by Adam Mickiewicz

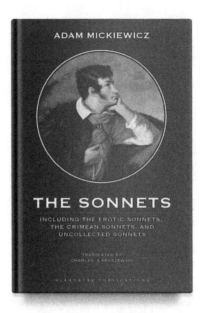

Because the poetry of Adam Mickiewicz is so closely identified with the history of the Polish nation, one often reads him as an institution, rather than a real person. In the *Crimean and Erotic Sonnets* of the national bard, we are presented with the fresh, real, and striking poetry of a living, breathing man of flesh and blood. Mickiewicz proved to be a master of Petrarchan form. His *Erotic Sonnets* chronicle the development of a love affair from its first stirrings to its disillusioning denouement, at times in a bitingly sardonic tone. *The Crimean Sonnets*, a verse account of his journeys through the beautiful Crimean Peninsula, constitute the most perfect cycle of descriptive sonnets since du Bellay. *The Sonnets* of Adam Mickiewicz are given in the original Polish, in facing-page format, with English verse translations by Charles S. Kraszewski. Along with the entirety of the Crimean and Erotic Sonnets, other "loose" sonnets by Mickiewicz are included, which provide the reader with the most comprehensive collection to date of Mickiewicz's sonneteering. Fronted with a critical introduction, *The Sonnets* of Adam Mickiewicz also contain generous textual notes by the poet and the translator.

Buy it > www.glagoslav.com

FOREFATHERS' EVE

by Adam Mickiewicz

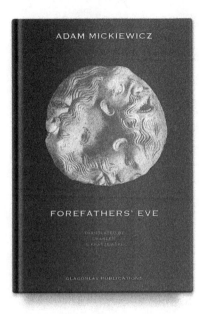

Forefathers' Eve [*Dziady*] is a four-part dramatic work begun circa 1820 and completed in 1832 – with Part I published only after the poet's death, in 1860. The drama's title refers to *Dziady*, an ancient Slavic and Lithuanian feast commemorating the dead. This is the grand work of Polish literature, and it is one that elevates Mickiewicz to a position among the "great Europeans" such as Dante and Goethe.

With its Christian background of the Communion of the Saints, revenant spirits, and the interpenetration of the worlds of time and eternity, *Forefathers' Eve* speaks to men and women of all times and places. While it is a truly Polish work – Polish actors covet the role of Gustaw/Konrad in the same way that Anglophone actors covet that of Hamlet – it is one of the most universal works of literature written during the nineteenth century. It has been compared to Goethe's Faust – and rightfully so...

Buy it > www.glagoslav.com

Four Plays:

Mary Stuart, Kordian, Balladyna, Horsztyński

The dramas in Glagoslav's edition of *Four Plays* include some of the poet's greatest dramatic works, all written before age twenty-five: *Mary Stuart*, *Balladyna* and *Horsztyński* weave carefully crafted motifs from *King Lear*, *Macbeth*, *Hamlet* and *A Midsummer Night's Dream* in astoundingly original works, and *Kordian* — Słowacki's riposte to Mickiewicz's *Forefathers' Eve*, constitutes the final word in the revolutionary period of Polish Romanticism.

Translated into English by Charles S. Kraszewski, the *Four Plays* of Juliusz Słowacki will be of interest to aficionados of Polish Romanticism, Shakespeare, and theatre in general.

Buy it > www.glagoslav.com

Olanda

by Rafał Wojasiński

I've been happy since the morning. Delighted, even. Everything seems so splendidly transient to me. That dust, from which thou art and unto which thou shalt return — it tempts me. And that's why I wander about these roads, these woods, among the nearby houses, from which waft the aromas of fried pork chops, chicken soup, fish, diapers, steamed potatoes for the pigs; I lose my eye-sight, and regain it again. I don't know what life is, Ola, but I'm holding on to it. Thus speaks the narrator of Rafał Wojasiński's novel *Olanda*. Awarded the prestigious Marek Nowakowski Prize for 2019, *Olanda* introduces us to a world we glimpse only through the window of our train, as we hurry from one important city to another: a provincial world of dilapidated farmhouses and sagging apartment blocks, overgrown cemeteries and village drunks; a world seemingly abandoned by God — and yet full of the basic human joy of life itself.

Buy it > www.glagoslav.com

Glagoslav Publications Catalogue

- *The Time of Women* by Elena Chizhova
- *Andrei Tarkovsky: A Life on the Cross* by Lyudmila Boyadzhieva
- *Sin* by Zakhar Prilepin
- *Hardly Ever Otherwise* by Maria Matios
- *Khatyn* by Ales Adamovich
- *The Lost Button* by Irene Rozdobudko
- *Christened with Crosses* by Eduard Kochergin
- *The Vital Needs of the Dead* by Igor Sakhnovsky
- *The Sarabande of Sara's Band* by Larysa Denysenko
- *A Poet and Bin Laden* by Hamid Ismailov
- *Zo Gaat Dat in Rusland* (Dutch Edition) by Maria Konjoekova
- *Kobzar* by Taras Shevchenko
- *The Stone Bridge* by Alexander Terekhov
- *Moryak* by Lee Mandel
- *King Stakh's Wild Hunt* by Uladzimir Karatkevich
- *The Hawks of Peace* by Dmitry Rogozin
- *Harlequin's Costume* by Leonid Yuzefovich
- *Depeche Mode* by Serhii Zhadan
- *Groot Slem en Andere Verhalen* (Dutch Edition) by Leonid Andrejev
- *METRO 2033* (Dutch Edition) by Dmitry Glukhovsky
- *METRO 2034* (Dutch Edition) by Dmitry Glukhovsky
- *A Russian Story* by Eugenia Kononenko
- *Herstories, An Anthology of New Ukrainian Women Prose Writers*
- *The Battle of the Sexes Russian Style* by Nadezhda Ptushkina
- *A Book Without Photographs* by Sergey Shargunov
- *Down Among The Fishes* by Natalka Babina
- *disUNITY* by Anatoly Kudryavitsky
- *Sankya* by Zakhar Prilepin
- *Wolf Messing* by Tatiana Lungin
- *Good Stalin* by Victor Erofeyev
- *Solar Plexus* by Rustam Ibragimbekov
- *Don't Call me a Victim!* by Dina Yafasova
- *Poetin* (Dutch Edition) by Chris Hutchins and Alexander Korobko

- *A History of Belarus* by Lubov Bazan
- *Children's Fashion of the Russian Empire* by Alexander Vasiliev
- *Empire of Corruption: The Russian National Pastime* by Vladimir Soloviev
- *Heroes of the 90s: People and Money. The Modern History of Russian Capitalism* by Alexander Solovev, Vladislav Dorofeev and Valeria Bashkirova
- *Fifty Highlights from the Russian Literature* (Dutch Edition) by Maarten Tengbergen
- *Bajesvolk* (Dutch Edition) by Michail Chodorkovsky
- *Dagboek van Keizerin Alexandra* (Dutch Edition)
- *Myths about Russia* by Vladimir Medinskiy
- *Boris Yeltsin: The Decade that Shook the World* by Boris Minaev
- *A Man Of Change: A study of the political life of Boris Yeltsin*
- *Sberbank: The Rebirth of Russia's Financial Giant* by Evgeny Karasyuk
- *To Get Ukraine* by Oleksandr Shyshko
- *Asystole* by Oleg Pavlov
- *Gnedich* by Maria Rybakova
- *Marina Tsvetaeva: The Essential Poetry*
- *Multiple Personalities* by Tatyana Shcherbina
- *The Investigator* by Margarita Khemlin
- *The Exile* by Zinaida Tulub
- *Leo Tolstoy: Flight from Paradise* by Pavel Basinsky
- *Moscow in the 1930* by Natalia Gromova
- *Laurus* (Dutch edition) by Evgenij Vodolazkin
- *Prisoner* by Anna Nemzer
- *The Crime of Chernobyl: The Nuclear Goulag* by Wladimir Tchertkoff
- *Alpine Ballad* by Vasil Bykau
- *The Complete Correspondence of Hryhory Skovoroda*
- *The Tale of Aypi* by Ak Welsapar
- *Selected Poems* by Lydia Grigorieva
- *The Fantastic Worlds of Yuri Vynnychuk*
- *The Garden of Divine Songs and Collected Poetry of Hryhory Skovoroda*
- *Adventures in the Slavic Kitchen: A Book of Essays with Recipes* by Igor Klekh
- *Seven Signs of the Lion* by Michael M. Naydan

- *Ravens before Noah* by Susanna Harutyunyan
- *An English Queen and Stalingrad* by Natalia Kulishenko
- *Point Zero* by Narek Malian
- *Absolute Zero* by Artem Chekh
- *Olanda* by Rafał Wojasiński
- *Robinsons* by Aram Pachyan
- *The Monastery* by Zakhar Prilepin
- *The Selected Poetry of Bohdan Rubchak: Songs of Love, Songs of Death, Songs of the Moon*
- *Mebet* by Alexander Grigorenko
- *The Orchestra* by Vladimir Gonik
- *Everyday Stories* by Mima Mihajlović
- *Slavdom* by Ľudovít Štúr
- *The Code of Civilization* by Vyacheslav Nikonov
- *Where Was the Angel Going?* by Jan Balaban
- *De Zwarte Kip* (Dutch Edition) by Antoni Pogorelski
- *Głosy / Voices* by Jan Polkowski
- *Sergei Tretyakov: A Revolutionary Writer in Stalin's Russia* by Robert Leach
- *Opstand* (Dutch Edition) by Władysław Reymont
- *The Night Reporter: A 1938 Lviv Murder Mystery* by Yuri Vynnychuk
- *Children's First Book of Chess* by Natalie Shevando and Matthew McMillion
- *The Revolt of the Animals* by Wladyslaw Reymont
- *Illegal Parnassus* by Bojan Babić
- *Liza's Waterfall: The hidden story of a Russian feminist* by Pavel Basinsky
- *Precursor* by Vasyl Shevchuk
- *The Vow: A Requiem for the Fifties* by Jiří Kratochvil
- *Duel* by Borys Antonenko-Davydovych
- *Subterranean Fire* by Natalka Bilotserkivets
- *Biography of Sergei Prokofiev* by Igor Vishnevetsky

More coming . . .

CPSIA information can be obtained
at www.ICGtesting.com
Printed in the USA
BVHW092052291221
624660BV00002B/72

9 781914 337314